Visions of the Past

Visions of the Past

Christopher Taylor and Richard Muir

J. M. Dent & Sons Ltd
London Melbourne

First published 1983
© Christopher Taylor and Richard Muir

This book is set in 10/12½ Lasercomp Photina
Printed in Great Britain by
The Alden Press, Oxford, for
J. M. Dent & Sons Ltd
Aldine House, 33 Welbeck Street, London W1M 8LX

Layout by Peter Matthews

British Library Cataloguing in Publication Data

Taylor, Christopher
    Visions of the past
    1. Great Britain—History
    I. Title   II. Muir, Richard
    941   DA30
    ISBN 0-460-04556-3

Contents

Contents

List of Colour Photographs

Colour and black-and-white photographs copyright of Richard Muir.

Introduction

When it was suggested that we should write an interpretative account of many of the monuments in the British legacy of historic places, our thoughts turned towards a theme or perspective which would link up the different sections. We have always thought that the history of the man-made landscape was essentially a story about people and agreed that there was much in favour of attempts to show first how former generations saw the world in which they lived and reacted to the landscape and social setting and, secondly, how historians have sought to interpret the past. In these ways, the theme of perception runs throughout the narrative.

The past can be perceived in many different ways, and often the durable evidence which has survived allows a variety of different interpretations. Towns, for example, have tended to be explained in terms of the geographical advantages of their chosen sites, while both churches and the greater houses have most often been appraised by the *cognoscenti* in terms of their aesthetic merits and the fashions current in architectural development. Here we adopt somewhat different perspectives, seeing towns rather as the creations of visionary entrepreneurs, churches as functional buildings provided to serve important communal purposes and evolving in harness with changing social and political conditions, while houses are presented in their most important role—as homes.

One of the more unfortunate tendencies colouring so many attempts to interpret the past concerns the idea that ancient or medieval people did things for rational and practical reasons, so that simple economic logic may be all that is needed to unravel and explain the patterns of the past. Why we should adopt this simplistic form of reasoning to explain the doings of our forbears is hard to see, since we all know how irrational the behaviour of modern decision-makers can be.

In modern Britain for example, where an urban population needs good access to unspoilt countryside and where there is widespread sympathy for conservational objectives, one might expect to find forceful and workman-like policies for the preservation of the good old landscapes, buildings and archaeological sites. Instead, however, we find that in a headlong drive to grow more cereal crops, hedgerows and woods are being ripped out, wetlands drained and permanent pastures ploughed up, with a massive destruction of all manner of potentially interesting archaeological sites, while scores of public footpaths are being closed or diverted around the scenes of environmental carnage. There might be some sort of logic in all this if the nation were afflicted by a grain shortage, but this is not so. It has been said that 'Ninety per cent of British farmers are growing for the (EEC) intervention board.' A large part of the destruction is being enacted because the Common Agricultural Policy offers support prices for grain that are higher than those which millers are prepared to pay—and the fruits of a vandalized heritage can be seen in mountains of unwanted wheat and barley and subsidized piles of rotting vegetables.

Yet there is a form of logic underlying almost all human deeds and creations: it need not, however, be of the most obvious and rational kind. The modern destruction of the British countryside can be ultimately traced to the need of French governments, in particular to placate their politically volatile and influential peasant farmers, buying support by securing inflated levels of EEC agricultural subsidies. In the same way, logic of a subtle or devious kind underlies older features: several medieval developments in castle design can be explained not in terms of the more obvious dictates of defence, but in relation to the role of the castle as a vital status symbol of its owner. Equally, some of the later medieval church developments were undertaken more to glorify the rich patrons who funded works than to glorify God. So to begin to understand the creations of long-lost generations we must first realize that people in the past were like ourselves in very many ways. We do things for the oddest reasons, yet underlying the apparent dottiness we will almost always find some obscure system of logic. So it was in ancient and medieval times.

To appreciate the past we must at least attempt to see the lost worlds as their inhabitants perceived them. But to do so perfectly is impossible, for we have all absorbed the outlooks and values of our own culture and civilization and could never wholly obliterate these perspectives to see the world through, for instance, Iron Age eyes. We would find it very hard to think in the way of the Alaskan eskimo tribe mentioned by Brian A. Orme who, even in times of great hardship, refused to fish a certain rich river because they believed that its valley was populated by 'wild babies', giant shrews and other fearsome creatures.

It is easy to adopt an air of superiority when encountering such 'primitive' outlooks, but it is worth remembering that we could not survive a fortnight in the settings where eskimo tribes endure; we should also appreciate that we have our own false perceptions about our native environment and heritage. This publisher has a fine reputation for producing a series of informative and uncomplicated books on landscape history. There is no doubt, however, that a popular understanding of the heritage and of the urgent needs for more and better conservation have been badly-served by the general tendency for popular books to present a most misleading picture. In a recent review of five books on aspects of landscape history, Paul Theroux wrote: 'As with many picture books, one has the feeling that one is being soft-soaped, reassured and told that all's right with the world.'

The effect of the tidal wave of glossy books on aspects of the heritage has been to create a new and unreal British world. The real Britain is packed with all manner of interesting details and afflicted by hordes of environmental challenges and conservational threats, but it is masked from public view by the synthetic world of sweet and simple fabrications. So long as people are encouraged to believe that all village landscapes are as tastefully preserved as that of Lacock in Wiltshire, all historic buildings as well protected as Windsor Castle or all archaeological sites as safe from destruction as Avebury then the destruction will continue. And once a historic site or monument has been destroyed, it can never be recovered.

In this book we mention a number of celebrated monuments, but the more important is the message that the byways and backstreets of Britain are still garnished with all sorts of fascinating relics from the past. There is interest and information to be found everywhere: in the way a living hedgerow will sweep and curve to reveal the outline of a former medieval field strip or deer-park, in crumbling walls which may still preserve the course of a Bronze Age territorial boundary or in the recognition that a neat Georgian façade is masking the timbers of a rambling fifteenth-century building. There is so much fascinating evidence locked in the backwaters of the landscape that each little parish offers a lifetime of study to those who can patiently accumulate the skills and clues needed to decipher it. And for those whose interest in the landscape heritage is less ardent than this, we hope to show that there is much more in Britain that is worth visiting and preserving than just the more famous stately homes and most majestic prehistoric monuments. Sites and buildings of all ages become interesting when one has a few insights and can begin to understand the motives of their creators—and so we have tried to offer ideas about the whys and wherefores of an enormous range of creations.

We begin by looking at the impact of religion on the landscape and then explore the ways in which countless generations partitioned the land into life-supporting territories whose boundaries and boundary marks may still loom through the handiwork of later ages. Territory, good land and privileges must be guarded and in the following section we look at conflict and the evolution of strongholds in Britain. The need for play has produced its own landscapes of recreation and these are explored following the sections which look at the history of settlement at different levels represented by the village, the town and the home.

The book which results is a condensation of our personal visions of the past—visions which the reader is invited to share, appraise and, perhaps, refine. It is the product of a very close collaboration; fortunately, we tend to see the past in similar ways. We both feel that many features in landscape history are much older than convention allowed and that ancient landscapes were more populous, and these populations more capable than has generally been thought. Fortunately again, new evidence periodically emerges to buttress these perspectives. We were also both originally trained as geographers, jumping ship when geography seemed to lose sight of the importance of man and place in an understanding of the landscape.

Although archaeologically much thumped and conservationally much abused, the British setting is still an inexhaustible source of fascinating historical evidence, providing more questions than answers, luring one ever deeper into its web of mystery and revelation until one is thoroughly but gladly entangled and entrapped.

Thanks are again due to Angela Taylor and Nina Muir for all kinds of help and all degrees of patience, and to Moira Hegerty for a great deal of hard work.

PART I

Landscapes of Belief

Introduction

There is nothing more powerful than a living belief, yet few things are as perishable and as difficult to reconstruct as a religion whose time has past. In the course of this book we explore a vast spectrum of human creations, monuments to man's need to secure and defend life-supporting territories; to produce food and sustenance; to create settlements and homes of many different kinds, and thereby satisfy the basic desires for nourishment, security and status. We begin, however, by exploring the monuments to a different kind of human need, one which does not concern the stomach, pride or earthly survival, but the spirit.

While man shares his urges for food and security with other members of the animal kingdom, so far as we know only mankind has the ability to ponder or become immersed in questions of creation, the supernatural and the after-life. Looking back across the millennia we find many epitaphs to the power of religious conviction. There were several periods when societies were motivated to create costly profusions of glorious temples: the church building and restoration bonanza of the Victorian era; the great monastic and cathedral building operations of the high Middle Ages, and the late Neolithic and Beaker periods which spawned an almost incredible legacy of ritual monuments.

There are several good reasons, however, why we should treat the interpretation of religious monuments with special caution. First it might be wrong to equate buildings narrowly with belief and so assume that the levels of conviction were low at the times when, or in places where few, if any, imposing ritual constructions were created. For example, the nineteenth-century Welsh Nonconformist might worship in a humble parlour but his conviction could have run stronger and deeper than those of many of the wealthy men who endowed great English Tudor churches. Secondly, we must learn not to evaluate religious buildings according to the aesthetic standards set by recent arbiters of artistic and architectural taste. Medieval churches and prehistoric circles or tombs were built—at great communal expense—to meet the contemporary needs of local worshippers, of priests and religious establishments and of rich and powerful men. If we attempt to judge them according to the standards which might be applied to a painting, a sculpture or a piece of music then we will lose sight of the bond between the temple, its setting and the people who created it—and it will be almost meaningless.

Thirdly, we must remember that where questions of belief are concerned, objectivity is a valuable and often controversial commodity. The human need to explain the meaning of life, the creation of the world, and the special role of mankind within it, and to believe in the existence of a spirit world and of life beyond the grave seem to be eternal. Therefore we hope that no readers will be offended by our various comparisons between pagan and Christian rituals and monuments. Fourthly, however, we are compelled to recognize the vast gulf in evidence which separates the Christian heritage from that of the pagan periods. Documentary evidence which explains the meaning of

Christian monuments is remarkably comprehensive, yet our very limited understanding of the pagan relics rests upon inference and guess-work.

To attempt to reconstruct lost religions from their legacy of landscape relics is like trying to unravel the depths and complexities of the human mind with an empty skull as one's only guide. Even so, we must accept that unless, by some unforeseen miracle of scientific enquiry, we become able to reconstruct the beliefs of ancient man we will never truly understand the meaning and layout of the remarkable megalithic tombs and circles of Britain, never know the purpose of the complex Bronze Age funeral assemblages which lie beneath scores of their blister-like burial mounds, and be ignorant of a vital facet of Iron Age life.

Modern excavation methods and the related scientific techniques may provide us with remarkably detailed information about the day-to-day lives of ancient people. They can give us a general picture of the landscape in which they lived: what crops were grown; which trees and weeds flourished in their surroundings and when; what crafts were practised, and what animals were kept. But one cannot excavate a belief, a ceremony or a myth concerning the creation and destiny of man. Thus, for example, the most recent excavations at the man-made mountain of Silbury Hill in Wiltshire have provided information which is so detailed in certain respects that we know which insects were airborne during a building season, but we still do not know what the hill *is*. We scarcely know any more about the great and compelling religion which suggests its creation.

Since religious ideas exist in the mind and cannot be excavated, the prehistorian is forced to fall back upon unprovable interpretations of those physical monuments to belief which have endured. The pitfalls which accompany such gropings for truth are recognized if we imagine how extra-terrestrial beings might interpret a Christian church ruin in the centuries following a nuclear holocaust which destroyed mankind and all our literature. It would soon become apparent that the temple stood amidst the remains of scores of buried corpses and the interplanetary excavators would be sorely tempted to regard it, wrongly, as a funerary monument of a death cult. They would note that the great majority of such temples were orientated on a rough east-west axis and they would probably come to the faulty conclusion that the church related to the rising and setting positions of the sun and so was also concerned with sun worship, with the tower or spire being built as a lofty platform for the observation of heavenly events. They would doubtless recognize the division between the lay and priestly worlds represented by the nave and chancel, but they would easily fail to understand the symbolic nature of the altar or the ceremonial function of the piscina—and so erect gory myths concerning human sacrifice and the washing away of blood. In short, we can be certain that one could never understand Christianity solely on the basis of the excavation of Christian churches. (On the other hand, recent excavations of various Saxon and medieval churches have provided much remarkable and unsuspected information about the first millennium of Christianity in Britain.)

1

Prehistoric Religion
and Monuments

Religion is surely no older than humanity, but at least it is older than humanity's sole surviving branch, *homo sapiens sapiens*. In some form it may be as old as *homo erectus*, whose wanderings may have brought him to East Anglia during a warm 'interglacial' interlude between Ice Ages. The evidence is controversial: some experts believe that the *homo erectus* communities who occupied caves around Choukontien in China about half a million years ago may have attempted to preserve the spirits of the deceased through the gruesome ritual of opening their skulls and eating their brains.

Our close cousin, *homo sapiens neanderthalis*, who survived until around 35,000 years ago certainly believed in the afterlife. We know of several ritual burials of Neanderthalers, including that of an Iraqi man of 60,000 years ago who was buried in a cave on a flowery bed of hollyhocks, hyacinths, thistles, ragwort and horsetails. It is hard to imagine that Britain lay outside the world of Neanderthal man although his remains were scarcely known here before 1981, when an early Neanderthal tooth of about 200,000 years ago was discovered in a cave in Clwyd, along with an outfit of flint tools and the bones of bears, rhinoceros, deer and voles.

Very little is known about the beliefs of our direct old Stone Age ancestors; the best evidence comes from cave paintings, however no evidence of cave art whatsoever has been found in Britain. The remarkably fluid and lively paintings of the Palaeolithic era which have been found in French and Spanish caves have traditionally been interpreted as 'hunting art', created to procure the slaughter of the beasts depicted. However, quite recently Bahn has suggested that the decorated caves might be linked with water cults associated with nearby streams noted for their purity and curative powers. The oldest known shrine, dating from the later stages of the Palaeolithic period (around 12,000 BC), was discovered in a northern Spanish cave in 1981 and is said to consist of an altar-like slab and a carved stone head, part human and part animal.

The hunting groups who trickled in to establish permanent occupation of Britain in the following centuries surely brought with them religions which were long evolved and sophisticated, complete with creation myths and rituals; possibly there were priests or witchdoctors. Next to nothing is known about Mesolithic beliefs, but since these hunting and gathering peoples moved around their territories, and had few if any continuously fully-occupied settlements, there may have been no ritual buildings.

The most important Mesolithic excavation site in Britain, although it has surrendered to agriculture, was at Star Carr in Yorkshire. The many finds included antler 'frontlets' which are thought to have been parts of an animal costume used in a hunting or dancing ritual. Several writers have noted the possible link between these Mesolithic ceremonial relics and the animal-headed figure scratched on bone and found in the Pin Hole Cave at Creswell Crags in Derbyshire. Perhaps dating from around 12,000 BC, the figure has sometimes been called 'the dancing sorcerer'. The same writers have also noted the link with the Horn Dancers of Abbots Bromley in Staffordshire, who still perform a ritual dance holding reindeer heads and antlers which are remarkable heirlooms from the Scandinavian Dark Ages.

From this scanty evidence and from analogies with enduring hunting cultures we might guess that Mesolithic religion involved sympathetic magic and hunting dances in which were enacted the capture and slaughter of animals of prey like the deer. It is possible that there were professional medicine men who worked to win the favour of the gods of the chase and predict the most rewarding directions for hunting and gathering, but it seems unlikely that the Mesolithic lifestyle would have supported a panoply of full-time priests or time-consuming religious projects. This is not to say that belief and superstition did not play a vital role in Mesolithic life. Many of the Stone Age hunting cultures, which survived to be studied by modern anthropologists, had philosophies which did not recognize a sharp division between the secular and spiritual world: animals, plants, rocks and streams each contained some kind of life spirit. In less extreme forms, such ideas permeated medieval religion and only quite recently perished.

Farming appeared in Britain in the centuries before 4800 BC and gradually displaced the hunting and gathering lifestyle. Hardly anything is known about the religions of the fifth millennium BC. During this period old Mesolithic beliefs must have been supplanted and remoulded by a powerful set of new convictions, for the fourth millennium BC witnessed an astonishing outburst of religious building: at first focussed on the 'causewayed enclosure' and the tomb it developed to produce as strange a collection of monuments as might be imagined.

These monuments can only be properly understood in terms of the theology and the society which caused their creation. Of the theology we know next to nothing, but a picture of Neolithic society is gradually coming into focus. In the earlier part of the fifth millennium BC there were localized efforts in pioneer farming. By the middle of the millennium, farming was established in a number of favoured areas—limestone and chalk lands and river valleys—while pioneer farming was reaching outwards into other settings. By around 4000 BC agriculture was widely established and expanding on a grand scale, supporting a rapidly-growing population.

Around this time peasant societies began to create the first generations of a series of ritual monuments which were hitherto unprecedented in Britain. These often embodied an enormous input of labour, and some survive today as imposing but mysterious monuments. They are the creations of a revolutionary age: the first agricultural revolution was no less important in the economic history of these islands than the Industrial Revolution of six thousand years later. They are also creations of a successful and expanding society, which may even have begun to experience the tensions of land hunger and conflict between crop-raising and stock-rearing interests; class divisions were becoming important as aristocrats, perhaps even warlords arose to provide leadership and organization—though the peasant may then, as ever, have paid a high price for these services.

It was thought that the earthen long barrows and megalithic ('big stone') tombs represented the first of the British forays in the field of monumental engineering. However, the date of around 4300 BC recently obtained from the 'causewayed camp' discovered at the new Northampton satellite of Briar Hill suggests these massive and puzzling enclosures are at least as venerable as the tombs. The causewayed camps probably served a variety of uses (for this reason they appear again in Parts II and III). Generally they were very loosely circular in shape, consisting of a large central area surrounded by one or more rings of broken or 'interrupted' ditches which have—or did have—banks or ramparts on the outer sides of the ditches.

Where these causewayed enclosures are concerned, our visions of the past have proved fickle. Initially they were regarded as livestock enclosures, then as religious ritual monuments. Now with the insights provided by painstaking modern excavations, such as Roger Mercer's exploration of Hambledon Hill, the enclosures seem to be multi-functional creations.

Although they vary considerably in size, form and setting, the interrupted ditch and bank is the hallmark of the class. The gaps or causeways which punctuate the ditches and ramparts have been interpreted as entrances to the open interior, although they are always far more numerous than required for access. Various building methods were employed and the ditches—in their time often massively impressive gorges—may be viewed as quarries providing materials for the adjacent ramparts. These banks were sometimes reinforced by timber revetments but on the whole they seem to have been rather poorly constructed, unstable and prone to slumping back into the ditches. This may help to explain why the camps, though remarkably imposing in their time, are seldom dominating features of the present landscape. Even so, their construction consumed prodigious amounts of organized labour, tens of thousands of man-hours in most cases; this fact alone provides proof of an organized, disciplined and motivated society.

No society will embark upon such monumental undertakings without good reason. But what purposes could the enclosures have served? The old notion that the camps were massive cattle pens is less unfashionable than it was a few years ago. The main argument against this, and also against the enclosures as settlement sites, is that most lie some distance from sources of water. Secondly, there is the possibility that they functioned as prominent trading centres, particularly in association with the vital trade in stone axes. Commerce requires places for transactions between buyers and sellers, and the camps, with their enormous ramparts and often hilltop locations, could scarcely be overlooked. Nevertheless, this could not have been the sole or probably even the primary use for such massive enclosures.

Then there is the question of defence (which we explore again in Part III). There is no doubt that battles were fought at some camps. At Crickley Hill rival forces of archers launched salvos of arrows and at Hambledon Hill there was a massive conflagration— one of the excavated skeletons was associated with the fatal arrowhead. Defensive considerations may explain the construction of once-imposing ramparts although, in comparison with a Bronze Age or Iron Age hillfort with its continuous girdle of stable ramparts and outer ditches, the causewayed enclosure, with its interrupted and unstable banks, would seem to be an unfortunate design.

The camps almost certainly had important religious functions. The most convincing evidence for this comes in the form of the numerous discoveries of both human and animal bones as ditch deposits. At several of the camps there is evidence that the ditches were periodically scoured and recut. While some of the human remains possibly represent burials and the animal bones may be the refuse from ritual feasts, it is very probable that corpses were exposed in the ditches where they decomposed. Most camps can be related to clusters of long barrows and there may have been an exchange of bones between the different monuments, with skeletons installed in the tombs after exposure in the camp ditches, or bones from the barrows being brought to the enclosures for use in rituals.

With these gory rituals in mind it is worth remembering that our visions of the past are governed by our own sensibilities. Today death is a subject which we exclude from conversation and it is quite easy to go through life without ever having seen a corpse. Many, perhaps most prehistoric people died in infancy; for those who survived the hazardous early years, death, often as a consequence of wounds, could strike at any time. Corpses had to be disposed of, prepared for the after-life in a proper and fitting manner, according to the methods which religion prescribed. The horrendous sights and stench of bodies en route to the after-life should not be taken as evidence of the uncouth barbarity of Stone Age peoples: rather, it seems to show a care and respect for the departed.

A religion in which a death cult or ancestor worship seems to have played an important part emerged in the revolutionary times which gave birth to the causewayed camps. Long barrows and megalithic tombs were majestic and costly repositories for the bones of the local élite. As ever, the full picture is more complicated and uncertain. The origins and prototypes of these tombs are not known, but recent excavations suggest that the tombs were individually preceded by the construction of mortuary houses, usually timber buildings, in which the corpses decomposed, perhaps to the periodic accompaniment of rituals. Skeletons seem to have been placed in the permanent tombs in a dry and partly disarticulated condition and although archaeology has revealed that some long barrows were built upon or around original timber structures, much remains to be learned about the design of the mortuary houses. Some may have been ritualized versions of the homes of the living, while in other places the ditches of causewayed camps or open compounds possibly served similar functions.

It would be easy to embark upon an inevitably lengthy and tortuous discussion of the typology of the tombs, exploring each particular local variant in design: at the end of the odyssey we might be no closer to understanding the fundamental questions of religious belief.

More important than the details of tomb construction are the questions which concern the origins of Neolithic religion, its spread and extent and, of course, its theology. In the first half of this century it seemed that the questions were being answered: the tombs were built by megalithic missionaries from the eastern

17

1. *A reproduction of an 'earth mother' figurine found in the Neolithic flint mines at Grimes Graves, Norfolk. To the left of the figurine is a pick of antler, as used by the flint miners.*

Mediterranean who settled in Iberia and proceeded to convert and settle in Britain and the rest of Atlantic Europe. Few experts would now accept this vision of the past in any of its forms: the carbon-14 dating evidence argues too strongly against it.

'Invasionism' in general is also unfashionable and we do not know the extent to which settlers from the continent, or just ideas from overseas, were responsible for introducing the innovations of the Neolithic period to Britain. What is indisputable is that around 4000 BC the communities that settled in a wide array of West European settings were adherents to religions which placed a mighty emphasis upon the construction of massive collective tombs in which the remains of selected ancestors were stored. The ritual may have begun in Brittany but it was soon adopted elsewhere and it is hard to imagine that nothing more than a coincidental convergence of ideas was involved. At the time, different communities were in contact with each other by land and sea and the development of the important stone axe trade will have cemented old contacts and created new ones. Religious beliefs could have been spread by casual trading contacts and by word of mouth; no actual invasions, religious or otherwise, need have been involved.

While the peasants of Wessex will have had at least an inkling of ideas current in, say, Wales, Brittany and Ireland and although the common emphasis on the collective tomb seems beyond the bounds of coincidence, one must also recognize the very considerable local and regional variations on the theme of the collective tomb.

The tombs were built in a rich diversity of forms. Some were successive within a particular region, suggesting subtle changes in belief and ritual. Others are specific to certain regions. In some cases the explanation must lie with the geology, with different ranges of building materials available in different places. But in some other cases one suspects that although a basic repertoire of beliefs united the communities of Atlantic Europe, the priesthood was too fragmented to preserve religious purity or agree on standardized doctrine and rituals and so local cults explored different modes of expression and architecture.

The most obvious distinction is between the earthen long barrows of lowland and downland England and the partly stone-built megalithic chambered tombs of the stone-rich areas of upland Britain, the West Midlands and Kent. They cover more or less the same timespan as the causewayed enclosures and their dates range from around 4200 BC for the Lambourn barrow in Berkshire to about 3000 BC for the Alfriston example in East Sussex. In terms of their present appearance, they can be well preserved (like the Pimperne long barrow in Dorset), be recognizable only as slight mounds, or be so assaulted by ploughing that they only emerge on air photographs or during

2. The great sarsen façade and entrance at Wayland's Smithy chambered tomb, Oxfordshire. The chambered tomb was built upon an older long barrow which itself had covered a mortuary house.

archaeological surveys: for instance, the numerous Lincolnshire and East Anglian examples recently discovered which demonstrate that the long barrow had an extensive eastern spread. Although they varied considerably when newly built, the classic form was that of a mound which was elongated and trapezoidal in plan, with a slightly wedge-shaped profile, and quarry ditches running parallel to the long sides of the barrow. The prototype for the long barrow may perhaps be found in the older mortuary enclosures which often seem to have existed as banked, ditched and palisaded areas in which corpses were exposed, either inside the enclosures in timber mortuary houses, or on the roofs of timber portal constructions.

The long barrows appear to have perpetuated the form of older mortuary enclosures which were sometimes trapezoidal in shape and in some cases they were built to cover and so inter a mortuary house, as at the Nutbane long barrow in Hampshire. Although the tomb has been levelled by ploughing, excavation revealed a complex of internal structures including a mortuary enclosure and two successive wooden mortuary houses: the site was already sacred when the barrow was erected. In other cases, different internal structures were found including the remains of fences, pits packed with flints or turf mounds which had provided the initial covering for burials. As with the later round barrows of the Bronze Age, the simplicity of the covering mound may mask complicated internal arrangements.

The long barrows, normally built on land that had already been cleared by farmers, are found in a variety of settings: the commonest siting factor concerned visibility. They were built to be seen and their probable role as territorial symbols is discussed in Part II. The earthen long barrows were erected in many of the prime farming centres of lowland and scarpland Britain, on or close to areas of limestone, chalk or alluvial soils. Before very long, the collective tomb was adopted in the hill and ridge country to the west, where the availability of boulder rubble allowed the builders to construct tombs with stone-built chambers. These could be temporarily sealed by massive blocking stones and reopened to admit new internments. Megalithic tombs appeared in Brittany in the latter part of the fifth millennium BC and there is some evidence that they superseded long barrows in the stone-rich areas. Wayland's Smithy, beside the Ridgeway on the Oxfordshire border, is one of the chambered tombs most worth visiting, particularly interesting because excavation has shown that it was built upon an older long barrow (around 3600 BC) which in turn covered a mortuary house.

An early variant of the megalithic tomb seems to have been the 'portal dolmen', in which an often gigantic stone slab forms a slightly sloping 'table top', supported by a few massive stone 'legs', two of which flank the tomb entrance. It may be that the design was inspired by the timber portals at the entrances to some mortuary enclosures and that prior to internment in the chamber formed by the vertical boulders, the corpse was placed on the roofing slab to decompose above the reach of dogs or pigs. Portal dolmens such as Chun Quoit and Trethevy Quoit in Cornwall, Poulnabrone in Co. Clare or Dyffryn in Gwynedd, are among the most visually spectacular exhibits in the archaeological showcase, aesthetically more moving than most modern forays into abstract sculpture. Their appreciation by the living did not last long however, for most portal dolmens were buried beneath earthen or rubble mounds.

Once established, some tombs were enlarged, while others were adapted, perhaps according to subtle changes in doctrine and ritual. Modern excavations show that the layout of chambered tombs were often acquired gradually, in the course of various rebuildings. Thus in the case of the Dyffryn tomb, the original portal dolmen, which was contained in a round cairn, was subsequently incorporated in a wedge-shaped long cairn following the construction of a second stone chamber which lay at the opposite end of the cairn. Now, with the covering mound eroded, both chambers are freestanding tilted stone tables which lie among the boulder rubble of the cairn.

The sophistication of the box-like portal dolmens perhaps produced the 'gallery graves' of types found in the Cotswolds and Severn area and around the River Clyde estuary; these tombs, however, often display covering mounds and quarry ditches which echo the classic long barrow form. The celebrated West Kennet tomb in Wiltshire and the less visited but thrillingly claustrophobic Stoney Littleton tomb in Avon are among the most visitworthy examples. Such tombs contain a number of box-like stone galleries in which bones were stored. These are set beside, and at the end of access passages. The imposing uprights and lintel of the portal have migrated in this design from the chamber itself to the mouth of the entrance passage. In some cases, the entrance was to be further dramatized by the erection of a great façade of upright boulders, as at West Kennett and Wayland's Smithy. In some of the Cotswolds tombs, a false portal was built in the 'normal' entrance position, perhaps to deceive the tomb robber, while the actual burial chambers were set in the long sides of the cairn. Belas Knap in Gloucestershire is a good example.

As the concept of the chambered tomb was adopted in areas far removed from the agricultural heartlands of England, many variations upon the theme were developed. It is not always easy to know whether these represent the religious deviations and developments of local cults, or whether they are more prosaic and simple responses to local geological or social conditions. Certainly geology must have played an important part, for a portal dolmen like Trethevy Quoit could not be built without easy access to massive moorstone slabs, while the Poulnabrone example exploits the potential of the silvery Carboniferous Limestone. Similarly, the stalled cairns of northern Scotland—in which the long flanks of the main chamber are neatly partitioned into side cells by vertical sheets of stone—could only be built in areas endowed with a fissile flagstone or slate. Midhowe on Rousay and Onstan on the Orkney mainland island are good examples, employing the local Caithness flagstone. Again, the imposing West Kennet façade exploits the monumental possibilities of massive sarsen boulders, while different qualities of stone are needed to create a dragon tooth façade like the one at Cairnholy I near Creetown in the south of Scotland.

Other local and regional fancies in chambered tomb architecture must relate to developments in funerary rituals. Some of the Clyde tombs have curved or horned façades: at the chambered tomb of Cashtal yn Ard on the Isle of Man, the upright boulders of the façade sweep out to form a crescent which embraces a semi-circular courtyard, and related 'court cairns' are common in the north of Ulster. These adaptations imply that the façades were developed to provide majestic settings for rituals performed in the courtyards, while at the spectacular 'full-court' tomb at

3. *Pentre Ifan near Fishguard is one of the most impressive of the Welsh chambered tombs.*

Creevykeel in Co. Sligo the forecourt is completely enclosed and entered through a small passageway.

Standing to the old portal dolmens as the Flying Scotsman might to the Rocket are the phenomenal 'passage graves', in which the burial chamber—possibly with a high, corbelled roof—is at the end of a long stone-lined entrance chamber, the whole being housed beneath a massive, often circular mound. The passage graves seem to represent a fairly late development in megalithic tomb architecture: Newgrange and Knowth in Co. Meath dates around 3300 BC, while the Maes Howe passage grave on Orkney appears to date from before 2700 BC (although Viking tomb robbers who entered Maes Howe in 1150 left runic inscriptions describing their discovery of 'treasure' and this might suggest that the tomb was in use in the ages of copper or bronze).

At Maes Howe the drystone walling of the chamber is of a remarkable quality and surprisingly 'modern' in appearance, while both Maes Howe and Newgrange display a mastery of the corbelling roofing method. Maes Howe, Newgrange and the other great Boyne valley tombs of Knowth and Dowth are exceptionally large, demonstrating a considerable competence in engineering and organization. The similarities between the widely-separated Boyne valley and Orcadian passage graves, and their similarities with the complicated passage grave at Bryn Celli Ddu on Anglesey, have led prehistorians to suggest an emigration of Irish passage grave builders. The best evidence to support this idea comes in the form of passage grave art: elaborate and richly-carved, if puzzling, geometrical motifs appear on stones in the chamber and at the entrance to Newgrange, meandering grooves appear on a stone inside the cairn of Bryn Celli Ddu, chevrons on one at the chambered tomb of Barclodiady Gawres on Anglesey, while 'eyebrow' and circular motifs are found in some of the Orcadian passage graves and other carvings are known in Breton tombs.

Wholesale invasions of far-flung territories by Irish passage grave builders seems an unlikely explanation, but the similarities between the tombs do hint at contacts and the exchange of religious ideas. Although the passage grave represents a remarkable sophistication of the simple concepts embodied in the portal dolmen, it also seems to have been simplified and reduced during its export to the west of Ireland to produce monuments resembling the old portal dolmens. In Ireland, the passage graves sometimes occur together in cemeteries and one of the most strikingly exciting but least visited of the prehistoric landscapes is to be seen at Carrowmore near Sligo, a cemetry of very early passage graves. The remains of around sixty tombs can be traced in this necropolis. Some small passage graves resemble portal dolmens, while others are ringed by circles of boulders, anticipating the stone circle which embraces Newgrange. Overlooking the cemetery from the peak of Knocknarea is the gigantic but unexcavated cairn of Miosgan Meadhbha, probably itself a passage grave and one of the most potent symbols of territorial control imaginable. It towers above the ruins of lesser summit passage graves.

Our knowledge of the grave architecture of the new Stone Age is weakest where the massive round earthen barrows are concerned. They include the enormous and complicated mound of Duggleby Howe in the east of Yorkshire (which lies inside a causewayed enclosure) and possibly the staggering artificial mountain of Silbury Hill in Wiltshire (see p. 102) as well as a variety of lesser mounds. Weak chains of association may link these monuments to the passage graves of the stone-rich lands, but the picture is still very blurred.

Had the later Neolithic people deliberately organized their religious lives and ritual landscapes in such a way as to baffle modern prehistorians, they could scarcely have created a more puzzling array of monuments than the one which we are still in the process of discovering. One problem concerns the strange diversity of 'ritual' monuments which existed. Medieval and modern Christians have found an orderly system of churches and chapels and monastic houses of different sizes quite adequate in meeting the physical needs of their complicated beliefs and rituals. Yet Neolithic people required causewayed enclosures and the broad spectrum of collective tombs which we have already encountered as well as a daunting assemblage of other often massive and costly ritual creations. These include the 'henge' in its many forms, the stone circle and the 'cursus', all of which are introduced below, as well as other monuments which do not seem to fit easily into any of these categories.

Categorization itself may be a part of our problem. When prehistory was a youthful subject it was convenient to segregate monuments into categories like 'tombs', 'circles' and 'causewayed camps'. As the scientific techniques of excavation have been refined, our simple visions of the past have been affronted by the baffling complexity of the information discovered. Today we know less that is certain about prehistoric belief than we thought we knew three decades ago.

The functions of the different monuments seem to overlap. Thus mortuary houses and enclosures, the roofing slabs of portal dolmens and the ditches of causewayed camps could all have been used for exposing corpses prior to internment; burials were sometimes made in causewayed camps and stone circles as well as in tombs; causewayed camps, earthen henges and stone circles could all have been trading centres associated with the stone axe industry. Religious ceremonies could have been held inside causewayed enclosures, henges or circles, in the courtyards of chambered tombs or in the cavernous interiors of the larger passage graves. Finally, the megalithic tombs and long barrows might not even have functioned primarily as tombs but as territorial symbols announcing a claim of 'ownership through occupation' over nearby land.

Probably the least visited of our truly stupendous Neolithic monuments is at Callanish on Lewis, where a recent excavation has underlined the fact that the monument defies classification. The most powerful single component of the complex is a mighty pillar-like slab of Lewisian Gneiss almost sixteen feet (five metres) in height. Near the foot of the pillar are the remains of a small chambered tomb. Thirteen massive gneiss slabs form a circle surrounding the pillar and tomb, towards which are turned their broad faces. An avenue and rows of tall monoliths radiate outwards on alignments which roughly correspond to the cardinal points; a long double avenue heads northwards and short lines run east, south and west. We know neither the range of uses which this great monument was built to serve nor even what we should call it since it is a circle, a tomb and probably several other things too.

The causewayed camp took its place on the British stage before 4000 BC and occupied it for most of the Neolithic period, while the camp at Hambledon Hill in Dorset served communities for a millennium, the final recutting of its ditch occurring early in the Beaker period. Long barrows and megalithic tombs had a comparable lifespan even if individual monuments had shorter useful lives. Around 3400 BC (long before the causewayed enclosures, tombs and barrows had become redundant) a new form of ritual monument appeared on the stage in the varied forms of the henge. The name itself is a sorry one, deriving from the 'hanging' stone lintels which are unique to Stonehenge. It is used to describe circular earthbanked and ditched ritual enclosures, including earthwork enclosures containing standing stones which are regarded as stone circles by the layman. Here we will take our lead from the layman and discuss stone circles later.

The earthen henges come in many different sizes: there are both small and large examples which are only visible from the air, while others, like one of the henges at Knowlton in Dorset, endure as imposing features. The largest may be up to a third of a mile (about half a kilometre) in diameter, the smallest less than 150 feet (forty-six metres) across. They are quite distinct from the causewayed enclosures, although also defined by a bank and inner ditch. Some have a single entrance through the earthworks, but many have two opposed entrances, producing the typical 'double banana' form. When newly built, the henges would have been prominent features: from the inside there might have been difficulty in seeing over the arcing rim of embankments, but from outside the entrance notches in the banks of two-entrance or 'Class II' henges appear like the gun-sights of later ages, leading the archaeologist Anthony Harding to suggest that the entrance might be sighted on significant features of the horizon.

As with all other prehistoric monuments, the important questions are: 'Who built and used them, and for what?' The builders and users of henges were the same Neolithic communities who were still partly preoccupied with causewayed enclosures and tombs. If the henges always occurred in isolation, and given the lack of firm evidence, we could simply assume they were a form of temple for religious rituals and celebrations: a sacred area defined by a prominent ring of banks and ditches. However, both the large henges like those at Priddy in Somerset or Thornborough near Ripon and small ones like the little flock discovered at Forteviot near Perth, often occur in groups. The henges probably were religious monuments, but it is hard to imagine why any community needed more than one. They often seem to occur in 'religious zones', where they are associated with cursus monuments and long barrow groupings. The henges may also be linked to an axe cult or to stone axe trading and evidence for an axe ritual comes from chalk axes, too soft to serve any practical purpose, which were buried at Woodhenge in Wiltshire.

The excavation of the smaller henges has tended to prove a rather fruitless activity, for their interiors are usually devoid of interesting contents. The larger examples however have yielded a most puzzling assortment of structures. A number of large and once imposing henges in Wessex have been excavated to reveal evidence of concentric arrangements of massive timber posts. They include Marden, Mount Pleasant, Durrington Walls and adjacent Woodhenge, the most famous example, where the positions of the posts are marked by a singularly unimaginative collection of concrete stumps.

The name 'Woodhenge' denotes the earlier interpretation of the site as a timber equivalent or parody of nearby Stonehenge. Following G. J. Wainwright's excavations at a number of these sites, it was proposed that instead of being wooden renditions of stone circles, the structures (which date from around 2500 BC) were enormous timber buildings—an interpretation which had been advanced for Woodhenge by Professor S. Piggot in 1940. While 'ethnographic parallels' are always to be handled with caution, one of our New Zealand readers writes: 'A Samoan would see the meaning of this at a glance. It is the meeting house of a tribe whose king sits near the centre on a 'Scone Stone', with a few squatting servants to feed him and fan him [in England?]. He is surrounded by an inner circle of twelve high chiefs, each with his column to lean against, and six more grades of titled men beyond. So that all can see the king, the posts are not set radially . . .' Certainly a sarsen stone was found at the centre of Woodhenge, but apparently it was installed after the decay of the timber structure. The experts' visions of the past are fickle and opinion seems to be drifting away from the concept of massive timber buildings, back to the circle theory. This brings us to the question of the origin of stone circles, but first a word must be said about the cursus monuments which are often important elements in the religious complexes of the Neolithic period.

Named by the eighteenth-century antiquary William Stukeley—who thought that the Stonehenge cursus was a track for funeral sports—the cursus monuments are as puzzling as any others in the repertoire of later Neolithic ritual works. One must beware of judging the original importance or impact of earthworks according to their present conditions. The Stonehenge cursus and sections of the Dorset cursus (which ran for some six miles and was more than three times the length of the Stonehenge example) are visible as parallel earthbanks flanking broad avenues. Most cursuses are only recognizable in air photographs and new examples are regularly discovered. However, particularly where the banks and outer quarry ditches were cut in chalk, the bright lines of freshly excavated ditches and banks will originally have been stunning features of the landscape. Erosion and ploughing have slighted their impact on the scene although phenomenal amounts of organized labour were needed in their construction.

Cursuses are often associated with other ritual monuments and a henge at Thornborough was built upon an older cursus. The current interpretation of the cursuses as magnificent processional avenues is not especially convincing, if preferable to the notion that they were prehistoric racetracks or astronomical sighting lines.

Infinitely more visually exciting today are the stone circles: not quite as exclusively British as the unique henge and cursus monuments, though seldom adopted outside these islands. The pedigree of the stone circle is still debated. Some circles, including Stonehenge itself, were built inside older henges. Some monuments which derived most of their impact from the henge earthworks contained a few standing stones. King Arthur's Round Table in Cumbria was such an example and the henge is still an impressive feature despite its vandalization by road-builders. At Arbor Low in Derbyshire, where—now at least—the stones lie flat, the boulders and the massive earthen bank and inner ditch competed for prominence, while at Avebury the quite phenomenal henge earthworks and the magnificent great sarsen circle and north and south inner circles were built at more or less the same time or all within a couple of centuries, around 2500 BC.

Since several circles were erected inside the ditches of older henge monuments while others were constructed with surrounding earthworks similar to the henges it seems likely that the circles evolved from them. The argument is supported by the excavation of post holes in circular or horseshoe arrangements inside henges, suggesting wooden circle prototypes. However, the oldest stone circle is the one surrounding Newgrange; the tomb is no later than 3200 BC and the circle, which is still impressive in its own right though incomplete, is thought to be no younger than the mound of the tomb. And so we have a different possible prototype for the stone circle. It should also be noted that the practice of surrounding a circular tomb by a ring or 'kerb' of stones which was sometimes enveloped by the covering mound was followed in some places in the Bronze Age. Following the erosion of the earthen mound, these kerbs can seem deceptively like small stone circles.

4. Part of the circumference of 'Long Meg and her Daughters' stone circle in Cumbria.

The stone circle tradition began in the Neolithic period but was pursued with more vigour in the 'Beaker period', which had its faint beginnings around 2900 BC, and it continued in the earlier part of the Bronze Age. Poor Beaker man! Bad enough to be named after a pot, but now his very existence is in question. If ever a vision of the past seemed rooted in fact, it was the belief in the burly, broad-headed Beaker folk immigrants who took their name from the practice of burying a beautifully-shaped and decorated beaker-like pot along with their dead. Very recently, prehistorians have become inclined to reject the idea of a large scale immigration of beaker-using people; the pot and the new beliefs and rituals which accompanied it are now seen in terms of the far-reaching exchange of new ideas rather than the arrival of new peoples. And so all the earnest work by a former generation of prehistorians who divided the 'immigrants' up into different groups and deduced where each group landed may have been for nought.

The adoption of the new pot symbolizes important changes in belief and ritual. The majority of beakers were probably used as prosaic domestic containers, but those which survive intact were ritual vessels, buried and protected in tombs. It now seems probable that these beakers provide proof of a belief in the after-life with an alcoholic drink that was flavoured with meadowsweet. The importance of a knowledge of brewing and the powers of command which it could endow upon the cognoscenti should not be

27

5. *A fine early Bronze Age Beaker from the collection at Bury St. Edmunds Museum.*

underrated—as the unhappy experiences of the North American Indians and Eskimos and Siberian tribesmen show. Whether the traditional Irish wake is rooted in the Beaker funeral ritual is another question.

The beaker-using people of the third millennium BC showed at least a passing interest in the old causewayed enclosures and megalithic tombs, but crucial changes in religion are represented on the whole by the rejection of the old rite of collective burial for

28

members of the élite by that of individual burial, with the corpse either being placed in a crouched position within a stone-lined box or 'cist', or buried beneath a relatively modest round barrow. In the west of Ireland, the wedge tombs, which are about the size of a small sports car and resemble slightly wedge-shaped stone chests, also seem to be a little later than the Neolithic chambered tombs.

In the past, prehistorians tended to relate the changes in burial practices to a change in belief from 'earth mother' worship to sun worship, although the evidence can hardly be said to exist. Converts to the new belief were clearly no less concerned than their forbears were for the souls or spirits of departed loved ones, although the emphasis on the ancestor cult may have been diminished. The Beaker burials also seem to show a more personal and individual concern for the departed. As most of the older types of monuments gradually sank into redundancy, the interest in stone circles increased.

While acknowledging the splendour, the skills in engineering, the organization and the investments in labour represented by great circles like Avebury, Stonehenge, the Ring of Brodgar, Castlerigg and the disappointing but once imposing Stanton Drew circle, we should not overlook the scores of lesser circles which exist in many unploughed and little-disturbed upland and moorland areas. The building of the greater circles will have mobilized the labour resources of considerable areas, but the small ones might have stood like chapels or parish churches to the great megalithic cathedrals. Even so, many that are classed as circles may really have been the kerbs of burial mounds which have since been eroded away.

We still do not know exactly what the circles were for. Perhaps more than in any other fields of enquiry, those who have delved for the meanings of the circles have allowed their visions of the past to be corrupted by the preoccupations of the present. In the eighteenth century, when the enthusiasm for ancient things that were Greek or Roman ran strongly, when scientific archaeology did not exist and when information about the ancient world could only be gleaned from the writings of Classical historians and commentators, the circles were of course the creations of Romans and druids. In the earlier part of this century, when crude Freudian psychology was much in vogue and was woven into equally crude concepts of mythology and folklore which trespassed on the territory of archaeology, the circles emerged as the creations of fertility cults. The twentieth century also witnessed a growing interest and competence in astronomy, mathematics and space travel—and so the circles could conveniently become the markers of 'significant' heavenly events. With the dawning of the computer age, computers could be applied to pick the brains of the circles. And Lo! The circles become astronomical computers.

This is also an intellectually lazy age when many alert brains are dulled by examination-orientated syllabuses. It is an age when many people have become disillusioned with science, the immorality of many scientists engaged in the warfare industry and the scientific prevarications on nuclear and environmental matters. At the same time it is an age when organized religion is in a deep decline, when science has robbed us of our mysteries and when hosts of imaginative people have turned to the dream worlds of psychadelia and Tolkienesque fantasy. For disillusioned souls in search of mysteries, deep meaning and occult thrills, the apostles of lunatic fringe

6. The Stones of Stenness on Orkney are the remains of a once majestic stone circle and the magnificent Ring of Brodgar stone circle lies just across the loch.

archaeology (in many cases quite cynically, we believe), have created a mumbo-jumbo world which has ignorance and deception as its hallmarks. It is packed with 'ley-lines', UFOs, earth forces, lost knowledge and—of course—the stone circle lies near the centre of its rickety stage.

In the existential world, the stone circle can be all things to all men. In the ancient world, the use and meaning of the circle will have been known to all. Today, it is *known* to nobody. If the circle is a religious and ceremonial monument, it could have been used as an amphitheatre of clearly defined sacred ground in which a congregation watched the performance of rituals, or it could have been used as a ring for dancing around until some kind of trance state was induced, or both. If the circles had secular uses, they could have served as meeting places or markets. The use of stone itself could symbolize the axe trade: axes and a bronze dagger are faintly carved on some of the Stonehenge stones, while several circles have outlying stones in locations which sometimes seem to signal the presence of the hidden circle to strangers.

The archaeologist Aubrey Burl, who has done much to catalogue and classify the multitude of British stone circles, sees them partly as components in fertility rituals and partly as the creations of societies threatened and overawed by the forces of Nature, which they sought to appease. A preoccupation with the mysterious forces governing fertility is common to many pagan agricultural societies, yet the fact of circle creation — particularly the creation of phenomenal constructions like Stonehenge, Avebury or Callanish — must tell of leisured, highly organized and competent societies which were capable of fulfilling long term goals. No community which was helplessly in the grip of wretchedness could contemplate such enterprises.

The astronomical case has been given many airings in recent years, but if anything, its influence on expert opinion is declining. Apart from other weaknesses, the choice of massive, knobbly boulders as precision sighting devices would seem inept. And prehistoric people were far from being inept. A much-needed and long-overdue objective study of the astronomical case was provided by Douglas C. Heggie in 1981. In general the survey is sceptical, if often inconclusive. This very inconclusiveness underlines the fact that any reasonably-preserved circle will offer a swarm of potential alignments between different stones. Some heavenly events, no matter how obscure, will coincide with some of them. It seems quite likely that some circles incorporate simple astronomical alignments, but most unlikely that sensible and capable people would have built anything as unwieldy as a stone circle primarily as an observatory.

There were several variations on the theme of the stone circle. Geology was obviously a key factor: there is not a single circle in the half of England lying south of the North York Moors and east of the Pennines and Cotswolds. Some circles were embraced by henge earthworks, others like Castlerigg were freestanding, while the Ring of Brodgar is ringed by a massive rock-cut ditch and excavation suggests that it perhaps had an outer bank. Some of the rings were perfectly circular, others slightly flattened or egg-shaped. A few, like Avebury and Stanton Drew, had rectangular or box-like settings of stone or 'coves' inside, it is not known whether these were inner sanctums or replicas of the sacred portals of megalithic tombs. Other circles, like the vandalized one at Cairnpapple Hill near Edinburgh (which was dismantled in the Bronze Age and reconstructed as a kerb), had later tombs inserted in their sanctified interiors.

The most obvious variation however concerns size. About a thousand stone circles are known in Britain, but only a small handful are of 'guide-book' proportions. The overwhelming majority have stones which stand only knee or shin-high; they could be obliterated in a few hours by a farmer with a horse and tackle or a sledge hammer, and many have been. Originally there may have been three or four thousand stone circles, but such dating evidence as is available seems to suggest that the large circles were built at relatively early dates and most of the small ones may be tiny replicas of them, built by families or small upland communities for local worship or as tomb kerbs. The little circles known as 'four posters' have only a quartet of stones.

The most distinctive sub-group is represented by the 'recumbent stone circles' of north-east Scotland, in which the standing stones rise in height towards the south west, where a large, horizontal altar-like stone, often pocked by 'cup-marks', lies between two tall vertical stone 'flankers'. Unlike most other stone circles, which tend not to yield very much when excavated, the recumbents release charcoal, cremated bone, pottery, scatters of white quartz pebbles and Bronze Age weapons. Burl, who has excavated several of these circles, believes that the recumbent stones were aligned on the axis of the moon's path in the sky. While astronomical arguments are becoming as stable as ninepins there must be some explanation for the enigmatic north-eastern circles, and this is perhaps the best to date.

Standing stones are usually attributed to the Bronze Age and recent excavations in Dyfed have shown that standing stones were not the simple structures that we thought they were. The Devil's Quoit standing stone was part of a complex archaeological site and was the dominating component in a Bronze Age setting of over 3000 upright stones set in rows which included a timber upright. Other evidence shows that standing stones elsewhere seem to have been surrounded by large collections of small stones and pebbles although the ritual and beliefs concerned with such monuments are unknown.

The Berrybrae recumbent stone circle was built in the Early Bronze Age, around 1900 BC. By this time the magnificent henge at Stenness on Orkney was already a thousand years old and the circle cult was passing from maturity into old age. The advanced and relatively opulent tribal societies of Wessex sustained their fascination with their majestic temple at Stonehenge, which did not assume its final form until about 1500 BC. By then the period which we label the later Bronze Age had arrived, and the centuries around 1000 BC were marked by climatic decay and land hunger. The construction of massive ritual monuments in stone ended and the subsequent adventures in landscape engineering concerned defence rather than belief.

We have said that archaeology can tell us a great deal about the day-to-day lives of prehistoric people, but it cannot exhume beliefs and doctrines. The excavations of ritual monuments tell us that the people who were concerned for the souls of the departed would occasionally consecrate their temples with a human sacrifice, sometimes an infant. Human bones often featured in their rituals but one cannot say whether this reveals a preoccupation with death itself or with ancestors. We know almost nothing about the identities of their god, goddess or gods although the burial of a set of antler picks on the completion of ditch-digging at Avebury, and the discovery of a fertility goddess figurine in a worked-out flint seam at the Grimes Graves flint mine in Norfolk, suggest efforts to appease Nature for the violation of the natural landscape and resources, or to secure future favours.

Many insights into ancient religion must be contained in excavation reports of the past and future but we should not overlook the evidence of our eyes or the impact of surviving monuments on our senses. When sunlit, the stones at great megalithic temples like Avebury, Stonehenge or Callanish flash and glow like brilliant icebergs, but in an instant they become dark and brooding in the shadows of passing clouds. Thus they mirror the elements which governed the destiny of prehistoric peasant farmers. The stone axe, as a tool for clearing woodland—perhaps hafted as a ploughshare and sometimes polished as a token of status—was a mainstay of Neolithic and Bronze Age life. A collection of boulders lies at the centre of Silbury Hill; exotic blue-stones from the Preseli Hills in Dyfed were brought across the Bristol Channel for use in Stonehenge (or perhaps originally to build a subsequently destroyed temple); quartz pebbles were scattered at many recumbent stone circles; the Newgrange tomb was iced with them and embraced by a circle of greywacke, slate and igneous boulders, some of syenite from a distant source, while the four great ritual basins in its recesses are of four different stones: granite, slate and two types of sandstone. And so it is not too bold to suggest that stone *itself* had a prominent place in ancient religion.

The nature of Bronze Age belief is no less enigmatic. The quest for understanding is made more difficult by the probability that the main centres of Bronze Age settlement, and perhaps the main religious monuments too were in riverside and low-lying places, now ploughed out or deeply buried by river deposits. The later stone circles apart, the archetypal religious monument of the Bronze Age is the round barrow. However, many different burial and cremation customs were followed; remembering that modern British Christians have been cremated, buried beneath a galaxy of different tombstones, iron or wooden crosses, laid in crypts or family vaults, it might be unwise to attempt to deduce too much about religion from the funeral practices. They tell us more about the lives and status of the deceased than they do about belief.

The burials seem to show a survival and merging of older and much older rituals. Beaker traditions continued into the earlier Bronze Age, while burials in cists and in earthen graves, which were accompanied by larger pots of 'food vessels', may have evolved from Beaker customs. Except in the northernmost extremities of England, the graves were marked by barrows; further north they tended to be clustered in level cemeteries. Other people were cremated and their remains were placed in pots known as 'cinerary urns' which were often buried in ancient barrows, henges or henge-like enclosed cemeteries. Where barrows of earth or cairns of gathered stones were built, they were only very loosely associated with the old Beaker practice of single burials; some, however, covered several original internments and many had later burials in the sides of the mounds, blending the English traditions of conservatism and 'making do'.

There is a well-known law of round barrows which holds that all are alike, and each is slightly different. When seen as monuments in the field they lack the presence and stony details of the chambered tombs, appearing as grass or tree-covered blisters. But excavations have shown that the superficial blandness can mask complicated internal structures of different kinds. This is apparent in the recent excavations of a barrow at Sproxton by the Leicestershire Museum's archaeological field unit. A man who died in his thirties around 1800 BC may have been placed firstly on a timber platform where the corpse was exposed and partly defleshed. Then a funeral pyre was built over the body and after burning the remains were covered by a small mound, probably carrying circles of wattle fencing. These were then burnt and the site was covered with a mound of earth and stones which was surrounded by inner and outer kerbs of low stone walling. A century later the barrow was capped with a rubble of limestone quarried from a ditch dug around the mound. At this time the remains of several young men and women were sealed in the capping materials. Perhaps at a slightly earlier date cremated remains and an urn were buried near the edge of the mound.

The same Leicestershire team excavated a round barrow of the same period at Eaton just six miles (ten kilometres) away and demonstrated that despite the apparent similarities between round barrows, there were considerable simultaneous local variations in funeral rituals. Here the first cremation had been placed in a wooden coffin; the next burial was uncremated and in a gouged-out tree-trunk; the next, a cremation which had probably been contained in a bag, while the fourth corpse was buried. Four concentric ditches corresponded to the Sproxton fences, and although stakes were erected they seemed to form a haphazard pattern; perhaps they carried fences supporting sections of the covering mound.

Barrows in Wessex, where the people of the earlier Bronze Age tended to be more cosmopolitan, richer and more hierarchically organized than elsewhere, were built in forms other than the common bowl shape. The names 'bell', 'disc', 'saucer' and 'pond' describe their various forms, but the significance of the different shapes is not clear. The nature of the grave goods accompanying different barrow burials led the archaeologist L. V. Grinsell to suggest that the bell barrows cover male burials and the disc barrows those of women. Particularly in Wessex, and sometimes elsewhere, the round barrows were clustered in cemeteries.

As the later Bronze Age gives way to the Iron Age our understanding of prehistoric belief becomes less rather than more clear. Yorkshire has always delighted in being different and the south-eastern part of the county contains many square barrows, often associated with heroic burials and rich in weapons and ornaments. Otherwise, there is little evidence of an Iron Age funeral rite and one does not even known whether corpses were normally buried. Neither is there any evidence of religious monuments, although the hillforts remind us that these talented but unsettled societies were capable of undertaking massive building operations. Some hillforts probably had ritual as well as defensive associations.

There is no reason to doubt that the Iron Age people had strong religious convictions and the absence of man-made monuments seems to show that there was a form of Nature worship, associated with natural features such as groves, water and wells and possibly certain animals or birds. There was a much nastier side to Iron Age ritual, which may reflect the tensions in a heavily-populated countryside which was in the grip of climatic decay. At Danebury hillfort in Hampshire there are hints of ritualized cannibalism, and the cult of the severed head permeated Iron Age society and mythology. At some hillforts such as Stanwick heads were displayed on poles or gateways and many carved stone heads with vacant and disturbing expressions have been discovered. The workmanship is often primitive; although some belong to quite recent periods most seem to be of the Iron Age.

The Classical references to the brutality of Celtic rituals are far too numerous to be dismissed as polemic and propaganda. The Classical literature and recorded Celtic folk traditions also reveal that the British had several key deities and sources of lesser gods: Lloyd Laing notes that the names of some 374 of them are known from inscriptions and that there are sixty-nine which have been coupled with Mars—an appropriate association considering the bloodthirsty nature of Celtic society. There was no prehistoric Golden Age in Britain: skirmishes were fought in the Neolithic period, infants were sacrificed in the Bronze Age and, while we of the Hiroshima age are in a weak position for moralizing, there is a pervasive nastiness to much of what we know about Iron Age Britain.

The true role of the druid caste in Iron Age society has been blurred by the apostles of lunatic fringe archaeology and by Celtic twilight romanticism. Caesar was not an unbiased commentator, but his descriptions of the druids as respected and privileged priests, teachers and judges may be accurate. He also tells how Britain was the seed-bed and focus of the West Europe druidic cult: '. . . the druidic doctrine is believed to have been found existing in Britain and thence imported into Gaul; even now those who want to study it deeply generally go to Britain.' Soon he would go there himself.

2

Roman Religion

The Roman army and administrative machine brought to Britain a new outlook on religion. The early Roman Empire was officially extremely tolerant of religious matters. There was indeed a State religion, but other beliefs were allowed providing that they were not thought to be offensive or dangerous to the State. Thus many 'harmless' water cults were allowed in Britain while the politically dangerous Druidism was ruthlessly crushed. This may seem to be rather a pragmatic or even irreligious attitude, but there was a basic, if simple, theology behind it. It held that there was not one god, but many, and that men could make a contract to carry out certain rituals to any or all of these gods in return for which the gods would give protection.

The 'official' gods were those derived from Classical Greek mythology but these were accompanied by the Imperial Cults whereby the Emperor of Rome became a god. Both the 'real' gods and the Imperial ones were widespread in Roman Britain at least at an official level. Far more popular were the old prehistoric gods, although often they were oddly transmuted.

The gods of late prehistoric times seem to have been based partly on natural forces but with the spread of Roman culture they were given physical attributes which could be represented by Roman sculpture and often pragmatically linked the Classical gods in various ways. Thus at Bath the existence of the hot springs led to the belief in a water

7. The Roman temple of Mithras at Carrawburgh beside Hadrian's Wall, looking through the entrance towards a trio of altars.

goddess who, in Roman times, was equated with the goddess Minerva. Even when there was no possible linkage with a Classical god the old Celtic gods were raised to an official status and often had temples erected to them.

These temples were mainly very simple in design. Some it is true, were large and elaborate and based on Mediterranean prototypes as at Bath, but most were small and relatively unpretentious. They consisted of a small, square structure surrounded by a verandah or portico ; occasionally the buildings were circular or even polygonal. These buildings stood within a walled enclosure. Many have been excavated but few survive to be seen. Among the remaining ones are those at Jordans Hill, near Weymouth, Dorset and within Maiden Castle in the same county, both now in the care of the Department of the Environment.

Throughout most of the Roman period there was a great diversity of religions and gods in Britain. In general they appear to have been very impersonal although it was thought that if the gods were prayed to or given gifts, they would assist the worshipper. Towards the end of Roman times, however, new religious ideas based on Middle Eastern cults spread across the Empire. These were very different in concept for they demanded not just recognition but also devotion and a code of living that went far beyond the earlier conventions. The most important of these new beliefs was, of course,

Christianity, although some of its features were shared with the Mithras cult.

Christianity arrived in Britain in the second century, but it remained a minority religion for some time. It gradually spread and, though never completely ousting the old beliefs, by the early fourth century was well established, at least from the organizational point of view, with a Diocesan structure with bishops and priests.

Few material traces have survived this widespread early Christianity. In the Roman town of Silchester in Hampshire what appears to be a small church of around AD 360 has been found, but its size hardly indicates a flourishing religious community there. A number of Roman villas are known to have contained private chapels. The wall-paintings at Lullingstone in Kent can still be seen, while the mosaic pavement containing a portrait of Christ from the villa at Hinton St Mary in Dorset is now in the British Museum. Other finds indicating Christian worship have been found at the villas at Chedworth in Gloucestershire, and Frampton in Dorset, as well as at the small Roman town at Oundle, in Northamptonshire.

It is clear that by the early fifth century, Christianity in Britain was a flourishing religion, its popularity fostered by the onset of the troubles which brought the final collapse of Roman Britain. It is likely that in these difficult times, Christianity put down its deep roots and began its growth as a truly popular religion.

3

The Christian Church

Despite the existence in the mid twentieth century of a largely agnostic society, the physical remains of the Christian church in Britain are as much admired, protected and lovingly preserved as they have ever been. More people visit York Minster in a year, than did in a century during its heyday as the religious centre of northern England. The reasons why so many people visit not only York Minster but remote parish churches are many. Some go out of deep religious conviction and find within the ancient walls a kind of peace which is increasingly rare in the world beyond. Others find pleasure in the architectural beauty of many of our churches, while a few find the complex exercise of unravelling the intricacies of the complicated building periods a fascinating task.

Yet to understand the remains of our great cathedrals, abbeys, parish churches or even the simple non-conformist chapels, we must try to place ourselves alongside those who, over the centuries, built and rebuilt, glorified and worshipped in these buildings. For although churches are the physical expression of Christianity at work through the ages, they are many other things as well.

They manifest the high structural engineering skills of their times, and thus are the past equivalents of the Humber Bridge or the Post Office Tower. They reflect great architectural ability in the same way as the finest modern secular buildings which have earned far less popular enthusiasm and admiration. Certainly nearly all the greater churches and abbeys were major engineering works and their story is a vital chapter in the history of the development of structural engineering. One of the main themes of this development is the attempt of builders to increase the dimensions of the structures while at the same time decreasing their bulk. The greatest difficulty was that of containing the forces of compression caused by the enormous weight of the structures themselves, particularly their roofs. Thus, the 'barrel-vaulting' of Norman times was constructed to carry the equal thrust of the roofs along continuous walls. The later pointed Gothic vaulting is characterized by ribs which concentrated these thrusts on to specific points on walls or piers. Whatever the aesthetic or symbolic values that the Gothic style may have, the pointed arch is structurally superior to the rounded and allows larger spans than the older forms. The resulting ribs, piers and buttresses could be ornately decorated in a variety of ways and the ribs of vaulting are themselves a form of decoration. Ultimately, however, the engineering considerations were probably predominant in producing the basic structural form of the medieval church. Most medieval churches express the achievements of generations of master masons who tested themselves and their materials to the limit.

The wholesale changes in church architecture of the seventeenth century, exemplified by the 'Wren' churches, largely originated in the concepts of construction. The intellectual and aesthetic ferment of the Renaissance led to the decline of the master craftsman and his replacement by the values of the 'new architecture' whose origins lay in the Mediterranean and Classical worlds. No mere home-grown craftsmen could easily acquire the new knowledge born of study rather than of practice. The knowledge of classical geometry, oval spaces and domes could only be learnt from books and visits, and not by experimentation. As a result, 'architects' replaced 'builders' with the former coming inevitably from the upper classes of society.

Though the influence of builders and architects on the form of churches was important, religious needs conditioned their layout and decoration. As Morris has said, churches are a 'theatre for the litany'. They were therefore designed primarily for the performance of services. Yet, despite the evidence to the contrary, the church, its theology and ritual observances were never static. The litany changed over time as society and theology evolved and architecture responded. For most of the medieval period the eastern end of the church—the chancel—was the most important, for it was there that the most sacred parts of the mass were performed. The nave was little more than an assembly area or auditorium. This had a number of consequences. One involved the actual building, for it was the east end of a church that was erected first. Thus, even when churches are apparently all of one date it is the east end which tends to be the oldest. Sometimes, especially in the thirteenth century when fashions of building style were evolving rapidly, these changes can be seen in the way that the structure differs in date, if only slightly, from east to west.

The importance of the eastern end, where almost all ritual was concentrated, was expressed not only in the chancel, but in Lady chapels and other side chapels. By the thirteenth century the necessity for dividing the sacred area of the chancel from the nave led to the development of ornate screens which proliferated in the fourteenth and fifteenth centuries. It is worthwhile remembering today, when so many of the medieval screens have been lost as a result of seventeenth or nineteenth-century 'reformers', that medieval worshippers rarely saw the architectural unity of nave and chancel produced by the builders for it was obscured by the rood screen. Now we see much more of the architectural structures than earlier people ever did.

The Reformation inevitably changed the emphasis of the litany in many ways: one of the most important of these was the increasing emphasis on preaching and the 'demystification' of the mass or Holy Communion. The result was the shortening of churches in the seventeenth century to become box-like structures with the rituals brought forward into the nave, the reduction or elimination of the chancel, and the installation of prominent pulpits to dominate the congregation. The trend persists today when many modern churches have almost abandoned the traditional form and have the altar placed in the centre of a circular or semi-circular auditorium. This trend was anticipated by many nonconformist sects who, by the nature of their beliefs, strove to eliminate the 'mystical remoteness' of Divine Service and to replace it by a more acceptable religious meeting between God and man.

Churches, and medieval churches in particular, had religious functions other than the purely formal ritual ones. In a largely illiterate society they were also designed for teaching, using what we would call visual aids. Symbolism of every kind lay behind each decoration, statue, painting, and was even vested in the architectural proportions and elevations of the buildings themselves. The church, as a physical structure, dominated its surroundings whether in the town or in the countryside in a way it is difficult for us to appreciate now. Most other buildings were small, crude, and insubstantial. The church stood above all of them emphasizing the power and the continuity of God and his works. Within the church, almost every wall was painted and there was painted glass; all articulating stories from the Bible, excerpts from the lives of the saints or, like the Doom paintings, giving horrific forewarnings of the fate awaiting the wicked in the next life. On the other hand, among the deeply religious decorations, the secular humour of contemporary society also shows through. Grotesque figures of fun are sometimes mixed in with those of saints and kings. Motifs, both bawdy and vulgar were not uncommon while the obscene Sheila-na-gigs and Green Man fertility figures were positively pagan.

All churches, including monastic buildings and nonconformist chapels have to be paid for, and here again they express the aims, ideals and values of the society that created them. At different times and in different ways, everyone in society contributed to the building and upkeep of churches: kings, bishops, lords, merchants, as well as the mass of society all surrendered resources needed to provide the places of worship. And the motives which created the great and not so great structures they left behind were not always those of high religious fervour. A host of decidedly non-Christian attitudes, such as the ruthless exercise of power, greed, pride and self-agrandisement are all visible. Certainly deeply held religious convictions played an important part in the creation of churches while penance for sin and an attempt to promote the soul in the hereafter were major considerations. However the physical expression of these desires changed through time. Thus in the twelfth and thirteenth centuries many monastic houses were the outcome of endowments provided to assist in saving the souls of benefactors. But by the fourteenth and fifteenth centuries, bequests gravitated to the parish churches and especially to the provision of Chantry chapels. At a much later date, the numerous, if often rather undistinguished Gothic churches of the new urban areas were often a genuine response to what the patrons saw as a vital need while hosts of nonconformist chapels were provided by earnest middle-class endowments.

Just as important as these religious motives for creating churches and their fittings were prestige and rivalry between individual communities. The great fifteenth-century wool churches were largely expressions of secular wealth, often built to serve communities so small that all would have fitted easily into one corner of one aisle, while the benefactor's arms encrusted the masonry and woodwork. Likewise the elaborate (and to many people, hideous) large marble monuments of the eighteenth century, which crowd many churches, are reminders of secular power and influence despite their pious verses. Even at worship the peasant congregations in churches like Exton in lost Rutland could not escape the domination of their masters.

Finally, we must remember that although many churches today have an entirely religious function, largely divorced from day-to-day life, this is a relatively modern attitude dating only from the nineteenth century. In earlier times the church was much more a part of the community it served. It was often used for purposes that would appal the twentieth-century church-goers though some modern churches are beginning to revert to the older pattern in parishes where enlightened clergy engage in social projects. Certainly medieval churches were used for a wide variety of communal events including the holding of fairs and courts in the churchyards, while schools were situated in the buildings themselves. As it was often the only secure structure in the village, the church had the important role of being the community store-house, and sometimes special rooms existed for the protection of valuables.

Thus the arrangement, shape, size and contents of every church and chapel in Britain, of whatever date, can tell us about the aims, desires, hopes and fears of individuals and society at large, as well as giving a history of Christianity. Everything is there if we care to look for it.

Having said that, when we return to the remains of the church in Britain we find that the early parts of the story are often unclear and difficult to unravel. As we have already seen, in late Roman times, there were certainly functioning church organizations with bishops and dioceses, although the evidence for churches themselves remains elusive. The picture is even more clouded when we move into the fifth century, after the enforced break with the Roman Empire. Certain factors are well established. The diocesan structure of the church seems to have continued, at least in the north and west of Britain, though it may have changed somewhat in detail. The dioceses seem to have been related to specific tribes or kingdoms which either already existed in some Celtic provinces, or which developed out of the ruins of the Roman administrative system elsewhere. In those parts of England which felt the full force of the early Saxon take-over there is less evidence: it may be that the system of bishops and church administration submerged with organized society at that time.

During the fifth and sixth centuries, a new wave of Christian activity took place, largely affecting Wales, Ireland, Scotland and south-west England and, as far as we can see, influenced by ideas and people from the continent. This is a difficult period to understand. It is usually described as the 'Age of Saints', when, it is alleged, the lands bounding the Irish Sea were filled with saints wandering the countryside and crossing the seas to convert the heathen to Christianity. Yet it is difficult to reconcile this missionary activity with the accompanying evidence for bishops and dioceses which certainly existed at the same time. That the saints lived cannot be doubted, but it is much more likely that they were preaching to the converted and vigorously introducing new concepts and ideas rather than a new religion. These saints have left many traces in the landscape: holy wells, caves, crosses and chapels. Later, churches dedicated to their names dotted the landscape in Wales, Cornwall and parts of Scotland. Exactly what these places were in the fifth or sixth century is not clear. Few definitive structures of the period are known and the sites are perhaps merely those where outdoor services or preaching took place and which then acquired a sacred significance. Subsequently, churches may have been built on some of these sites. On the other hand, flimsy timber structures used as chapels or oratories, which certainly existed later, may have been built in such places and remain to be found.

The main surviving structures of this period are memorial stones which exist in many places. A few are inscribed in Latin, many in the Celtic Ogam alphabet, or in hybrid variants of the two. They all commemorate secular and religious notables in contemporary society and indicate the continued existence of some form of Christian worship.

The 'saints' were rapidly followed by a new form of Christian activity, which was also initially confined to the western seaways, originating from the continent, and more importantly, from the Mediterranean. This was monasticism, which probably arrived in south-west Britain in the fifth century and spread gradually during the next century to cover most of the north and west of Britain; it also had some adherents in the Saxon areas. It was this monasticism which gradually submerged the surviving diocesan system in these regions and produced a new form of ecclesiastical life.

The early monasteries were quite different from the later more familiar ones. They usually consisted of a group of crude stone or timber huts, lying within an enclosure bounded by a bank and ditch. The sparse severity of the buildings reflected the beginnings of monasticism in the hermit communities of the Mediterranean world. The earlier enclosures were often rectangular, as at Iona which covers some ten acres, but there are also many smaller circular enclosures as at Inchcleraun, in Ireland, and Applecross, in Scotland. Sometimes older fortifications were used to form the enclosure: either Iron Age forts or Roman forts. The site at Holyhead, on Anglesey, used the Roman fort of Caer Gybi, while an English example lay inside the Roman fort at Reculver in Kent.

These monasteries were in effect small enclosed villages, the enclosure banks being used to define the sanctity of the interior rather than for defence. They contained groups of crude buildings, which included small cells for the monks, a guest-house, refectory,

8. *One of the lofty round towers commonly associated with early monastic sites in Ireland. This example stands beside the living church near Turlough, Co. Mayo.*

working or writing rooms, as well as barns, cowsheds and stables. The crudely austere churches were equally simple, consisting of rectangular or sometimes circular one-cell buildings, often less than fifteen feet (4.6 m) across and originally built of timber. Normally there was not one church (or more correctly oratory) but several; later these were reduced to a single chapel of stone, and developed separate compartments to provide a chancel and a nave. One of the earliest of these monasteries is at Tintagel in Cornwall, now in the care of the State, and many exist elsewhere.

The strength of Celtic monasticism was considerable and it was a long time before it was replaced by a more familiar form of Christian activity. Eventually it was overtaken by a new tradition coming again from the continent. In 597 St. Augustine arrived in Kent with orders to convert the Saxons. After many difficulties, most of England became, at least nominally, Christian. A new diocesan organization was established, and the church, usually under royal patronage, began to accumulate power and strength. Gradually the first churches appeared, but not in any centrally planned way.

There are a number of ways from which the earliest churches came into being. The first, exemplified by Canterbury Cathedral, were those set up at the seats of political powers that had initially encouraged the earliest missionaries. Several of these were destined to become cathedrals or diocesan centres. It is not without interest to note that of the first seventeen dioceses established, ten were centred on former Roman towns; this suggests a continuity of political and administrative power from Roman times, even where religious and urban communities had failed. Few of these early churches now survive as upstanding monuments and others have only been discovered as a result of detailed and meticulous excavation carried out under extremely difficult conditions.

One such early church was discovered recently at Lincoln. We know from the Venerable Bede that St. Paulinus of York, while helping St. Augustine to Christianize the people of England, came to Lincoln, converted a royal official and his household, and built a church. The actual site of the church was discovered on the site of the later St. Paul-in-the-Bail Church, beneath some seventeen different phases and rebuildings. The excavation showed that the small building, only fifty feet by ten feet (15 m by 3 m), had a perfect Roman-style plan, consisting of a rectangular nave and a semi-circular eastern apse or chancel. Such a plan would be expected of a first generation missionary from Rome. A similar church, fragments of which still stand, is at St. Pancras, Canterbury, with an equally 'Roman' plan. Another identical one existed at Rochester, also in Kent, and its outlines are preserved in the markings on the floor of the present cathedral. Here again, Bede tells us that Rochester had a church built by King Ethelbert and in 604 St. Augustine consecrated Justus as Bishop of Rochester.

Recent excavations at Northampton have revealed the remains of a large stone church, lying to one side of the present St. Peter's Church there, probably built in the eighth century. It has been shown that, at that time, Northampton did not exist as a true town. Its urban functions were only to develop in the tenth century, under the impetus of the Danes. Yet it is clear that Northampton was an important administrative centre, controlling a large royal estate, which was possibly inherited from Roman times.

At Northampton then we have an early church positioned at a political focus, even though that centre was based on administration rather than commerce. How did these early power-centred churches function? They seem to have been 'proprietorial

9. *Canterbury Cathedral, the original church being established in the Dark Ages at the seat of a sympathetic political power.*

churches', belonging to the kings or lords who founded them and used by the families and households of these people. Perhaps St. Paul's, in Lincoln, had this function. Examples, like Rochester, were either initially or later the seats of bishops and were duly elevated to cathedral status, and some, while sharing such functions, certainly had others. In particular there were those churches which lay at the administrative centres of extensive rural estates and which assumed the task of ministering to the inhabitants of the whole estate, rather than just to the congregations in the administrative or commercial centres. These churches did not have a single priest, but became 'collegiate': they were run by a college or group of priests. The colleges, as well as fulfilling duties in the church itself, travelled to other places on the estate and held services there. In this way, the Minster churches were born and by the tenth century at the latest they existed over most of England. Many of these still survive and display architectural evidence of their often considerable size, although in many cases other non-architectural evidence has to be used to prove their original purpose. One example may be noted to illustrate the evidence for Minster churches: Canford Magna, in Dorset.

At Canford, the large church contains works from almost every century from the twelfth to the nineteenth, and comprises a tower, nave, chancel, north and south aisles, a south chapel and a south aisle to the chancel. Careful investigation has shown that the chancel is actually of eleventh century date and until about 1200, when the present nave was built, it existed as the chancel of a smaller church which had a cruciform plan. Such plans often suggest an elaborate Minster church, and at Canford there is additional evidence. In the late twelfth-century document, when the church was given to the Priory of Bradenstoke, in Wiltshire, it was mentioned that in earlier times the church was held by three clerics. This again suggests that the building was a Minster church served by a small ecclesiastical community. But there is still more evidence: while the modern parish of Canford is quite small, until the late nineteenth-century reorganization of parishes in the area it was huge, and contained what is now the town of Poole, six miles to the south. The medieval church at Poole was not strictly a church at all but a chapel dependent on Canford Church. Clearly the large Canford Parish was the estate or Minster Parish that was served from Canford Church. Later when Poole was founded as a 'new town' it was given a building where its worshippers could conveniently worship. But this church remained dependent on Canford and it was thus a 'parochial chapel'.

Elsewhere in Dorset, both place-names of the present parishes and the evidence of dependent chapels allow us to reconstruct the greater part of the late Saxon ecclesiastical pattern of Minster churches. A little to the west of Canford is Sturminster Marshall. As the name indicates, its church was also a Minster, although nothing survives in the present fabric. But again, until the nineteenth century, the churches in the adjacent parishes of Corfe Mullen and Lychett Minster were both dependent chapels of Sturminster. Thus all these parishes together show the original territory served by the late Saxon Minster church at Sturminster itself.

Many of the earlier monasteries previously discussed were wiped out in the Danish raids of the ninth century. Some were subsequently refounded and we shall discuss these later, but others were transformed into Minster churches to serve the inhabitants of the surrounding areas in late Saxon times. One such is Hadstock, in Essex, which was the site of a monastery founded in 654 and destroyed by the Danes in 870. Excavations at the existing church have shown that it began life in the seventh century as a large cruciform building which was probably the original monastic church. In late Saxon

10. *Wimborne Minster church, Dorset, one of several minster sites established in this county during the early days of English Christianity.*

times it was massively rebuilt (though still with the basic cruciform plan), probably when it acquired its status as a Minster church.

So far we have looked at the origin of churches of the Minster type as well as those resulting from the influence of powerful lords. But these represent only a small proportion of the total number of medieval churches. The majority have different and varied origins, not all of which are fully understood. One reason behind the development of many parish churches, which we have already touched upon, involved the establishment of dependent chapels from original Minsters. Gradually the peripatetic clergy from the central Minster, who held services either in the open air or on traditional sacred sites which were often marked by crosses or by small timber structures, were superseded by resident clergy serving the local community from a permanent stone 'field' church.

At first many of these buildings remained chapels of the 'mother' or Minster church, largely for financial reasons. If they had become totally independent then the 'mother' church would have lost valuable revenue from tithes and fees accruing from weddings and funerals. In some places, as we have seen, these dependent links survived until relatively recent times, so enabling us to reconstruct the original Minster Parishes with ease. Elsewhere these links were cut, either in late Saxon times, or more gradually during the medieval period. There are frequent documentary references to financial and tenurial links between various churches which indicate the origins of many churches as dependent chapels, although for all practical purposes these churches had gained full independent parochial status.

Exactly how these dependent chapels, as they originally were, came into being is not clearly understood. Most likely, local lords established them on their lands in places close to centres of population for reasons of status and piety. At the same time, it seems that in areas where the Minster system was still developing, other major landowners established their own private or proprietorial churches for themselves and their tenants and dependents. Gradually, churches or chapels spread so that by the late twelfth or early thirteenth century almost all the familiar parish churches in rural Britain were in existence.

The casual traveller in the countryside will quickly realize that the actual positions of churches vary widely. Some stand on hills, others in valleys. Some are quite isolated while others are in the centres of villages or tucked into a village backwater. A study of the position of churches, regardless of their architecture, can be very important and can tell us not only about the origins of the church itself but often about the history of the area.

Isolated churches, for example, are a very common feature all over Britain. However, the reasons for their isolation are varied and almost every case has to be examined carefully before any firm conclusion can be reached. Many churches that stand alone do so because the village which was once around them disappeared in later centuries. Often the traces of the former villages, either as the banks or ditches of former house sites, gardens and paddocks, or as scraps of pottery in ploughed land, can still be found in the surrounding area. In such instances it is clear that the church was once within a flourishing community. There are many examples of such churches, especially in the

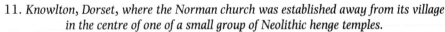

11. *Knowlton, Dorset, where the Norman church was established away from its village in the centre of one of a small group of Neolithic henge temples.*

Midlands, north-east England and East Anglia. But other churches stand alone for mysterious reasons.

Many in south-west England, Scotland, Wales and Ireland, lie near springs or wells with holy connections. Others have prehistoric monuments close by. The church at Knowlton in Dorset stands quite remote from the site of the village it once served; deserted, and inside one of a group of neolithic henges or temples. The now ruinous and isolated St. Columba's Church at Southend on Kintyre in Scotland has no known connection with St. Columba and indeed has nothing dating before the thirteenth century in its structure. Even in the Saxon areas of England, the same feature occurs. Stow Church in Cambridgeshire stands alone on a low hill, a quarter of a mile from the village of Stow. Here it is the place that is significant: Stow probably means 'holy place' in this context.

This brings us to the real purpose behind these isolated churches. They were built in such places not because they were centres of population, but because the site had been regarded as sacred, albeit not based on Christian religions—or cults—for centuries or perhaps millennia. In the initial stages of the establishment of churches in what were perhaps only nominally Christian areas, it was important to continue the traditional use of sacred sites. In the chapter which follows we explore the continuity between the different religions and then resume the story of the evolution of landscapes of belief.

4

Hallowed by Time

In this brief chapter we explore some of the ways in which holy places and sacred structures have proved themselves more durable than the religions they originally served. Matters of pure theology lie outside our scope, but we are interested in questions about how man has applied and manipulated religion. Often one finds dogmatism, intolerance and bigotry; but there are also surprising levels of flexibility and accommodation. It seems that adherents to new creeds have often regarded the sanctity of old holy places as overriding the unacceptable features of the religions which they served. Thus holy sites, monuments and even ideas have been freely transferred as one set of beliefs has yielded to another. As in so many fields of landscape history, continuity is a remarkably potent and enduring force.

We introduce several examples of the adoption of pagan focuses by Christians, but the tradition of assimilation also retreats deeply into prehistoric time. Often it is represented by the juxtaposition of ritual monuments of different ages and one frequently wonders whether or not the associations are merely coincidental? In this way the proximity between the fine but partly destroyed Neolithic long barrow at Lambourn in Berkshire and the remarkable Bronze Age cemetery of bell, disc, bowl and double bowl barrows is challenging and puzzling, but not at all unique. The use of the same ground for the Neolithic causewayed enclosure and round barrow at Duggleby in Yorkshire can hardly be accidental, while in the same county the henge, cursus, monolith and round barrow complexes of the Thornborough area and the cursus, barrow and monolith associations at Rudston reveal areas which were especially venerated.

The thread of a sanctity linking places, monuments and belief can remain unbroken during quite dramatic changes in the orthodoxy of religion. The religions of the Bronze Age may have been as different from those of the Neolithic as Christianity was from Saxon paganism, but there is no doubt that Bronze Age communities held many of the already ancient Stone Age ritual works in reverence and awe. This is shown in the case of the great stone circle at Castlerigg in Cumbria, which contained at least one and probably three later, but now levelled Bronze Age cairns. It is shown at the great stone-studded henge of Arbor Low in Derbyshire, where a large round barrow containing a food vessel burial was built upon the rim of the old and sanctified earthworks. Close by is Gib Hill where the original oval barrow formed a nucleus for a later round barrow. There are many other cases where the erection of round barrows seems to show an attempt to allow the Bronze Age dead to slumber in the reflected glory of redundant Stone Age temples.

In surveying the many intriguing examples of continuity in sanctity it is necessary—where possible—to distinguish between cases where the ideological newcomers have adopted an ancient ritual focus, knowing full well the beliefs of its previous users, and other cases, where an 'odd' and imposing feature has been assimilated into folk myths in complete ignorance of its original religious meaning. Many ancient monuments bear Saxon names and it is obvious that the Saxons and their successors were wont to attribute 'weird' monuments to the handiwork of a god, the Devil or giants. Whether or not the pagan Saxons built any of the several different linear earthworks known as Devil's Dyke, once their frontier or defensive functions had been forgotten, they were deemed Satanic creations. There are Devil's Humps and Devil's Jumps barrows and the name Devil's Punchbowl was given to an Isle of Wight bowl barrow and a natural mere in the East Anglian Brecklands. In a naïve but charming way, long barrows and round barrows were often held to be the graves of giants and many still bear a name based on the Saxon *hlaw*. Other ancient ritual earthworks were no less naïvely assumed to be fortresses and many still carry a Saxon '*burh*' name, as with Silbury Hill, Avebury or Mayburgh henge, while Arbor Low or *eordburh hlaw* combines both Saxon elements.

In all such cases we are meeting folk myth rather than continuity in the use of sacred sites. Sadly, like lost inebriates, accounts of folklore and mythology weave and ramble across the stamping grounds of archaeology. Taken as folklore, stories such as those of the mythical blacksmith Wayland, who had his smithy in the Ridgeway chambered tomb or the petrified army, knights and king which compose the Rollright Stones circle, portal dolmen and monolith in Oxfordshire, are interesting. But they are unlikely to have any archaeological value.

Folk myths, like some successful salesmen, tend to be spontaneous, dynamic—and quite unreliable. The case of the deserted village of Snap in Wiltshire provides a good example. In the early years of this century the village was depopulated by a butcher from Ramsbury who used its lands as a clearing house for his trade in sheep. In less than half a century the causes of Snap's downfall had been forgotten and M. W. Smith's research showed that folklore has invented the myth that the village perished through the failure of its water supply.

Still, it would be wrong to dismiss folk myths and customs entirely as sources of archaeological information. With continuity as our theme it is worth mentioning the survival of apparently pagan fertility rites in many folk customs. In many versions of the St. George Mumming play, St. George fights and slays or else is slain by a character who is variously 'Bold Slasher, King of Egypt' or the 'Turkish Champion'. A doctor is then summoned and the fallen warrior is resurrected. Similar fertility themes of death and resurrection are found in the Padstow May Day rites (which can only be traced to 1835 but are probably much older), and the Abbots' Bromley Horn Dance, which was bowdlerized by a nineteenth-century vicar's wife. The Mumming play can be traced back through literary sources to 1596, but St. George was an eastern resurrection cult figure, perhaps introduced to England at the time of the crusades and grafted on to indigenous fertility rituals.

It has been suggested that the medieval church in Britain only provided a veneer of respectability which masked the strong survival of an old pagan religion. The idea is regularly dusted down and proffered by modern witches, who are more dotty than dangerous. It is quite incredible. While some members of the medieval church and royal establishment were odiously unChristian in their behaviour, almost all were—according to their own and contemporary standards—devout and convinced members of the church. And so it is much more likely that Christianity and fertility cult practices were considered to be compatible and the 'pagan' practices might as easily have been medieval as prehistoric in origin.

In terms of monuments, this compatibility is evident in the cases of fertility symbols such as the Sheila-na-gigs and Green Men which adorn many of our medieval churches. They can be found openly displayed cheek by jowl with images of angels, mortals or animals. Medieval bishops were not sympathetic to witchcraft and heresy and would certainly have noticed the effigies in the course of their parochial inspections. Thus one can only conclude that the church, which had responsibilities for the renewal of fertility and successful harvest, saw no harm or conflict in taking aboard overt fertility symbols. Indeed, death and resurrection were central to the Christian doctrine. Sheila-na-gigs are explicit female figures which are distinctly reminiscent of prehistoric earth mother figurines like the one found in the Neolithic flint mine at Grimes Graves. There is a well-known example on the exterior cornice frieze at Kilpeck Church in Herefordshire; less publicized is the Sheila-na-gig and man-goat tableau, perhaps Celtic or Northumbrian and probably reused, which is built into the medieval church tower at Whittlesford in Cambridgeshire.

The Green Man, Woodwose or Man o' the Woods occurs widely in both ecclesiastical and domestic carving. He often has a cap of leaves, while fertility is symbolized by vines growing vigourously from his mouth. He can be seen, for example, at Crowcombe Church in Somerset and Melbourne Church in Derbyshire. Several new examples have been recently discovered during roof repairs at Landbeach Church in Cambridgeshire.

The Green Man provides a link with the May Day ceremonies, sometimes featuring as the May King or Jack in the Green, a leaf-festooned character who is symbolically killed at the climax of the rituals.

Just as Bronze Age peoples revered the older Neolithic ritual sites, so Christianity inherited many sites which were sanctified in pagan customs. The official seal of approval was conferred at an early stage in the life of British Christianity. Because it is so explicit, the following passage from a letter sent by Pope Gregory to Abbot Mellitus on his departure to Britain in 601 has often been quoted:

> ... we have given careful thought to the affairs of the English, and have come to the conclusion that the temples of the idols among that people should on no account be destroyed. The idols are to be destroyed, but the temples themselves are to be aspersed with holy water, altars set up in them, and relics deposited there ... the people, seeing that their temples are not destroyed, may abandon their error and, flocking more readily to their accustomed resorts, may come to know and adore the true God. [Bede, *A History of the English Church People*, translated by L. Sherley-Price]

Such attitudes may not have been confined to Roman missionary work in England. Earlier, in the sixth century, St. Columcille is reputed to have founded his church at Derry by a pagan sacred grove, preserved the trees and prayed for their safety.

When we come to look for specific landscape monuments to Gregory's policy at work there are many candidates, although one is forced to rely upon suggestive juxtapositions of pagan and Christian monuments which might be accidental. One of the least ambiguous is the Norman church at Knowlton in Dorset which lies at the centre of a very imposing henge. This does not imply a survival of Neolithic religion into Christian times, but shows that the henge was used in pagan rites long after its original ritual function had been forgotten. The positioning of the church is quite deliberate, for the Knowlton church was not set in the village which it served, but some distance away. The remains of the deserted village were found in a valley in the course of an RCHM survey. Almost equally striking is the case of the Norman church at Rudston near Bridlington which stands right beside an enormous monolith which is more than twenty-five feet in height. The church founders may have been unaware of the nearby cursuses but the great stone, which had probably attracted ritual ceremonies since the Bronze Age, acted like a magnet. In contrast, the church at Avebury stands conspicuously at the end of the village which is outside the pagan temple.

One often reads of churches which are built upon mounds. In the cases of Glastonbury and Burrow Mump in Somerset, or Wadenhoe in Northamptonshire, the hills are largely or completely natural features. There are examples where the chosen hilltop church site is so inconvenient that one suspects that the hill concerned must have been especially revered in pagan times. Brent Tor church, which crowns an 1130 foot (344 metres) high granite outcrop in Devon, seems to be such a case. It was built in the second quarter of the twelfth century by the lord of a nearby manor and it is one of many hilltop churches with a St. Michael dedication.

51

12. *The hilltop church of Llanfyhangel-Traethan near Harlech stands upon what was formerly a tidal island, is dedicated to St. Michael of the Sands and was affiliated to St. Michael's Mount in Cornwall. In the churchyard is an inscribed stone which tells (in Latin) how Lledr mother of Hoedliw caused it to be erected in the reign of Owen Gwynedd (1137–70).*

Not all hilltop churches are dedicated in this way while many St. Michael churches do not stand on hills. However, the remarkably long-lived enthusiasm for dedications to the Archangel is a striking example of continuity within the Christian church. There are sixty-seven Welsh dedications to St. Michael, more than 600 English examples and more than a quarter of Lancashire churches honour the saint. Professor Finberg has suggested that St. Michael was a favoured substitution for pagan deities at religious sites that were taken over during Dark Age conversions, superseding Mercury, Hermes or their equivalents as guardian and escort to the dying and dead. During the wars against the Danes and Norsemen the warrior saint attracted new dedications, while the Normans with their military culture were particularly well disposed to St. Michael. He was able to maintain his popularity after the Reformation because he was a biblical figure and therefore did not owe his canonization to Vatican decisions. St. Michael's Mount in Cornwall, which was occupied by a prior and twelve monks from the great French foundation at Mont-Saint-Michel is our most spectacular example of a hilltop St. Michael dedication, even though the roots of the link between the cult and hilltops may involve more than the rededication of pagan sites. Lovely in a less spectacular way is the hilltop church at Wadenhoe in Northamptonshire which overlooks a strange and undated fortified enclosure.

There are other cases still where the church mound is apparently man-made and presumed to be a pagan creation. Such mounds range in size from the gently-sloping example at Maxey in Cambridgeshire, through bulges like that at Edlesborough in Buckinghamshire, to mighty earthworks like the one at Llanddewi Brefi in Dyfed. Of course, one is obliged to ask what the mounds were before they acquired Christian churches? They seem much too large for Bronze Age barrows, while massive Neolithic round barrows seem to be rather rare. Some might not be pagan but the remains of great Norman mottes and the church at Buckingham stands on a known motte mound. A village church was always the most imposing building that a community or, more usually, its masters could afford and it is not surprising that prominent sites were often favoured, as at Earls Barton in Northamptonshire where the small Saxon church and its great defensive tower were set amidst the earthworks of a presumed Iron Age promontory fort. Only where the church position imposed upon its congregation a long or arduous walk to worship do we have strong grounds for suspecting the reuse of a pagan site.

Away from the south west of England, isolated churches, either in ruinous or well-maintained conditions, are generally epitaphs to the now deserted villages which once accompanied them. There are scores of examples, like Nidd in Yorkshire, Fawsley in Northamptonshire and Castle Camps in Cambridgeshire. There are few others which seem always to have been sited in remote places, often presumably on anciently sanctified sites; the example at Stow in Cambridgeshire, joined to its village by recent development, carries a Saxon 'holy places' name. *Hearh* is another Saxon name denoting a sacred site and it can surface in names like Harrow, where the hill overlooks the capital. England had probably not lapsed completely into paganism by the time of the Saxon conversion and Celtic *egles* or 'church' names which can emerge in English as Eccles (-ton, -field, -hall) may reveal ancient Christian foundations.

13. *St. Madron's Well, Cornwall, perhaps a place for baptism that was inherited from the ancient pagan water cults.*

Not only parish churches, but also some minsters and even cathedrals, like Lichfield, were sometimes erected on empty sites. The first cathedral here dated from 700 and was erected on an early seventh-century Celtic church site to enshrine the remains of St. Chad, bishop of the Mercians, who died in 672. St. Chad administered his vast diocese from his cell at Stowe, just half a mile from the cathedral. The cathedral site may have been hallowed in prehistoric times, for a massive boulder is buried behind the cathedral's high altar, while the cathedral setting is traditionally near the place where a thousand native Christians were murdered in the reign of Diocletian (284–305). Professor Finberg has shown that, contrary to popular opinion, the name Lichfield derives from the Roman town of *Letocetum*. Perhaps more important than St. Chad's Church as a forerunner of the cathedral was the hilltop church which was absorbed during the medieval expansion of the town and which had a St. Michael dedication and an association with a number of springs.

Water may have been an important place in religion since the Palaeolithic period and springs or wells were revered in the late Bronze Age, receiving costly votive offerings including bronze weapons, as well as in Celtic and certain Roman pagan religions. A number of quite early Christian churches, like Stevington in Bedfordshire, are close to wells which were held to be holy in the medieval period and which, in some cases, must have been pagan holy wells which first attracted the church foundation. Such wells could have been Christianized by subtle rededications and it has been suggested that some at least of the various St. Anne's wells could have been inherited from the terrifying Celtic goddess, Annis. There are many interesting and challenging examples, such as the holy well at Stoke St. Milborough in Shropshire. The settlement appears in Domesday as *Godestoch* and was a significant earlier Saxon estate and church focus. The renaming in honour of the seventh-century saint presumably occurred later, denoting the tradition that, pursued by men and bloodhounds, the saint fell from her horse here. She ordered it to strike a rock with its hoof, and a spring gushed forth. Peasants ran to her aid and she commanded the barley that they had been sowing to grow. By the evening it was ready for harvest and the pursuers were told that St. Milburga had not been seen since the grain was sown. Originally, a stone lying beside this unspectacular well was said to be stained with her blood. Not forgetting our doubts about the reliability of folk myths, the legend's close links to the well, blood and fertility suggest the pagan origin of the holy site.

The case of Wells Cathedral is also worthy of note. The antiquity of the church site can be traced right back to a minster of about AD 705 and excavations in 1978-9 by Warwick Rodwell suggest that a Roman settlement might lie deep beneath the cathedral complex. For years experts had been puzzled by the lack of alignment between the standing medieval church buildings and the town's market place. The excavations helped to prove that the ancient holy well of St. Andrew and the planned Saxon cathedral and town were on the same axis; it was in the late twelfth century that work began on a new cathedral which adopted the more orthodox east-west alignment.

The study of the form and building materials of a church may give some insights into the early life of the foundation. Even so, it is difficult to offer suggestions that a particular foundation may incorporate older pagan elements—partly because we know very little about the nature of pagan temples as they existed on the eve of conversion. Pope Gregory in his letter to Mellitus mentions 'temples of the idols', although he was probably repeating hearsay; elsewhere, he wrote that the English worshipped sticks and stones. Pagan Saxon temples of some kind may well have existed and Bede described how the canny and lately apostate King Redwald of the East Angles 'had in the same temple an altar for the holy Sacrifice of Christ side by side with an altar on which victims were offered to devils'.

The fabric of many old churches reveals the use of materials from ruined and presumably domestic buildings. The missionary and bishop St. Cedd built the nave of

14. *Wells, showing the peculiar lack of alignment between the market place and the medieval cathedral, in shadow in the background.*

the church at Bradwell-on-Sea in Essex around 654, using bricks pillaged from the surrounding Roman fort of Otona. The magnificent Saxon church at Brixworth is also of the seventh century and incorporates some Roman bricks, while some experts believe that the piers in the recently burned and restored church at Ickleton in Cambridgeshire derived from a Roman building. The first English martyr, St. Alban, now a shadowy figure, became an important cult hero in the early days of Christianity in England. A church was erected on the site of his martyrdom and in the eighth century the church was rebuilt, a Mercian abbey established, and the remains of the saint placed in a special tomb. The cathedral was begun after the Norman Conquest, using massive quantities of bricks pillaged from the Roman ruins of Verulamium and incorporating the columns from the Saxon church in the 'triforium' or upper arcade of the transept.

Some of the most intriguing relics are to be found in the church at Llanddewi Brefi. We have already mentioned that the church is built on a 'pagan mound' and there is an ancient tradition that a synod was held here around 519 to refute Pelagianism; St. David is said to have attended and the church mound 'sprang from the ground' at his command to provide a speaking platform. Nearby stood the ruined Roman camp of Loventium, while early links with Ireland are suggested by one of the ancient Christian stones housed inside the church tower. Perhaps a Pelagian tombstone, it carries an Irish Ogham inscription and a later cross. In a corner of the nave are the remains of the Idnert Stone. Broken, probably in the nineteenth century, its inscription was recorded in 1698; it provides a further link with St. David and was the tombstone of Idnert '—who was slain because of the plunder of the Sanctuary of David'. The present building largely represents the remains of a massive, once transepted church in the Early English style of about 1200, but the various associated tombstones and fragments support the legends of an early church and give evidence of Christian burials here from the early seventh century onwards. There is even a fragment of a Roman soldier's tombstone built into the masonry.

Less thought provoking but still informative are the many cases of incorporated masonry fragments which denote predecessors to surviving medieval churches. There are scores of instances and examples from Cambridgeshire which include the Saxon tombslab in the walls of Little Shelford church, the Norman chevron fragments in the later church at Cottenham or the late Saxon or Norman masonry incorporated in the medieval church at Grantchester, as well as the Whittlesford case quoted above.

A theme which repeatedly emerges from modern studies of archaeology and landscape history is one that tells us that things are older than we thought they were. Often our visions of the past need to be recalibrated backwards in time. This may also prove true in terms of our understanding of the layout of religious buildings—as some recent excavations by M. Popham, H. Sackett and E. Touloupa suggest.

The apse is an important feature of continental church architecture. It was adopted in many Saxon churches, such as Wing in Buckinghamshire or North Elham cathedral in Norfolk, and was common in Norman churches, as at Kilpeck—although for some reason it was rejected by the insular British in later medieval churches. In the apse, facing towards the chancel and fronted by the altar, the Saxon or medieval bishop sat enthroned, surrounded by a horseshoe array of clergy. As a focus of attention for congregations, the apse was inherited—via a variety of domestic and civic building forms—from the pagan basilicas of Rome. In 1982 it was announced that a joint Greek and British archaeological team working on the island of Euboea had discovered the earliest known Greek temple. Constructed on top of a Bronze Age chambered tomb it was dated to about 1000 BC, yet it incorporated important features of later Classical temples. Although of humble thatch and mud brick on footings of rubble, it was surrounded by a 'peristyle'—not of imposing marble pillars but of squared wooden posts—and one end was rounded to form an apse. It was associated with a burial and cremation which were rich in grave goods. Thus the construction of apsed churches provides a link between early medieval Christianity and the Greek Bronze Age.

From our brief survey it emerges that while the converts of a new creed could find the beliefs and rituals of the older religion repugnant (in the way that early Christians of Britain despised the pagan beliefs), throughout the different shifts in ideology, sacred places often tended to retain their sanctity. One set of values seems to have been applied to matters of doctrine and belief, but other perceptions were brought to bear on holy places. Whether or not this simply reflects the sort of pragmatism which is implicit in Pope Gregory's letter to Abbot Mellitus, one cannot tell; but some of the prehistoric juxtapositions at least seem to reflect the notion that the sanctity of places and monuments could override the issues of theology.

5

Exploring the Medieval Church

Once the churches were established, by whatever means, they were constantly altered and rebuilt. There are few if any churches in Britain that consist of only one phase of building. Almost all have evidence of many phases of alteration and reconstruction. In the modern climate of conservation and preservation, it is difficult to appreciate the attitudes of medieval church builders, who repeatedly tore down and then rebuilt their predecessor's work. By modern standards this would be regarded as verging on vandalism, yet it produced our many faceted architectural heritage. The fact that today we tend to preserve rather than to build anew is very much a reflection of a lack of confidence in our own society and architecture. As Richard Morris has said: 'Medieval churchmen and builders were possessed of almost unassailable confidence in the artistic validity of their new work which enabled them to undertake such operations as a matter of routine.'

On the other hand it should be stressed that 'total rebuilding' is less common than it appears at first sight. Most academic reports and the ubiquitous parish church guidebooks usually state firmly that, for example, 'the nave was rebuilt in the thirteenth century' or boldly hatch the entire plan of the chancel as 'early fourteenth century'. Such statements or cartographic details have, in recent years, been seen to be travesties of the truth. The confident assertions of date are made because, to follow the examples given above, the piers, arcades and capitals of the nave are in an architectural style which indicates they were constructed at that time, while the chancel has windows and a piscina which can confidently be attributed to the early fourteenth-century style. But in the last few years, archaeologists have stripped plaster from the walls of fourteenth-century arcades and examined more carefully the layouts, arrangements and proportions of naves and chancels. They have found that, in many cases, the datable features such as window-tracery, capitals and piers have merely been inserted or added to much older walls and structures; a chancel which appears to be entirely fourteenth century in date may actually be twelfth century in origin. All that the fourteenth-century builders might have done was to replace old fashioned windows with more 'fashionable' ones or punch holes through the walls to enable fourteenth-century arcades to be fitted inside the existing structure. As always, such archaeological research gives us a new perception of the way medieval church builders or 'modernizers' worked.

One result of this constant rebuilding or alteration is that it is often difficult to trace development of medieval churches by looking at a group of 'perfect type-sites'. For most periods they do not exist. To fully understand the aims of church builders and the architectural and liturgical fashions they were following, involves complex analyses of hundreds of individual churches, each contributing a little to the story. In the following pages we shall attempt to indicate the main thrusts of parish church development, but with our emphasis on the overall structure of the churches rather than on the details of the architecture. The complexities of 'ogee-headed arches' or 'stiff-leafed foliage' will be ignored, as will be the difference between 'dog-tooth' and 'nail-head' ornaments. Such features and their dates are covered in numerous excellent publications and we can add little to this oft-retold story.

It is particularly difficult to understand the earliest churches because, for obvious reasons, they are the ones which have been rebuilt or altered most often. The very first chapels or churches were almost certainly simple wooden structures of which none survive with the possible exception of the well-known but much restored example at Greenstead-Juxta-Ongar in Essex which is probably by no means typical. Recent excavations have revealed the former existence of small wooden churches comprising only a wooden cell, and also a number of rather larger churches. Sometimes these timber structures were rebuilt in stone, and in an equally simple form.

As so often happens when we attempt to understand the past, it is highly dangerous to equate simplicity with an early date and so to assume that constant improvement and refinement then takes place. This is particularly true of churches. When the church was established in Britain it was not as an unsophisticated prototype; it was already a fully-developed administrative and religious organization with well-established ideas, particularly in terms of church building. As a result the first churches were often

15. *Nevern near Fishguard, where the medieval church incorporates older stones with Ogam inscriptions and has several fine old crosses nearby, like this splendid Celtic example.*

complicated structures and owed their forms to Christian and even non-Christian traditions which had evolved on the continent over many centuries.

This is now apparent at the recently excavated original seventh-century church at St. Paul-in-the-Bail, Lincoln. It had an elaborate Roman-style plan consisting of a rectangular nave and a semicircular eastern apse or chancel. Other early churches were even more complex in plan, often with lateral chapels arranged along the sides of the building which were used for special services and for the burial of important benefactors, ecclesiastics, or other highly-placed personages, since burial in the main body of the church was then forbidden. Splendid examples of such side chapels are at St. Augustine's Abbey, Canterbury, where the early seventh-century plan of the first church is now displayed on the ground. Similar plans are once known to have existed at Bradwell-on-Sea in Essex.

Perhaps the most impressive example of an early church is seen at Brixworth in Northamptonshire, although the church there was not a parochial structure in origin. While only the majestic nave now survives, it is obvious that it was originally furnished with side chapels, for the blocked arches on the nave walls still exist. Brixworth is also important for preserving the high level of sophistication displayed in one of the earliest English churches. The spire is much later, but it can be seen that the western tower was a two-storey porch with single-storey annexes to either side and that the nave, with its clerestory windows, was also part of the original structure. Here again we must try to appreciate the factors which lay behind the building of Saxon, or indeed the later churches. It was quite possible, given the necessary will, political power, or religious fervour to build as at Brixworth a noble building of cathedral-like proportions, even in the seventh century. Likewise, even amid the splendours of the fourteenth century, a remote and poverty-stricken village which lacked a resident lord might gain only a humble church with a simple nave and chancel. Brixworth shows that by the seventh century, the complexities of structural engineering—as involved in the use of clerestories to solve the problem of lighting a large nave flanked by aisles of chapels—were known and could be applied if the necessary resources were available.

Similarly complex 'transeptal' churches (those having a central compartment with arches leading into four narrow cross-like arms) were known in Saxon times. Many late Saxon churches are of such a form as to puzzle the casual visitor who might not understand how they functioned. One reason for this was that they were built for liturgical purposes which were later changed or modified, while fashions in buildings have altered. The church at Barton-on-Humber is a good example. In its original tenth-century form it consisted of a tall central tower of two storeys, flanked on two sides by very small rectangular chambers. The tower and the western chamber still survive, although the body of the later medieval church now lies on the east covering the remains of the other chamber. Recent excavations have shown that the missing chamber was the chancel. The tower base was the original nave which seems to have had an upper room, or more likely a gallery, which may have provided private accommodation for the proprietorial lord and his family during services. The western chamber was a baptistry for the excavations there have revealed the original font base. Over the baptistry was another small upper chamber, perhaps the living quarters of the resident priest.

The use of apparent towers as naves is seen at a number of other places. The remarkably splendid and ornate tower at Earls Barton in Northamptonshire (which, like the one at Barton-on-Humber, is characterized by the long, narrow stone plaster or 'flatband' decoration typical of late Saxon work) was also once the compact nave of a church whose chancel was later destroyed by the construction of the present nave.

While the late Saxon concept of a church may seem strange to our eyes it is also clear that by the twelfth century all the familiar features of later medieval churches such as

16. *The spectacular Norman church ruins at Reculver, Kent, occupy the site of a Roman Saxon Shore fort.*

aisles, clerestories and porches were common and long established. Thereafter the decorations would change as new fashions developed and methods of spanning roofs, supporting walls and constructing arcades evolved; changes in liturgy also caused modifications. But with the basic plan of the church established, the differences between a twelfth-century church and one of the fifteenth century were largely differences in architectural fashion, engineering techniques and liturgy, or were rooted in the relative wealth or poverty of the individuals or local societies that supported the church. The basic concept of the arrangement of a church did not alter much.

This is a vitally important point. Many books on churches and the ubiquitous guide books tell us that Norman churches of the twelfth century were small, unaisled structures with 'apsidal-ended' chancels; that aisles were added and the east end of the church made square in the thirteenth century; that porches and other extensions came in the fourteenth century; and that great towers and chapels appeared in the fifteenth century. This was not always the case. A simple Norman church such as that at Winterbourne Thomson in Dorset or the one at Hales in Norfolk was not necessarily representative of its period. Such churches were built by little communities which remained too small and impoverished to countenance great alterations. Larger and richer communities, or those enjoying the advantages of rich patrons, often had large and complex churches in the twelfth century which acquired many later additions. A good example may be seen at Melbourne in Derbyshire.

The change from the rather disparate church forms of late Saxon times to the ordered and settled forms of the twelfth century is sometimes said to have resulted from the influence of Norman administration and control. Though this may be partly true, there are undoubtedly other reasons too. As an international organization, the church was reformed and reordered in the eleventh century. Britain became increasingly locked into European civilization and it was probably inevitable that both the new and the rebuilt churches came to take on a somewhat standardized pattern. That said, it is one of the great joys of British ecclesiastical architecture that, while firmly rooted in continental origins and concepts, it always had a life of its own and produced buildings which could never have been conceived outside these islands.

The Norman churches of Britain are characterized by what may be described as 'great mass'. Their walls are thick, with the dressed stones masking the rubble filling within; such massive walls were needed to support the heavy roofs and arches which pressed down on them. Buttresses were broad flat strips extending well up the walls to accentuate the heavy oppressive appearance. Columns were large and cylindrical, arches massive and rounded. Towers, where they existed, tended to be short and dumpy. On the other hand, this illusion of solidity was, in the late twelfth century at least, gloriously relieved by ornament that offset the weight and made Norman architecture so much more vital and florid than the rigidly stereotyped subsequent Gothic ornamentation. This decoration reaches its finest flowering in the fabulous ornamentation at Kilpeck in Herefordshire or Barfreston in Kent, but there are countless less noted examples such as the arcades at St. Peter's, Northampton.

Norman architecture in Britain is strangely and surprisingly insular and certainly more so than the succeeding early Gothic which came fully developed into Britain in the late twelfth century. Yet the Gothic style did not impose itself suddenly and was not thoroughly accepted in Britain for thirty or forty years after its appearance around 1200. Except in a few large and important buildings, the new ideas were slowly grafted on to those that already existed. Clearly builders were cautiously experimenting with the new designs: rounded arches and heavy Norman capitals

17. *Norman arches forming part of the older monastic remains at Fountains Abbey, Yorkshire.*

were set on octagonal piers, while pointed arches sometimes rose from heavy rounded piers.

It was well into the thirteenth century before the average parish church builder grasped the full potential of the first Gothic design which is usually known as 'Early English' and even then it tended to be executed in a rather hesitant and piecemeal way. In the greater buildings—one thinks particularly of Salisbury Cathedral—the Early English style is seen at its finest and purest. Admittedly, there are a number of parish churches, such as Warmington in Northamptonshire and West Walton in Norfolk where the style is complete, assured and exquisite. More usually in the parish churches, the style is seen in the insertion of narrow lancet windows which were often grouped, and in the provision of new arcades with increasingly slender round or octagonal piers. These piers sometimes had thin attached or free-standing shafts

64

18. *Many small and simple Welsh churches have scarcely been altered since the twelfth or thirteenth century. Here we see the simple porch and bell house at Llangelynnin on the cliffs near Harlech, a twelfth-century church thought to stand on the site of a seventh-century foundation.*

19. *A Mid-Anglian broach spire at Bythorn in the north west of Cambridgeshire. This unfortunate example extends no higher than the top of our photograph, having been drastically shortened during World War II, when it was thought to present a threat to allied bomber aircraft.*

grouped around them and supported pointed arches with lines of complex ribs. At the same time towers and spires acquired a unity of design not seen before. Groups of windows or arcading were arranged in stages separated by 'string courses' and often a harmonious spire rose from the summit of the tower, carrying its lines upwards to a disappearing point in the sky.

Such artistic achievements were not attained by accident. This can be well seen in the East Midlands, where the almost ubiquitous broach-spires of the thirteenth and early fourteenth centuries have been rightly described by Cox as 'aesthetically and structurally one of the supreme achievements of their age'. These octagonal spires rise from the summit platforms of square towers and the flowing transition from one shape to another was made possible in structural terms by semi-arches across the interior angles of the tower and realized visually by undecorated triangular masses of masonry called 'broaches' linking the tower top to the lower part of the alternate faces of the spire. Like all such bland descriptions of church architecture this one cannot convey the real beauty of broach spires. One of the most memorable periods in this writer's life involved thrice-weekly drives across western Cambridgeshire and eastern

Northamptonshire made via as many different routes as possible in order to enjoy the broach spires. The views on a clear, frosty, sunny morning with at least four hill-top churches showing their spires stark against the blue sky is something that is never forgotten.

The thirteenth century was also marked by a period of numerous massive enlargements of narrow Norman churches. Chancels were lengthened, chancel arches heightened and porches added. It was at this period, rather than later, that the wholesale removal or destruction of Saxon or Norman work took place. Many churches in England, if examined carefully, can be seen to be basically thirteenth century in form if not in detail. For the first time churches became really spacious, with large openings and broad lofty arcades.

20. *Early English architecture in the nave of Salisbury Cathedral.*

21. *Sharply pointed Early English arches at Bolton priory near Skipton, Yorkshire.*

In the early fourteenth century, decoration and design changed again as the so-called 'Decorated' style made its impact. Having achieved the basic spacious structural framework in the thirteenth century, it became possible to develop the decorative embellishments in new and exciting ways. This was most marked in windows which became larger and were then filled with increasingly elaborate and exuberant 'flowing tracery'. Outside, towers and spires, while they continued to be built or rebuilt, also changed. Broach spires, for example, were gradually superseded by spires which simply sat within the tower summit, with the point of junction masked by an ornate parapet. The parapet often had pinnacles at its corners and occasionally flying

22. A fine example of window tracery in the Decorative style at Bolton priory near Skipton.

buttresses linked them to the tower, as at Kings Sutton in Northamptonshire. The Great Pestilence of 1348–51 and the confusion and economic chaos of the late fourteenth century brought a deceleration in church building and design. Yet suddenly out of the confusion appeared a new and almost fully-developed style which was almost purely English, the 'Perpendicular'. This was to be the final achievement in medieval church architecture in Britain. The Perpendicular style had two aspects: structurally, the designers reached the epitome of engineering in stone, while decoration achieved its most elaborate and yet its most mechanical expression.

It is not easy to see which of these two aspects led the development; perhaps it was neither. The masons were persisting in their attempts to make churches taller and lighter by the creation of ever larger windows. They solved the challenge by using flat roofs and depressed arches which allowed the main thrusts to be directed straight down the walls and piers at set points. This provided not only the spaces for the large window openings, but also flat surfaces on walls, roofs and windows for more decoration.

Whatever the evolutionary process, the result is clearly expressed in the great Perpendicular churches such as Salle in Norfolk or Saffron Walden in Essex. The ultimate objective was a broad high hall, walled with glass. The later development of fan-vaulting (really nothing but applied decoration again) is only the crowning glory of this concept of a church by the mid fifteenth century.

Arguably the greatest achievement of the Perpendicular style lay in its breathtaking towers. No visitor to East Anglia or Somerset can fail to be moved by the array of great towers of this period. Some are relatively plain, others have panel decoration all over. At others still the ornamentation is restrained until the top is reached when it culminates in a crescendo of battlements and pinnacles.

These great perpendicular structures are often termed 'wool churches' for they are a physical expression of the great wealth produced by the fifteenth-century wool trade. However, there was much more involved in churches than just the wool industry. In south-west England, for example, similar towering structures, like the one at Widecombe-in-the-Moor in Devon, could equally be termed 'tin-churches', as the wealth which created them ultimately came from the local tin-mining industry. But to explain these churches merely in terms of wealth and wool, tin or any other commodity is to fail to see the real social, religious and economic backgrounds to the period. The church at Lavenham in Suffolk is sometimes said to be the ideal of a wool-church; yet while the Spryngs, a rich local cloth family, certainly paid for part of the cost of the building, the rest came from John de Vere, Earl of Oxford and lord of the manor. Here, new and old wealth combined to produce the staggering beauty that survives. Likewise, the 'Fenland Glasshouse' at Burwell, in Cambridgeshire, was largely paid for by the parish priest and not by any local merchant or lord. In other places, the whole congregation combined their resources to finance the rebuilding of their church—an interesting social development, and one quite different from the earlier situation when kings, lords, abbots and bishops provided most of the resources for new churches.

An interesting and related facet of late medieval life which changed the character of many churches at this time concerned the activities of the religious guilds. They flourished in the fifteenth century in the form of religious 'friendly societies' whose

23. *A soaring Perpendicular church tower at the parish church at Wells, Somerset.*

24. *The Mompesson tomb in Salisbury Cathedral. Sir Richard Mompesson died in 1627 and his monument marks an intermediate stage between the solemnity of the medieval monuments and the elaborate and melodramatic styles of tomb architecture which were favoured in the eighteenth century.*

main purpose was to protect the interests of members who could be from the same trade or locality. Such organizations saw an important aspect of their work as support for regular masses for the souls of dead members. And so, many guilds provided chapels within the local church where a resident chaplain could recite the necessary rituals. Elsewhere, a part of a church might be appropriated to the guild. The guilds achieved not only the addition of many new side-chapels in aisles, or transepts—all constructed in the up-to-date Perpendicular style—but sometimes also considerable rebuilding of the entire church. A related form of addition or alteration derived from individual endowments for the provision of chantry chapels. These were similar to guild chapels, but were intended for the performances of services or masses for the souls of individuals concerned—usually lords, other rich landowners or merchants. Again while money was given for the chapels themselves, it was often invested in refurbishing the main structure as well.

This brings us to another aspect of the Perpendicular style, which is sometimes overlooked. Almost every medieval church, of whatever period of construction, if looked at carefully reveals major alterations in the Perpendicular style. This may be expressed in the complete rebuilding of a tower, or the heightening of the nave by the addition of a clerestory. More often it is seen in the insertion of undistinguished fifteenth-century windows in an older aisle, or the addition of a few pinnacles to a tower. What these features represent is the 'updating' of churches by their parishioners. Often the changes were small, but collectively they represent an enormous outpouring of communal resources. These minor works show the impact of religion on almost every level of society and must be taken into account when looking at late medieval churches.

There is another point which also has to be remembered: for the great majority of churches the Perpendicular work, whether on a major or minor scale, was the last work apart from restoration which was ever carried out. Thus the Perpendicular style tends to figure largest in many churches where it obliterates all that had gone before. What we do not always see is the earlier work, which surrendered to the impetus for the new and fashionable style.

It is interesting, if hardly practical, to speculate on what would have happened if the architectural break brought by the Renaissance had not taken place and the Gothic style had continued to evolve. On past form it is probable that the amount of surviving Perpendicular architecture would be severely limited, having itself been destroyed by the next wave of fashionable updating.

The discerning explorer of the countryside will have already realized that this general survey of the development of the parish church does not adequately explain all that he sees. He will have looked in vain for fine Perpendicular architecture in the parish churches of Scotland, or have been puzzled by the round towers of Norfolk. For behind the generalizations of the previous pages lies a rich variation in local styles, fashions and details. A fifteenth-century church in Norfolk, though similar in outline to one in Gloucestershire, is very different in detail and materials. Some of the reasons for the local differences are, of course, the results of the readily available building materials. In Cornwall there is always a coarser decoration as a result of carving in tough crystalline granite, while in parts of East Anglia, the interior use of clunch, a hard form of chalk, allows the most exquisite details in carving. On a larger scale the flint churches of Norfolk look quite different from those of the same period in Northamptonshire, where the brown ironstone is mixed with the paler Jurassic limestone. The tyranny of poor transport facilities ensured the widespread use of local stones—with fortunate consequences for most medieval churches mirror the geological building blocks of the regional landscape.

Yet there is more to regional variation than building materials, important as these are. In many places the churches subtly reflect the whole character of the countryside in which they lie. In the Pennine Dales they have an austerity and toughness which reflect the landscape from which they seem to have been hewn. In south-east England they tend to be low with sloping roofs that appear to merge into the rounded hill or wooded vales. Especially interesting are the local fashions which will almost always identify a region. We have already mentioned the delightful broach-spires of Northamptonshire, north Bedfordshire and western Cambridgeshire, but the small

25. *Salisbury Cathedral, one of the finest and purest examples of Early English architecture.*

wooden belfries of Surrey, Kent and Sussex are as distinctive as the leaded 'spirelets' of Hertfordshire.

Parish churches form the great majority of medieval ecclesiastical buildings in Britain, but they are of course equalled in design and excelled in size by the great medieval cathedrals and the remains of monastic houses. Space will not allow us to dwell on the details of individual cathedrals or abbeys; everyone has their favourite, whether it be the heavy dignity of Durham, the graceful setting of Salisbury or the towering pinnacles of Ely. Cathedrals have their own particular importance and interest in terms of architecture and design, quite apart from their administrative and religious functions as the centres of dioceses.

In the medieval period it was in fact cathedrals and abbeys which directed architectural advance by their experimentation with innovatory styles which were often tried out and developed there before reaching the parish church level. It is no accident that the earliest English exercise in the true Perpendicular style occurs at Gloucester Cathedral, even it is 'hung' on a Norman frame. The same is true of the great monastic churches: the influence of Fountains Abbey on the decorative style of the parish churches of North Yorkshire was profound.

The great cathedrals and monastic sites of Britain embody many features of the society that created them, while the amount of constructional work they represent is staggering. It is obvious, for example, that in the late eleventh and early twelfth centuries there would have been some reconstruction and new structures as a result of the reorganization of the Benedictine Order and the establishment of new sees or diocesan centres. As these administrative and religious changes took place in generally unsettled times it would not have been surprising if the new building work had taken place on a minor scale. The reverse was true: the period was one of building on a prodigious scale. Morris had estimated that no less than thirty cathedrals and major monastic houses were begun in England alone between 1070 and 1100. In modern terms this might be the equivalent of building a Humber Bridge every year for three decades. What such a building programme meant in terms of human, financial and material resources is almost beyond comprehension, and it was carried out by a society which was in the middle of social and political upheavals and at the same time engaged in producing hundreds of parish churches. Yet our perceptions of this society, which is so much closer to us in time than the prehistoric temple builders, still remains clouded.

Much of what was achieved during these years has, of course, been removed by later work. Even so, enough remains to remind us of the achievements of earlier master masons, builders, clerics, lords and kings. Tewkesbury, Rochester and, of course, Durham still stand as gigantic monuments to this period.

During the early twelfth century there was much less new building, largely because so much had already been provided. But after 1150, a new wave of construction

26. Norman architecture at its best, in Durham cathedral.

began. It was partly triggered by the arrival in Britain of new reformed monastic orders, particularly the Cistercians, as well as the introduction of the new Gothic style which encouraged builders and benefactors to update their work.

By 1170–80 fully integrated Gothic designs had been accepted and places such as Wells, Ripon and Worcester led the fashionable movement. At all these places, and others, the work partly involved the replacement of what had been built less than a century before; only Salisbury, begun about 1220, was an entirely new structure. However, the new monastic houses were obviously newly built and the Cistercian Order was notably at the forefront of development. The relatively austere Early English style was admirably suited to the bleak ascetic ideals of that Order and it was the Cistercians who seem to have pushed the development of this Gothic style to the limits of its potential. The Cistercians also influenced the arrangements of cathedrals and parish churches, especially the designs of each end and the transepts. In Norman abbeys and cathedrals there was a multiplicity of altars usually accommodated in apsidal chapels. The Cistercians simplified this by having rectangular or square chapels resulting in widespread acceptance of this design.

This burst of Gothic rebuilding of cathedrals and abbeys continued until well into the fourteenth century. Part of the stimulus was the unrestrained artistic development of the Gothic style: as soon as a new form of moulding or tracery was established it was superseded by another. The severe Early English style flowered into the Decorated with ever more elaboration. Masons and churchmen alike vied with each other to produce and embellish their churches; meanwhile England's population was rising rapidly and its wealth increasing. Around 1300 the monastic population of this country reached its height. It had to be provided with suitable buildings and the growth of popularity of pilgrimage and of shrines meant that many cathedrals needed vast extensions, as at Lichfield where a new and sumptuous east end was added.

Then, quite suddenly, almost everything came to a halt. After 1350 little rebuilding took place and, with some notable exceptions, no additions were made to cathedrals and abbeys. Obviously the economic decline of the mid fourteenth century and the ensuing Black Death had an important role in this suspension of construction which also affected parish churches. However, as we have already seen, within a few years the Perpendicular style imposed itself on parish churches thus producing the culmination of English Gothic building. Yet there were no new Perpendicular cathedrals. Why was this so? There are many reasons: but perhaps the most important was a general shift in the relationship between church and people. In a subtle way the perception of the church by the laity began to change almost as its congregations were anticipating the mighty upheavals of the Reformation.

The trend was visible in a number of ways. First there was a growing lack of enthusiasm for the monastic orders, perhaps brought about by their increasing isolation from and indifference to the outside world, as well as by their often well-publicized laxity. As a result, far less money in the form of benefactions for massive new works was available. At the same time such resources as were on offer were ploughed into routine maintenance and repair of the work of the previous century rather than in massive rebuilding. Meanwhile fewer people were choosing to enter monastic orders so that many monasteries were half empty. Economic conditions also played a part. Lay lords were able to adjust to the post-Black Death conditions, but the institutional organizations of cathedrals and abbeys found it more difficult. There was a major decline in profits from agricultural land and this severely afflicted the wealth of many abbeys. At the same time religious ideals were changing. The influence of Friars, with their missionary zeal and emphasis on preaching the gospel to the world rather than seeking seclusion from it as their predecessors had done, led to new attitudes among the laity. On another level it became more fashionable to endow parochial chantry chapels than to give money to the relatively impersonal cathedrals and abbeys. All these features combined to produce the new perception of the church held by the increasingly wealthy merchants, small farmers and traders. As a result, money that in earlier times went to build or endow the great Cistercian abbeys or the vast provincial cathedrals was invested more locally in the parish church. It was therefore in the rural parish churches like Lavenham and Cullompton, or in the urban churches like St. Mary Redcliffe, Bristol, that the new Perpendicular style flourished.

Not all cathedrals and abbeys were left entirely untouched by the new style. There were always places which still managed to amass the necessary fortunes for improvements or essential rebuilding either by gift or by astute estate management. Some especially notable work was also carried out at monastic centres where there was no separate parish church and where parishioners attended services in the nave of the monastic church or where disasters forced a massive rebuilding programme. At such places a Perpendicular style was achieved as at Sherborne in Dorset which was massively altered after a riot and fire in 1437.

A curious aspect of very late Perpendicular rebuilding can be seen in a number of monastic houses which show considerable alterations dating from well on into the sixteenth century. The splendid gate houses at Cerne Abbas in Dorset and at Ramsey in Cambridgeshire illustrate this well. Here we seem to see attempts by abbots and priors to rid themselves of capital by investing in new buildings, thus preventing its threatened confiscation by the crown. Presumably the possibility of a complete Dissolution was not contemplated.

The Reformation as a major component of the English Renaissance changed the intellectual, social, political and economic basis of the realm. The origins, development and overall effect of the Reformation are topics too vast to be covered in this book, though the consequences for the religious structures in the landscape were profound. The most obvious effect is seen in the ruined monastic houses that dot the countryside. The political events that led up to the Dissolution of the monasteries produced what many people have seen as an 'orgy of destruction'. Within a few years, abbeys great and small were emptied of their inhabitants, torn down, and their treasures broken up and dispersed. At no other period in our history—except perhaps during the 1950s and 1960s when a similar 'orgy' destroyed many of our historic towns or in the contemporary assault on the countryside—has there been such a massive obliteration of our visual heritage. In most cases, all that has come down to us are the fragmentary hints of a glory that once existed.

While appreciating what has gone, we must note that not everything was destroyed.

On the whole the buildings of the older and larger Benedictine House survived much better than those of the later Orders. This was because the Benedictine foundations had integrated into the society that surrounded them. They had either become the centres of dioceses with bishops/abbots at their head or they had allowed the naves of their churches to be used as parish churches. As a result, great abbeys such as Ely and Peterborough survived and even their claustral buildings were remodelled and reused. Elsewhere, though these latter buildings were removed and the naves and transepts of the main church destroyed, the naves and sometimes an aisle remained as the parish church. Binham Priory in Norfolk, Boxgrove in Sussex and Crowland in Lincolnshire are all examples of this. In contrast, Cistercian houses, in accordance with the rules of the Order, were physically and socially remote; they were ruthlessly destroyed, often without trace, so that ultimately the Cistercians paid the price for the depopulation which had often accompanied the establishment of a house or estate.

On the other hand, most of the great cathedrals and all of the parish churches survived. It is true that many suffered damage in the mid sixteenth-century traumas and even more during the excesses in the drive for true puritan liturgical ideals in the first half of the seventeenth century. Most medieval painted glass was assiduously smashed, wall paintings obliterated, chantry chapels removed and all decorations and carvings of an 'idolatory nature' swept away. Parish church interiors became plainer and simpler, in keeping with the new theology. On the other hand, new times brought new features. The emphasis on preaching and prayer produced pulpits and sounding boards, pews, galleries and wooden altar tables. Social changes also produced new forms of monument. The knightly effigies of the medieval period were replaced by coloured tombs or wall monuments in elaborate sub-Renaissance styles. These monuments, in many cases repainted in their original colours, add much to the visual attraction of our parish churches.

6

After the Reformation

The turmoil of the Reformation and its aftermath led to a reduction in church building. Few new or rebuilt churches appeared in the century after the Reformation and most of those that did continued to be in the late Gothic style, as at Whiston in Northamptonshire. However, by the late seventeenth century new churches again appeared, led by the rebuilding of the London churches after the Great Fire of 1666 and were principally the works of Christopher Wren or his followers. These churches were of a completely different form and style.

Architecturally they mirrored the post-Renaissance age, being symmetrical in arrangement and classical in decoration. Pediments, classical columns, and pilasters are featured. Although based on continental parallels and still retaining the overall layout of chancel, nave and aisles of the medieval tradition, there was often a subtle change in emphasis to conform to the Protestant ideals of preaching and the reduction of the mystery of the sacraments. As a result, chancels were either not provided, with the altar being set against the end wall of the nave, or they were reduced to small annexes attached to the nave. Likewise, while 'aisles' still existed, columns were extended to the roof level and arcades disappeared. The effect was to draw the congregation physically and spiritually closer to each other and to the preacher. The construction of galleries both in the 'aisles' and in the 'nave' also had the same effect.

Not all of these Classical churches exactly conformed to this pattern. The traditions of the past were not easily broken and often chancels remained relatively long and narrow and occasionally they were even separated from the nave by screens, as at St. Paul's Warden in Hertfordshire. These classical churches continued to be constructed into the late eighteenth century and even into the early nineteenth century, yet the Gothic tradition did not die out completely: there are scatterings of churches in a generally Gothic style of seventeenth and eighteenth century dates.

One important feature marks these churches. They were designed by true architects, many of whom like Wren, Gibbs and Hawkesmore are known by name. The medieval master masons and the craft tradition of experimentation and building had gone. Such churches reflect the intellectual development of their age as do the contemporary great houses and parks. An even greater reflection of the age is seen in the interiors of all churches. This is especially true of their monuments. The warm, colourful memorials of the sixteenth and early seventeenth centuries were gradually replaced by colder white marble monuments in a strictly Classical idiom. Draped weeping figures, urns, seated dignitaries appeared in profusion. Many churches, it seems to us now, became the private memorial chapels of the upper classes. While this was not strictly true these monuments do reflect a change in the attitudes of the church in the eighteenth century which became more and more a part of the Establishment, set in its ways and little concerned with the needs and problems of the rapidly increasing mass of working people. Meanwhile the Nonconformist sects sought to provide these people with real spiritual comfort. The elitist attitudes of the established church persisted well into the nineteenth century although in the end action was demanded by the vast problems that emerged from the industrialization of Britain.

As a result, the nineteenth century saw enormous changes in the parish churches of Britain. The reasons for these changes are many. The most obvious one was the rapidly increasing urban population. Thousands of new buildings resulted as the church struggled to bring Christian teaching to the masses and more new churches were built in Britain than at any time since the eleventh and twelfth centuries.

Another important factor was the need for repair and restoration after, in many cases, nearly two hundred years of neglect. By the eighteenth century many existing churches needed massive repairs almost amounting to total rebuilding and all needed some refurbishing. Coupled with these factors were the emergence of new building

27. The Dutch Reform Church at the planned industrial town of Saltaire, Yorkshire, built by Sir Titus Salt after 1850 in a fairly consistent Italianate style. Salt's textile mill appears in the background.

techniques and new architectural ideas. Church architecture in the nineteenth century was not cut off from the rest of society for architects attempted to mirror contemporary preferences. As a result, there was a wholesale return to the Gothic style, as it underlined the identity of the true church as well as the romantic visions of a past that never was. Yet perceptions of Gothic architecture which were blurred by nineteenth-century preferences produced many forms of church architecture. There was no one 'Victorian Gothic' but a sequence of changing ideas. These ideas ranged from the rather whimsical romantic Gothik to the 'pure' Gothic slavishly imitating what was thought to have been the best of medieval designs and 'derived Gothic'. There was also some experimentation with later Classical styles and widespread use of materials now available cheaply as a result of the Industrial Revolution. Brick, terracotta, and artificial stone were all used widely. Nor should we forget the introduction of heating into churches which introduced the miles of piping, cast iron floor grills, and attached boiler houses.

The restoration of existing churches and the provision of new ones required vast quantities of capital and this came from a variety of sources. Much was provided by individual lords, priests and parishioners, especially in rural parishes where bene-factors were motivated by a sense of duty, religious idealism or local pride. In the New

Towns especially, public subscriptions, local and national bodies concerned with spreading the gospel or providing churches, and private individuals all poured money into building projects. The nature of the donations had an immense effect on the structures that finally appeared. If money was available then large churches in the favoured Decorated style could be produced. Elsewhere when money was short, a derived form of Early English was often chosen—largely because it was cheaper to build.

Theology too had its effect on the appearance of churches, especially on their interiors. Much of the second half of the nineteenth century was marked by interminable and often vitriolic disputes within the church and the Oxford Movement for church reform was deeply involved. These were, essentially, arguments over whether the strict Protestant tradition of worship, organization and Christian beliefs, or the older Catholic attitudes were 'correct'. Visually they produced the difference between what we might call 'high' and 'low' churches and which led, when the 'high' ideals were favoured, to the appearance of more elaborately decorated churches, coloured glass, stencilled and painted walls, tiled floors, choir stalls and much ornamental brass and metal work. At the same time, much of this new decoration also reflected the tastes of Victorian society as a whole, with somewhat cluttered and garish churches merely imitating the modes already established in middle or upper class drawing rooms.

Equally Victorian in taste and outlook was the new generation of monuments which were usually less massive but at the same time less elegant than those of the eighteenth century. Particularly common in the larger churches and cathedrals was the flaunting of all the trappings of Imperial Power. Memorials to the dead of long forgotten colonial skirmishes and the now threadbare regimental colours are still very obvious visual reminders of this era, while, from more recent times most parish churches have monuments on which are carved the names of men who perished in the grotesque carnage of the two World Wars.

From the seventeenth century onwards a new form of ecclesiastical structure began to appear in the landscape, the Nonconformist chapel. Protestant Nonconformism emerged out of the ferment of the Reformation as a radical religious movement embracing many different beliefs, and despite many changes it has, on the whole, remained a divided tradition. Though of considerable importance in the religious and political events of the seventeenth century, Nonconformism has left little trace of those years in the landscape. This is partly because the movement suffered from discrimination and persecution in its early years and its adherents were forced to worship either in private houses or in crudely built chapels, few of which have survived. At the same time many Nonconformist sects actively discouraged the construction of specialized buildings for worship, preferring to hold services in a domestic setting, without the ritual and formality of the established church which had been rejected. It was not until the eighteenth century that Nonconformism came of age, partly as a result of the teaching of John Wesley, and then as a reluctant offshoot of the Church of England rather than as a movement evolving from older sects. Eighteenth-century Noncon-formism succeeded partly because it was aimed at the people that the Church of

England had abandoned or ignored and partly because it addressed itself to their very real spiritual needs in a way that was not patronizing. The result was the explosion of building and rebuilding that continued into the end of the nineteenth century producing the thousands of chapels which now dot our landscape.

It has to be admitted that, with a few notable exceptions like the delightful early nineteenth-century thatched chapel at Roxton in Bedfordshire, most Nonconformist chapels are not and did not seek to be aesthetically pleasing when seen from the outside. They tend to be barn-like structures either with the minimum of decoration or gauche details which are often completely out of character with their surroundings. Many that are of mid or late nineteenth-century date have been rebuilt on several occasions as a result of the great upsurge in Nonconformism.

On the other hand, many interiors are plain and unadorned but in fine taste, sometimes with galleries; they genuinely express the simple and uncomplicated rituals which are the visual manifestations of Nonconformist belief. Others display carpentry of an exceptional quality. Altars, if they exist, are plain and are set close to, or within the congregation and lecterns or pulpits for the vital preaching component of worship are a prominent feature. Nonconformist chapels can be found over most of Protestant Britain, though they tend to be more numerous in some areas than in others. For example, Nonconformism was always strong in East Anglia, even from the seventeenth century and as a result there are more chapels per village there than in the adjoining counties. The chapels are also numerous in areas like the Yorkshire Dales which supported the first difficult stages of the Industrial Revolution.

It is in Wales, however, where we find the greatest wealth of chapels: in some places the streets are lined with them. Here we see Nonconformism taken to its final logical, or illogical conclusion whereby devout people, obsessed by the quest for purity in religion, became divided and subdivided into a multitude of sects, each with a slightly different but very important view of the proprieties of worship and belief. The forces of fragmentation even produced semi-detached chapels as a result of continuous sectarian quarrels, inter-communal disputes and the forceful influence of charismatic local preachers.

Today most of these often inexplicably huge chapels are abandoned, underused or attended by a mere handful of worshippers and indeed, many were always far larger than the most optimistic visions of the congregations. Although they may be somewhat depressing in visual terms, they do mark an important aspect of English social and religious history: one which has had a profound effect on British life, attitudes and politics.

The churches of Britain too are now often underused, half empty, or even deserted. Only in Ireland, where religious fervour has remained, for better or worse, an integral part of the political and social fabric of the society, are churches and chapels still functioning in anything like the traditional way. Elsewhere, a handful of believers tend or protect vast structures whose social and spiritual purposes were, at least until very recently, taken-over by the welfare state and the medical profession. The conflict between the need to protect or preserve these great monuments to our heritage and the lack of material or spiritual support for them is now obvious. A new 'industry' has developed in the search for uses for the redundant urban churches. They have been turned into theatres, social centres, warehouses and even places of worship for new beliefs brought in by immigrants from other parts of the world. In rural areas the problems of underuse and dereliction are even worse. Depopulation and religious apathy have left hundreds of redundant churches which have no viable religious function. Many have been virtually 'mothballed', waiting in hope for a new generation of worshippers to return. Others slowly decay and are lost for ever. The problems that beset our ancient churches remain almost insoluble, as a society which is partly indifferent towards them, except as historical monuments, searches blindly for the comfort and help that the churches were built to provide.

At the same time, new churches continue to appear, particularly in the New Towns and suburbs of the mid twentieth century. Most are simple and relatively poor in visual terms, though a few, notably Liverpool's Catholic cathedral, are both impressive and exciting in their applications of modern building technology and in their use of designs adapted to worship in a democratic society. It may be that from these there might emerge a new tradition of church building to continue the long story of man's search for ritual stimulation and spiritual comfort.

Reflections

In the modern era, life has increasingly tended to be dominated by the perspectives of the economist, with his austere models, proclamations and exhortations. In these widely-influential visions of the world, man was reduced to the role of the mindless but 'rational' consuming or producing cog in the great economic machine of state. Spiritual fulfillment was seen in terms of incomes, mortgages and purchasing power, while individuality or eccentricity could not be embraced by the economic calculations. Having endured the latest bout of fashionable economic philosophy—with all its false predictions, implications for the society and for the heritage of monuments—this may be a good time to consider other philosophies. Religion has no role in the illusory world of 'economic man', yet in the past it has played vital and sometimes dominating roles in shaping human behaviour, customs and creativity. It may have no obvious economic rationale or identifiable value in the struggle for human survival, but over countless centuries it was a major influence on man's perception of society and the world and his proper place within them.

In the prehistoric era men saw no formal boundaries between the day-to-day world of hunting, farming and play and the world of belief and ritual. A man would worship his gods at the circle, tomb or grove not only to satisfy social conventions or assuage an inner need for ritual, mystery or belief in a world beyond the grave, but also because the religious observances were thought essential to the success of the chase, the health and fecundity of the livestock and the fertility of the soil. The modern economist might regard the time and energies expended in religious ceremonies or the construction of stupendous monuments as squandered resources, but without his religious convictions the ancient peasant would have known little but the colourless drudgery of survival and would have been deprived of the essential explanations of the nature, origins and dynamics of the world.

Many of the ancient roles and responsibilities of organized religion endured in the era of medieval Christianity. Until recently, accounts of the medieval church tended to be based on the historians' interpretations of early Christian documents and legends or on Fine Art evaluations of whether particular items of church architecture were 'good' or 'bad', 'unique' or 'stereotyped'. Recent developments in church archaeology are beginning to offer new insights into the formative years of the Christian church in Britain; as a result the legends of the founding saints are being nudged from the centre of the stage by rather more complicated appreciations of the ways that the earlier churches may be related to estates and the policies of estate owners, as well as sometimes being established on sites held sacred in pagan times. While archaeology is also adding extra dimensions of complexity to the already complex story of the architectural evolution of particular churches, we should attempt to see the churches not so much as architectural exhibits to be praised or damned by the connoisseurs, but as functional buildings. As such, the medieval churches served all manner of useful purposes and were elaborated, enlarged or reduced according to the needs and fortunes of communities and the changing preferences of their patrons.

Some of the evolutionary stages in the development of churches can be explained 'rationally' by reference to the advancing technological capabilities of their masons, the varying availability of local building materials, fluctuating economic circumstances or changing social or political conditions. Yet there are other features which fly in the face of any sort of determinism. No computer programme could have predicted the ornate vitality of Decorated embellishments or local infatuations like the Northamptonshire enthusiasm for broach spires. Similarly, we can offer no practical explanation for the vast dimensions of many Welsh chapels. While the exteriors of these buildings are almost invariably austere, the structures were often built so large that even the conversion of the entire locality to the particular doctrine on offer would have failed to fill the benches.

Today, popular interest in organized religion in Britain is at an all time low. Most people probably regard churches more as attractive elements in the architectural heritage than as venues for essential worship and spiritual refreshment. And yet it is hard to imagine that we have trudged so far along the bleak road to becoming 'rational economic man' that all spiritual needs have been abandoned and cast off along the evolutionary track. The brave new worlds which the twentieth century appeared to offer are increasingly seeming threadbare, unpredictable and tarnished. Disillusionment may breed its own spiritual revival in Britain, but we cannot know whether it will lead to a gimcrack spiritualism of a Californian type in which bizarre cults and populist political dogma produce grotesque parodies of old and dignified theologies, a revival of traditional beliefs and churches, or something else quite different. But we are fairly confident that the continuing story of the impact of belief upon the British landscape will involve more than just the scrabble for funds to preserve neglected churches.

PART II

Territory: The Communal Stage

'The new men took over as landlords but farming still had to go on'
W. G. Hoskins, 1973

Introduction

Land was life. In pre-industrial societies the landless or dispossessed family faced starvation. The same fate threatened those communities whose land resources were too small, were deteriorating in the face of soil exhaustion or a worsening climate, or were lacking in vital components such as pasture or hay meadows. The ownership of land gave more than mere sustenance, for territory also bestowed rank and privilege upon the controlling magnate or chieftain.

Much of what happened in history might be encapsulated as the struggles, operating at many levels, to win and retain territory. Few would deny the supremacy of questions of land ownership in medieval feudal society, but such questions can hardly have loomed less largely among prehistoric communities, whose dependence on the land and its food resources were no less. Our understanding of the Dark Ages and all preceding periods will be woefully weak until we can understand the patterns of territorial cells that sustained the many different and successive communities, underpinning their social customs and determining their political outlooks. But the evidence is hard to come by. A little can be gleaned from excavation or field-work, more from 'retrogressive analysis', tracing boundaries back through time from documentary evidence; much more has probably been lost forever.

Even so, the historical period provides plenty of examples which show us that simple economic logic and technological advance are inadequate as explanations of man's organization of the landscape. In some places the factors of politics and ownership have had a greater impact than elsewhere. The Highlands of Scotland provide an example: a clan system which was in some ways tribal and in others feudal surrendered to its fate on Culloden Moor in 1746. Hitherto, the clan chieftains had been the ultimate powers within their respective territories, vast estates which were finely divided into tenancies and sub-tenancies. The autocratic chieftains derived their wealth, status and security by raising black cattle and impoverished warriors. Although the loyalty of the clansmen is legendary, the success of the clan muster was insured by the practice of granting tenancies on short leases—and eviction threatened the warrior who ignored the call to arms. While the aristocratic warlords were uninterested in land improvement, the tenant on a short-term lease had neither the resources nor the incentive to improve or even maintain the vulnerable Highland soils. The preoccupation with politics, status and war overrode all economic considerations; as a result, by the time of Culloden, the Highland zone of Scotland was a worn out and grievously over-populated agricultural wasteland. Only when the English overlordship forced political habits to change did the logic of economics begin to govern the pattern of land use. The grotesque sheep clearances of the 1760s to 1880s were the result.

In our attempts to understand the past we tend to assume—despite all the contrary evidence from the modern world—that human behaviour was governed by logic. We may, however, find ourselves in pursuit of the wrong system of logic and to be relying on economic yardsticks when we should be concerned with the forces of politics, status or religion. The clan system of the Highlands created a landscape which was ravaged by over-grazing and soil exhaustion and within which most people lived in conditions of extreme deprivation. Yet the system *did* have a logic of its own and it *did* persist for countless centuries.

The Highlands clan territory was one member of a galaxy of different types of territories existing in Britain in different places and at different times. Every territory must have a useful role to play or else it will be discarded. All territories have areas and limits or boundaries; some have 'central places' or foci resembling a cell with its decision centre or nucleus, internal components and outer membrane. But territories are also very diverse. A medieval village-centred field system was an economic or agricultural territory not necessarily corresponding to a manor, or a Roman villa-centred estate, which was a tenurial unit, or a church-centred ecclesiastical and administrative parish. A shire was one thing, and an Iron Age tribal territory was much more. Territories have different functions and they change and evolve along with the communities who adopt, preserve or adapt them.

At the same time, we are just beginning to appreciate the durability of many ancient land cells. A territory can be like the hard shell of a fertile egg, which remains rigid and unchanged while all sorts of important changes are going on inside. Another analogy is that of the billiard table that preserves its form while the enclosed balls, which may be likened to settlements, take up changing positions within its fixed bounds.

So many of the most important questions in archaeology would be answered if we could unravel the patterns and layouts of former territories. We would know the sizes of the communities which worked the different economic land cells, the combination of the different hunting, grazing and ploughland resources needed to sustain them, and the ways in which smaller communities combined in larger political or tenurial units. We would also know whether the supposed invasions and introductions of new technologies had traumatic effects, or whether the older political and social territorial patterns endured. We do know that many of the partitions in the British landscape are old—and we suspect that many partitions are older than has generally been allowed. But as yet, hints and hypotheses are almost all that we have to cling to.

What follows is divided into four parts. First we will explore some of the psychological aspects of territory. Then we will look at territories in terms of the one watchword of landscape history: change. Next, we will introduce a spectrum of boundary markers that endure as prominent or subtle monuments to man's urge to define, defend and organize. Finally, we turn to the other great watchword of landscape study–continuity—and describe some of the remarkable new insights concerning the durability of territories.

7

Territory in Mind

Because the use of land was essential to human survival, it is not easy to disentangle the pursuit and defence of basic economic needs from behaviour that was rooted more in psychological factors. Since territory was such a fundamental factor in human life and history, studies of territoriality embrace politics, psychology and a flock of other –ologies.

Ethology, the behavioural branch of zoology, is more prone than most subjects to statements of the obvious; but it does offer some interesting insights into the biological bases of human behaviour. Workers in this field (which has Konrad Lorenz as its most famous practitioner), have been fascinated by territorial behaviour in the animal world and its relevance to understanding man. The most widely read book on the subject is *The Territorial Imperative* by Robert Ardrey. Ardrey rose to fame with his books *African Genesis* and *The Social Contract.* Many of his sweeping proposals were ultimately based on dubious interpretations of Australopithecine skeletal remains. Man was presented (probably wrongly) as the latest of a line of blood-thirsty hunters and cannibals, his behaviour forever governed by his violent and intensely territorial instincts. With no little ingenuity, Ardrey sought to produce a biological support for his own reactionary and pessimistic political outlooks. Now it seems that the slaughter and murders attributed to *Australopithecus* were wrought on the human bones concerned by leopards and hyenas.

In fact, the territorial component of human behaviour is not yet understood. In the animal kingdom some species are territorial and some are not. Where territoriality is apparent it seems to have a definite survival value for the species concerned. It may operate at the level of the group, like a troop of monkeys which will guard the boundaries of an area which supports them, or at the level of the individual breeding pair. It is normally only concerned with aggression towards members of the same species. The great advantage which territoriality offers is that of adjusting the breeding population to the available resources. In some species the readiness to reproduce has the possession of a territory as its prerequisite. Those males which lack the measure of dominance necessary to secure a territory are not accepted by potential mates. In this way the young which are produced have access to an adequate supply of food and an overpopulation of undernourished and vulnerable youngsters is avoided. In the various territorial conflicts the possessor of territory is often seen to enjoy a psychological dominance over the intruder, irrespective of their relative physiques. And so there may be psychology as well as legal experience in the old saw that 'possession is nine tenths of the law'.

This is all very well, but we still have much to learn about the biological foundations of human territoriality. Does it only operate on a very localized level, as implied by the saying 'An Englishman's home is his castle', or can it—as writers such as Desmond Morris have suggested—explain the behaviour of nations, football crowds or car-owners? Whether one be a hunter and gatherer, a herder or farmer, the possession of lands and the ability to exclude threatening competitors is essential to survival. This is a fact of economic life irrespective of any more subtle psychological pressures or instincts.

Even so, psychological factors, particularly those concerning the perception of territories, are much too important to ignore. Everyone, whether a modern commuter, a Dark Age peasant or a Mesolithic hunter and gatherer has a clear perception of 'the homeland' and what constitutes it. To most intents and purposes however, there were no maps before the Middle Ages—a crucially important fact. The homeland was not a precise drawing on a piece of paper, but a composite of many mental pictures of ploughlands, pastures and trails, places where roots could be grubbed and of killing grounds. The old or ancient farmers or hunters could not draw their territories; their ideas about their actual shapes were probably quite inaccurate, but the boundaries, the no man's lands and the no-go areas will have been well known and oft retold.

Each group will have had a clear perception of what it owned and must defend, which resources were shared, which intrusions could be tolerated and which strategic areas must, at all costs, be secured. Though rooted in experience, these feelings about territory were perceptions rather than facts, but every group must have had its own ideas about what the political scientist K. E. Boulding has termed 'critical boundaries'. These are lines or zones which policy-makers perceive as being crucial to the survival and well-being of the group concerned. We all have a pretty good idea about where the critical boundaries of the modern world lie—and our survival may rest on the hope that this perception is respected by potential adversaries. The western powers accept Warsaw Pact troops on the Odra, but not on the Elbe. President Johnson put the western perception of critical boundaries into words when he said: 'We must say in south-east Asia—as we did in Europe—in the words of the Bible, "Hitherto shalt thou come but no further".' Offa's Dyke and Hadrian's Wall were surely expressing such sentiments in different ways. One also thinks of the Rogationtide ritual of 'beating the bounds' of a parish which goes back at least to the eighth century in some form. To assist the learning process, choir boys were beaten at various points on the boundaries, for them an unforgettable experience which underlines the fact that in times past everyone knew or had to learn where the bounds of their landcell lay.

Attitudes to territory are fluid and change with time and from one individual to another. The Neolithic peasant was probably preoccupied with maintaining critical boundaries which lay within a few miles of his homestead; his perception of the territories beyond may have been blurred, with the great ritual monuments and meeting places, which he might visit occasionally or labour upon, standing as familiar islands in a fuzzy middle distance, while the exotic stone axes which the traders brought may have come from mythical or unimaginable places. At the start of the fifteenth century England began to feel the influences of the Hussites of Bohemia, but for the average Englishman these ideas might almost as well have come from the moon. More

28. A section of Hadrian's Wall near Housesteads fort.

than five centuries later it suited Prime Minister Chamberlain to perceive Bohemia—or rather, Czechoslovakia—as 'a faraway land' which was populated by 'people of whom we know nothing'. Even today most British people perceive that country faintly, as a rather faceless component of the Eastern bloc. Yet, visas apart, Prague is far more accessible to the Londoner than is Kirkwall in Orkney, and scarcely more distant.

One would love to learn the perceptions and expectations of Britain which were held by those ancient peoples who chose to settle in these islands—and whether or not the reality disappointed them. Perhaps their attitudes would have surprised us in the same way that the following description of the Americas seems somewhat off-beam: 'It is to the South, not to the icy North, that everyone in search of fortune should turn, below the equator everything is rich.' This was written by Peter Martyr in 1525 and reflects the preoccupation with instant wealth in the form of gold or gems. Attitudes to what was eventually to become the USA and Canada were summarized in Admiral Morison's remark that 'America was discovered accidentally, when discovered it was not wanted; and most of the exploration for the next fifty years was done in the hope of getting through or round it.'

These comments reflect the important fact that peoples of different cultural backgrounds respond to territory in different ways. If we could resurrect a group of Mesolithic clansmen and set them down in the Lake District they might share the modern conservationist's feelings that the coniferous plantations are an ecological disaster zone—but on the whole they might not be displeased with the lake and moorland setting. Peasants brought from Normandy on the other hand might think it a foul place with its interminable rain, rock exposures and thin, acid soils. Attitudes to landscape can change quite swiftly: 'after travelling . . . over this region of stone and sorrow, life begins to be a burden, and you wish to perish'. Sidney South was providing a description of our beloved Cotswolds which was quite in keeping with those of his contemporary early nineteenth-century arbiters of scenic taste!

Attitudes towards the homeland will also vary according to whereabouts within it one dwells. While the fourteenth-century Scottish invasions might have been irksome or even irrelevant to people living in the south of England, they were catastrophic events for others living in the north. The territories of the Mesolithic and early Neolithic periods may have been so small and the settlements so ephemeral that everyone may have been a frontiersman. As the territories expanded and amalgamated, the frontier communities will have assumed special roles and attitudes within their societies. At all periods the frontiersman is the first to suffer when his territory is attacked and he often forms the vanguard for territorial expansion. Not surprisingly, his political awareness is heightened; it is no accident that the extreme forms of Republicanism are most commonly espoused in the Irish counties which lie closest to the Ulster border.

However, the frontiersman is much more than a political activist and the frontier is more than a sensitive territorial skin. The frontier can be a place where different cultures meet and exchange ideas, as well as the setting of confrontations. To F. J. Turner, writing in 1893, American nationhood was born at the advancing frontiers of the USA. In these zones the Old World outlooks were shed, people from diverse back-grounds met and mixed and co-operated and—according to this romantic version— a nation of independent and resourceful Americanized Europeans emerged, with each new phase of frontier advance serving a process of national renewal. Of course, we wonder about the relevance of ideas such as these to events in prehistoric Britain; for example, the cultural interactions at the shifting frontiers between the early Bronze Age Beaker ideas and the indigenous late Neolithic societies. As we have said, we do not know much about the Beaker movement and whether we should see it in terms of new ideas or actual immigration on a large scale; but we do know something about the outcome of the influences and the revitalization of old beliefs with the extension and elaboration of old monuments such as Stonehenge, the building of new temples and the insertion of Beaker burials in old tombs like West Kennet.

During the Neolithic and Beaker periods the great monument-building projects must have had enormous social and political side-effects, with labour being recruited from all corners of the tribal territories concerned. Contacts will have been made, ideas, beliefs and customs exchanged and in this way the social and political coherence of the

29. Stonehenge, Wiltshire. The construction of this great monument must have exploited the labour resources of a wide area.

territory must have been strengthened and expanded. The great ritual monuments like causewayed camps and major circles demonstrate that the necessary capacities to mobilize and organize large and heterogeneous labour forces already existed. The organizational abilities of the controlling chieftains, priests or demagogues can only have been strengthened by the experiences of these great operations.

Medieval local communities were probably less parochial than we have imagined and events like pilgrimages or the muster of great feudal armies must have periodically broken the bonds of parochialism and created the contacts between peoples from widely separated areas which were essential to the process of nation building. Like the frontiers of nineteenth-century America, the great cathedral and castle-building operations were also places where people from widely different provincial backgrounds met and mixed. This will have been particularly true in the cases of the great Edwardian castles in Wales. The records tell of the 100 English masons conscripted by the Justice of Chester in 1295 for work at Caernarfon castle, of other masons from Yorkshire, Northamptonshire and Dorset, ditch-diggers from Lincolnshire, carpenters from Derbyshire, of local carters contracted to shift building materials and similar deals with Welsh ship-owners. At Harlech in 1286 some 950 men were employed on the castle site, 546 labourers and a complement of skilled workers, masons, quarriers, smiths and carpenters. They will have conversed with each other and with the scores of transport workers and the locals who provided the many back-up services. Whether in the prehistoric or the medieval period, the great building site must have been a cultural melting pot where perceptions of the homeland were broadened and enriched.

The homeland may seem a rather different place when it is perceived from its heartland rather than its periphery. The political scientist L. D. Kristof has contrasted the differing perspectives of the inner-orientated interior dweller and the outward-looking frontiersman. Central control often diminishes towards the margins of a territory; for example, the medieval Scottish kings had difficulty in controlling the English raiding activities of powerful Border families, although these raids created a threat of crippling and far-reaching English reprisals. Faced with the difficulties of transmitting power to the territorial frontiers, central authorities have sometimes delegated responsibilities for the defence and advancement of marchlands, offering quasi-independence in return. The Cossacks performed such roles on the expanding Asiatic frontiers of tsarist Russia, as did the lords of the Anglo-Welsh and Anglo-Scottish marches. Needless to say, these privileges were withdrawn when the capacity for effective central government could be extended over the marchlands. In Wales the successive advances are marked by the motte and bailey strongholds of freebooting Norman lords, speculative plantation towns, the great Edwardian citadels of the late thirteenth century and new generations of urban plantations.

A measure of psychology must have been involved in the gradual process of territorial amalgamation and expansion which began with the establishment of small clan hunting and gathering territories in the later phases of the Upper Palaeolithic period, culminating in the political unions which produced the United Kingdom. As

30. *This enormous unexcavated cairn, probably a passage grave, occupies the summit of Knocknarea mountain near Sligo and is a very prominent landmark dominating the surrounding territory. It is ringed by the ruins of several lesser passage graves.*

we shall see, it is interesting that while the Romans had no difficulty in forming a perception of Britain as a complete and integrated province, there is no evidence that the immediately preceding dynasties of Celtic tribal rulers were capable of perceiving such a British union. Their ambitions seem to have ended at the regional level and it was only in the later centuries of the Saxon era that the formation of a united English kingdom became a feasible ambition (although the Mercian king, Offa, AD 757-96, had unrealistically styled himself as 'Emperor' and 'King of the English').

8

Territory and Change

Here we describe how different types of territories may have evolved along with the societies which created and used them. The other side of the territorial coin, as represented by continuity and the retention of ancient territories, we discuss in Chapter 10 which concludes this part.

Apart from mentioning that lake and riverside sites in the southern parts of England seem to have been the most favoured places for settlement during the Old Stone Age or Palaeolithic period, there is next to nothing that can yet be said about the hunting territories of these really ancient Britons. Whatever territories may have existed, they will probably have been made redundant by the sweeping environmental changes of the period around 12,000-8,000 BC, the establishment of a lush and diverse forest cover and the replacement of the great tundra herbivores by woodland creatures.

We may not be able to delimit a single Mesolithic territory, but we can make some informed guesses about the general features of these homelands. The hunting and gathering lifestyle will have ensured that population densities were relatively light and that the society consisted of many small and self-sufficient groups—extended families, perhaps. Most of these groups will have had to range widely in search of food, towed along in the slipstreams of migratory animals upon which they preyed, while exploiting each vegetational flush of edible shoots, grass seeds, fruits and nuts which the changing seasons offered.

Even though population densities must have been rather light, we would be wrong to imagine the bands being like lost souls, forever on the move through a dark, unknown and threatening forest. More than any other lifestyle, that of the hunter and gatherer hinges upon an expert and intimate knowledge of the environment, its grazings and migration trails and the different habitats which provide roots and fruits and seeds at different times of the year. Neither should we imagine that vast areas of Britain remained vacant and unexplored, with the bountiful produce of the lush and humid woodlands and life-teeming marshes unharvested. Man is exceptionally resourceful, mobile and adaptable and will swiftly colonize any niche which the environment offers.

One estimate has put the Mesolithic population of Britain at around 10,000, but this assumes that venison from the red deer was the cornerstone of human existence. However, David Clarke has pointed out that so-called hunting cultures rely heavily on the gathering of vegetable food and he guesses that sixty to eighty per cent by weight of the Mesolithic diet was provided by vegetable foods. He has described how temperate oak/hazel forests will produce up to 1,000 litres of edible acorns per tree, half a tonne of hazel nuts a hectare; twenty to fifty tonnes of edible bracken root per square kilometre; prodigious quantities of fungi and berries, and green mountains of edible leaves, shoots and herbs.

With all this in mind it seems probable that the small clan or family group of Mesolithic hunter-gatherers would, in the course of each year, progress around a circuit and that this circuit formed the framework of their territory. They would know their territory and its bounds very well and at a given time of the year they would be found in a specific place where a particular food resource was ready to be culled. In many places these territorial stepping-stones or temporary campsites might be integrated in a pattern which followed the seasonal movements of red deer from lowland wintering places to open or less heavily wooded upland summer grazings.

People as ingenious as were our Mesolithic ancestors undoubtedly would never starve in the seasons of plenty between the spring and the great autumn fruit and berry harvests. The crunch would come in winter when the natural food factories were shut down. At this time of the year the bands would head for base camps in low-lying and sheltered places, retreating downslope with the deer and living beside rivers, lakes or marshes which continued to supply fish and wildfowl, while vast stores of gathered nuts, roots and dried fruit could be stored in pits as hard rations in a seasonally hard environment. Many of these base-camp sites have been found; they are marked by dense scatters of worked flints and microlith blades and by storage pits, and it is possible that some of these excavated hollows may have been covered in skin awnings to serve as dwellings.

Archaeological work suggests that the 'typical' territory might contain four types of settlement sites. First there was the winter base camp which was left in the charge of the old, the very young and their mothers during other seasons of the year. Settlement at this site might persist for several years until its surroundings had been depleted of small game. Secondly, there were 'gathering camps' which were periodically occupied as bases for spring and autumn hunting and food-gathering and repeatedly visited over a number of years. Thirdly, there were 'light exploitation camps' which seem to have been visited at certain seasons by very small hunting and gathering parties, perhaps in search of a specific type of food—shellfish, a nut or a fruit—while finally, there were bivouac sites where small hunting and foraging parties would camp overnight.

As long ago as 1937, J. D. G. Clark and W. Rankine mapped the flint and dwelling-pit sites of the Mesolithic in the Weald; they correlate remarkably with the sandy soils of the Greensand and Tunbridge Wells Beds which would have been particularly productive of hazel nuts, acorns, bracken rhizomes, fungi and berries. Of this 'Horsham

Group' of base camps Clarke writes: 'Radial territories from this common core could conveniently run across several ecological zones, north to the Thames valley, marshes and estuary, or south to the lost Sussex and Hampshire coastline on the sheltered South Channel bay.' (For much of the Mesolithic period a low land-bridge linked south-east England and France.) Elsewhere in Britain the different environments will have supported different territories. Around the upland margins we can imagine winter base camps in valleys, with the adjoining territories running up-valley and upslope to embrace the summer grazings of the upland plateaux; other territories may have fanned outwards from well-endowed lakeside foci, while coastal environments will probably have had their own specially adapted territorial divisions.

We can only wonder whether there was any tendency for territories established in the Mesolithic period to survive the transformations of the environment which were enacted by Neolithic farmers. As yet we do not know the extent to which the farmers concerned were immigrants from the continent or agricultural converts from among the indigenous Mesolithic people. While the earlier farming efforts may not have produced dramatic increases in the production of food, there are good reasons for thinking that the old hunting and gathering economy and the new farming lifestyle were incompatible. First hunting, whether mainly for sustenance or recreation, remained important in the Neolithic period and the activities of 'weekend' Neolithic huntsmen in pursuit of quarry which they might have regarded as crop-gobbling vermin could have played havoc with the game supply that was essential to the professional hunters. Secondly, every territorial frontier of the Mesolithic clan must have been a 'critical frontier' because the circuit would have linked essential local food-producing environments. The expansion of farming activities across a part of a hunting territory would also be disruptive in rather the same way that the modern afforestation of slopes in the Scottish Highlands and the accompanying construction of forest-top deer fences puts a barrier across the red deer 'migration trails' from upland pastures to lowland wintering places.

The nature of Neolithic territories is also largely mysterious, particularly for the earlier part of the period. We cannot be sure whether the emphasis should be placed on a shifting form of agriculture based on slash-and-burn clearance followed by phases of desertion and forest regrowth, or on more advanced and permanent methods, with the revitalization of tired croplands under pasture providing the fallow role. Each system would surely give rise to different territorial patterns. The pollen evidence is not clearcut although some experts have visualized the Neolithic landscape as a very detailed mosaic of croplands, pasture, upland grazing and woodland; some emphasize the survival of woodland. Other evidence comes from snail shells which can survive long periods of burial and it is known that different types of snail flourish in open and in shaded and wooded environments. The snail-shell evidence can be studied along with that of buried soils which may be found preserved beneath datable monuments like tombs.

In the chalk and limestone areas, the evidence is quite striking, for the vast majority of Neolithic monuments are found to have been constructed on lands which had long been cleared of woodland. In many parts of Neolithic Britain the landscape will have

31. *Long barrows and chambered tombs like this re-erected example, Lanyon Quoit, Cornwall, seem to have served as the foci of Neolithic territories.*

been covered by extensive systems of fields rather than dotted with island clearings. Given that more than four millennia of agricultural activities have masked or obliterated the traces of Neolithic farming, it is not surprising that hardly any clear evidence of Neolithic field systems has survived. However, from the 1970s onwards Neolithic fields of sizes around three to four acres bounded by continuous straight walls of up to a mile in length have been emerging from beneath the blanket peat around Behy in Co. Mayo, in an area which can never have been especially inviting to the farmer.

Since our vision of the Neolithic environment is blurred because we know little about the settlements and the jigsaw patterns of fields, pastures, commons and woodlands which supported them, our ideas about the territories of the period can only be vague. There is, however, one type of monument—the collective tomb—which seems particularly suggestive.

The Neolithic tombs may have had several roles. Clearly they were places where the remains of selected corpses were eventually stored and laid to rest. But the tombs are also likely to have been important territorial markers and symbols. They often seem to be associated with pockets or packages of land which would have supported small

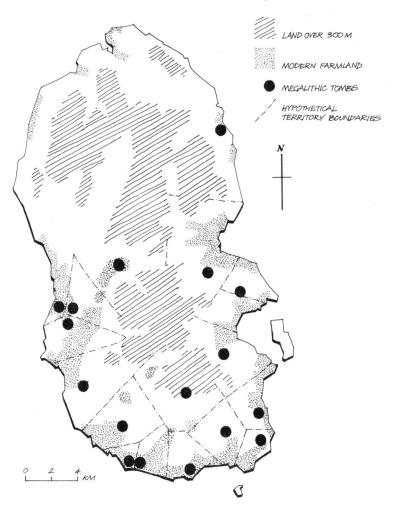

Fig. 1. *Map of Arran, Scotland, showing the distribution of Megalithic tombs in relation to modern farming land (from C. Renfrew,* Before Civilisation, *Penguin 1976).*

communities. Often too, they seem to have been placed in prominent, eye-catching positions. In staking claims of group ownership it may well have been important to demonstrate that one's ancestors had controlled and worked the lands concerned; how better to announce this fact to would-be interlopers than by storing their remains in a dominating and monumental mausoleum?

If we are correct, then the tombs must tell of a situation in the fourth millennium BC in which territories were being claimed if not fought over and empty farmland was a limited commodity. Some estimates of the population of Neolithic Britain which have been offered must be wildly inaccurate, such as Professor R. J. C. Atkinson's suggestion that at one stage the population of Lowland England was between 70 and 140. Plainly, such a minute population could not have prevented a rapid recolonization of the landscape by forest, let alone have continued to remove woodland. Dr. G. J. Wainwright has noted that southern England contains rather less than 200 earthen long barrows and around 130 chambered tombs (more of both have since been found); he suggests that these tombs may well have been reserved for the burial of selected members of the population, while the majority of corpses were disposed of in ways which are hard to identify.

The tombs then were the mausoleums for the top people in the Neolithic communities and, in a few cases, anatomists have been able to recognize family resemblances between some of the different skeletons in particular tombs. Whether the members of the élites were landlords, priests, petty-chieftains or all of these things, we do not know. Although the tombs in some areas form loose clusters when plotted on small-scale maps, in general each tomb often seems to serve as the focal point of a small local territory. The relationship between a tomb (often situated upon a raised beach) and a geographical land cell seems clearest in the cases of a number of small Scottish islands. Professor Colin Renfrew has shown that on the islands of Arran and Rousay, each tomb seems to be associated with a coastal strip of arable land. Meanwhile, in many areas of English ridge and valley country it often appears that a tomb has been deliberately sited not upon a real crest line, but on the skyline as seen from the plain or valley beneath. In this way, the magnificent West Kennet chambered tomb in Wiltshire lies just above the 550 foot (168 metres) contour on a northern spur of the All Canning Down which rises to heights of over 800 feet (244 metres). Yet from the vale of the River Kennet it is a prominent skyline feature which seems to be watching over the lowland landscape.

As an area in which a particular local dynasty or élite was revered and in which the aristocratic mausoleum was normally the most imposing and durable construction, the tomb territory would seem to have been the basic social, religious and, perhaps, political unit over most if not all of Neolithic Britain.

The construction of a collective tomb would be well within the capacity of the people of most 'tomb territories'. Estimates of the amount of labour involved, based on experimental constructions such as those at Overton Down in Wiltshire and Wareham in Dorset, suggest that a 'typical' long barrow might be built by twenty men in less than a month or that a very large example of a long barrow some 400 feet (122 metres) in length would take a labour force of eighty more than a month to build.

Causewayed camps are roughly the contemporaries of chambered tombs and it is clear that they embody a different magnitude of toil. Windmill Hill in Wiltshire is the type-site and estimates of the amounts of labour involved in excavating the triple ring of interrupted ditches range from 40,000 to 120,000 man-hours. Clearly the pooling of labour contributed by a number of tomb territories would be necessary for the construction of a causewayed camp. The next question is obvious: do the causewayed camps of southern and eastern England represent the foci of a second or top tier of territories, with each camp territory embracing a number of barrow territories?

As yet, we do not even know what a causewayed camp was for. Each camp was some sort of focus or 'central place', and defensive, religious, economic and social interpretations are all on offer. Most Neolithic monuments may have served several

Fig. 2. *The emergence of late Neolithic chiefdoms in Wessex, with the distribution of causewayed camps plotted in relation to long barrows (from C. Renfrew,* Before Civilisation, *Penguin 1976).*

purposes and the camps could have been used for social or religious gatherings and as market and distribution centres for the trading of livestock, stone axes and other commodities. Windmill Hill dates from around 3200 BC and there are older examples of causewayed camps, such as Abingdon in Oxfordshire which dates back to around 3900 BC.

Professor Renfrew has suggested that this period witnessed the emergence of chiefdoms and that the camps could represent the focal point of each chiefdom in Wessex. He showed how the landscape could be divided up into a series of camp-centred social territories. His suggestions were updated and amended by G. Barker and D. Webley, who proposed that each of the resultant territories would encompass roughly similar amounts of high pasture, arable soils, lowland grazing and browse. Of the thirteen camps which they map, some, like Maiden Castle, Hambledon Hill, and Whitesheet Hill seem to be situated beside rather than among loose clusters of long barrows. However, the even nature of the territorial partitioning between camp foci would be even more impressive were it not for two trios of closely-spaced camps, Rybury, Knap Hill and Windmill Hill in one group, Broadwell, Langford and Eastleach in another. Distributions such as this can provide the basis for many an inconclusive game and one can, for example, relate the camp locations to the upper reaches of the rivers Frome, Stour, Hampshire, Avon, Kennet and Thames.

On balance, a two-tiered division of the Wessex landscape into barrow-centred and camp-centred territories seems more probable than improbable. Not all tomb sites have been discovered and not all tombs were in use at the same time—so one can only guess that the average tomb territory might have been parish-sized and in places, smaller. But this is not the end of the story. It has been suggested that there may be some sort of association between long barrow groups and the 6.2 mile-long (10 km) Dorset cursus, an avenue-like feature flanked by banks, which are around ninety yards apart, and outer quarry ditches. It had been said that the cursus represents 1,300,000 man-hours worth of toil, sufficient to occupy 500 men for 260 days; at least ten times the amount of organized effort needed to construct a causewayed camp.

The man-made mountain of Silbury Hill in Wiltshire dates from around 2800 BC and it has been calculated that it embodies a staggering 18,000,000 man-hours of effort. If a permanent labour force of around fifty men had been employed continuously on the creation of Silbury Hill, they would have had little time to down tools before work began on hauling and erecting the great sarsens of the inner ring at nearby Avebury, around 2600 BC. It is hard to avoid the conclusion that at a fairly early stage in the third millennium, much if not all of Wessex was responding to a powerful and capable central authority and that this authority was so well entrenched that ideas and ambitions could pass from one generation to the next. Between the great landmarks of Windmill Hill, Silbury Hill and West Kennet chambered tomb, the prestige of this authority was further enhanced with the construction of the uniquely impressive circle, henge and stone-avenue complex at Avebury.

We are left to wonder whether Wessex should be regarded as a political unit, or whether some enormously influential religious organization was integrating the labour forces contributed by a number of perhaps secular chiefdoms?

32. The enormous artificial mound of Silbury Hill, Wiltshire, must express the might of the same territorial dynasty that created the Avebury monument nearby.

Work on the perimeter ditch and inner bank at Stonehenge began about the same time as the inner circles were erected at Avebury, or a little before. In the middle of the third millennium at least eighty bluestones were imported, originally from South Wales, and erected in a double ring. Subsequent constructional stages involved the dismantling of these rings, the levelling of the site, the importation of massive sarsen slabs (probably from the Marlborough Downs) to form a new circle and a horseshoe formation of 'trilithons', the re-use of some of the bluestones in an oval setting, and finally, around 1600 BC, the construction of a bluestone circle and horseshoe within the sarsen circle and trilithon arrangements. Much later, around 1100 BC, the avenue was extended down to the banks of the River Avon.

We can only wonder whether the two great religious monuments of Avebury and Stonehenge were complimentary or whether they represented two different political and religious territorial powers? Stonehenge is interesting in another political way. It would have been difficult for the Wessex powers to have accomplished the transport of the ponderous bluestones from their origins on the slopes of the Prescelly mountains down to the waiting rafts on the Bristol Channel without the agreement of the local chieftains. Either religious influences were so powerful and widespread that they overrode all political considerations, or else the Wessex and Welsh authorities were partners in effective diplomacy. The bluestones however offer other challenges: one has been found inside a long barrow near Heytesbury in Wiltshire which must be much older than Stonehenge. And so Stonehenge might have been constructed from materials imported to Wessex long before.

The so-called 'megalithic' religion, with its emphasis on the dead, the afterlife and the building of monumental mausoleums or houses for the dead probably had many regional variations or cults, but in some loose sense it embraced Britain and the western seaboard and peninsulas of Europe. The details of the religion and the levels of cultural

102

or ethnic similarity uniting its far-flung communities of followers remain mysterious; this is equally true of the beliefs and adherents of the Beaker creed.

The evidence for territories in the Beaker period and early Bronze Age is more difficult to recognize. The oldest Beaker pots in Britain date from around 2700 BC; copper working was introduced around 2500 BC and late beakers and the manufacture of bronze objects are associated with the period 2200–1900 BC. In the course of these centuries the ritual of collective burial in aristocratic tombs was replaced by burial of either a single corpse in a stone-lined cist, or of one or a few bodies beneath a round barrow. The crouched corpse was generally provided with items of domestic or military equipment and a Beaker pot, which may have contained a ritual mead and meadow-sweet brew. By the closing centuries of the third millennium the collective tomb was obsolete and the old tomb territories may likewise have become redundant.

While the round barrows are sometimes grouped closely in cemeteries and include groups which may be related to other features of the man-made landscape—like Stonehenge, the Dorset cursus and the Ridgeway route—it is not easy to relate them to territories. Again, though, there are scores of examples which were sited on skylines and seem to be watching over a particular land cell. Andrew Fleming has suggested that Wessex may have been some kind of early Bronze Age 'proto-state' in which a stock-raising aristocracy dominated sedentary farming peoples and that the pastoralist

33. *Some of the surviving stones in the great circle at Avebury. Beyond the stones is the encircling henge ditch and then the still imposing henge ramparts.*

groups congregated in areas of upland grazing in summer and autumn, when they constructed their barrows and barrow cemeteries. The barrows could thus be seen as the religious landmarks of seasonally occupied territories—but this interpretation is controversial.

Although Renfrew's view that, in the course of the Neolithic period, the emerging chiefdoms became fully fledged is attractive, the Bronze Age presents some problems. We would expect the chiefdoms or tribal territories to become larger, more coherent and more sharply defined. We know from the archaeological evidence that Bronze Age society was a class society dominated by chiefs, aristocrats or warriors wielding costly bronze swords or daggers and wearing bronze and gold ornaments. Even so, Stonehenge apart, early second millennium societies did not tend to create the enormous and durable monuments which visibly survive to tell us of the wholesale mobilization and organization of large provincial populations. If extensive chiefdoms existed—as they probably did—we are still unable to locate them. It now seems that in the later Bronze Age the main social and trading centres were located in lowland valleys and so the evidence we seek may be buried beneath great thicknesses of slope wash and river silt. In the latter half of the second millennium, however, the sporadic construction of hillforts marked a revival of the monumental traditions.

Much more positive evidence is forthcoming of the more localized Bronze Age territorial divisions. The work accomplished in recent years on the Dartmoor 'reaves' is most valuable. The reaves are low stone walls which were built as land boundaries. Andrew Fleming has used the evidence of the reave networks to produce a convincing account of how, in the Bronze Age, the upper moorland of South Moor was used as common grazing by six or seven fringing communities. Each community had its own lower valley grazing land near to the settlement enclosures, and other areas which were divided by networks of 'parallel reaves' and used partly for cultivation and partly for grazing. Other reaves clearly demarcated the boundaries between neighbouring territories, sometimes running to streams or rivers which continued the boundary. The 'contour reaves' which divided the group-owned from the common land may have been less important or later than the boundary-marking reaves.

On Dartmoor the ancient patterns of field and territorial divisions have survived; there is no reason to suppose that most other parts of Bronze Age Britain did not have similarly comprehensive and well-organized systems of division. In many places the evidence will have been obliterated, while in others it probably endures unnoticed in the patterns of streams, old banks, wall footings and boundary stones; some of the reaves which Fleming has mapped still carry existing boundaries. According to the reaves scheme, the shared commons will have been areas where neighbouring territorial communities made contact and these contacts may have been important in furthering the process of political development. The reave period on Dartmoor may only have lasted for two or three centuries, in the middle Bronze Age.

As the archaeological evidence accumulates, it seems that the competition for control of territory intensified in the later part of the Bronze Age, when rural population levels may have been comparable to those of the medieval period. As population pressure grew, so the definition and demarcation of territories became more exact and forcefully stated. If we can generalize from some local evidence it seems that boundaries marked by chains of round barrows were then marked out by 'pit alignments' or lines of pits, which were in turn superseded by prominent 'linear earthworks'—long distance banks and ditches. (Important new evidence of this from the North York Moors is

Fig. 3. *General map of south Dartmoor plotting the reaves (from A. Selkirk in* Proceedings of Prehistoric Society, *1978*).

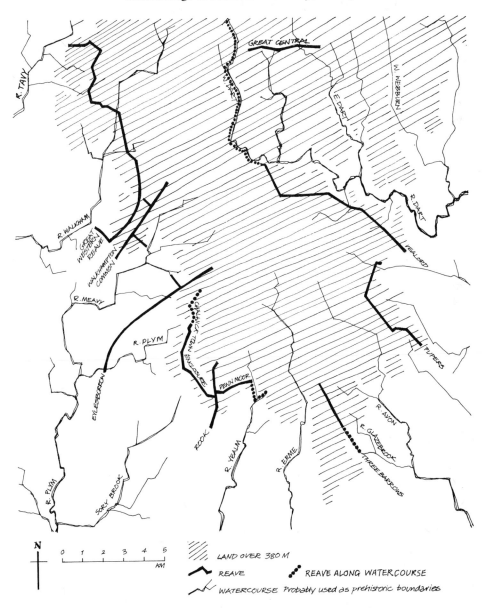

described in the following chapter.) In the later Bronze Age, hillforts—the most obvious symbols of competition and conflict for territorial control—began to appear in growing numbers.

As one might expect, the evidence for the Iron Age is much more comprehensive, but in some ways it seems to be contradictory. The classical writers who described England in the period before the Roman Conquest tell of extensive tribal territories like that of the Catuvellauni of Essex and Hertfordshire, capitals like Camulodunum and chieftains like Cunobelinus. Several tribes had their own coinage and the archaeological evidence based on coin distributions may even demonstrate the annexation of parts of one territory by a neighbouring tribe. Clearly a division of Britain into advanced tribal provinces had been accomplished at least by the later stages of the pre-Roman Iron Age. The hillforts on the other hand would seem to tell a different story, for they could be interpreted as regional or local strongholds in a finely-partitioned and unstable landscape; it is interesting that some tribes, like those of Wessex, built numerous massive forts, others built far fewer and others still had lots of small hillforts. Finally, homestead defences in the forms of the ditched, banked or walled compounds surrounding most farmsteads or hamlets could be read as evidence of an anarchic and turbulent political situation in which each family or small community had to look to its own defences. (All these problems are explored in more detail in Part III.)

The only correct answer must be one which assimilates all this apparently conflicting evidence. The discrepancy between the extensive or provincial nature of the major tribal territories and the local or regional impact of the hillfort may fade when we realize that the tribal units were unstable, often subject to wars and intrigues and therefore frequently gaining or losing peripheral territories while, at the same time, Iron Age society was intensely hierarchical. Caesar wrote of *druides* or learned men, *nobiles* or aristocrats, *equites* who were warriors or 'knights' and *plebes* or common folk sometimes dismissed as *servi* or slaves, as well as the great tribal kings. There were also *obaerati* and *ambacti* who might be compared to grades of feudal peasants.

The territorial divisions of Iron Age Britain surely reflected a society which was politically complex and the presence of grades of sub-chiefs and lesser nobles. Thus the hillfort territory could be the Iron Age equivalent of the domain controlled by a medieval baron from a motte and bailey or stone keep.

When exploring the many puzzles which the hillforts evoke, we must remember that they were a long-lived feature of a troubled landscape, with a lifespan of more than a millennium. There have been several attempts to relate the hillfort to the territory which it may have served or dominated, but some interesting new possibilities are suggested in the work of Richard Bradley and his research students. Like the Neolithic tomb, the hillfort could have played several roles—and these roles could have evolved during the long hillfort era. Among other things, the hillforts could have been fortified food stores. Many of the earlier hillforts are known to have been packed with rectangular buildings, presumed to have been granaries. The later hillforts often contained scores of storage pits. It has been argued that the older hillforts served as distribution centres for grain produced in the surrounding territory. While a granary can be opened at any time to extract the stored grain, pits are sealed and grain cannot be removed piecemeal. And so it seems that the later hillforts may have served in the hoarding of tribute extracted from an expanded and more extensive area. Thus they had perhaps become colonial centres as well as local strongholds and grain banks.

We have seen that, by the late Neolithic period, forms of centralized control existed which could mobilize and command the labour resources of county-sized or larger areas. Some writers have compared the Wessex of the earlier Bronze Age to a tribal kingdom or 'proto-state'. As yet we do not know the extent to which the tribal territories of the Bronze Age governed those of the Celtic period, but some strong influences must have existed. However, in the growing climate of unrest and environmental decay which marked the transition from the Age of Bronze to that of Iron, in southern England at least the centres of political control moved firstly upslope from valley foci to defended hilltops, and then, in the later pre-Roman phase, downslope to native capitals or *oppida*. In the uplands at least, the Bronze Age/Iron Age transition was marked by the creation of purposeful linear earthwork boundaries which superseded the symbolic barrow boundary-markers, as we shall describe. At the local level however, we strongly suspect that pre-Roman land cell territories often endured into the Middle Ages and sometimes to the present day.

Although we understand some aspects of the history of Roman Britain very well, in other respects, this remains a prehistoric period and the documents have little to tell us about the smaller territories and estates. Archaeology provides strong hints that Roman estates entered the Dark Ages and emerged more or less intact in the form of estates described in Saxon charters. While many modern experts seem to believe that this was the case, actual proof is another matter.

As tenurial units, estates or manors would be less durable than the fundamental economic land cells or local territories sustaining small farming communities. Before the principle of primogeniture became established, Norman and Saxon estates or manors had been subdivided between male heirs and so division and recombination of lands was only to be expected. The basic territorial building block of the medieval landscape was not the manor or the parish, but the tūn or vill. Vills persisted because they were useful and were needed. They were the fundamental units of communal farming and survival and if they were not the geographically exact equivalents of the land cells which had nurtured Neolithic, Bronze Age and Iron Age communities, then they resembled them in most other ways.

In a few cases the vill or township corresponded with the medieval manor or the parish, but in most cases the tenurial, legal and ecclesiastical divisions were federations of smaller vills. Some 'multiple estates' and parishes spanned a dozen or even two dozen vills, but if we are to seek really impressive examples of territorial antiquity, then we are more likely to find them among the jigsaw patterns of the medieval vills.

We know little about the complexity of the prehistoric territorial divisions of Britain, but it is clear that medieval Britain supported a tangled labyrinth of different jurisdictions, estates and special purpose areas. Rather than becoming trapped in this maze, we will describe the boundary relics and markers which may help to resurrect old divisions before exploring the fascinating topic of continuity in the partitioning of the British landscape.

9

Boundary Monuments

Quite recently, the recognition of the fundamental importance of territory to an understanding of old and ancient societies has produced an upsurge in boundary studies. Boundary-hunting is a challenging and often frustrating pursuit, but physical relics of old boundaries are numerous—if not always easy to recognize or understand.

Most of the old boundaries in Britain, whether they defined small economic land cells, tenurial, administrative or political areas, will have been well known by the people of their time and plainly marked out upon the landscape. Today, many of these boundaries are difficult or impossible to discover, although there are probably many more old boundary markers surviving than we are able to recognize. There are two basic reasons for our difficulties: first geographical features like rivers, streams and watersheds are the most durable of boundary-marking features, but after the boundary concerned has been extinguished and forgotten there is no means of distinguishing between a boundary river or crest-line and any other watercourse or watershed. Secondly, man-made boundary markers, like linear earthbanks and ditches, hedge-banks, barrows, monoliths or crosses, may closely resemble similar man-made earthworks or standing stones which were erected for other purposes. A third facet to the problem is where a boundary had been described in an old document, but the markers have perished or the place-names have changed.

Trees, buildings, hedgerows and woods are all perishable features, although prominent in the landscape during their lifetime. Bewerley (with a name which probably refers to the long extinct British beaver) is today a small satellite of Pateley Bridge in Yorkshire. It was probably a pre-Conquest vill which perished in the Harrying of the North of 1069–71 and did not exist as a village throughout the Middle Ages. A twelfth-century charter mentions a boundary as 'the stream of Bewerley flowing into the Nidd where the old chapel was'; unfortunately we cannot pinpoint the boundary with certainty because there is no longer any trace of this ruined Saxon chapel.

The two boundary descriptions which follow (the first an extract from a Saxon charter of 904 and the second dating only from 1877) show the difficulties of resurrecting old boundaries when place-names change or when the boundary is linked to perishable or commonplace features:

> . . . from Wringforde to the hedgerow east to the large spring of Schire-bourne. From the large spring to Carstie, to the hedgerow. Again, along the hedgerow to Wythescombe. From the combe to Brokenanbrugge. From the Brugge to Stanbrugge. From Stanbrugge to Wet Meadow . . .
> (Reconfirmation of a grant of Wrington in Somerset to Duke Ethelfrith, 904).

In this case the 'Wringforde', 'Shirebourne', 'Carstie', 'Wythescombe', 'Brokenan-brugge' and 'Stanbrugge' names have all perished (although local enthusiasts were able to identify many of the topographical features described since the estate boundary of 904 corresponded quite closely to the Wrington parish boundary as mapped by John Rocque in 1738).

The use of ephemeral and geographical boundary-marking features is apparent in the following description of part of the now defunct county of Morayshire provided by 'A Pedestrian' in 1877:

> From Fuaran Laoigh Well the boundary line runs in a southerly direction over some moorland to the Burn of Lyneriach, which it crosses at a point about one-third of a mile above the ruin of Lyneriach [these were abandoned farm buildings] . . . a pile of sods on the south side of the burn marks the boundary line—thence in a SSW direction over the Hill of Knocknashalg, by piles of stones and piles of sods to a point on the Burn of Knocknashalg or Altdurnan, about half a mile above the farm houses of Knocknashalg . . .

In this case, old maps will preserve the boundary which would otherwise have become undetectable once the sod piles and ruins are perished and the significance of the well, hills and streams, forgotten.

With the problems of boundary resurrection still in mind, it is worth noting the confusion which can exist even when boundary features are—or appear to be—well preserved. First there are the mistaken Iron Age 'provinces' of northern Scotland which experts quite reasonably believed they had identified on the basis of 'broch' and 'vitrified fort' territories (for explanations of the brochs and forts see pp. 140 and 139). From their interlocking distribution maps it seemed that the northern and western margins of Scotland were home to a 'broch people', while the interior and north east were inhabited by 'vitrified fort people'; and there was discussion about frontier wars between the two groups and suggestions that forts had been fired and so vitrified by brochland warriors. Only when Carbon-14 dating techniques were brought to bear was it confirmed that, while the brochs mainly belonged to the Roman Iron Age, the vitrified forts are of a different and older period.

One daunting possibility that confronts the searcher for prehistoric boundaries is the chance that in the marking out of medieval or later boundaries, most prehistoric tombs or cairns may have been removed, leaving only those which conveniently signposted the course of the new boundary! Because stonepiles or cairns were built as boundary markers in the historical period, the opportunity for confusion is considerable. For example, the authors of a recent archaeological survey of West Yorkshire quote the case of the boundary between Wadsworth and Midgley townships defined in 1594. The documents mention 'one heap of stones then newly made, called Foster Clough Head'. However, not all the cairns marking this boundary were newly made for some bore the name 'law', which derives from a Saxon word often used to describe prehistoric tombs.

Then there are the difficulties concerning the dykes or 'linear earthworks' of Wessex and Ulster. In Wessex, Wansdyke, which is likely to belong to the fifth or sixth century, was probably more important as a prominent and unambiguous boundary marker than as a defencework; it was judged to be a fifty-mile-long (80 km) frontier work, perhaps constructed by the British to stem the westward advances of Saxons. In 1958 however, A. and C. Fox showed that it is in fact two distinct earthworks and that presumed sections of 'Wansdyke' east of the Savernake Forest seem to be local independent constructions. The picture is even more confused in the case of 'Black Pig's Dyke' which was associated with the frontiers of the Kingdom of Ulster. When D. Davies looked at this and some other presumed 'great frontier earthworks' he found only short lengths of independent ditches which seemed to be of various ages and to be constructed to concentrate traffic at various defined and chosen crossings. As such they make more sense when viewed as local constructions to obstruct the removal of rustled cattle. Finally, there is the case of the Welsh 'prehistoric boundaries' which eventually proved to be defects in the emulsion of the air photograph concerned!

Man-made territorial symbols come in many forms, but we could make a distinction between those which are prominent symbols of the *heartland* and those which define, defend or control the *boundaries* or *frontiers* of territories. Heartland monuments—such as estate-guarding Norman mottes, ritual monuments like churches as the foci of parishes, or Neolithic long barrows as those of Neolithic land cells—clearly served important functions concerning defence or religion, but they are also symbols of territorial control of different kinds. While long barrows often provided conveniently prominent pegs upon which Saxon estate or parish boundaries could be hung, originally, during the Neolithic period when the tombs were almost invariably the most costly, durable and imposing monuments of their territories, they may typically have been placed neither at the centres nor upon the boundaries of their territories. As we have said, widely visible and commanding positions were often favoured. However, in some cases the tombs may have been placed beside boundaries, perhaps to underline the ownership of the land. One thinks here of the case of the two Cairnholy chambered tombs overlooking Wigtown Bay and sited only 150 yards apart. If both served the same territory or local dynasty one wonders why two tombs were built when an original single tomb could easily have been enlarged if necessary? Could they be the key monuments of adjacent territories, watching over the shared boundary which ran between them? Of course, we can only guess.

In some ways the round barrows of the Beaker and Bronze Ages offer more interesting challenges as territorial symbols. In an important recent study of the North York Moors, D. A. Spratt has probably succeeded in rediscovering a number of Bronze Age territories. The main settlements in each territory seem to have been situated in valleys and most are lost; around, or a little above the 600 foot (183 metres) contour are 'cairnfields', assemblages of a few or more than a hundred small heaps of stone, each around ten feet (3 m) in diameter. The cairns are normally piles of stone cleared from the surrounding fields rather than burial mounds, and occasionally the remains of circular huts can still be detected among the cairns. The cairnfield sites were occupied in the summer season, mainly in association with the grazing of the upland pastures although there was some arable farming around these sites. Well above the cairnfields

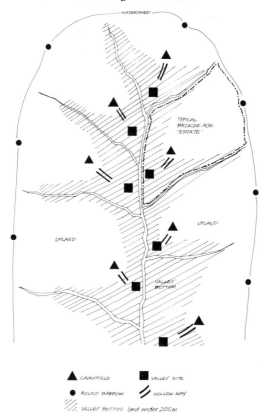

Fig. 4. *A model of Bronze Age 'estates' in North York Moors. The valley settlements (huts, enclosures, fields, cairns) are permanently occupied for a mainly arable system with some pastoralism; the cairnfields are seasonally occupied for a mainly pastoral system with some arable farming. Hollowways link the two parts of the system, and barrows mark the watershed boundaries (from D. A. Spratt in* Prehistoric Communities in Northern England, *ed. G. Barker, pub. Dept. of Prehistory, University of Sheffield).*

are lines of round barrows situated on watersheds and forming chains up to sixteen miles (26 km) in length. It seems clear that streams (which were tributaries to rivers such as the Rye) were used to define the 'sides' of the valley settlement and cairnfield territories, while the upper limits of territories were marked on the landscape by the lines of watershed barrows. In due course, some of the barrow chain boundaries were demarcated by linear earthworks.

Not all round barrows are boundary markers, but work by Hawke-Smith in Derbyshire suggests that perhaps burial monuments which are not on boundaries may be used to reconstruct Bronze Age territories. In the area between the rivers Wye and Dove it was noted that cremation and inhumation burials were not mixed at random, but that the people of some areas seemed to prefer one type of burial rite, those of others, another. The burial mounds were traditionally sited in grazing areas and it was argued that those containing both cremations and inhumations might denote grazings which were shared or 'intercommoned' by adjacent groups with different preferences. When the distributions of cremation, inhumation and shared barrow burials are mapped, the pattern which emerges could reveal the areas controlled by territorial groups which were similar in many ways but had different burial preferences.

In some ways comparable is the recent study of stone axe distributions by W. A. Cummins. It is argued that the trading spheres of the leading stone axe factories might represent the extents of three great Neolithic tribal territories. Thus northern and central England is dominated by the products of the Langdale factories of the Lake District, Wales and the Welsh marches by Welsh axes, and southern England by Cornish 'greenstone' axes. The arguments are challenging though one must remember that trading areas and political provinces can have quite different extents. Thus the spread of the Datsun car does not (we assume) mark the expansion of Japanese political control.

In the later Bronze Age it seems that many societies, particularly those living in the uplands and upland margins, faced environmental stresses. Soils which had been worked for centuries had become exhausted; the problems were exacerbated by the onset of a deterioration in the climate. In the course of the increasing competition for land, defended settlements, enclosures and hillfort strongholds began to appear. In a number of places (notably in the northern English uplands where monuments are more likely to endure than in the lowlands), it is clear that the 'symbolic' boundary markers such as barrows were superseded by more prominent and purposeful constructions in the form of linear earthworks. In the case of the Hambleton Hills in Yorkshire, Spratt shows that the old barrow-line boundary was supplemented by a 'pit alignment' which was then converted into the unambiguous linear ditch and banks of the Cleave Dyke system. At Thwing in the east of the Yorkshire Wolds, a heavily defended homestead or 'mini-hillfort' lies close to the junction of an extensive double-dyke system. Examples from the modern world, such as the frontier defences of the 'Iron Curtain', show that the greater the political tensions between neighbours, the more purposeful and imposing the boundary works are likely to be.

The construction of linear earthworks must represent a determined attempt to stamp a territorial boundary upon the landscape in a way that provides a clear statement of ownership and gives warning to would-be trespassers or land grabbers. Distinctions have been made between the smaller earthworks, as boundary markers, and the larger ones which are said to have defensive dimensions. However, to offer real defensive advantages it could be argued that a linear earthwork would need to be of a size comparable to the Antonine Wall (see p. 146) and be strongly manned by a large and permanent garrison. Even the largely stone-built Hadrian's Wall, the ultimate in linear defences, was occasionally overrun.

The effective defence of a linear earthwork depends too much upon the co-operation of the attacking force: they must not cross the boundary until the defenders have had time to muster, and then they must oblige by attacking only the section of the earthwork which the defenders have chosen to man. Even then they must resist the obvious logic of attacking the line of defenders who are strung-out thinly along the rampart crest in a column, and use the strongest and best-armoured warriors in its

34. *The Ta Dyke, an undated linear earthwork in the Pennines with its ditch hacked into the rock at the foot of a natural low cliff face marked by the stone wall. It barred the cross-watershed route from Wharfedale into Wensleydale.*

spearhead. A tall order indeed, though it should be noted that items of Saxon military equipment have been recovered from the ditches of Cambridgeshire dykes, suggesting battles around the dykes.

Linear earthworks or dykes were built in several different periods and need not always mark boundaries. Some of the northern examples are boundary markers of the later Bronze Age, others in the south appear to have been built late in the pre-Roman Iron Age as the defensive outworks of tribal capitals or *oppida*: the Lexen, Sheepen and Shrub End dykes seem to have defended the approaches to the Catuvellaunian capital of Camulodunum near Colchester. The Bokerley Dyke, forming part of the Hampshire–Dorset boundary, may have been built by Romans to control a routeway between *Sorviodunum* (Old Sarum) and Badbury Rings hillfort. The four Cambridgeshire dykes may be of the late Roman or early Saxon periods, as may Wansdyke(s); Offa's Dyke dates from the late eighth century, while the Normans in Ireland utilized dykes barring routes through passes.

The Antonine Wall apart, of all the linear earthworks Offa's Dyke is the least ambiguous. Whether or not sections of the rampart originally carried a palisade, it was undoubtedly built by King Offa of Mercia (757–96) to provide a clear-cut and threatening statement of the limits of Mercia which the Welsh leaders could not afford

35. *Devil's Dyke, Cambridgeshire, dates from the late-Roman or early-Saxon period and is a linear earthwork of a most impressive size.*

to ignore. This does not rule out the possibility that the line of the dyke was fixed by negotiation, for Fox has pointed out that anchorages on both banks of the lower Wye were left available to Welsh sailors.

In other respects, the Cambridgeshire dykes are more interesting and challenging, for here we possibly have evidence of a boundary which may have been shifted under force of arms. There are four dykes in the series; the northernmost is Devil's Dyke, seven and a half miles long and still a massive and formidable construction, then Fleam Dyke which is still imposing, while Brent Dyke and Heydon Dyke are largely destroyed.

It is plain that the dykes were constructed to straddle and thus control or bar the swarms of parallel and branching trackways which composed the Icknield Way route, and there is no evidence that crossing places were provided. The dykes are roughly parallel, but some seventeen miles separate Devil's Dyke from the most southerly, Heydon Dyke. Since the dykes are too far apart to constitute a single defensive or territorial system it seems likely that the complex represents stages in the advance and retreat of the frontiers of a Saxon or Roman East Anglian polity. If dyke building began at Devil's, then the other dykes could have been built to secure the territory gained by successive advantages. On the other hand, Devil's Dyke, which might have taken 500 labourers more than a year to complete, could have been the desperate creation of a threatened and retreating society whose other frontier defences had been overrun. Though few dykes survive in such imposing forms, scores of others are known and most are frontier works of Iron Age, Roman or Dark Age communities.

We have seen that, depending on the local circumstances, cairns, barrows and linear earthworks may or may not be boundary markers. The same is true of isolated standing stones, 'menhirs' or 'monoliths' and shaped stones such as crosses. Monoliths too come in many shapes and sizes and date from a wide range of periods. There are some striking prehistoric examples like the Rudston Stone near Bridlington, more than twenty-five feet (eight metres) tall, which attracted the establishment of the nearby church, and the Clach an Trushal standing stone on Lewis which is nineteen feet (six metres) in height. Other monoliths are only knee-high while many are relatively recent creations provided to mark post-medieval parish boundaries or erected to serve prosaic functions as gateposts or rubbing posts for cattle.

In the cases of prehistoric monoliths, excavation has not solved many problems although a monolith near Glynllifon in Snowdonia was found to be associated with a burial accompanied by a cinerary urn, and a small proportion of monoliths was associated with scatters of cremated bone. It is also possible that some monoliths were both grave markers and boundary stones: it was customary in some early Irish societies for a person to be buried on the boundary of his land with a monolith to mark the spot. Here again we seem to have an example of the remains of ancestors being used to guard and claim territory. Other monoliths were probably used to mark trackways and near Llanbedr village, near Harlech, a chain of thirteen standing stones are thought to be route markers. The majority of monoliths were probably erected for ritual purposes, and although one might speculate that the monolith was conceived as some sort of 'conductor' linking solar and atmospheric 'forces' to those of the earth, the details of belief may never be recovered.

There remain a few examples of monoliths with clear territorial connections. Perhaps the best example is 'Long Tom' in Wiltshire, which P. J. Fowler has described. Not only does this tall sarsen slab lie on the present boundary between Fyfield and Clatford parishes but it also stands upon a boundary-marking bank which is younger than nearby 'Celtic' fields, but older than adjacent medieval plough ridges. Whether the stone and bank are contemporary, and if not, which is the older, we do not know.

One of the most visitworthy if little-known prehistoric sites in Britain is near Merrivale on Dartmoor. Here, within a stone's throw of the ruins of Bronze Age stone huts stand a group of monuments—a small stone circle, a monolith (perhaps erected as a signpost to the nearby circle) and double stone rows—triply puzzling because we do not know the exact purposes that any of the elements served. Small stone rows of various forms abound on these moors and the double ones have their rows too closely spaced to have served as impressive processional avenues, while blocking stones sometimes close their ends. With their linear forms one might be tempted to guess that the rows mark boundaries.

In the course of his work on the Dartmoor reaves, Fleming explored the association between stone rows and reaves. No simple answer emerged. The stone rows are generally associated with the Beaker period and the reaves with a later stage in the

36. *The Blind Fiddler in Cornwall, one of the better known of the mysterious British monoliths.*

Bronze Age. In some cases the reaves were seen to have cut or destroyed stone rows, but in others it seemed that the reaves had been set out to run beside rows, just on their downslope side (although at Merrivale the reave runs above the row). The rows were probably ritual monuments of some kind, often sited just inside a zone of permanent grazing and Fleming suggests that at a later stage the reaves may have marked the traditional divide between the lower and upper moorland farming zones. Stone cairns and 'prestigious' barrows on Dartmoor also predate the reaves and seem to be territorial symbols which have been placed on hilltops or on the moorland rim to stake claims of ownership.

The cross is a sophisticated form of monolith and Christian crosses served a wide variety of purposes: inviting divine protection for structures like bridges or places where disasters had occurred, or might happen; marking or guarding routeways; denoting places where events like markets or preaching would take place or marking the boundaries of church lands. Most of the older crosses are broken, often as a consequence of Protestant fanaticism and an Act of 1643 which ordered that crosses be defaced and superstitious monuments demolished. Crosses of all types were very common in the medieval era. The antiquarian Stanhope White has painstakingly recorded almost seventy examples, mostly damaged, in the neighbourhood of the North York Moors. Some crosses certainly staked out the bounds of parishes or townships and in 1571 the Archbishop of York issued instructions for the Rogationtide or 'Cross-week' perambulations, requiring the ministers to stick to the orthodox litany 'without wearing any surplice, carrying of banners or handbells or staying at crosses or such like Popish ceremonies'.

The interpretation of crosses may be a tricky exercise, for while some must have originated as boundary markers, others will have been moved from original sites to serve new functions as boundary markers and some will have been erected as way marks. White notes a popular treatise, 'Dives et Pauper', of 1496 which states 'For this reason be Crosses by the waye, that when folks passynge see the Crosses, they shold thinke on Hym that deyed on the Crosse and worshypp Hym above all thynge'. In Ireland, scores of pagan monoliths were Christianized through the addition of cross symbols, but which of these stones originated as boundary marks is impossible to say.

37. One of the two double stone rows at Merrivale on Dartmoor. The territorial significance of these peculiar monuments is still uncertain.

38. *Bennett's Cross on the roadside near Postbridge on Dartmoor. The original function of the cross is uncertain, but the letters 'W B' carved on one of the faces show that at one stage the cross was used to mark a (rabbit) warren boundary.*

However, White quotes the interesting case of the 'Bridestones', including the 'Craw Stone' on the North York Moors which he believes originated as Bronze Age boundary stones. They were listed as contemporary boundary features in 1716 when the Lord of Gisborough Manor, with a company of 200 pedestrians and horsemen, rode his boundaries; the 'Craw Stone' was probably the pagan stone which has acquired a cross symbol. He also mentions John O'Man's Cross, destroyed in the nineteenth century, but with a name which probably derives from the Celtic *maen* or 'standing stone', implying a pre-Christian origin.

Some monuments remain so inscrutable and unresponsive to conventional archaeological techniques that we must wonder whether their secrets will ever be unlocked: cup-and-ring marks and even stone circles may be in this category. There are others which are even more tantalizing because we feel that we should be within a hair's breadth of cracking their code, yet still the mysteries endure. The Pictish symbol stones are a remarkable example. There are around 250 of these stones surviving, mainly in north-east Scotland, and it has long been recognized that they appear to belong to three classes. The first and oldest class bears only pagan symbols and presumably belongs to the sixth century and earlier; the second class includes stones which bear both Christian and pagan emblems and seem to belong to the conversion period of the late sixth and seventh centuries, while the third group of stones is unambiguous—stones bear the cross alone.

The pagan symbols include stylish representations of contemporary animals—the wolf, boar, bear, eagle and salmon—outlandish beasts, notably the 'Pictish beast' with dolphin and elephant-like features; but most interesting are the abstract symbols. These are far too intricate and sophisticated to be geometrical motifs and frequently recurring emblems are the 'serpent and Z-rod', the 'double disc and Z-rod' and the 'crescent and V-rod'. Most of the stones display a group of several symbols and evidence of the erasure and replacement of symbols suggests that the groupings were intentional and meaningful rather than arbitrary.

The stones were probably not tombstones, although as many have been moved it is not easy to relate the distribution to topography or burials. Most probably they are elaborate territorial markers originally erected at the boundaries of clan or tribal territories. The clustered symbols probably proclaimed a message to the traveller which was quite intelligible, perhaps a statement of ownership, a boast or a warning. It has been suggested that the animal symbols are tribal emblems or totems and it is conceivable that the stones carry an early form of heraldry with other symbols relating to the lineage of a tribal dynasty. Because the symbols often occur in pairs, sometimes accompanied by a mirror and comb symbol, A. Jackson has suggested that they may proclaim marriages between different lineages, with the common 'mirror and comb' emblem signifying the payment of a bride price. The truth is lost and the memory of a Pictish code must have faded along with the Pictish language after the conquest and absorption of Pictland by Kenneth McAlpin's Scots in AD 843. After more than a century of modern endeavour the chastity of the secret remains intact.

A completely different type of boundary marker is represented by the place-name; as ever, where place-names are concerned, the evidence must be handled with great care.

39. *The Pictish symbol stone known as the 'Picardy Stone' near Insch, Grampian. The undeciphered double disc and Z-rod and serpent and Z-rod symbols are clearly seen, and a mirror symbol can just be discerned below them.*

40. *Many old boundaries are preserved in surviving place-names. This Mere Lane is on the margins of Fornham All Saints near Bury St. Edmunds and 'mere' usually derives from a Saxon word for a boundary.*

'Mere', the commonest boundary name, is Saxon in origin but the same word can also derive from the Saxon name for a pond. Other Saxon words often denoting boundaries include *mearc* and *hār*, which may now emerge as 'Merke-' or 'Hare-', while *(ge)flit* emerging as 'Flit-' and *prēap* emerging as 'Threp-' or 'Threap-' often denote boundary woods and disputed lands respectively. Pagan Saxon burials were often made on boundaries while Dark Age and medieval gallows also stood on boundaries and surviving names like 'Thieves Grave' can reveal old execution sites. Roman roads were often adopted as convenient boundary markers, while Saxon roads which now bear the name 'Way' generally ran between territories. All the names mentioned, however, can create confusion: *hār* can mean 'grey', while 'burgh', which we normally associate with an early medieval fortification, can occasionally derive from the Saxon *burgaesn* denoting a burial or cairn.

So far, we have looked at the territorial symbols of heartlands and boundaries, but another class of relics comprises the fossils of extinct frontiers. It is a broad class embracing monuments of many ages and includes the fortified Saxon *burhs* (see p. 240), the Scandinavian earthen fortresses and harbours of the Danelaw frontier—a class of monuments which we do not explore because many of the supposed Danish constructions have dubious attributions—and the chains of World War II pillboxes marking frontiers of confrontation which, fortunately, were never activated.

While boundaries are (to most intents and purposes) linear features, in the language of the political geographer a frontier is not a line on a map, but a zone of territory with its own population, outlooks and political characteristics. Often monuments may persist to fossilize a frontier, long after the political conditions which sustained it have perished. This is true of the Anglo-Scottish marchlands, which contain not only Hadrian's Wall (see p. 146) and patterns of strategically-placed Roman fortresses, but also the relics of medieval conflict and insecurity including the great citadels of feudal warlords, the stark tower houses of lesser nobles and the pele towers and defensive farmsteads or 'bastles', the refuges of priests and yeomen (all described in Chapter 14).

While the towns of the Welsh borders may preserve fragments of the advancing frontier of the Roman Empire in Chester, Caerleon and Gloucester, or of insecure Saxon penetration as at Chester, Hereford and Gloucester, where the defences of *burhs* rose upon Roman footings, the rolling frontiers of Anglo-Norman medieval subjugation and colonization are particularly well preserved. One can still trace the advance of English conquest and feudalism across the face of Wales in the form and layout or 'morphology' of Welsh towns. Thus at Clun in Shropshire we see the Norman successor town to a Saxon frontier village poised at the gateway to Wales, with its Norman church and massive motte and its little gridwork of planned streets and burgage plots, some of them hacked out of woodland. At Grosmont in Gwent, the thirteenth-century stone castle stands on a Norman motte and bailey site but the accompanying town, once said to have been the third largest in South Wales, has withered and contracted into a road-hugging village. Meanwhile in the west of Wales, at great Edwardian castle sites like Caernarfon, Flint, Harlech and Denbigh, the planned layouts of defended towns which were at first peopled by allied traders, craftsmen and entrepreneurs are still plainly discerned. Between the Norman frontier towns and the fortress towns of the west which symbolize the Edwardian conquest are others which mark stages in the advance of the frontiers of English control: like New Radnor of the mid thirteenth century, which still nestles in the shelter of a great oval castle mound, with a main street which preserves the planned alignment between the gateways in the urban defences.

Similarly, the Irish landscape preserves old conflicts and the fluctuating frontiers of alien rule. There are the many deserted Norman village foundations which flourished only so long as a foreign feudalism could curb old settlement traditions and pen the peasants in villages. Then there are the crumbling hovels of Catholic peasants driven from the better lands. Elsewhere are the strongholds of alien aristocrats—and also the youngest relics, the burned-out mansions of a landowning élite which departed during the birth pangs of the independent state. One can only wonder where the frontier will finally come to rest and how many more ruins will be created before it does?

10

Continuity:
The Old Boundaries Live On

Our knowledge of the past is a mass of assumptions salted with a sprinkling of facts. To some extent the history that we learn is the creation of historians. In the field of prehistory the facts are like flotsam on a restless ocean of inferences; sometimes even the facts prove to be guesses. The assumptions from which we build our visions of the past are human perceptions of what was or might have been. As such they are often faulty and the greatest body of flawed dogma concerns the antiquity of so many facets of the landscape. Things are frequently much older than we thought they were. It was commonly assumed that for most intents and purposes, landscape history began with the Roman collapse around AD 410. Even today many accounts begin with a token short and uncomfortable survey of the prehistoric era, merely to set the table for the real meal which is to follow. But slowly dawning is a realization that pre-Saxon communities contributed enormously to the layout of our living landscape. In terms of territories, the lasting contribution was much greater at the small-scale or local level, but we begin with an example from higher up the political pyramid.

In 1970 the authorities in the threadbare little Scottish county of Kincardineshire spent £3,000 on a public relations exercise designed to prevent the county being split between reformed local government areas centred upon Aberdeen and Dundee. The emotional and tradition-based argument triumphed over the logic of social and economic realities, and the county was handed over intact to the new Grampian Region. The previous history of Kincardineshire reveals the forces of continuity at work, with a territorial unit surviving across the centuries despite many changes in the nature of its political function.

Stonehaven was the last administrative centre of Kincardineshire, but before 1607 Kincardine had been the county town. In 1296 Edward I and his invasion force of 35,000 men had stayed at Kincardine where a castle guarding the Cairn-a-mounth route northwards had existed since at least 1119. A village grew around the castle site and in 1562 the settlement was elevated to the status of a county town. The old market cross of Kincardine is now at Fettercairn village; the earthworks and footings of the castle are overgrown and, as a lost or deserted county focus, Kincardine is exceptional. However, the county (or in Scottish medieval terminology, the 'Sheriffdom') was older than Kincardine. It was originally known as the sheriffdom of 'the Mearns' and could be several decades older than its first surviving mention, which dates from about 1170.

The institution of sheriffs and sheriffdoms was a feudal device, borrowed from England, by which insecure medieval Scottish kings sought to pacify and administer their realms and extend the frontiers of effective central control. However, the Mearns was older than the twelfth century. It had a brief existence as an Earldom which seems to have been extinguished at an early date in the Middle Ages. The Earldoms however were older than the dignity of *Comes* or Earl, for it is clear that the title and office simply represented an anglicization and feudalization of the high Celtic rank of *mormaer*, meaning either 'sea steward' or 'high steward'. The switch probably took place in the reign of Malcolm Ceannmor (1057–93) when the king, who had a Saxon princess as his queen, used the introduction of English feudal practices as a means of strengthening his control over the unsettled Celtic provinces.

The mormaerships of Scotland, of which the Mearns was one, seem to have appeared about the tenth century, but the territory of the Mearns was older than this. Dark Age Pictland did not have a literature of its own, but references to Pictland were made in Irish annals and traditions were recorded in early medieval manuscripts. The political geography of the Pictish realm seems to have been unusual and complicated, for it was apparently divided into northern and southern components, each in turn divided into provinces with each province, Caithness apart, consisting of two territorial units. These provinces can be identified from two documents: the late-Pictish quatrain in the *Pictish Chronicle* which tells how Alba was divided into seven provinces to be ruled by the seven sons of 'Cruithne', and the tract *De Situ Albanie* in which a twelfth-century Bishop of Caithness described the Scottish provincial boundaries of the mid ninth century. The Mearns emerges as one component of Angus and Mearns, appearing as 'Enegus cum Moerne' in the younger record and 'Circinn' in the older.

Thus we can trace the territorial integrity of Kincardineshire backwards through time for well over a thousand years to a period in which Scotland was, in many respects, a prehistoric land. This does not mean that the territory was not older still, but the Roman accounts of contemporary tribal territories in Scotland are vague and ambiguous. The county which died but escaped dismemberment on the altar of administrative reform could look back on a coherent territorial existence which disappears into the mists before recorded history.

While the similarities between some English counties like Kent, Sussex and Essex, Saxon kingdoms and Celtic tribal territories have often been noted, the most exciting work on the continuity of territories concerns the durability of small land cells. The main technique involved is that of retrogressive analysis, in which, as with the example of Kincardineshire, one attempts to trace a territory backwards through time. There will come a point where the evidence from old documents runs out and the hunch must take over from proof. The oldest items of 'proof' which may, if one is fortunate, be found to exist are estate charters of the middle or later Saxon periods. Beyond these, the landscape detective must resort to interpreting archaeological evidence. Even so, information is accumulating which hints that many agricultural units which existed in the Middle Ages and which sometimes endure today, existed in Roman Britain, probably in stages of the pre-Roman Iron Age, and possibly even in the Bronze Age.

Let us underline the fact that we are talking about the endurance of small economic or agricultural units—the little packages of land and resources which can sustain small or village-sized communities—and not, for example, about more complicated areas such as parishes often are. In the past there has been a mistaken tendency to equate the village and its lands with the manor, and the manor with the parish. Many parishes are composite areas which take their name from a still-living village, but include that village's lands along with those of one or more lost villages and those of several other townships, hamlets and farmsteads. Thus Marton-cum-Moxby parish near York is shaped like a semicolon, with the dot-like block of territory on the end of the tail of the Marton comma representing the acquired lands of the lost villages or hamlet of Moxby. Similarly, Michael Aston has shown that Mudford parish in Somerset comprises the territory of Mudford village and also those of the very shrunken village of Hinton, West Mudford and Up Mudford and of the lost village of Mudford Terry. In the north, where parishes tend to be larger, Halifax parish contains twenty-two smaller townships.

David Michelmore and his colleagues in the West Yorkshire Archaeological Unit have studied the ancient and basic communal building blocks of the landscape. These were the tuns or vills mentioned in Chapter 8 and all of medieval England seems to have been divided into vills. Not estates or parishes, they were the small territorial packages each of which supported a peasant community. As such, they were essential to life—and hence they persisted. We do not yet know the antiquity of vills: they can often be traced back to Domesday Book of 1086, they occasionally emerge in Saxon charters although these are concerned with estates rather than vills, and they then recede into the shadows of the Dark Ages. Quite probably, a large proportion of the medieval vills had prehistoric pedigrees.

The townships were often smaller than parishes and sometimes corresponded to the vills. These were usually effective through a peasant assembly or 'byelaw' and they seem to have predated the manor and its court while often continuing to operate at a lower level during the medieval period.

Vills and townships were the most durable components in a very complicated system of medieval divisions. If we could reconstruct the maps of Saxon and Norman England, we would find a multitude of different and overlapping territories of different kinds: administrative areas like shires or counties, wapentakes, hundreds and bailiwicks; land measures like virgates, carucates and hides; tenurial and judicial divisions like 'multiple estates' embracing great packages of smaller tenures or manors, detached estates or 'berewicks', manors, honours and liberties; special status areas like royal hunting forests; areas which are not yet completely understood like sokes, rapes and lathes; and ecclesiastical units like dioceses, parishes and more obscure and specialized divisions—like the three British 'circaries' of the Premonstratensian monastic order or the 'leuga' within a radius of one and a half miles of Battle Abbey in which the abbot had special rights. Overlain by these twining networks of boundaries, the already ancient agricultural territories tended to persist, although they might be combined, separated and recombined in changing parish or manor groupings.

One may be able to find old agricultural territories which do not coincide with parish boundaries. In 1980 we rediscovered the lost Bedfordshire village of Picts Hill which was unusual because the boundary between Stevington and Turvey parishes ran directly along the 'holloway' or trough which represented the old village main street. This boundary seems to have fluctuated during recent centuries. The name Picts Hill is first mentioned in 1227, but this could be a Saxon settlement founded by the followers of somebody with a name like 'Pica' and inserted into an area of higher boulder clay-smeared terrain between the Saxon valley villages of Stevington and Turvey in an as yet unpartitioned no-man's land. When the site was mapped by Angela Simcoe, some twelfth-century pottery was found; but there were other sherds which could be of Iron Age date and it was noted that the surrounding field patterns and the layout of old roads seemed to demarcate an oval package of land. And so it is possible that medieval Picts Hill assumed control of an older, perhaps prehistoric agricultural territory which had been in existence long enough to guide the field and road patterns.

In other cases the relationships between old territories and parish boundaries are interesting and suggestive. Several of the boundaries of the Bronze Age reave territories on Dartmoor coincide with parish boundaries, while the western boundary of Bilsdale Midcable parish on the North York Moors links up a chain of eight Bronze Age boundary barrows. In the Hambleton Hills the situation is more complex: the boundaries follow some of the ancient divisions which are preserved by both the Bronze Age barrow lines and the subsequent earthworks of the Cleave Dyke system in some places, but elsewhere adopt the younger line of the straightened Hambleton Street Ridgeway.

Work done by Desmond Bonney in Wessex is particularly important: it shows that in places the patterns of Roman or pre-Roman estates and territories were so deeply entrenched as to govern the forms of parishes which developed in the Saxon era. East Wansdyke is largely ignored by parish boundaries—which strongly implies that the territories whose bounds were later to be adopted by the parishes were older than the Dark Age earthwork. The relationships between parish boundaries and Roman roads in different parts of Wessex were found to vary. In some places, a road had clearly been adopted as a convenient boundary marker, but in others a road would be completely ignored by parish boundaries. Where this happens it seems that the divisions of the countryside which the parishes were to perpetuate were complete and ingrained before the roads were built.

In recent years, boundaries have begun to receive some of the attention that they merit, while old ideas about the traumatic effects of Celtic, Roman and Saxon invasions on the organization of the landscape are being disproved. Ecclesiastical, political and economic wheeling and dealing in land, the accidents of marriage or inheritance and different phases of administrative boundary reform have all tended to blur the pattern, causing the fission and fusion of units, but the antiquity of so many patterns and the durability of the ancient land cells can still be discerned.

The evidence is flowing in from many quarters. There is other work by Bonney which shows how pagan Saxon burials—which were commonly made on territorial boundaries—are often found to coincide with later parish boundaries. At a much grander scale there are the cases of the large medieval 'multiple estates' which seem to have gradually fragmented from extensive Roman estates. Professor Glanville Jones has described the example of Burghshire which occupied the land between the rivers Wharfe and Ure in Yorkshire and took its name from the Roman cantonical capital of the Brigantes tribe, *Isurium Brigantum* or Aldborough. By the time that Domesday Book was compiled in 1086 some fragmentation had taken place, but the Burghshire Wapentake then had two royal multiple estates as its main components, one centred on

Knaresborough and one on Aldborough. Returning to the local level, Rodwell's intensely detailed study of Rivenhall parish in Essex seems to confirm that the medieval parish was an agricultural land cell in Roman times.

In areas where dispersed farmsteads have always predominated it may be possible to demonstrate continuity at a still more local level. Hoskins has shown that many of the farms of nineteenth-century Devon existed as farms at the time of Domesday and could have their origins in Dark Age, Roman or even prehistoric times. Similarly, current work by the Cornwall Committee for Rescue Archaeology in showing that some of the boundaries of farms in the Zennor area match up with the limits of field systems which were worked from Romano-British farmsteads.

The older studies of continuity in the British landscape tended to focus on settlements but it is becoming clear that most of our villages and hamlets date not from the Roman or early Saxon periods, but from the later Saxon centuries and Norman times. In the prehistoric period, and perhaps for the greater part of the Dark Ages, communities who built villages and hamlets did not presume to be creating permanent settlements, and most such places perished before they were a couple of centuries old. However, while settlements rose, declined and were shifted the land cells which contained them tended to endure. Once a viable little package of ploughlands, meadows, pasture and woodland had been put together, it was not abandoned or dismembered without good cause. Thus, the man-made patterns on the landscapes of Britain are sometimes far older than we thought. While hardly giving a face-lift to the countryside, modern farming and development is tending to erase the lines and wrinkles which could tell us just how old the features are. Even so, the search for old territories offers many interesting challenges to the dedicated local historian.

Reflections

Our survey of the evidence for old territories brings us back to our opening quotation from Professor Hoskins: 'The new men took over as landlords but farming still had to go on.' Until a little more than a century ago, the destiny of Britain lay in her farming resources. Aristocrats strutted or rampaged, dynasties rose and fell, estates large and small were amassed and collapsed according to the whims and accidents of time and inheritance. But these gaudy vessels of history were buoyed up by the deep currents of peasant toil and tillage.

We have seen that man may share the territorial instincts which exist in many members of the animal kingdom. These may intensify his attitudes to property and his reactions to interlopers. But even without these instincts, the control of territory would have remained the mainstay of human existence. Manageable, diversely-endowed little land cells which became known as 'vills' in the Middle Ages were created and preserved because they were the essential theatres, factories and homelands of the peasants whose labour and production allowed society to exist.

Long before the people of Britain were able to comprehend the meaning of statehood or nationhood the myriad of local peasant communities had learned the importance of forging, maintaining and defending territories. While the ancient land cells are often difficult to detect and less colourful and glamorous subjects for study than, say, prehistoric monuments, castles or churches, they gave birth and sustenance to all pre-industrial monuments and endeavours. Also, it is quite probable that the most important advances of the next few decades, those which will most help us to improve our flawed visions of the past, will result from new investigations into the territorial building blocks of the British landscape.

PART III

Landscapes of Conflict

Introduction

All around us we see the evidence of man's natural instinct to defend his dependants, home and land. But these remains are of a very varied nature. An Iron Age hillfort covering, perhaps, twenty hectares, and bounded by massive ramparts encircling a hilltop is clearly a defensive system with much the same military aims as a small eleventh-century motte and bailey tucked into the corner of a village, or a line of concrete pillboxes dating from 1940. Although the differences between them are, at the most obvious level, the results of technological changes and advances, they are much more importantly the result of differences in the outlook and political and social needs and aims of the societies that created them.

It is just as important to understand man's perception of those factors of home and homeland which should be defended, and by what means, as it is to understand the developments in military technology. This perception of what should be defended, or attacked, did not develop steadily through time, but constantly changed along with the underlying social and political organization of society.

Thus in late Iron Age southern England, if we read the evidence correctly, the values of the day required not merely the protection of the political and religious élite but also of the peasant masses. As a result huge defensive works, often covering large areas of land, were created. In the medieval period different attitudes held sway: while the aristocrats sought to protect themselves, their status and possessions by creating formidable castles, the bulk of the population lay outside the defensive walls and were left to the mercies of aggressive neighbours. The achievement of a politically unified country—as in the different cases of the Roman province, the emerging Tudor state or the modern nation state—produced different forms of defence. To the state, the greatest threat has usually been that of external enemies. The state has to protect, not only its élite, but—for economic, social or political reasons—the total population and its agricultural or industrial resources. This need resulted in the defence of territory by ringing it with military works. At one stage in the Roman period this involved linear frontier defences, such as Hadrian's Wall and the Antonine Wall and, at another, strongholds along the boundaries of Britain—the so-called Saxon Shore Forts. At least one Saxon kingdom protected its territory with linear works, as with Offa's Dyke and other examples include Wansdyke and perhaps the Cambridgeshire dyke system. Even the dense distribution of small earthern mottes along the Welsh Marches is a reflection of the way the early Norman kings attempted, within the limits of their power, to protect the vulnerable western boundaries of their domain.

Over the last 400 years, the almost continuous threat from external enemies has meant that Britain's defences have lain along the edges of its land with coastal protection as the major concern. The Henrican gun platforms, the gigantic Victorian coastal fortresses and the more prosaic Emergency Batteries of the 1940s all reflect this concern. But the state can also be threatened by civil war or internal dissent by groups of people of greatly varying sizes, ideologies and aims. Thus the underlying strategy behind the siting of early Roman forts and the layout of the accompanying road system in Britain were responses to the threat of guerrilla warfare by dissident tribesmen. The building of the unique series of twelfth-century Fen-edge fortresses in East Anglia was a royal retort to a single dissident, Geoffrey de Mandeville, whose ambitions threatened the crown. The forts and road systems of eighteenth-century Scotland were England's response to another form of threat, largely in the form of guerrilla warfare. On the other hand, the military works of the mid seventeenth century, which can be found all over England, were the result of a civil strife of a very different character: that of ideological conflict, involving two groups whose views of society were incompatible to the point of outright war. The defended police stations, observation posts and barracks in Northern Ireland today are yet another type of reaction to internal dissent.

The state also has needed to provide military bases from which to launch attacks on external enemies. Until recently this primarily involved harbours for the navy, which not only had to contain the structures and the technology for storage, repair and manufacture, but also the necessary protection for them. And so, structures like the rope-houses and warehouses at Portsmouth and Chatham, the nineteenth-century breakwaters and moles at Portland and Dover, and others like the frigate refitting shed at Devonport (arguably one of the most aesthetically pleasing military buildings of the twentieth century) were created. Cases of continuity can often be recognized, for the Romans too had naval bases and stores which had to be protected and the castles at Richborough or Porchester reflect this much older aggressive strategy.

In this century new technology, notably the development of military aircraft, has forced the state to develop internal protection for its people as well as for its own bases, whether they are for attack or for the storage and manufacture of war materials. Anti-aircraft and searchlight batteries, radar towers and barrage balloon posts appeared. Indeed, the Doomsday weapons, the nuclear bombers and the ICBM—now with multiple nuclear war-heads—have produced what may be seen as a very uncharacteristic response by a democratic society: the construction of heavily protected fortresses, solely for the governmental élite. The concrete bunkers, usually called Regional Seats of Government, are more akin to the medieval baronial castle, where a chosen few survived in relative comfort while the surrounding land was devastated.

Other necessities for all armed conflicts are training facilities. An organized military force has to be trained and these preparations can leave permanent marks on the landscape. The elaborate trench systems, dating from 1915–18, on the Wiltshire downlands are a modern expression of this necessity, while the RAF College, Cranwell, Lincolnshire, dating from the 1920s, is a more permanent and perhaps more obvious example. The earthen redoubt at Weedon Barracks, Northamptonshire, probably dating from the early nineteenth century, is a reminder that training was important then, while the apparently functionless 'sconce' or battery near March in Cambridgeshire, dating from the 1640s, tells us that practice was considered important even in the seventeenth-century civil war. In much earlier times the practice camps of the Roman period, perhaps most notably those at Clifton, just outside York, also show the same need to rehearse war.

There are other aspects to man's perception of danger and his response to it which may still puzzle us. Before the state could assume the responsibility for defence, it might be assumed that, when danger threatened, there would be a need to protect home and family: thus, most settlements, whether towns, villages, hamlets or farmsteads, would have had some form of defence. This was certainly so in the latter part of the prehistoric period, when almost every settlement had some form of protection. Yet for Dark Age England, there is no real evidence of defensive works in most settlements, despite the obvious and very real threat from Norse and Danish raiders. Either we have not yet recognized such works or, much more probably, there were subtle differences between the organization and attitudes of Iron Age and Saxon societies which we do not yet understand.

A feature of many strongholds which was often important—if today not always easily understood—concerns status. This is represented by a wish to display the power or importance of an owner or builder though the results may have little or nothing whatsoever to do with the military necessities. At one level this can involve mere decorations: the Royal Cypher on the entrances to Victorian coastal forts, the Royal Coat of Arms on the gates of the sixteenth-century Henrican forts. But much more important are whole classes of fortifications whose primary purpose was to enhance the status of those living within. The many thousands of medieval moated sites which can be found in almost every part of England are perhaps the most obvious. They almost all date from the twelfth or thirteenth centuries. They have no real defensive value, and must surely represent a phase in fashion when any man with social pretentions surrounded his home with a water-filled ditch, in direct imitation of the moated castles of his social superiors in their castles. Irish Iron Age raths with their circular embankments or the flimsy smaller stone forts of the Burren in Co. Clare are almost equally unimpressive as defenceworks.

Not only individuals sought to impress their neighbours. The appearance of new and rebuilt town defences in the thirteenth and fourteenth centuries, often with sophisticated towers and gates, was much more related to the development of civic pride and ambitions than to the necessities of defence. It is true that the walls and gateways had economic functions too, for they could help control the ingress of traders whose taxes helped to swell the urban coffers. But militarily they had almost no function at all.

Another important aspect related to status, which can be seen in many military works, concerns their use as homes or 'offices' for the occupants. Many sites, whatever their original functions, frequently became administrative centres or dwelling places housing considerable numbers of people with non-military requirements. Such needs often caused major adaptations to the structures; sometimes the alterations merely fulfilled a special military need, as at Launceston Castle in Cornwall, where in the eleventh century specially built structures, best described as 'flatlets', were erected in the outer bailey to house the families of men summoned from outlying manors to fulfil their feudal dues as members of the garrison.

More common were the products of the military needs for office accommodation for clerks and messengers, together with extra storage and stabling. The social needs of an owner might also necessitate specialized dwellings, with kitchens, halls and other rooms for family and important visitors. Towards the end of the medieval period—when pure defensive needs receded while new ideas of improved living conditions were acquired—a subtle architectural struggle developed which in the end was won by domestic aspirations. Narrow slits and gun ports were gradually replaced by broad mullioned windows, crenellation became decoration, and the country house was born.

There are some purely military considerations which link defence systems of all periods. Perhaps the most obvious examples occur where a single site is reused by successive generations, each perceiving it to have identical or similar tactical or strategic advantages. Dover is a prime example. The geographical position of this relatively poor harbour always endowed it with a strategic importance which far outweighed its tactical situation. As a result, in the Iron Age a defensive work of some form stood on the cliff edge. In Roman times a fort was built below it. The great castle above the town was certainly frequently rebuilt and strengthened during the medieval period, while harbour and town were protected by sixteenth, seventeenth and eighteenth-century forts and ringed by gigantic batteries. New forts appeared in the nineteenth century; more batteries and then radar towers were acquired in this century. Traces of all still remain, along with the stump of a Roman *pharos* or lighthouse.

Less obvious, but equally important aspects of the military mind, as preserved in the landscape, include manifestations that may be termed 'going by the book'. This produces a number of results, two of which are particularly noteworthy. First there is the tendency to construct works on a scale that may be totally unnecessary. Thus the great Wessex Iron Age hillforts were almost certainly far stronger than was strictly necessary for contemporary indigenous warfare and far more than just 'impregnable'. Similarly Hadrian's Wall was undoubtedly built much stronger than circumstances at the time of its building demanded. Many medieval castles show the same tendency. At a later date Fort George at Inverness, built in the mid eighteenth century to the highest military standards of the time, is a prime example of 'over-kill' to face enemies who were likely to be either undisciplined Scots or small numbers of their French allies.

The second result, a corollary of the above, is that having expended vast sums of money and huge efforts on defence works it often proves that they are unnecessary or—more seriously—out-moded before they are completed because of the developments in the military technology of the attackers. The Wessex Iron Age hillforts seem to have reached their most elaborate form just at the moment when the Roman legions, with their advanced military equipment, arrived to reduce them with little effort. The designers of the great nineteenth-century coastal forts could not keep up with the advances in designs for the guns which were meant to go in them, let alone with the developing fire-power of the weapons of their potential enemies. In all such cases, perception plays an important role for each defencework is a response to a perceived threat. Change this threat, and the fortress may fall or have no purpose whatsoever.

The landscape relics can therefore tell us much about the changing patterns of human aggression. They not only tell of the constant dialectic of defence and attack as weapon technology develops, but also of political, social and economic pressures, changes and ideas.

11

Defence and the
Prehistoric Societies

The evidence for defenceworks in prehistoric times is extensive, yet any attempt to understand more than their obvious military functions is fraught with difficulties. Unlike the works of the Roman, medieval and later periods, we have little or no idea of the details of social and political organization which lay behind the construction of defences in prehistoric time. Without this information (which, by its nature, archaeology can never supply), it is often impossible to understand the real purpose behind the outward appearances of early defenceworks. In most cases we can only guess—and our guesses may well be quite wrong. Further, it is clear that throughout prehistoric times there were wide variations in military engineering from one province to another. Thus, the Late Iron Age people of Wessex defended their homes in a quite different way from those in Cornwall, Northern England or Scotland, and this must reflect different social and political conditions. Thus any generalizations are likely to be quite untrue to the details of local defenceworks.

From the end of the last Ice Age, about 12,000 BC, men have occupied these islands in growing numbers. Yet for over two-thirds of these 14,000 years we have no real evidence for purpose-built defences of any kind. In fact it is not until the last millennium BC, late in prehistoric times, that strongholds became common in the landscape. This is not because prehistoric people were incapable of constructing defences. Many other aspects of their lives—notably their tombs and temples—show clearly that prehistoric societies could be organized to construct massive earthworks or assemble and erect gigantic stones. Nor was it because prehistoric people lived in a world free of aggression, where warfare was unknown. They certainly fought with each other for the archaeological record is full of weapons such as maces, axes, spearheads, arrowheads and daggers all of which, though primarily for hunting purposes, or ceremonial display were probably also used for war. But throughout the long centuries during which man advanced from being a hunter and gatherer (the Mesolithic period) to a pottery-making farmer with a sophisticated religious organization (the Neolithic period), and then to a bronze-using agriculturalist with complex trade and social relations (the early Bronze Age), the archaeologist finds little trace of defence construction.

In the later Neolithic period (3500 to 2000 BC) people did indeed construct concentric encampments bounded by banks and ditches, known as causewayed camps. The most famous of these is on Windmill Hill near Avebury, Wiltshire; other good examples include one which is partly overlaid by a later Iron Age fort at Rybury, Wiltshire or beside the huge Iron Age fortress on Hambledon Hill, Dorset. Another lay within the grandest of all the later hillforts, at Maiden Castle, also in Dorset. Yet while all these have commanding positions which may indicate the importance of such sites as the bases of local power, causewayed camps themselves usually have rather poor defensive attributes. Their very name (taken from their characteristic features—the numerous causeways which cross ditches and banks to give easy access to their interiors) indicated that causewayed camps were not primarily fortresses; although archaeologists are still uncertain as to their exact purpose. The fact that large numbers of similar causewayed enclosures have more recently been discovered in low-lying positions makes their purpose even more puzzling.

This said, recent excavations imply that at times some causewayed camps *were* defended. Crickley Hill, near Cheltenham, Gloucestershire, certainly began life as a normal causewayed enclosure. But later it was abandoned and replaced by a continuous bank and ditch with a wooden stockade and just two narrow entrances, perhaps secured by gates. A remarkable discovery showed that the stockaded enclosure was destroyed by methods which included fire and that attackers had fired hundreds of flint-tipped arrows, many arrowheads being found at the entrance and along the bank. So it seems that a major battle took place on the site. The causewayed camp at Hambledon Hill, Dorset, was not altered in this way, but it did have massive 'outworks' added to it which were of defensive proportions and enclosed an area of perhaps a hundred acres. And this camp too, the excavator has suggested, was destroyed by violent means.

The recent discoveries underline how little we know about warfare in these distant times. The same is true of the minor settlements of the Neolithic period. Until recently the majority of settlements excavated showed few attempts at defence. Then a site at Carn Brea near St. Austell, Cornwall, was examined. This proved to be a hilltop 'village' containing perhaps as many as a 100-120 people. Initially these people lived in undefended huts scattered over the hill, but soon after 3050 BC the village was surrounded by a massive stone wall which can only be interpreted as a defensive structure. Other similar but unexcavated sites are known elsewhere in Cornwall, but it may be years before archaeology can reveal the true form of Neolithic defences.

For the early part of the Bronze Age, there is even less evidence for defenceworks. It would be easy to explain this deficiency by suggesting that warfare declined and that society became more simply organized. Unfortunately this is unlikely, for all aspects of human activity at this time—be they field systems, burial rights or technological advances—show a very complex way of life. It is possible that either warfare (and thus by implication, society) was being run on different lines than before, or that—much more probable—archaeologists have not recognized the defences of this period.

Even so, there is a lack of firm evidence for large numbers of defensive structures until the latter part of the Bronze Age—and this must be explained. Obviously, the social and political bases of prehistoric society will have influenced military practice. Also, it is possible that the population of the country during the millennia up to perhaps 1000 BC was relatively small, preventing economic, social and political pressures from developing to the point of regular conflict and large-scale warfare. Until the latter part of the Bronze Age, land may still have been available for the expansion of settlement, fields and hunting areas so that although occasional conflict (as witnessed at Crickley Hill in the earlier Neolithic times) was no doubt always a possibility, imposing and time-consuming defences were not needed.

41. *The ramparts of the Iron Age hillfort of Hambledon Hill, Dorset, which was constructed on the site of an enormous Neolithic defensive complex.*

This idyllic stage—if indeed it ever existed—came to an end around 1200–1400 BC. Archaeology plainly shows that there was a great change in the way of life of most occupants of the British Isles at this time. The reasons for these changes are quite unknown, but underlying them was a massive increase in the population. It is possible that soon after 1000 BC there were as many or more people in these islands as there were in, say, the eleventh century AD. The relics of this population explosion can be seen in scores of Bronze Age settlements, massive territorial boundary works, and vast areas of field systems and grazing grounds. They reveal the exploitation of the entire landscape whether upland or lowland.

The archaeological record is explicit and informative. At one level, it consists of great numbers of artifacts which can be described as perhaps the first real weapons designed for hand-to-hand combat and not merely as an adjunct to hunting. Swords, spears, shields and daggers become increasingly common and, at the same time, the first of the true hillforts appear in the landscape as well as defended settlements of all types.

The first forts, as one might expect, did not appear in the landscape suddenly and fully fledged. The earliest tend to be simple defensive enclosures. One of the earliest is at Norton Fitzwarren, near Taunton, Somerset, on a site which was later refortified by Iron Age people. Here, the five-acre (2-hectare) hilltop was surrounded by an irregular V-shaped ditch of defensive proportions and there is some evidence of quite extensive and permanent occupation within it, probably dating from well before 1000 BC. An almost contemporary example is the fort at Mam Tor near Castleton, Derbyshire. It consists of a great tongue-shaped area, covering some sixteen acres (6.5 hectares) and bounded by a single rampart and ditch. Within the defences large numbers of hut sites can be seen, cut like dimples into the rising hillside. These two forts belong to the middle Bronze Age.

Later in the Bronze Age, other forts appeared although they were often very different in character. For example, at Thwing in the Yorkshire Wolds excavations of two concentric ditches, thought to be the site of a Neolithic henge monument, led to the discovery of what has been called a mini hillfort, dating from around 1000 BC. The outer ditch, more than ten feet (three metres) deep, was separated from the inner one by an earthen rampart revetted in timber, and enclosing an area only fifty yards (forty-six metres) across. In the centre were the remains of a single very large wooden structure, possibly a house. The site on the peak of South Barrule on the Isle of Man is much later. Here, dated to about 600 BC, is a massive fortress enclosing dozens of hut circles, indicating permanent occupation on a very large scale.

In a very different setting, close to the River Thames at Egham, excavations have discovered not only an important late Bronze Age settlement, probably of the eighth century BC and perhaps covering as much as twenty-five acres (10 hectares), together with evidence of riverside wharves, but also some indication that the whole site was surrounded by a defensive ditch. The site has been interpreted as a major settlement and trading centre and this has led to suggestions that, in the late Bronze Age, the largest and most important of all settlements lay in the lowland valleys of the British Isles.

These examples indicate clearly that even in the later part of the Bronze Age there was a great variety of structures which can be termed 'defensive'. And, as we move into the Iron Age, after about 700 BC, the picture becomes even more confusing. The defences themselves become more complex, with great earthen ramparts replacing the earlier timber-faced ones, and complex entrances with out-works and barbicans superseding simple gateways. Most important of all, there is an immense variety in size and considerable differences in the distribution of the various types of structures.

Our view of the Iron Age is dominated by the truly gigantic hillforts of southern England, such as Maiden Castle, Hambledon and Hod Hill, all in Dorset, or Yarnbury and Old Sarum in Wiltshire. Four aspects of them are notable. First most of them only reach the form that we now see after a long process of development. Hambledon, for instance, started life as a small simple uni-vallate fort on the end of its great hilltop. It was progressively enlarged and given multiple ramparts and a great barbican entrance only after a long period of time. Likewise, Yarnbury appears to have started life as a relatively insignificant circular fortress whose original ramparts are only just visible today. It only acquired its present massive defences towards the end of its life as a fort.

Secondly, although the large forts are the best known, there are many others which, though by no means as impressive, cannot be ignored when we try to understand the distribution and function of such forts. Thus, while Maiden Castle seems to be large and important enough to have dominated all of south Dorset, within just three miles (5 km) of it are the forts of Poundbury near Dorchester and Chalbury near Bincombe. Both are minor forts by Wessex standards, but match or exceed many outside southern England. Similarly, although the great adjacent hillforts of Hambledon and Hod Hill dominate the Dorset chalk scarp, they are only two of a line of smaller and much less impressive forts, including those at Dungeon Hill, Nettlecombe Tout and Rawlesbury.

Thirdly, not only do the hillforts of Wessex range greatly in size and shape, but when excavated they prove to have had very different functions which often changed in

42. *The stunning rampart and ditch defences at Maiden Castle hillfort in Dorset. The silhouette (upper right) suggests the scale of the enormous defensive earthworks.*

the course of time. Some again—such as Hambledon, Hod Hill, Maiden Castle—were tightly packed with numerous huts, showing little or no coherent arrangement. In contrast, at Danebury, near Stockbridge, Hampshire, excavations have shown that streets lined with rectangular huts were laid out, indicating an element of deliberate planning. At Winkelbury near Basingstoke, also in Hampshire, it is clear that at one period the fort was only occupied by very few people who, oddly, seemed to have needed far more grain storage pits than was normal, implying perhaps that it was used as a temporary refuge for larger numbers at certain times. Excavations at Balksbury, in the same county, where housing and a bypass have largely ruined the fort, have indicated that throughout its life it never had anything more than a handful of people living in it and then, only on a very intermittent basis.

Even where there is evidence of permanent occupation this is not always a feature of the whole life-span of the fort, and many places seem to have been unused for long periods. At Winkelbury, for example, the fort was constructed with a timber-faced rampart in the fifth century BC and used, as was noted above, by relatively few people. Soon afterwards it was abandoned for about 200 years. It was then rebuilt with an earthen rampart and another small group of people occupied it.

While the variation in size, form, distribution and function of the forts of southern England is difficult to understand, the problems are much harder when we look at hillforts over the whole of Britain. In some areas, notably the Midlands and East Anglia, hillforts of any size are relatively few on the ground. In the Welsh Marches there is a dense distribution of forts of very varying size and complexity, while in the rest of Wales they are far fewer; except along the coastal plain of the south west, where small cliff-edge promontary forts consisting of a rampart cutting off a spur are very common. In south-west England too, the forts are usually quite small, again favouring coastal promontaries. In central northern England hillforts are very rare indeed, until one reaches the Border country where the pattern changes again. Stanwick and Ingleborough are massive exceptions. In the Borders, while there are many forts most are very small indeed, the most characteristic type being tiny ramparted sites less than two acres (0.8 hectares) in area, which may not be true forts at all.

South-western Scotland, however, has very few forts; 'vitrified' forts surround the Grampians but there are hardly any in the north west of Scotland. The vitrified forts of central Scotland are certainly the most puzzling of all British defenceworks. The process of vitrification, in the course of which rubble ramparts were baked and converted into masses of glassy slag, was achieved by the burning of lacing timbers which were used to bind and strengthen the rubble ramparts. The vitrified fort is therefore a 'normal' timber-laced fort which has *been* vitrified. Yet vitrification did not improve a fort and would not be contemplated by fort-builders. Even so, experiments in the late 1930s showed that prodigious quantities of brushwood were needed to accomplish the conflagration of the lacing timbers while recent chemical analysis shows that temperatures of around 1000°C are needed to vitrify stone. Defenders would hardly stand idle to allow attackers to heap brushwood upon their ramparts while the vitrified forts are both too numerous and too localized to be explained in terms of accidental fires affecting beginning in adjacent huts. The only explanation which we can offer is that vitrification was a ritual which might have been performed after the conquest of a hillfort or else to accompany an orgy of destruction comparable to the *potlach* ceremonies of North Western American Indians.

In the whole of Ireland there are only about fifty true hillforts but thousands of defended farmsteads known as 'raths' and hundreds of little stone-walled ringforts, along with about 200 promontory forts. As in Wessex, the hillforts of other parts of Britain also show great variety in types of ramparts as well as in their apparent usage, function and longevity. For example, while most forts in southern England have a long history of development and permanent or intermittent occupation sometimes spanning 500 years, few of the larger forts in southern Scotland seem to date before the first century BC as fortresses and they were often refurbished during the Roman occupation of England. On the other hand, many of the tiny forts appear to have begun life as timber palisaded farmsteads as early as the fifth or sixth century BC and were then refortified with stone or earthen ramparts.

Similarly, while the numerous small forts in north-eastern England were indeed only protecting single homesteads or small family groups, the larger ones were often well populated. Thus, the site at Yeavering Bell, Northumberland, is thirteen acres (5.3 hectares) in extent and has some 130 'hut platforms' still visible in the interior.

The existence of these small defence sites, which can hardly be termed 'forts', introduces us to other types of defenceworks which can be generally dated to the Iron

Age and occur either in areas totally devoid of true forts, or inextricably mixed up within them. One important type is the small defended homestead widespread in south-west England, south Wales and Ireland and variously called 'raths', 'cashels' or 'rounds'. An excavated example at Walesland Rath, Pembrokeshire, comprised an area only 210 feet (sixty-four metres) by 160 feet (forty-nine metres) bounded by a massive earthen bank and ditch. The gateways were defended by a timber tower in one instance and by a stone-faced wall and wooden gate in the other. The interior was packed with circular huts and other timber structures were built against the rear of the rampart.

A similar site, also totally excavated, is at Trethurgy near St. Austell, Cornwall. Here, a circular rampart and ditch enclosed an area only about 150 feet (forty-six metres) in diameter. Inside, the stone foundations of a group of five circular huts lie behind the rampart while the centre is open. This site, like other raths or rounds, was occupied not only in the later part of the Iron Age, but throughout the Roman period.

Another form of defended homestead is the 'dun', largely confined to the western part of Scotland though with curious and unexplained outliers elsewhere in northern Britain. These are small stone-built structures with thick vertical rubble walls, basically no more than single homesteads, but clearly erected for defence. A good example can be seen on the shore at Kildonan Bay on Kintyre in Argyll. Some, especially examples in Argyll, have outer defensive walls. Duns vary greatly in size and shape, in the date of their construction and the duration and frequency of occupation. Of those that have been excavated, dates ranging from the later Iron Age right through the Roman period into the Dark Ages have been established. In some the occupation was continuous; at others occupation appears to have been restricted to short periods of time, although often with later reoccupation.

Perhaps related to duns are the remarkable 'brochs' which are found beside the western Scottish seaboard, the northern fringe, Orkney and Shetland. They were great stone towers up to forty-five (fourteen metres) or fifty feet (fifteen metres) high, with rooms or galleries set within their massive thick walls. The origins of the brochs is still fiercely debated. They represent a highly sophisticated way of protecting family groups or local communities who may have only retired to them in times of danger. They range in date from the later Iron Age to well into the Roman period and were occasionally reused during the Norse threat. However, the broch known as 'the Howe' on Orkney has yielded a much earlier date to fuel the broch debate.

Yet another Iron Age structure, perhaps only marginally related to defence and yet widespread in the western part of Britain, is the 'fogon' or 'souterrain'. These are underground passages or chambers, usually stone lined, though in some cases once apparently roofed in timber. They are usually associated with open or lightly-defended settlements and have been variously interpreted as winter houses, food or grain storage places, refuges for livestock, places for worship or ritual, or, least convincingly, places to hide when the settlement was under attack. Again, no clear proof of any of these explanations has been forthcoming and it has been suggested that such a relatively simple structure could have been used for a multitude of purposes. Some associated with forts in Ireland, may be refuges for livestock, while the excavated souterrain at Newmills near Perth, Scotland, is said to have been used for grain storage. Perhaps the best-known example is at Carn Euny near Penzance, Cornwall, beneath the centre of the extensive Iron Age village. The settlement itself was occupied from perhaps 500 BC until at least the second century AD, a typical date range. The excavator suggested that the structure was a ritual one connected with the worship of an earth god or goddess. More impressively claustrophobic is the souterrain at Culsh near Aboyne, Grampian.

Of the many concepts of the defended homestead, that of the 'crannog' was the most durable. A crannog consists of a great platform of brushwood and rubble, supporting one or more dwelling, and set in a natural lake. Though crannogs are normally associated with the Iron Age, recent underwater explorations in Scotland have yielded some Bronze Age dates, while Irish crannogs are known to have been defended in the seventeenth century AD. It would probably be wrong to regard crannog-dwellers as a separate culture, they were simply families who exploited the natural defensive potential of a neighbouring lake. Even so, the building of a crannog island involved many times the efforts and resources needed for hut building and it reflects the obsessive need for defence at the parochial level of Iron Age society. Many crannog islands survive in Scotland and Ireland while a complete reconstruction is on display at Craggaunowen in Co. Clare.

The list of (roughly) Iron Age defences can still be lengthened: over much of England, and probably beyond, archaeological work is showing that one of the commonest types of rural settlement was the hut or groups of huts, set in a roughly circular enclosure which was usually defined by a bank and outer ditch. The ditches were usually only about three feet deep and such enclosures are generally described as 'courtyards', 'stockyards', 'farmyards' and so on. That they did indeed function as yards in which various domestic, agricultural or even industrial work was carried out is clear. But if such enclosures are reconstructed to their original form—as has been done at the Butser Hill Experimental Project in Hampshire—a curious fact emerges. The surrounding ditch, plus the three to four foot (0.9 m–1.2 m) high bank with its crowning wooden palisade forms a boundary of a surprisingly massive character, far in excess of what might be necessary merely to impound animals or separate domestic areas from fields or tracks. In fact, these banks and ditches have minor defensive proportions. Whether this was intended is quite unknown, but it is certainly worthwhile considering that perhaps the great majority of Iron Age settlements were protected by minor defenceworks guarding them against small bands of marauders rather than concerted assaults. Also, the excavations of the enclosed late Iron Age farmstead at Woodcutts, Dorset, revealed its destruction by Roman soldiers who employed a *ballista* or bolt-firing field gun. This suggests that it could, in the last resort, be used as a defensive site and was perhaps regarded as such by both its inhabitants and their enemies.

Having briefly explored the defensive works of the last centuries of the prehistoric period we find that the great variety of structures makes it difficult for us to relate them to any single clearly defined military strategy or political organization. As we shall see in the historic period, there is an equally diverse range of military creations but evidence from historic documentation allows their political and military setting to be at least partly understood. If we had to rely solely on the physical remains of, say,

43. *The gatehouse and palisade at the reconstruction of a 'crannog' or artificial defensive and inhabited island at Craggaunowen near Shannon airport. Crannogs in different parts of Britain were occupied from the Bronze Age until after the close of the Middle Ages.*

medieval defencework with no knowledge of the political, social and economic history of Britain, they would be as perplexing as Iron Age sites.

Such evidence as there is for the later stages of the Iron Age only seems to confuse the picture, but political background is sketched in the chapter on territory. In fact, it is clear that there was no neat political organization in Britain, only confused and shifting patterns of political control and allegiances, among societies which were either involved in almost continuous warfare, at all levels, or at least engaged in the preparations of such warfare. In the mid first century BC there are records of wars between, for example, Catuvellauni of the Home Counties and the Trinovantes of Essex and in the following century the Trinovantes were virtually eclipsed and their Roman client king fled to Rome. Meanwhile, detailed analysis of the coins point to continual strife between the various kingdoms of south-east England generally, the details of which will perhaps never be understood.

It is therefore not surprising that it is difficult to interpret the distribution, size, type and function of later Iron Age defence structures. In southern England no obvious line of forts marks the assumed boundary between the Durotriges of Dorset and Somerset and the Dobunni of Gloucestershire and west Wiltshire. Indeed, there are more and larger forts in the centre of the territories than on the edges. On the other hand, in the north-west Welsh Marches, where the lands of the Deceangli of north Wales and the Ordovices of mid Wales met that of the Cornovii of the west Midlands, hillforts large and small are common even though on the other presumed boundaries of the Cornovii they are rare or non existent.

It has been suggested that the large numbers of small rounds or raths found in south Wales, amounting to seventy-five per cent of all raths known in the modern Principality, are related to the Demetae tribe which occupied that area. On the other hand it is said that the similarly large numbers of rounds in south-west England, along with the coastal promontory fort and hill-slope enclosures, may reflect the pastoral way of life of the inhabitants there rather than tribal preferences. Here, the preoccupation with cattle may have favoured structures which were defensive animal enclosures; the same explanation may apply to the multitudes of Irish raths. Yet the comparable numbers of very small forts in north-east England and south-east Scotland have been interpreted in terms of a highly fragmented society with a multitude of minor chieftains, contrasting with the apparently centralized aristocratic rule of southern England.

This argument, however, ignores the very nature and distribution of numerous southern English forts, which seem to indicate that while indeed there were tribal kingdoms these were probably very fragmented and based on either loose federations of minor chiefdoms or perhaps something akin to the patchwork feudal organization of medieval times. And here, as for example on Kintyre where there were numerous fortified rural settlements or duns as well as minor but substantial hillforts, the existence of semi-protected minor settlements seems to imply that warfare on a local scale was indigenous. Further north in Scotland, the numerous coastal brochs may imply the constant threat to small communities from slave raiders from across the sea; or else, like the chambered tombs of much earlier times, reflect the coastal location of the contemporary undefended settlements. The paucity of fortresses in the central part of northern England which became home to the Brigantes, the greatest tribe of all, has never been satisfactorily explained.

It is one thing to describe the physical appearance and construction of fortresses, but quite another to solve the larger questions about their meaning and use. In short, the late prehistoric defence systems remain the physical manifestation of a warrior society that as yet we understand but little.

12

The Roman Military Mind

With the arrival of the Roman army in Britain in AD 43 the whole story of defensive works changes. For the first time in its history a great part of Britain passed under the control of a unified political system with clear aims and purposeful methods supported by a technically advanced, well-trained and disciplined army with a tradition of military tactics and strategy which had been developing for over 500 years.

Yet it must not be assumed for the thirty-seven decades of the Roman occupation that military works remained static and unchanged. Not only were there inevitably alterations in the weapons and methods of warfare but there were also considerable changes in the overall strategy. These resulted from internal and external imperial politics, changing pressure from the enemies of the Roman Empire and fluctuating frontiers as well as important economic trends. At any one time, the layout and disposition of defenceworks in the Roman period reflected contemporary military tactics, local military and political considerations as well as topography, imperial politics and strategy. They also reflected the level of economic resources, the length and ease of communication systems and the organization, numbers and equipment and aims of the actual or potential foes—as well as many other factors, all of which might change suddenly for a variety of reasons. What remains for us to study therefore, are merely the physical remains of all these varied forces which governed military works.

These works can be classified into specific types, according to their functions and garrisons. In the early part of the Roman period, at least, there was a basic division of the Roman army into legions, each of some 5300 men and auxiliary troops formed into units of 'cohorts' for infantry and 'alae' for cavalry, nominally either 500 or 1000 strong. The permanent legionary stations are called fortresses. Those at York, Chester and Caerleon were the most permanent, but there were others occupied for shorter periods in places such as Lincoln, Exeter, Gloucester, Wroxeter and at Inchtuthil in Scotland. These fortresses were major strongholds, usually fifty acres in extent, placed at strategic locations and often near navigable rivers which acted as supply lines. They held perhaps 6000 men and had permanent headquarter buildings, a chapel, a hospital, store sheds, workshops and barracks. The 'amphitheatres' which survive at Chester and Caerleon were not merely for garrison entertainment but were parade grounds for continuous arms-drill, vital for the success of the army.

Next in importance to the major fortresses was a group of twenty-five to thirty acre (10–12-hectares) forts, also known as fortresses. Little is known about them and most are only recorded as soil and crop-marks visible from the air, as at Longthorpe near Peterborough. Parts of one still exist, however, at Malton in North Yorkshire. These fortresses appear to have been used by half-legions, perhaps supported by auxiliary troops and were often only used for short periods.

The forts used by auxiliary troops were usually miniature versions of the larger fortresses. They ranged from two to ten acres (0.8 to 4 hectares) depending on the type and size of the unit based there. Thus an auxiliary cohort of 500 men usually needed a fort of three and a half acres (1.4 hectares), while an ala of the same strength needed a fort of five and a half acres (2.2 hectares) in order to house its horses. Likewise, a cohort of 1000 normally had a five-acre (2-hectare) fort while an ala of a 1000 required one of nine acres (3.6 hectares). These forts had a similar range of buildings to those in the fortresses and the length of time during which they were occupied varied considerably. In addition many of these forts had external features as did the larger fortresses. These include detached bath houses, which have been frequently identified, and parade grounds, which only survive at Hardknott Fort in the Lake District where the carefully levelled mountainside also shows the remains of a saluting-base.

All these forts vary in detail, usually as a result of various alterations or changes in military methods. The earliest were bounded by earthen ramparts and ditches surmounted by timber palisades and with wooden gate towers. Some of these later had stone walls added to the rampart and others were often built in stone from the outset. On the other hand, turf forts continued to be built until the second half of the second century AD. All internal buildings were initially of wood; later the principal administrative buildings at least tended to be replaced in stone. Many forts gained enclosures or annexes, while others had platforms on the ramparts to take *ballistae*. On rare occasions there are much larger emplacements to take the stone-throwing *onager* as at High Rochester fort.

Other types of Roman military works include the very common 'marching camps'. These are merely temporary fortifications constructed by an army or a unit on the march; they range from less than one acre to 165 acres (0.4 to 67 hectares) in size, depending on the size of unit involved. A full legion required a camp of about twenty acres (8 hectares). These were usually rectangular with rounded corners and, of course, contained no buildings. Equally important, especially for the day-to-day running of the army, were the 'practice camps' where soldiers were trained in the rapid erection of turf ramparts and the digging of complex ditches designed to trap attackers, features shared with the permanent forts.

A large number of these practice camps exist, though many are very small and apparently incomplete. They seem to mark the result of short-term field exercises. Among the finest are those of Haltwhistle near Hadrian's Wall, at Dolddinas in north Wales and especially in central Wales on Llandrindod Common. Most of these appear to have been constructed by auxiliary troops but the huge camps at Bootham outside York and the even more remarkable ones at Cawthorne in North Yorkshire are the remains of exercises by at least half-legionary units.

It is also clear that full-scale battle training was sometimes undertaken. The best known are the incomplete lines of siege-works around the hillfort at Woden Law in Roxburghshire which consist of encircling lines of ramparts and ditches, carefully positioned just beyond the range of hand-thrown missiles, accompanied by emplacements for siege engines. There is no doubt these were only practice works, for the hillfort was unoccupied at the time and is itself relatively small and unimportant. That such works had a practical objective may be seen at the hillfort of Birrenswalk in Dumfriesshire, where similar siege works, as well as raised earthen battery mounds for the *ballistae* seem to have been erected for an actual attack on the fort.

Other military works included the signal stations, erected in chains along which messages could be transmitted. These were usually small embanked enclosures surrounding a tall timber tower. The remains of these stations are well known in the north of England with the greater part of one system surviving in the Stainmore Pass.

There are, in addition, other less obvious military works of the Roman period. Most of the Roman roads in England, and almost all those in Wales, northern England and Scotland, were primarily part of the military communication system, whatever their subsequent use, and were built by the army. Indeed the great Fosse Way which stretches across England from Lincoln to the south coast was initially part of an early frontier defence system. Other aspects of military work in Roman Britain relate to the economic role of the army rather than to its purely military activities. The legions made their own tiles and even pottery at Holt near Chester. The factory, which belonged to the Twentieth Legion, covered twenty acres and included barracks for the troops engaged in the work. At Corbridge, in the north of England, walled compounds held sheds used for the manufacture of weapons, while the lead mines in Derbyshire, Somerset and Northumberland were directly under military control. At Catterick, the depot where leather was prepared for footwear, tents and uniforms, has been discovered. These are just a few of the many examples indicating both the self-sufficiency and the wide-ranging activities of the Roman army.

The best known of all Roman military defenceworks, that of Hadrian's Wall and its near neighbour the Antonine Wall, are also noted in the chapter on territories and boundaries (see p. 108ff). Hadrian's Wall is the finest example of what was, in the early second century, a fairly new venture in military strategy. The early imperial boundaries had been formed by natural frontiers such as rivers or deserts. But first in Germany and then in Britain, military strategy and events urged the construction of defensive frontiers. The German ones were little more than lines of forts linked by a palisade, but in Britain a much stronger line was required. There was not only a question of keeping out northern invaders but also that of separating tribes on different sides of the frontier who might ally with each other, and of securing the stability of the communities on both sides of the wall. Thus Hadrian's Wall was not merely a barrier but also a component in a system of defence in great depth which at first covered much of northern England, and later parts of southern Scotland.

The actual wall, its ditch, mile castles or fortlets, turrets, main garrison forts, the *Vallum* or great ditch on its southern side and the military way running behind the wall were only portions of the system. In addition, a line of forts and signal stations followed the Cumbrian coast. No less important were the thirty or more forts behind the wall spread over northern England and connected by roads with links to the legionary fortresses at Chester and York. The less complex Antonine Wall across the Clyde Forth isthmus in Scotland was built of stacked turves. Forts, fortlets and a military way formed part of a much more complicated defensive system which included forts scattered across southern Scotland. Scholars have often wondered why, having built

44. The foreground earthworks and the flint wall beyond represent successive stages in the development of the Saxon Shore fort at Richborough, Kent. The triple ditches in the foreground represent the defences of an early phase and surrounded a signal tower ; they were filled in when the shore fort masonry was built.

the complicated defences of Hadrian's Wall in the AD 120s, the Romans quickly abandoned it and built the Antonine Wall to replace it?

This brings us to the broader political and military background to the Roman period in Britain. Space prevents a full analysis of Roman military history in this country, but a few general points are worth making and may give some understanding of the factors influencing the siting and forms of defenceworks.

The initial conquest of Britain, began in AD 43, was carried out swiftly by the four Roman legions and their auxiliaries in the space of four years. Thus the various Roman fortifications in the area south east of the Fosse Way all relate to this initial conquest. The half-legion fortresses at Longthorpe near Peterborough and at Newton-on-Trent are almost certainly the temporary camps of the Ninth Legion, which probably split into two sections as it pushed north skirting the fens towards the Trent and the Humber. The Second Legion also advanced rapidly across Southern England smashing its way into at least twenty of the great hillforts and leaving a scatter of auxiliary forts behind as its lines of communication and to keep control of the newly conquered land. The most striking example of what was achieved may be seen at Hod Hill, Dorset, where excavations on the great Iron Age fortress have shown that it was attacked by the Roman army who advanced under the protection of a hail of *ballista* bolts fired from mobile batteries. Having captured the fortress, its interior was cleared, the closely packed huts of the inhabitants destroyed and a small auxiliary fort constructed in the north-west corner. From the arrangement of the interior, the excavator was able to show that it was garrisoned by a mixed unit consisting of a cohort of legionary infantry and an auxiliary cavalry unit of about 250 men. This shows the use of improvisation in day-to-day fighting and the ability of infantry and cavalry to adapt to particular circumstances; they gained a strong base from which free-ranging cavalry could control the surrounding areas.

By AD 47 all of Britain south east of the line of the Fosse Way was in Roman control. The subsequent advances into Wales, northern England and Scotland can also be seen as a fine example of integrated tactics and strategy. Legionary fortresses were established at Caerleon, and at Wroxeter which was later moved to Chester; so from north and south the legions marched into Wales. The process of conquest was carried out by rapid advances, followed by the establishment of a military road system punctuated by auxiliary forts. In essence, the whole country was divided into blocks bounded by roads which could be easily patrolled and along which supplies would reach forts set at nodal points. The system as we perceive it from the identifiable roads and forts efficiently secured the conquest and subjugation of the fragmented Iron Age societies, which were only able to respond to the initial conquest with guerrilla warfare.

The same method of conquest and control is visible in the north of England. Major roads were laid out running northwards on either side of the Pennines from the legionary fortresses at Chester and York, while the Pennines themselves were crossed by linking roads. Marching camps marked initial advances and these were quickly replaced by auxiliary forts, again erected to control blocks of territory. The beautifully-preserved fort at Hardknott Pass on the only Roman road across the Lakeland hills, set on the craggy mountainside which dominates even the great stone walls of the fort, is perhaps the most evocative relic of this strategy. In this wild and inhospitable place generations of Roman soldiers lived, trained, fought and died in the service of the Emperor. Many will have dreamed of postings to more equable outposts of the Empire!

The subsequent story of the advances into Scotland and the later retreats is more complex and more related to local and imperial politics than mere tactics or strategy. Even accepting the fierce resistance of the local tribesmen and the difficult terrain, there is no reason to suppose that the Roman army could not have conquered the whole of the British mainland. There were defeats and setbacks but external factors were paramount. The Dacian Wars of the Emperor Trajan in 101–2 and 105–6, which demanded a reduction in the British army, meant that it was impossible to sustain adequate numbers of troops and so the first retreat from Scotland took place. The resulting consolidation led to the construction of Hadrian's Wall. This consolidation was not just a British phenomenon: this period marked the end of expansion for the whole empire. Henceforth the imperial policy was, for a variety of reasons, one of consolidation and retrenchment: the barbarians beyond the Empire were to be excluded rather than incorporated.

The actual position of Hadrian's Wall also caused problems. Though perfectly sound in terms of military considerations, politically it spanned the wrong places. It divided

45. *The northern angle of the wall of the Roman fort at Hard Knott in the Lake District.*

the Brigantes from their neighbours and old allies the Selgovae of south-east Scotland. To obviate this problem a readvance into Scotland and the construction of the Antonine Wall was undertaken. Yet this tactic failed, for revolt by the Brigantes in 154–8 and a lack of reinforcements caused another retreat, although the army later resumed control of southern Scotland. After the disastrous overrunning of the Antonine Wall by northern tribes in AD 180 and a continuing shortage of military resources there was another change in political and military strategy: Hadrian's Wall was refurbished and fortified, and independent buffer states with garrisons at tactical centres were established to the north.

The external pressures on the Empire as well as internal political intrigues and crises were the main reasons behind the gradual military collapse of Roman Britain in the third and fourth centuries. Though the constant barbarian attacks on the frontiers and the raging inflation within intensified, the political disturbances were perhaps more destructive. It is often forgotten that between AD 244 and 284 at least fifty-five emperors were proclaimed—and in many cases murdered shortly afterwards. Britain's insular position shielded her from the worst excesses of Rome's political decay and, indeed, the country was relatively prosperous in the early fourth century. Even so, she was not immune. The army was repeatedly stripped of units which were taken away to fight for claimants to the imperial purple.

This situation was exacerbated by worsening attacks on Britain by sea-raiders who appeared for the first time in the late second century. The majority of them came from north Germany, the so-called Saxons, but Scots arrived from Ireland and Picts raided from northern Scotland. The responses to these problems were two-fold. One involved the introduction of a new type of army unit, the *numeri*, composed of lightly-armed barbarian troops who served either as mercenaries or as levies drafted from continental tribes under treaty conditions. The employment of such troops, as well as locally recruited units, the lack of fully disciplined legionaries and the continuing internal revolt and invasions from the north is still evident in the forts of northern England and along Hadrian's Wall. Repairs were often badly executed, the regular planning of interiors was abandoned and some buildings appear to have been used by families, rather than military units. The defences seem to have been garrisoned by what might be termed 'irregular militia' rather than fully trained and disciplined troops. Even so other forts, further south, still seemed to retain the old style military methods and troops.

The other response, directed at the sea-borne raiders was the establishment of the so-called Saxon shore forts. These represent a departure in military tactics. Previously, Roman forts had been bases primarily used in offensive operations. Now they became heavily defended and protected strong-points, usually designed to hold mounted troops who, with the co-operation of naval scouting units, could intercept raiders landing from the sea. The first forts, particularly the one at Reculver in Kent which was designed to protect the vital Thames estuary, were bounded by earthen ramparts in the traditional way. These appeared in the early third century when the Saxon threat first became serious. But it was in the late third century, after 268, that the main blows fell. Between then and the end of the century, the whole of the coast of south-east England from Brancaster in Norfolk to Portsmouth (Porchester) in Hampshire was punctuated by massive forts. These had freestanding stone walls up to twelve feet (4 m) thick and twenty-five feet (8 m) high of a kind best seen at Richborough in Kent, Burgh Castle in Norfolk, or at Porchester, with external bastions or towers built or added to take artillery. Other forts guarded the west coast and are known to have existed at Cardiff, Caernarfon, Holyhead and Lancaster. Later, towards the end of the fourth century, the system was extended by the introduction of lightly defended signal stations along the north east coast.

Many of the Roman towns in Britain also had defences. Some were provided with earthen ramparts, ditches and wooden gates soon after their foundation in the first century, but during the second century almost all the major urban centres acquired similar earthen ramparts. The reason for these defences is not easy to ascertain and dates of their appearance cover a number of years from about AD 150 to 200. Though attempts have been made to see an external threat, such as an invasion from the north, it is more likely that these defences had more to do with civic pride and a need to control and tax the comings and goings of traders than any military consideration. However, a century later, probably between 250 and 280, most of these earthen defences were strengthened by the construction of massive stone walls on their external faces. These appeared at the same time as the main Saxon shore forts, and probably protected the towns from the same threats. That these walls were successful cannot be doubted, for all the evidence suggests that, behind them, the towns of Roman Britain continued to flourish.

Shortly after the middle of the fourth century these urban defences were improved by the addition of towers or bastions of various shapes to carry defensive artillery, probably *ballistae*. It is likely that this work was part of a unified plan and perhaps the work of Theodosius who played a major role in the reorganization of Britain following the great barbarian invasions of 367. The defence of these urban areas was vital to the well being of the Province, for the administration of the country lay within them. If the towns could be protected, even when the surrounding countryside was wasted, the government of the country could survive. Indeed, in the end, it was probably these walled towns manned by the locally raised militia, that enabled a Romanized Britain to endure during the fifth century, long after the official Roman army had collapsed.

Beyond the limits of the Roman occupation and indeed in places within them, the tradition of Iron Age military works continued, almost unaltered by Roman civilization. Older forts continued to be occupied, although where Roman military rule existed, even in its final attenuated form, they were sometimes no longer fortified. For example, at the Iron Age fort at Hownam Rings, Roxburghshire, the area of settlement in the third century AD spread over and defaced the earlier ramparts, while in south-west England and Wales, raths and rounds continued to be occupied though no longer having defensive functions. Elsewhere, beyond imperial frontiers, the old fortifications were still used, sometimes with minor modifications, showing that the old habits of inter-tribal strife continued into the Dark Ages.

13

Defence in the Dark Ages

With the collapse of the Roman power and the mounting attacks on Britain from outside, it is not surprising that the unified government and defence systems decayed in the early fifth century. Political power and therefore responsibility for defenceworks passed gradually into the hands of the remnants of Roman local government and from there to petty chieftains and leaders. Despite some attempts at national or regional co-operation (which the Arthurian legends dimly recall) Britain gradually returned to a later prehistoric system of political organization: Iron Age defenceworks based on fortified strongpoints which were also the administrative centres of local tribes or kingdoms.

Coming first as raiders and from the mid fifth century perhaps as settlers, the Saxons generally followed the same system. Some chieftains or kings used the existing Roman towns and forts, partly for their defences and partly because of their traditional role as administrative centres. Thus Wroxeter in Shropshire was certainly used as the headquarters of a local chieftain in the fifth century while the Saxon shore fort at Porchester was apparently used both by Romano-British survivors and by incoming Saxon warlords. But gradually most of these places were abandoned and the seats of power seemed to have returned to some of the old hillforts. This is particularly true of Wales, the west and northern England which may reflect the underlying tradition of hillforts as political centres more than any conscious military decisions. For example, excavations at two Iron Age hillforts in Somerset, both called Cadbury, have shown that both were refortified in the fifth and sixth centuries AD and apparently used by local kings as their capitals. Elsewhere, other instances are now coming to light. In Wales it is clear that many older hillforts were reoccupied at the end of the Roman period as the traditional Celtic system of chieftains and minor tribes was reasserted. The hillfort at Dinorben in north Wales was one such a place.

Yet it must be stressed that this picture of strongly fortified places dispersed throughout Britain was not a static one. The tribes and kingdoms were in an almost constant state of war with each other and with invaders and raiders from overseas. Kingdoms came and went, grew and declined, split and amalgamated with almost monotonous regularity. Space precludes a detailed history of these events, but it should be remembered that defence sites changed their status, were rebuilt and extended, dancing to the tune of the unstable military societies which used and created them. Indeed new strongholds were erected to cope with the ephemeral aims of petty kings. For example, in south-west Scotland, on the northern side of the Solway Firth, the timber-faced rampart fort at the Mote of Mark appears to have been built in the late fifth century around an earlier undefended hamlet. By the sixth century it was probably one of a number of strongholds associated with the kingdom of Reget and the excavator discovered a variety of rich and even princely finds. The fort was apparently attacked and destroyed in the early seventh century, probably when the kingdom was absorbed into that of Northumbria.

Likewise in Ireland, among the many small kingdoms of the Dark Ages was one near Dublin known as Brega. In 688 this kingdom was divided and the capital or stronghold of North Brega was transferred to Knowth where the mighty Neolithic chambered tomb mound, covering one acre and thirty feet (nine metres) high, was fortified by an encircling ditch; it became a Royal residence of the living for a short time.

As the centuries passed there was a slow development towards larger political units, particularly in England. Again the details are complex, but the size of the kingdoms gradually increased so that eventually, by the eighth century, England was divided into large areas ruled by individual kings: Wessex, Mercia, East Anglia, and so on. Finally, there was precarious growth towards a unified English kingdom, although its final fruition was disrupted by the Danish invasions and settlement which produced the temporary hiving off of the Danelaw.

Military architecture mirrored the political developments. While Dark Age kingdoms cannot, by any definition, be called Nation States, the basic essentials of governmental administration—notably tax collection and what may be called 'the defence of the realm'—required more than merely royal strongholds or sophisticated administrative centres. This period therefore saw two major developments in defenceworks. One was the construction of linear frontier works which clearly defined the limits of political control and a number of examples are introduced in the section on territories (p. 86ff). As we say there, these works were not primarily military ones. Certainly they are of such lengths that they can hardly have been manned along their entirety, even in dire emergencies. They may more fittingly be regarded as a mixture of political status symbols, anti-rustling devices, territorial markers and trade control barriers as much as, or more than, purely defenceworks. Nevertheless, they do represent an important change in perception of territorial kingship and the need to define and vouchsafe its limits.

The second development, coming towards the end of the Dark Ages, was more important. This was the establishment of the so-called 'burghs' which first appeared in Wessex in the late ninth century. The onset of the Danish invasions and more especially the ravaging of Wessex in 871 made it clear to all that the use of locally recruited levies, who had no firm bases from which to operate was totally inadequate when faced with the 'Fury of the Northmen'. Alfred, King of Wessex, not only reorganized his armies and made them capable of sustaining long campaigns over vast distances, but also devised a system of defence for his kingdom whereby no place in Wessex was more than twenty miles from a fortress. The work was not completed until after Alfred's death, but ultimately Wessex was ringed and traversed by forts, each being kept in repair and garrisoned in times of danger by men from the surroundng area. The individual fortresses varied considerably. Many such as those at Bath, Winchester, Portchester, Chichester and Exeter merely made use of their existing Roman defences of the town or fort walls. Others were built anew and were given massive earthen ramparts. Some of the latter were laid out in almost precise rectangles, giving them the appearances of Roman towns. These mighty ramparts still exist at Wareham in Dorset, Cricklade in Wiltshire and Wallingford in Oxfordshire, all of which enclose the cores of the modern towns. At other places the natural topography was exploited: at Shaftesbury in Dorset, Lydford in Devon and Burpham in Sussex the fortresses were set on spurs with long ramparts constructed, cutting across the necks of the salients. Such ramparts survive at Burpham and Lydford.

The concept of the burgh was also adopted by the Danes and a number appeared within the area which they controlled, as at Stamford, Derby, and Leicester which made use of the Roman defences. Burghs continued to be constructed in the tenth century during the continuing Anglo-Danish wars. Bedford, Hereford and Shrewsbury all began life as burghs. The Roman defences of Towcester in Northamptonshire were rebuilt, and places such as Stamford and Nottingham had English burghs added to the Danish ones when they fell into English hands.

As so often in the story of defence systems, these burghs were much more than just forts. This is underlined by the fact that the majority of them became major medieval towns: it was intended that they should rise as trading places and local administrative centres. They acquired marketing functions, and in many cases, mints. In a very real sense they were the first towns in England after the Roman period. To view burghs as merely military works is to misunderstand the complexities of late Saxon society.

One final point should be made: like the hillforts and Roman towns, burghs served to protect communities. We are specifically told how Ethelfled, a daughter of King Alfred, built the burgh of Worcester 'to shelter all the folk'. This concept of communal defence came to a sudden end with the arrival of a new social order which required a very different form of protection: the medieval castle.

14

The Medieval Period: The Castle Comes of Age

Sometime in the eleventh century, a new type of fortification, the castle, appeared in Britain. Much ink has been spilt by scholars debating the origin and development of the castle. It also emerged on the continent of Europe and the most likely answer is that its arrival was associated with a new way of organizing society which arose in this medieval period: the feudal system.

This system had many aspects. It developed in Western Europe with the disintegration of the Carolingian empire in the face of Viking raids. As with the collapse of Roman power in Britain, this allowed the emergence of warlords who carved out new lordships from the wreckage. Again, these developed into minor kingdoms and a complex web of social relationships evolved. It was based on bonds between the king and his vassals whereby lands were held from the king by vassals in return for military service which the king employed in the protection of the whole kingdom. Society was thus organized for war—and a form of war which gradually came to depend on heavily-armoured mounted knights.

But knights were expensive to recruit, equip, train and keep. As a result two other developments took place. The terms of military service by which most land was held became dependent on the number of knights the vassal could furnish for his overlord. In addition, these knights had to be housed and protected as did their lord and his family. And so, fortified residences emerged which differed greatly from the burgh or the Iron Age fortress. Within them dwelled an élite; from them issued administration, power and armed might.

These true castles seem to have come into existence in the tenth century in France and soon afterwards they appeared in Britain. Their gradual introduction into this country became an avalanche after the Norman Conquest of 1066 which introduced a fully-fledged and more refined feudal society to Britain. Within a few years castles by the score appeared in England and soon they spread to other parts of these islands. Some

46. *The great castle mound at Old Sarum, Wiltshire, where the Normans redeveloped the site of a massive Iron Age hillfort.*

earthen 'mottes' predated the Conquest and there are indications that even before the introduction of the castle, in England at least, there was an indigenous growth of fortified residences—but this has yet to be firmly established.

From the beginning, the essence of the castle was the 'keep' or stronghold. This could vary from a massive stone-built tower like the Tower of London to an earthen mound or motte, crowned by a timber palisade or a tower. These keeps had two distinct functions. One was purely military, with the keep as the ultimate refuge for the lord and his household. The other—less obvious, but in feudal society equally important—was symbolic, with the keep serving to proclaim the power and status of its owner. The arrival of the Normans in 1066 thus introduced not only a new form of defencework but also a new arrangement of society. As long as that society persisted castles would exist; as that society declined, so also did castles. In due course we explore details of castle development in Britain, but we must not forget that in broad terms the castle was more an expression of contemporary society than a mere military stronghold.

The classic form of Norman castles is that known as the 'motte and bailey', the motte or mound being for the keep and the bailey, a fortified enclosure attached to it. Mottes vary greatly in size, the tallest being those at Thetford in Norfolk and Clifford Hill in Northamptonshire. Many others were very small and were merely embanked enclosures. Normally the motte had a ditch around its base and in most cases beyond it lay the attached bailey, bounded by a rampart and ditch with examples of numerous sizes.

47. Hedingham Castle in Essex, a well-preserved Norman stone keep.

Many of the early mottes had timber towers on their summits, while in some castles the tower projected from the motte which was erected around it. Other mottes had stone towers or keeps from the beginning as at Farnham in Surrey. With some castles the great stone keeps were added at a later date. Most famous is that at Rochester in Kent which was probably built soon after 1127; the almost identical keep at Castle Hedingham, in Essex, was built around 1138. Most of these early keeps were rectangular in plan and splendidly display the ideal of the fortified residence. They were certainly well fortified, with massive walls, protected entrances and tiny windows, but

156

inside they were homes and offices. The narrow external windows usually had wide 'splays' and were recessed into the walls. There were basements for storage, great halls and chambers, chapels, kitchens, internal wells, and often elaborate sanitary arrangements. In the bailey lay other buildings such as warehouses, barns, stables and servants' quarters, all protected by the lesser defences of the surrounding rampart or walls. Some of the castles of the greater lords, and certainly many belonging to the crown, had more than one bailey.

Many hundreds of motte and bailey castles were constructed in Britain in the late tenth and eleventh centuries. They lie dispersed across England, sometimes little altered, often greatly modified by later owners, but all symbolizing the power of the feudal lord. They were carried into Wales by the Norman lords where they protected newly conquered lands and were swiftly adopted by the Welsh chieftains. The same developments occurred in Scotland and especially in Ireland, where again the Norman warlords staked out their lands and erected their castles as military and administrative centres. Motte and bailey castles, usually with little or no evidence of stone keeps or walls, are particularly common in the Welsh Marches. They not only reflect the more disturbed conditions in an area under constant attack from Welsh raiders, but also deliberate royal political policies of devolving the difficult task of policing the frontier on local lords.

Once castles had been established they were continually modified as the military engineer responded to advances in warfare and changes in fashion. These changes were very complex and, in the new light cast by detailed modern research, not as simple as used to be believed. Nevertheless, certain trends can be seen. One involved the replacement of the square keeps by circular or polygonal ones. Having no sharp angles to be sapped or blind spots to defend, the round keeps were a significant improvement. Castles such as Pembroke, Conisbrough in Yorkshire and Launceston in Cornwall, are examples. Similarly, as a result of the increasing awareness that other features and functions of the castle needed to be protected as well as the main residence, there was a gradual concentration of the defences on the castle perimeter or bailey. The former earthen ramparts were replaced by 'curtain' walls and the walls then protected by square interval towers—particularly well displayed at Framlingham Castle in Suffolk. These towers, which had the same function as the bastions on late Roman forts and towns, enabled the curtain walls to be swept by flanking fire. The advantages of circular towers or bastions were also soon appreciated and these became common. The importance of defending the entrances in the outworks was equally appreciated and elaborate and complex bastion gatehouses with flanking drum towers developed. All these advances and developments may best be seen at Dover Castle, whose position as a royal stronghold on a site of supreme strategic and tactical importance ensured that the castle was kept in the forefront of military architectural development.

As the thirteenth century progressed, the idea of increasing the strength of castle perimeters while lessening reliance on the fortified keep spread across the British Isles. The culmination of the process was the so-called 'concentric castle'. As always, these developments were not purely inspired by military functions. They reflected changes in society and more particularly, in the way that people—or at least those who aspired to

48. *The hall keep at Castle Rising, Norfolk, represents a less common variation on the Norman keep. Some experts suspect that a portion of the adjacent defensive earthworks may have been inherited from the Roman period.*

castles—thought they ought to live. The great keeps, although they continued to be occupied, were not adequate or sufficiently adaptable to accommodate the increasing demands for a more comfortable lifestyle for the lords, their families and their retainers. Increasing numbers of servants, goods, animals and so on had to be included within the protective walls. In addition, status and fashion were as constantly in the minds of medieval societies as in our own. No great magnate could afford to be seen to be living in an old-fashioned castle, even if from the purely military point of view it provided more than adequate protection. As a result most castles were periodically remodelled to produce the complex architectural development that the castle visitor so often finds.

Near perfection in contemporary castle design may be seen in those built by Edward I in Wales around the end of the thirteenth century as part of his conquest of that country. Though, as we shall see, they are militarily sophisticated, they are much more than just structures for defence. They were built by a king who was arguably the greatest in Christendom and who was prepared to spend almost any amount of money. They were more than superb military strongholds designed to cow the defeated Welsh: they were also major status symbols, and expressions of total kingship. The best known of these castles is Caernarfon which forms one integrated and defensible unit bounded by a huge curtain wall punctuated by great polygonal towers, which could cover the whole circumference with flanking fire. As Alan Brown has said, these 'must have provided one of the most formidable concentrations of fire-power to be found in the Middle Ages.' Yet there was more to Caernarfon than defence. The great west or Eagle tower was given added architectural distinction and provided with sumptuous residential accommodation intended for the King's Vice-Regent in north Wales, and perhaps

49. *Caernarfon Castle, one of the most formidable and best preserved of the great Edwardian castles of Wales.*

50. *The moat and outer walls of the concentric Edwardian castle at Beaumaris on Anglesey. The more formidable inner wall can be seen rising above the outer defences.*

ultimately for the Prince of Wales. In addition, there was spacious accommodation for the king and queen and also for the constable and members of their various households. All the Welsh castles of Edward I show the combinations of concentric design and lordly accommodation, none more so than the last in the series, Beaumaris on Anglesey, which is regarded by many as the most perfectly designed medieval castle in Britain.

After the fourteenth century in most of England the castle entered into decline. Few new ones were built and on the whole alterations to existing ones were of a non-military nature—usually in the form of more luxurious residential accommodation. Some were in fact largely abandoned. Many of the smaller castles of the thirteenth, fourteenth and fifteenth centuries were more the reflections of the pursuit of the status which battlements and turrets bequeathed to their owners than of the realities of defensive needs. Such small castles and fortified manors did not threaten the stability of the realm, while medieval kings were pleased to sell the necessary 'licences to crenellate'; much of their income derived from the sale of licences to do this, or that. Thus some of the so-called castles which were then built only aped the defensive image. Tattershall Castle, Lincolnshire, built between 1430 and 1450 has, it is true, a moat and its great towers have battlements. But it also has wide windows, simple undefended doors and bogus machiolations as decorative features. Of the same tradition and general period is Kirby Muxlowe in Leicestershire.

Why did these changes occur? It is true that military advances were involved, especially the arrival of gunpowder and improved cannons which eventually blasted castles into redundancy. But these were of lesser importance, for even in the Civil War of the seventeenth century many medieval castles withstood the battering of artillery far more advanced than that of the fifteenth. Likewise the increasing emphasis on pitched set-piece battles rather than long sieges also played a part, as did the relative poverty of some late medieval kings who could not maintain large numbers of royal castles but sometimes invested in formidable mercenary forces.

As always, however, the real answer lay in changes in the contemporary society. For the decline of the castle in England was matched by the rise of the country house. Gradually the castle crept into obsolescence and its position as the residence of a lord was assumed by the mansion house, at first with crenellations, moats and great undefendable towers, such as those at Oxburgh Hall, Norfolk, of 1482, or the alterations to Hever Castle, Kent, in the same year, and finally in the sixteenth century at Hampton Court Palace. Even the most costly work on all English Royal castles, that at Windsor between 1350 and 1370 by Edward III, was almost entirely for non-military purposes and involved the construction of splendid suites of royal apartments. The same is true of later baronial castles as at Warwick, where in the late fourteenth century the castle was generally strengthened in a true military fashion though its residential accommodation underlined the political might of a great earl.

The changes in society which were reflected in the movement from the medieval castle to the country house were signifying the end of feudalism in England. This was not a sudden occurrence and the reasons are complex in detail and not fully understood. The changes involved many aspects of life including the increasing wealth and political power of the middle classes, evident in the gradual growth of the influence

51. *Markenfield Hall near Ripon, a well-defended medieval hall with a moat and gatehouse.*

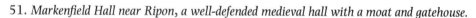

52. Lemeneagh Castle in Co. Clare, a tower house which results from the addition of a seventeenth-century mansion to a fifteenth-century residential tower.

of the House of Commons. Yet, paradoxically, they also involved the expansion of the royal power and its consolidation in terms of justice and administration. At the same time, less tangible changes in outlook involved greater freedom (for certain people), the growth of nationalism and more practical events and developments including printing, increasing standards of living (which again, only some people enjoyed) and the gradual

162

influences of new aesthetic, scientific and religious ideas that together made up the Renaissance. Out of this maelstrom of change gradually emerged the centralized and unified state which was based on new concepts of political power, economic wealth and social aims and ideals. In this new world there was no place for private fortified residences, nor the provincial royal castle. The new world needed new citadels and created its own custom-built defences.

Outside the areas of effective royal control the story was slightly different. In Wales, the north of England, Scotland and Ireland defensive local and private structures continued to be built; in places they proliferated. Even in Wales, which was at least nominally under English control, the nature of Welsh society favoured more conservative processes than were taking place in England. The greatest of the late medieval Welsh castles is that at Raglan, almost entirely a fifteenth-century structure, yet even here the splendour of the contemporary residential accommodation is noteworthy and still more lavish appointments were gained in the sixteenth century.

Castles, however, were retained in the north of England, and more particularly in Scotland, where the Scottish victory at Bannockburn in 1314 was reinforced by the auld alliance with France. They proliferated in the Borders where, after the English defeat, there followed three troubled centuries of war and raiding while England itself lived under the shadow of concerted French and Scottish invasion. The old medieval castles such as those at Bamburgh and Durham continued to be updated and remained as major fortresses. Elsewhere, the period produced minor castles and defenceworks of types unknown elsewhere on the British mainland. These can generally be classified as Tower Houses, Bastles, Pele towers and Pele houses. They are very different to true castles, and reflect the fact that the needs of many different levels in society sought protection in a period of continuous if sporadic warfare. Tower houses, which occur widely in Scotland and Ireland, and range in date from the fourteenth to the sixteenth centuries were the homes of larger local potentates. They were primarily residences, whose major apartments were often elaborate and sophisticated though sometimes spartan; they were designed to protect lords and their families against minor if often perilous attacks. The tower houses could be rectangular in plan but were often 'L' or 'Z'-shaped and many had attached lightly defended stone-walled or even earthen-ramparted enclosures which were used to protect cattle or stores. Many survive in the Border counties; Neidpath Castle near Peebles is a good example which withstood a Cromwellian siege in 1650 while Etal and Edlingham, both in Northumberland, are English examples. Lemeneach Castle in Co. Clare is a tower house of 1480 to which a mansion was added in the seventeenth century. Below them in social status were pele towers which are merely smaller versions of tower houses, usually rectangular, with small window openings and again with a walled enclosure or 'barmkin' attached. These towers often only had two floors and a basement. Many were quite small and simple like the Vicar's Pele at Corbridge, in Northumberland, although others were sometimes more sophisticated. In the Scottish Borders almost every minor lord or noble had a pele tower and as a result individual villages acquired groups of them. Thus at Langton in Roxburghshire there were three, while the town of Jedburgh had six.

53. *The parson's pele at Corbridge. Such small private defenceworks were numerous in the strife-torn Anglo-Scottish borders.*

Lower down the social scale came bastles which were erected by most of the minor Border gentry and well-to-do farmers in the fifteenth and sixteenth centuries and sometimes by local villagers as communal refuges. These were still smaller towers, usually of two storeys. They occur in large numbers right across the Borders and indeed in 1544 the village of Lessudden, again in Roxburghshire, had no less than sixteen. With their general emphasis on defence at the first floor level they slightly resemble Norman stone manor houses.

Near the bottom of the social scale came pele houses which were built by individual farmers, to protect themselves against raiders and cattle rustlers. They simply consisted of a stone-built first-floor hall with a storage basement below and had tiny windows and occasional loops for hand-guns. These small-scale defensive structures are vivid reminders of the great differences in the way of life 'enjoyed' by the people in northern Britain and stand in sharp contrast to the emerging peace and unity of Tudor England beyond the Borders. In Ireland too the late medieval period is marked in the landscape by rebuilt castles and the great and smaller tower houses of the lesser nobles which commonly survive to remind us of the ceaseless warfare taking place in that country.

In England itself there are other forms of apparently defensive structures which belong to the medieval period and which, like pele towers and bastles, were constructed by others than the top people of their time. One is the 'fortified' manor house. Not everyone in medieval times wanted or could afford a castle. As a result, there were many small manor houses which appeared to be fortified, but which were much more a reflection of their owner's aspirations, smaller facsimiles of the great true castles. Prettiest of all is Stokesay Castle in Shropshire which was built by Lawrence Ludlow, the richest wool merchant in England, between 1285 and 1296. It had a moat, a 'mini-keep' and crenellated curtain wall but all this is largely sham masking a normal hall and chamber block. It is an expression of status sought rather than defence. The same was true of many similar structures.

Of more consequence, particularly in view of their numbers, are the almost ubi-quitous moated sites which can be found all over England and which occur in vast numbers in certain areas of East Anglia and the Midlands. These usually survive only as small rectangular or circular islands surrounded by broad shallow ditches or 'moats', often with attached ditched or moated enclosures. Numerous excavations have shown

54. *The ruins of an abandoned Scottish tower house near Insch, Grampian.*

55. *Herstmonceux Castle, East Sussex, was built in 1440 at a time when the private castle was being superseded by the stately home. The castle was partly dismantled in 1777 and restored in 1933.*

that they were formerly occupied by timber or stone-built halls with associated barns, stables, farmyards and gardens, and documents indicate that their owners were minor local lords, wealthy yeomen or rising gentry. Almost all of them date from the twelfth to the early fourteenth century. Much discussion as to their function has taken place, but with the best will in the world, they cannot be conceived of as 'defensive' except in terms of minor protection against the local hooligans. The social status of their owners,

166

their indefensible nature and short period of flowering, all point to another example of status symbolism within medieval society and reflect the social aims and desires of the castle builders, albeit writ small.

One exception to this explanation of moated sites should however be made. In Ireland, and especially in southern Ireland there are also numerous moated sites. These too were built by small farmers and lesser lords and over roughly the same period as in England. But work on them by Barry has shown that they are more viably fortified than their English cousins and have raised interiors. Barry has suggested that these are much more likely to have been true defensive structures and, as such, much more necessary in unstable contemporary Irish society than in the almost completely pacified English situation.

One final form of pseudo-defence is medieval town walls. They also proclaim status but have economic significance too. Very many English towns acquired walls in the medieval period and where the town had a long pedigree these sometimes rose on Roman footings. While those in Wales—notably those built by Edward I at Caernarfon and Flint—were indeed designed to give protection to the new towns within, most had little military function and were built to low standards. The majority never had a shot fired against them in anger, nor was it expected that they would. As with the 'defences'

56. *A well-preserved section of the medieval town walls of Canterbury.*

of early Roman towns, they were perhaps primarily built as status symbols either by their lords or their burgesses but they also performed a useful economic function in controlling the entry and exit of traders.

Thus, as with most medieval fortifications, town defences were built for the display of power and status, either actual or desired. They reflect the demands of society at peace as much or more than those of a society at war.

15

Post-Medieval Fortifications: Defending the State

From the sixteenth century onwards, with one or two notable exceptions, the defensive sites of Britain are the physical expression of the needs, demands and aspirations of the emergent nation state. From the reign of Henry VII onwards, the primary motivation was the defence of the realm against external enemies. Thus for most of the period the major defensive structures lay on the periphery of the country, protecting it from invasion and defending the coastal bases from which attacks could be launched against its enemies. For the first time since the Roman period, the boundaries of the kingdom were clearly defined and protected by a ring of permanent defenceworks whose purpose was to protect, not only the upper echelons of society, their families and goods, but all the king's subjects whoever and wherever they may have been.

Such radical concepts did not appear overnight; they emerged slowly from the ferment of late medieval times and the Renaissance. They were tested in the fires of seventeenth-century civil war, codified in the late seventeenth-century political settlement, further developed in the eighteenth and nineteenth centuries and reached their most explicit form this century. Once more it was society not military developments that controlled the overall pattern of fortifications. Military techniques only determined the details.

The final break with the medieval feudal tradition came under Henry VIII. If not the first king to conceive the total defence of his kingdom, he was the first to express it in physical terms. His, and his daughter Elizabeth's main concerns were to protect strategically vital ports at times of threatened invasion.

The event which triggered off the process was the threat of invasion in 1538 following Henry's break with the Pope who then preached crusade against him. Over the next few years defences were constructed along the coasts of England from Hull to Milford Haven. While some older castles were brought up to date, the main innovations were a series of batteries or 'block-houses'. Though they were, and still are, called 'castles', this is a misleading term for they marked a major advance in military technology. These new structures were actually stone-built protected batteries from which large calibre cannon could cover the adjacent sea and coastline. Here then, for the first time, we find fortifications designed and built for artillery. The block-houses varied considerably in design but most had central towers or 'keeps' containing the

57. Like other south-coast ports, medieval Rye was continually threatened by French raiding and was razed by the French in 1377. The Baddings tower is a defensive post dating from about 1250 and was rebuilt around 1420 and sold to one John de Ypres.

living quarters of the garrison and a basement for stores and ammunition. The keeps were either completely surrounded or partly surrounded by a lower curtain wall behind which were casements or vaulted rooms for the guns and a parapet above surrounding other open gun emplacements. The curtain walls were sometimes circular but more often arranged to form a series of semi-circular or semi-hexagonal bastions. In front was a deep ditch or moat across which a drawbridge allowed access to a heavily defended gate tower.

These batteries or block-houses were positioned not (except in one locality) to resist invasion across open beaches, but to protect major ports or estuaries which might be used as bridgeheads by invaders who required sheltered places in which to disembark their armies. Thus the major positions that were so protected included Portsmouth and the Solent (where Southsea Castle and Hurst Castle survive), Carrick Roads, Falmouth in Cornwall (where St. Denis and St. Mawes Castles still stand), the entrance to Portland Harbour, Dorset (still overlooked by Portland Castle), Dover, where a new and enlarged harbour required special protection, and along the lower Thames Estuary. Only the block-houses at Deal and Walmer, in Kent, together with the almost destroyed Sandown Castle were covering open beaches; here the protection of merchant shipping, sheltered in The Downs between the coast and the Goodwin Sands, was perhaps a more important consideration.

Henry VIII's work was well executed, showing such strategic and tactical skill that little new work was needed during the reign of Elizabeth, despite the threats of invasion. Minor modifications and repairs were carried out and a few new block-houses built, including Upnor Castle on the Thames Estuary, to protect the dockyard at Chatham. The greatest defence work of the period was directed towards an invasion threat from a different direction: the Scottish challenge led to the complete refortification of the town Berwick-on-Tweed, over the period from 1559 to 1640. Here the massive walls and their projecting bastions echo continental but un-British urban defences.

Both Upnor Castle and Berwick, though on vastly different scales, introduced a new and long-lasting concept of military engineering into Britain, for both had 'angle bastions', a very advanced form of defensive work only recently invented. An angle bastion is a projection from a curtain wall, with a plan in the form of an arrowhead; such bastions, set at corners or at intervals along the curtain wall enabled the defenders not only to sweep the flanks of the curtains with fire, but the adjacent bastions and every possible angle across the land outside the wall were covered. In addition, their pointed shapes made them difficult to attack by mining, bombardment or direct assault. Berwick is a superb example of this type of defensive structure. The surrounding moat, stone-faced curtain walls and bastions, surmounted by gun emplacements, provided an impregnable fortress guarding the main route to the north.

In the early seventeenth century little work was carried out on the defence of this country. But although England was at peace with the outside world, internally there was political argument and ferment which, in 1642, erupted in civil war. This was quite without precedent. There had indeed been civil wars of a kind in the medieval period, but these were usually fought over fairly restricted areas between the king and some of his dissatisfied nobles. There were campaigns of marching, punctuated by

58. *Deal, a castle for national defence, built about 1540 in the face of a threat of French invasion.*

battles and sieges which did not, at least directly, involve the mass of people, except on a relatively minor scale.

Now the emerging nation was at war with itself, fighting for new though deeply-held political and religious ideals. Except at the very lowest levels of society, everyone had to choose a side. The result was a gory conflict which involved the mass of the people in a way which was not to recur in England until 1914. Unprecedented at least since the Roman period, the Civil War involved the use of professional soldiers led by experienced and trained officers. For the few years of this war, towns were besieged, taken and retaken, medieval castles refortified, strategic areas protected, and tactical points fought over. Even churches were not spared and Lichfield cathedral was severely bombarded. As a result, thousands of fortifications of all types were constructed, often rapidly, and then swiftly abandoned as the tide of war swept on.

Few of these fortifications survive today. Unlike the earlier castles, the block-houses and the later defenceworks, most civil-war fortifications were not built of stone or brick but were constructed hastily of earth with timber palisades. As a result, most have long disappeared under the later expanding towns or beneath the plough. Yet enough remains to give some insight into the bitter conflict.

The professionalism of the armies involved meant that defenceworks followed the mainstream of European techniques which were developed and refined in the tragic religious war of the early seventeenth century. A whole new vocabulary describing defence sites and their details passed into the language including sconces, redoubts, raised batteries, ravelins and so on. Military manuals giving precise instructions for their construction, defence and attack were printed and widely circulated and trained military engineers accompanied most armies. The result was that even the most temporary work often had the most formidable sophistication.

The best of the surviving remains are those at Newark, Nottinghamshire, which include the Queen's Sconce, a large rectangular fort with huge angle bastions; a small redoubt or detached strongpoint, surrounded by a ditch and a rampart; a flanked redoubt with projecting semi-bastions at the corners to provide flanking fire; as well as parts of the 'lines of circumvallation' or ditches dug round the town to link the strong points.

Many other towns with massive defenceworks around them include London, Oxford, Colchester and Reading. At Oxford, a few traces of angle bastions and ramparts still remain, while at King's Lynn in Norfolk long sections of the defensive ramparts, moats and bastions survive, sometimes in the middle of modern housing estates. Outside the towns, forts and batteries raised at strategic points have occasionally been accidently preserved as at Earith in Cambridgeshire where the great bastioned fort known as 'The Bulwarks'—perhaps the finest civil-war construction in England—still stands close to the River Ouse. The gun emplacements, surrounding ditches, ramparts, infantry walkways and assembly points and complex outworks to protect both the river and the main road between Huntingdon and Ely are all visible. Another fort lies at Horsey Hill near Peterborough. Not far away, and built to guard the Great North Road at Sawtry in Huntingdonshire, is the small embanked depression for a gun battery, while at Leverington near Wisbech a flat-topped mound marks the site of a raised battery built to protect a temporary assembly area for Parliamentary troops.

These all show the impact of the professional engineer in the Civil War. Yet as we have noted, the Civil War was to some extent a people's war which involved more than just the professional soldiers. Untrained levies or volunteers were also involved and they too have left their mark. At the crossing of the Old West River near Stretham in Cambridgeshire is a small civil-war fortification. Its purpose was to control the main road to Ely. It was certainly intended as a flanked redoubt, but it was apparently built by men who had never seen one and who only knew that the rectangular earthwork had to have projecting areas extending beyond each side. The result is a curious and irregular mound which reflects the 'Dad's Army' aspect of the Civil War. Rather superior is the small sconce near March in the same county, yet with only three ill-shaped bastions, set on a site of no tactical or strategic importance whatsoever, it seems to be the result of a training exercise, by local and equally unversed troops.

The peace of 1649, and more importantly, the Restoration of the Monarchy in 1660, brought an end to the construction of internal defenceworks. But no sooner had Charles II taken the throne, than the external threat to the country reappeared and was most vividly demonstrated by the Dutch raid on the Medway in 1665. The response to this was a new wave of coastal defences, again concentrated on the protection of the major naval bases: by now the importance of the navy as both the main defensive and offensive arm of the state had become established. The new king had, during his exile on the continent, been well aware of the latest development in military engineering and he employed as his chief engineer Sir Bernard de Gomme. De Gomme designed and built a new series of forts based on the then highly-developed system of bastion fortification used on the continent, whereby defensive works were composed of a series of massively defended lines and/or outworks, all protected by bastions. De Gomme's earliest work was involved in the refortification of the Medway for obvious reasons, but he later designed and built the great Citadel at Plymouth and between 1670 and 1680 created Tilbury Fort on the Thames. The latter is probably the finest surviving example of his work. The core of the fort has a pentagonal plan, bounded by massive earthen ramparts faced in stone and with huge bastions on four of the corners, all with emplacements for guns. Within are barracks, officers' quarters, storehouses, magazines and a chapel. Below it, on the riverside, are emplacements for two separate batteries to cover the Thames, while the fort itself is surrounded by a moat which has within it and opposite the main entrance a triangular island or 'ravelin', which not only protected the gates but acted as a strong point to cover both the north side of the fort and the so-called 'covered-way' beyond the moat. The latter is a flat berm or terrace protected by an earthen rampart which projects forward at intervals as triangular bastions or spurs. In front of it is an outer moat. Within this moat, again on the north side, is another triangular defended island or redoubt, originally another stronghold covering the outer ditch and the covered-way. Tilbury provides our finest example of the seventeenth-century military engineer at his most inspired.

Yet none of the coastal fortifications ever heard a shot fired in anger. Their buildings consumed vast quantities of money, but they were obsolete almost before they were finished. The main reasons for obsolescence were both political and military. On the political side, the eighteenth century saw Britain in a world where land warfare was a continental or colonial affair, while at the same time Britain was usually at peace with her neighbours. Militarily, the defences became obsolete because of the increasing power of the Royal Navy. Thus for most of the eighteenth century such structures as were built tended not to be primarily for defence but for the support of the Navy in its home bases. Among the most notable of these are the magnificent rope houses and stores at Chatham and Portsmouth. The brick store houses of the late eighteenth century at Portsmouth are monumental structures, well deserving of the protected status they now receive.

Thus, for almost a century Britain slumbered under the protection of its navy and the unrelated defensive works fell into disuse. There was only one exception, although it was a considerable one. With the Jacobite uprisings of 1715 and 1745 the English monarchy and State were threatened from Scotland. The union of the crowns of 1603 had little effect, particularly on the warring Highlanders and the first English attempt to pacify the Highlanders was not made until 1652 when Cromwell sent an army there. Several typical seventeenth-century bastion forts were constructed and two in particular were erected in the far north, one at Inverness and the other at Inverlochy (Fort William). That in Inverness was abandoned in 1660 but, with the arrival of the Protestant King William III in 1689, Inverlochy Fort was rebuilt and renamed Fort William in his honour. The existence of this solitary stronghold did nothing to prevent the 1715 uprising; once it had been crushed, the British government ordered the construction of infantry barracks in strategic places to act as strongholds against an essentially guerrilla form of warfare. One of these, Ruthven Barracks near Kingussie, Invernesshire, still survives. It consists of two large Georgian-styled barrack blocks protected by a stout stone wall pierced for muskets and with projecting flanks to cover each side. These barracks proved ineffective and, in the face of political disaffection and lawlessness, a new tactic was introduced in 1724. The barracks were supported by new forts, and linked by new military roads and so the strategy pioneered by the Roman army in similar terrain and against similar enemies was reintroduced.

This time the system failed. In the 1745–6 rebellion the forts at Inverness and Fort Augustus were besieged and taken by the Bonny Prince's Highlanders; the British army, although subsequently victorious at Culloden, was humiliated. Action had to be taken and it was on an almost ludicrously grandiose scale. Many more military roads were built and further strongholds established. Fort Augustus was rebuilt but at Inverness a new and almost incredibly formidable fortress, Fort George, was built. The building of Fort George began in 1748 and was not completed until 1770, by which time its original need had long since evaporated and it was reduced to the military barracks station which it still holds. But it remains as perhaps the best example of eighteenth-century defensive work in Britain with several hints that the military minds had triumphed over common sense. The main fort, containing the barracks, storehouses and chapel, is defended by stone curtain walls, angle bastions and demi-bastions. Below the ramparts are mortar-bomb-proof casements for magazines and barracks. The eastern landward side is the most heavily defended and the actual curtain wall and bastions are only the inner defences. In front of them is a ditched ravelin with a covered way beyond, with assembly points or 'places of arms'. Beyond is a 'glacis' or broad area of ground gently sloping down from the parapets of the covered way so that the whole area could be swept by fire.

In England, meanwhile, various minor invasion threats in 1756 and 1799 led to the construction of new gun batteries, especially in south-eastern England and around the major naval installations. It was not however, until the beginning of the Napoleonic Wars that governments, reluctant to invest in costly defensive programmes, instituted a new phase of defence work. At first, the new work was a continuation of the old. Major estuaries and ports were strengthened but with new and different types of artillery platforms. As well as masonry walls there was now an emphasis on earthen ramparts which could better absorb a battering from the increasingly powerful naval guns. Huge ditches still protected the ramparts but to give additional strength, brick-built bomb-proof galleries were inserted in the sides of the ditches or extended into, or even across the ditches. The latter are known as *carponiers* and enabled the floors of the ditches to be swept by fire. Such work still survives at Dover, around and to the west of the medieval castle.

The threat of cross-Channel invasion by Napoleon in 1803 brought new problems. It was clear that the invasion was likely to be launched across open beaches rather than at existing harbours. At the same time, the growing industrialized organization of Britain; the clear dependence of the armed forces on the strategic industries, and a growing political awareness at all social levels influenced in part by the French

59. *Dover Castle is an accumulation of many centuries of military engineering. Here, the Norman keep flies the flag in the centre of the photograph.*

Revolution itself, led to a need for the total protection of the country in the face of armies of quite unprecedented size. The military response to these events and attitudes was the construction, along the coasts of south-eastern England, of the 'Martello Towers', spaced as little as half a mile apart. These were tall brick and stone towers, each mounting a large cannon on its roof and garrisoned by a small detachment of men, and were intended to pin down any invasion force as it came ashore. The towers were backed up by massive entrenched camps where whole corps of 5000 to 6000 men could be held in readiness to strike at the chosen point of invasion. The great earthen ramparts, bastions and ditches on the Western Heights at Dover represent one of these strongholds. In places where an invading force could not be prevented from landing, special measures were taken. The exposed beaches of Dungeness and the flat lands of Romney Marsh were not protected, but were cut off from the rising ground to the north by the Royal Military Canal, comparable to a massive modern anti-tank ditch, protected at each end by a tower and batteries.

The threat of the Napoleonic attack also left its marks far from the invasion coast. In the very centre of England, at Weedon in Northamptonshire, at the hub of a main road system, a large barracks and storage complex was built, where regiments stood ready to be dispatched to any point in the country. The movement of these troops and military materials was not intended to be made merely by road. The newly-built Grand Junction Canal—the late eighteenth century's equivalent of a motorway—passed the gate of Weedon Barracks. From it a spur led to wharves and basins inside the barracks. Outside

60. *A Martello tower standing on a small platform which nestles at the foot of old sea cliffs near Folkestone.*

the barracks, troops practised manoeuvres from which we inherit the earthen remains of detached redoubt, a model for ones that, in the event, never had to be built.

There was no invasion, for the Royal Navy defeated the enemy in far-off waters and confirmed the nation's trust. The continued confidence in the Navy during the long peace of 1815 to 1854, during which Britain's military activities were confined to suppressing ill-disciplined natives in the far-flung corners of the Empire, resulted in little indigenous work of a defensive nature being undertaken. Indeed, the major military buildings of this period largely reflected the demands of the navy. Again, Portsmouth Dockyard provides good examples of this period, with its elegant terraced houses for the dockyard admiral and his staff and the beautiful cast iron Fire Engine House of 1847.

New developments were to follow. The late Victorian progress towards a more democratic society brought new aspirations and demands for protection. Meanwhile, the ebullient nationalism or jingoism and the ever growing importance of the industrial base of Britain which had to service armed forces with increasingly complex military technology, all led to a general sense of the sanctity of the boundaries of Britain. They had to be defended at all costs. In military terms, the results of the Crimean War and especially the fruitless naval operations at Sebastopol (where well protected coastal guns battered what had been thought of as an invincible fleet) showed the need for massive protection. And when in 1858 the French launched their first iron-clad warship and thus at a stroke rendered the Royal Navy outmoded, the call for action was deafening. The Report of a Royal Commission, set up to consider the defences of the United Kingdom in 1860, triggered off the most intensive phases of military construction that had ever been seen in Britain. Nor was this period one of simple military building. In Britain and on the continent, industrial, scientific and military complexes worked at a frantic pace to improve old weapons and weapon systems and to invent new ones. In the space of ten years, artillery converted from smooth-bore cannon with an effective range of 400 yards (366 metres) to rifled guns whose shells could penetrate nine inches of iron plate at 2400 yards (2195 metres). Whatever defences were designed, by the time that they were constructed, they were out of date. But the race went on. For half a century millions of pounds were spent as thousands toiled to produce outmoded hardware.

All the work was concentrated on the traditionally threatened areas: Portsmouth, Plymouth, the Thames, Milford Haven and some Irish harbours, for total protection of the coastline was out of the question. It was assumed that these places had to be protected, not only from the sea, but also from landward attack by invaders landing elsewhere. Thus, two main types of forts were initially built, although there were many minor variations. Those with the primary task of defending the sea approaches were long curved batteries consisting of massive granite walls pierced by openings behind which, and under huge earthen ramparts, were vaulted casements holding guns. Attached barracks and storage blocks were erected at the rear. Coalhouse Fort near Tilbury on the Thames, is a good example of this type of fort. Secondly, those forts built to protect the main naval bases from attack from the rear were usually polygonal in shape, surrounded by a massive wall of granite. Again, these had casements for guns and magazines set behind the wall in the thickness of the ramparts. Above were other gun platforms on open sites, the guns firing through embrazures. The whole circuit was surrounded by a deep ditch across which carponiers or protected galleries extended at the angles. Other galleries, for sweeping the ditch bottoms with fire, were set into the outer sides of the ditches. Some forts, notably Fort Widley, at Portsmouth, had an inner 'keep' of barracks blocks, and these were also ditched.

Other associated works included breakwaters with batteries mounted on them as at Plymouth and Portland, and at Portsmouth huge granite-faced towers of concrete and steel, positioned in the approaches to the harbour—the so-called 'Spit Head Forts'.

All these works were continually altered—often in the planning stage—as military technology advanced. Stone walls were superseded by earthen banks which could better withstand the shock of the increasingly powerful shells. Perhaps the most important change was the abandonment of the heavily protected casements in favour of open batteries. These casements had proved far too small to hold anything but the smallest of the new breach-loading guns while their narrow gun ports and unfortunate tendency to fill with smoke when the gun was fired made them hopelessly inefficient. Many of the forts were changed. At Coalhouse Fort, Tilbury, the underground casements were abandoned, the granite walls covered by massive earthen banks and open batteries mounted above them. At the huge citadel on The Verne, Portland, built in the 1870s, large numbers of open batteries were laid out beyond the fort itself in the 1890s. Many older forts were also altered. At Tilbury fort, for example, new open batteries were built on top of the seventeenth-century ramparts, while at Dover vast lines of new open batteries were constructed both at the medieval castle on the Western Heights and below them on the seashore.

By 1900 the coastal defences of Britain were massive, complex and, to contemporary observers, impregnable. But when war finally came in 1914, it proved to be a war in which such defences were largely unnecessary: most of the action took place on the continent and elsewhere. The Royal Navy managed to contain German sea power and invasion was never threatened. Extra defences were indeed constructed, along the north-east coast and at the mouth of the Humber in particular, but few saw any real action. All the efforts of the Victorian engineers had been for nought.

The late nineteenth century also saw great changes in other aspects of defence. Up until the 1850s Britain's professional army had been relatively small, and although usually well-trained and organized, when not engaged in active service it was treated with scant regard by the government and the nation. The technological advances in warfare—and especially the changes in social awareness marked by the public outcry following the Crimean War concerning both the ability of officers and treatment of men—all led to massive reorganization. The 1872 Army Reform Act improved the professional abilities of the officer class, and it also reorganized the army putting it on a territorial footing, whereby regiments were located and associated with particular places or areas: the familiar County Regiments emerged, each with their own local barracks, headquarters, administration and training grounds. Instead of soldiers being in billets or unsuitable barracks, new regimental centres appeared. The barracks on Whittington Heath, Lichfield, with the necessary areas for training grounds, is a good example: they have late nineteenth-century barracks and stores, a mock-medieval guard house and administrative block. On a larger scale was Aldershot, transformed from a small village to a considerable town supporting the thousands of troops living in new barracks and training on the adjacent heathland. The same period also saw the development of the training and barracks areas on Salisbury plain and elsewhere.

The growing threat of war, after 1900, also led to the reorganization of a long-standing but hardly efficient part of the armed services: the part-time yeomanry and the militia. These small units had existed since the eighteenth century and were created for local defence in times of danger. Many were organized by the local gentry in a haphazard fashion and some had their own barracks and defenceworks. In North Wales, Thomas Wynn, later the first Lord Newborough, built two small 'forts' in the 1760s, one known as Fort Belan and the other Fort Williamsburg. These housed the loyal 'Newborough Volunteers'. Though it had angle bastions, a ditch, an internal barracks and headquarters buildings, Fort Williamsburg could not have been a serious obstacle to invaders and was more a social centre for a military-minded lord.

In 1907, these militia regiments were reorganized into the Territorial Force, the predecessor of the Territorial Army and their epitaphs are the familiar Drill Halls which still exist in many large towns. These varied from crudely-constructed steel-framed halls to quite large and imposing neo-Georgian offices and stores.

Though Britain remained outside the main theatre of action in World War I, the war inevitably brought new forms of military works. As before, some of these were the results of advances in military technology; others reflected the developing social attitudes. The war was regarded as 'the War to end all wars'! No longer a war between professional armies however large, the whole nation was committed. And because of the scale of the war, the whole nation had to be mobilized, not only to fight, but also to produce the necessary equipment. As a result entire new factory complexes appeared. The numerous Royal Ordnance Factories (many of which still exist with their workshops hidden behind standardized high brick walls, as at Branston, near Burton-on-Trent) are relics of this period.

The organization, housing and training of men for the new conscript armies required thousands of acres of land, vast barrack complexes and storage and repair facilities. Cheap standardized buildings, often of a temporary nature, sprang up and many still remain in army control as at Tidworth in Hampshire and Aldershot. On the enlarged training areas, especially Salisbury Plain, all kinds of earthworks and other structures appeared. Practice trench systems, artillery observation bunkers, rifle ranges and other related features appeared by the thousand and many can still be seen, but often only as 'crop marks' or 'soil marks', visible solely from the air. In addition, new railway systems were built to supply the military bases. Most of these have gone, although traces still remain, as in the case of the line from Sleaford to RAF Cranwell in Lincolnshire.

Despite playing only a relatively minor part in the War, the new aircraft produced original and very specialized forms of military works which were to become much more important later on. Bombing by the German Air Force (although on a small scale compared to that of the 1939–45 War) produced the first anti-aircraft defences, a few of which still remain. Most important was the need for airfields and especially structures in which aircraft could be housed and serviced. Thus military aircraft hangars made their first appearance. The earliest were very temporary indeed, but by 1917 permanent hangars based on a modified standard warehouse design were being built. Many still survive at the sites of World War I airfields such as those at Southampton Airport; RAF Old Sarum, Salisbury; RAF Duxford, Cambridgeshire (now part of the Imperial War Museum); and at RAF Hendon (now the RAF Museum).

With the end of the war, most of these structures were abandoned, or put into a state of 'care and maintenance'. The growing threat of another war in the 1930s produced little in the form of new military works, except in terms of aerial warfare. The realization of the potency of aerial bombardment and the acceptance that bombing constituted a special threat is a rare example of preparation for an event which actually took place. In the late 1930s many new airfields were constructed, all with standardized buildings in the neo-Georgian style currently popular with establishment architects. RAF Duxford, with its neo-Georgian administrative block, guardrooms, officers mess and barracks is a good example while there we also see another new aspect of military demands in an increasingly democratic society: the provision of married quarters for the lower ranks as well as the officers. Rows of neat but oddly old-fashioned houses, which might be dated to about 1910 were it not for the numbers '1937' on their rainwater-heads, show this trend well. Despite the urgency of this situation, the changing social climate is reflected in the fact that the designs of many of the buildings of this period were subject to approval and review by the Royal Fine Arts Commission. At RAF Hullavington, for example, the structures were not of brick but were faced with local Cotswold stone.

At the same time new and much larger hangars appeared, some helpfully dated, like those of '1938' at RAF Mildenhall, in Suffolk. Unique military works which also appeared just before the war were the early radar towers, a set of which remain at Dover. High technology had arrived.

World War II marked perhaps the greatest change of all in military structures. It was again a war of mass armies and mass weapons but, even more than in 1914–18, it was The People's War, fought in defence of democracy. Yet military works had to protect more than just an idea. The United Kingdom had to be entirely fortified to protect the industrial base, and after 1940 to act as a spring board for the ultimate liberation of Europe.

The traditional goal of defence against invasion was again pursued, this time through the construction of hundreds of Emergency Batteries, installed on every likely invasion beach. Many of these, together with pillboxes and observation towers, still litter our coastline. The immediate prospect of an invasion which was likely to be at least initially successful, led to the construction of thousands of pillboxes, ditches, anti-tank barriers and other more esoteric constructions often contrived by the Local Defence Volunteer Force. These pillboxes, at least, can now be recognized as having a conscious strategic background, for they were arranged in lines across south-eastern England to serve as a kind of military frontier, whose parallels can be seen in Roman times with the Fosse Way and Hadrian's Wall.

Once again however, invasion did not come and the boundaries of the state remained inviolate from the sea, although not from the air. The fears of the 1930s became a reality. New technology had created a situation in which enemy assaults could strike at the soft interior of the realm. The airborne threat challenged the survival of civilians and the national industrial base. Thus appeared the anti-aircraft emplacements, barrage balloon sites and listening and observation posts. Like the fortifications of the seventeenth century these were almost all earthworks, and most have now disappeared. Yet some still survive as low circular banks of earth, while others, notably around Northampton, have been described by archaeologists as the sites of Bronze Age burial mounds: when viewed from the air they now present themselves as circular rings in ploughed soil almost indistinguishable from real burial mounds.

61. *Medieval and modern responses to the threat of invasion in southern England;*
Bodiam Castle is in the background while the pillbox in the foreground dates from
World War II.

1. *Carn Brea in Cornwall, where the hill has been the setting of a fortified Neolithic 'town',
an Iron Age hillfort and a small medieval castle.*

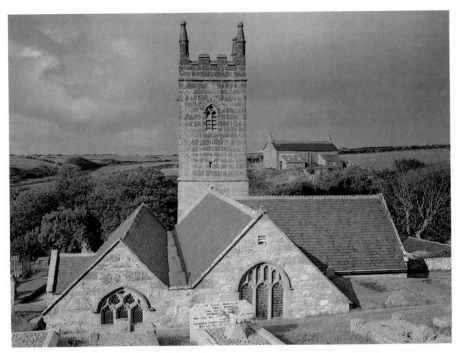

2. *St. Levan's Church in Cornwall, the probable successor to the cliff-top holy site of St. Levan's well; a typically small and rugged Cornish stone church.*

3. *Earls Barton church in Northamptonshire with its celebrated Saxon tower.*

4. The superb Norman carving at Barfreston in Kent.

5. *Fortifications of different ages in Derbyshire; in the background is the great hillfort of Mam Tor, which could date from the Bronze Age, while the Norman keep known as Peveril Castle stands on the limestone cliff above Castleton.*

6. *The modest Norman motte at Laxton, now colonized by trees.*

7. *The Neo-Gothic extravaganza of Knebworth House in Hertfordshire in its
well-manicured setting.*

8. *One of the small Neolithic passage graves which nestle on the lowlands beneath the great territorial symbol of a much larger tomb on the summit of Knocknarea.*

9. *St. Levan's well in Cornwall, one of the many sites in western Britain associated with the dimly-glimpsed Age of the Saints.*

10. *Wadenhoe church in Northamptonshire showing the late-Norman tower. This is one of the many hilltop churches with a St. Michael dedication.*

11. *Oxburgh Hall in Norfolk, of 1482, symbolizing the transition from castle to stately home.*

12. *Lower Slaughter in Gloucestershire, a picture book English village with houses and cottages in the little changing vernacular style of the Cotswolds.*

62. *The unworldly landscape of conflict in the Space Age: Menwith Hill, Yorkshire.*

The bombing campaign against Germany and the preparations for the invasion of Europe turned Britain into a vast military camp. Hundreds of airfields with standard or improved hangers, hutments, bomb storage bays, runways and dispersal stands mushroomed. Even airfield control towers had their own architecture. The American Army Air Force introduced its own design, very loosely based on the 'International Modernist School'. Army camps with the ubiquitous Nissen Hut and its variants multiplied. Many of these can still be recognized today.

The end of the war was marked by the arrival of two new weapons: the ballistic missile and the atomic bomb. They combined to represent a weapon against which there is, arguably, no real escape or defence. Yet, despite this, new structures have appeared. The Fylingdales Early Warning Station, on the North Yorkshire Moors—arguably one of the most aesthetically pleasing of all military works—is one such, while the Stonehenge-like steel and lattice amphitheatre at RAF Chicksands, Bedfordshire, and the mysterious Doomsday surrealism of Menwith Hill, Yorkshire, are others. Meanwhile traditional defenceworks have continued to be built and modified to suit modern social conditions. Modern accommodation for the army and airforce now includes large numbers of married quarters and fewer of the old-fashioned barrack blocks.

This then is the story of defensive structures in Britain. Unlike other aspects of the landscape, it would seem that today we have reached the end of that story for what else is left but Armageddon? Technological advance has helped to fuel the processes of evolution in defenceworks and one is left to wonder about the next stages in the process. Perceived from our present standpoint, the culmination of the story which began with the mysterious Neolithic defences seems awesomely impending.

Reflections

It is true that the need for defenceworks to evolve apace with innovations and refinements in offensive warfare added an urgency to the story of the development of strongholds. Even more important, however, was the fact that—like most other of man's creations—the citadel was a mirror of the society which gave it birth. Each was a manifestation of the needs of the castle builder—or rather, his perceived needs. Where perception and reality were in accord a successful fortress would result, and it would be no more elaborate and costly than the prevailing military circumstances required. False perceptions of future needs could create disastrously costly and ineffectual strongholds. The Maginot Line is the most obvious example, but Britain yields others. They include the redundancy of even the most magnificent and 'modern' hillforts when faced with the disciplined might of the Roman legions and the vast sums expended in the nineteenth century to create coastal defence systems which were both outmoded and unnecessary.

But strongholds were not solely, or even always primarily the products of perceived needs in the fields of defence. Some of the most impressive Roman defenceworks— perhaps most notably the Antonine Wall—seem to have been built to produce an impact on politics in Rome rather than upon their immediate military environments. Many examples have also been given to show that status rather than security featured largest in the minds of the builder. At different times, the quest to establish a social position in the world as perceived by one's equals and betters affected every field of fortification from at least the moated manor house upwards. At certain stages in history and prehistory, and most particularly in the age of popular democracy, decisions about defenceworks have been taken not only by the mighty, but also by the population at large. The results are evident in the ubiquitous fortified homesteads of the Iron Age, but also, for example, in the fervent early twentieth-century support for building dread-noughts. Without a strong measure of public concern to support Winston Churchill's demands for an enlarged fighter force, the Battle of Britain might have been lost—and our freedom with it. The road that leads away from Armageddon may yet be the choice of the masses.

Today we see the strongholds of times past as crumbling relics, tourist attractions or weathered earthworks. Yet these creations are only meaningful in the context of their periods and circumstances. They are in fact fossilized decisions, some good and some bad, but all having some credibility in the thoughts and times of their builders. Could we enter the minds and ages of the makers of prehistoric creations like causewayed camps or vitrified forts, then we would surely find a logic that was deeply rooted in contemporary society, its beliefs, values and fears.

Human ingenuity and adaptability have brought us this far. However, our animal heritage has in some way equipped us badly, for we are unable to curb or direct our instinctive aggression and defensive responses. In the animal kingdom, aggression has considerable survival value although conflict between members of the same species is generally ritualized and very seldom pursued to the point of killing. Our landscape is littered with broken hillforts, tattered fortresses, incredibly costly coastal defences which were stillborn into redundancy and vast acreages of war cemeteries. Yet so far our response to danger and challenge has not evolved since before the hillfort era. We no longer go to war with slingstones or arrows and the inflexibility of the human perception of threats and counter-measures may prove the downfall of the species.

PART IV

The Village in its Fields

Introduction

'Geography is about man and the land'—at least, in our schooldays it was. This same simple definition could equally be applied to the study of prehistory or to the key themes in British domestic history up to the Industrial Revolution. So anyone seeking to understand the evolution of a landscape must wrestle with problems of who owned the land, how it was tenanted, worked and organized? The intense and enduring association between man and the land has produced a remarkable legacy of monuments in the forms of fields and settlements, some living and others only apparent as relics. The literature on the village alone would stock a library and we have each added a morsel to the banquet—yet for all this, the most important questions concerning the evolution of villages and fields remain unanswered.

In very general terms, we can trace the development of fields and the settlements which they succoured up to and into the Dark Ages. We can also visualize, to an extent, how they evolved during the Middle Ages, and we can describe the transformation of the old feudal patterns in later centuries in great detail. But the history of the rural landscape in the centuries immediately preceding the Norman Conquest remains a tantalizing mystery. This dark chasm in our knowledge would not matter so much were it not for the fact that, in the course of this dimly perceived period, a remaking of the English landscape was in progress which was to affect the whole course of later development and lay the foundations of many surviving countrysides.

In this way, the archaeologist can see an essentially prehistoric tradition of fields, hamlets and farmsteads being carried forward on the rivers of time, through the Roman period and through the first few centuries of the Dark Ages. The currents of change then sweep into a dark tunnel, and what later emerges to view is a lowland countryside that has been transformed, reorganized into the complicated but comprehensible patterns of open field farming, each field system focused on one of the thousands of new villages created, while the traditional hamlet and farmstead patterns have partly disintegrated.

Even in its present ghostly form, this vision of the past contradicts the more venerable visions which have dominated landscape study for generations and which are still standard fare in the classroom and in most media accounts. The old view was more romantic and decisive and ran more or less as follows: after the collapse of Roman rule, England was invaded, conquered and settled by Saxon hordes which then set about the archaic, almost primeval landscape in a most determined, business-like and revolutionary fashion. They cleared away vast expanses of wild wood, established most of the villages which endure to this day and imported open field farming from their continental homelands.

Archaeology, however, paints a very different if much more tentative picture. If the prime achievement in the shaping of the British landscape involved the removal of the primeval forest, then the foundations of scenery were laid in the Neolithic period, between three and five thousand years before ever a Saxon foot trod on British soil. As for the Saxon hordes, it now seems that Saxon settlement was far lighter and more sporadic than was thought, so that even by the end of immigration, the Saxon element in the population of these islands probably amounted to only a single percentage figure—perhaps even less. Also, it is now clear that the early centuries of the Saxon era did not witness a dramatic remodelling of the landscape: field patterns probably remained much as they were, while hamlets and farmsteads remained the most ubiquitous types of rural settlement.

Modern archaeological work also consigns another myth to the scrap-heap. This is the long-cherished vision of the village as a timeless, immovable, inflexible and inevitable feature of the landscape. It was a vision created partly by able historians who struggled to build a picture of the past from evidence which scarcely existed, and partly by popular writers, some poetic, some skilful and many neither, who sought to fulfil the popular need for a stable, deeply-rooted and romantic counterpoint to the heartless, impersonal and insatiable world of the town, whose influences hold most of us in thrall.

But now it is clear that villages will only appear under special conditions and are by no means an inevitable and unchanging facet of the countryside. It is also plain that once established, a village is likely to undergo several quite dramatic transformations: it will probably change its layout on more than one occasion, is footloose and quite likely to migrate across its fields, and is ever vulnerable to changes which may cause it to shrink or to perish completely. This much we know, yet when we try to peel back the layers of the village onion to understand how settlements have gradually acquired their present forms, we enter another realm of mystery. Most of the vigorous action took place in centuries before village plans were drawn and so the clues to most of the formative stages in the development of a village may consist only of a few faint earthworks in the nearby fields, an ambiguous entry in the Domesday Book and some equally ambiguous and hopelessly brief mentions in medieval taxation documents.

New visions of the past, illuminating key passages in the story of the evolution of the countryside, are slowly in the making. Modern archaeology has urged us to reject the heroic vision of the Saxon founding fathers and if we do not yet have the answers, at least we know where to look for them if adequate funds ever become available. It seems that the evidence for the remaking of the English landscape will be found by excavating the remains at areas in and around the now-deserted settlements appearing in the centuries which bracket the Norman Conquest. In the meantime we can but bemoan the fact that, while old documents express the human preoccupation with the ownership of land and the various obligations and dues attached to land tenancy, their writers always assume that the reader is familiar with all the commonplace features of life and landscape, so that the obvious is not stated. Bede could probably have described a countryside as it existed on the eve of the remaking of the English landscape; the Wessex propagandists who contributed to the Anglo Saxon Chronicle could have mentioned the revolutionary transformations of the countryside, but were silent, while the Domesday clerks, who provided a unique register of taxable assets, present their information in such a way that one does not know whether a settlement mentioned is a single village, a complex of villages and hamlets or one or more farmsteads.

16

Prehistoric Fields and Farms

The pioneering phase in British farming arrived around 5000 BC. By around 4300 BC most attractive and amenable soils like those of the chalk downlands, limestone slopes and alluvial vales had been cleared and settled and the pioneering communities were then active in many remote and modestly-endowed settings. It is sometimes said that prehistoric people had no knowledge of soil fertility and manuring so that, throughout the Neolithic period, cleared areas were abandoned to the encroaching wilderness after just a few years of cultivation. Theories based upon the premise of the ignorant savage have always struck us as rather weak, and here one should remember that at least 3000 years worth of farming experience had been acquired in the Middle East before agriculture diffused into Britain. As if to lay the myth of the incompetent British farmer who scrabbles in a remote ephemeral clearing, there is evidence from more than one Irish site of extensive networks of stone-walled fields which date right back to the Neolithic era. Elsewhere, most traces of Stone Age farming will have been destroyed by later activities but it is probable that as farming succeeded and population rose quite dramatically, the wasteful system of slash and burn clearance and then abandonment will have been superseded by the division of large areas of countryside into permanent fields.

We cannot write in any detail about Neolithic fields and farms, for as yet we do not know what, if anything, was typical, but if clues are to be found in the later prehistoric periods then we must imagine that estates and territories were durable, the field divisions quite long lived but adaptable, while settlements would migrate within these firmer frameworks in a lively fashion. The traces of Neolithic settlements are more numerous than is often supposed, although generally very fragmentary. They seem to have been very varied, for the spectrum includes the massively fortified settlement which lay behind a mighty palisade in a river-girt peninsula at Meldon Bridge near Peebles; humble farmsteads, which could be circular or rectangular, of timber or of stone, and large communal long houses (not related to the medieval and later peasant long-houses described in Chapter 23) which are known to have existed on the continent and of which controversial examples are known in Britain. The best-preserved examples are likely to be atypical, for the near-complete relics of Skara Brae on Orkney represent a distinctly Orcadian fishing and farming village built from the remarkably amenable local flagstones, while the huts at Carn Brea near Redruth belonged to an important fortified hilltop settlement which seems to have had significant political and trading roles.

Villages were probably greatly outnumbered by hamlets and farmsteads. Of the latter, the best surviving example is Knap of Howar on Papa Westray island, which consists of two small rectangular stone buildings linked by a short passageway and which probably represent the dwelling of a self-sufficient farming family and their attached store room and workshop.

The centuries around 2500 BC represent something of an archaeological no man's land between the Ages of Stone and Bronze, a time when new religious ideas were circulating and when the celebrated 'Beaker' pottery was being used for both domestic and ritual purposes. Until very recently, everybody believed in the immigrant 'Beaker folk', but not necessarily in their settlements. Very few dwelling traces had been found and so it was argued that the Beaker folk had introduced a much more pastoral lifestyle and had lived beside their roaming herds and flocks in temporary encampments. Belief in the Beaker folk as invaders and settlers is now passing out of fashion, while a number of dwellings of the period have been discovered! Again, they are of various designs, and we will not really be able to understand the nature of the rural life of the period until archaeologists are able to explore not only an entire settlement, but also the little farming empire of contemporary fields, paddocks, gardens and commons that support it.

At Lough Gur in Co. Limerick, circular enclosures of around ninety feet (27 metres) diameter were originally thought to have been stone circles. More thorough explorations show that these enclosures of the third millennium BC had walls of earth and rubble which were revetted with stones and one excavated enclosure had a wooden gate and contained a rectangular post-built dwelling. It could be interpreted as a farmstead set within a protective compound for livestock. Potentially even more informative are the excavations currently in progress at the well-known stone-hut settlement site on the southern slopes of Holyhead Mountain on Anglesey. Until the latest of a long series of digs here, everyone was content to regard the prominent dwelling remains as being those of a Romano-British upland village—a view that was supported by the discovery of a small cache of second-century Roman coins in one of the huts during the 1860s. However, a recently obtained Carbon-14 date suggests that the huts which compose this familiar monument may belong to the late Neolithic-early Bronze Age era. Also, rather than belonging to a loose unenclosed village, the circular huts can now be regarded as farmsteads that were strung out along the hillside. They were linked to terraced fields and it seems that the field boundaries were established in a piecemeal fashion as the slopes were gradually cleared of stones. When W. O. Stanley explored the settlement in the 1860s, the traces of some fifty huts were visible, more than survive today, and perhaps the settlement expanded piecemeal as stone clearances made new arable fields available. One of the excavated dwellings, a circular stone hut of eight metres in diameter, was found to have an underfloor drainage channel leading to a sump which probably served as a watering place for cattle, while a farmyard adjoined the hut.

The field and settlement remains for the Bronze Age proper are more numerous and comprehensive, so that in some places one can begin to picture the appearance of a slice of prehistoric countryside and the day-to-day lives of those who toiled in it. Excavations currently in progress on the Isle of Arran are painting such a picture, for they are exposing the traces of hut farmsteads, fields, gardens, land boundaries, burial cairns

63. *The remains of a circular stone-walled dwelling on the slopes of Holyhead Mountain on Anglesey. Recent excavations have suggested that this collection of farmsteads should be redated to the late Neolithic/early Bronze Age period.*

and other cairns which accumulated as repositories for stones cleared from the ploughland. As interesting and revealing as any site in the British Bronze Age portfolio, the area will soon be completely destroyed by ploughing and planted with conifers by the Forestry Commission.

One of the huts excavated by John Barber's Arran team was uniquely informative. It was most unusual in that it had been occupied throughout almost the whole of the Bronze Age and had gone through many rebuilding operations, in the course of which it drifted gradually southwards. Finally it burned down and the burning carbonized and preserved evidence of the vast amount of grain that it had stored, showed that at the time of the burning a cow had been tethered to one of the walls and that the inner face of the low earth and rubble wall was lined with a screen of wickerwork. The farming landscape was divided by banks of earth and rubble which seemed to represent the boundaries of land holdings rather than of fields, while painstaking excavation revealed some areas where the land had been ridged into corduroy-like corrugations, probably by spade cultivation. One ridged area was a small kitchen-garden plot, but another was much more extensive. Finally, even in the warmer drier climate of the Bronze Age before the spread of peat, Arran can hardly have been an agricultural utopia, but the archaeologists discovered the evidence for dense rural settlement and population which we now presume to have been typical in prehistoric Britain, with archaeological sites discovered at the level of 200 per square kilometre.

In other parts of Britain which were abandoned when peat began to spread across the uplands at the end of the Bronze Age (and which are variously threatened by afforestation or ploughing and seeding as pasture), quite substantial fragments of a Bronze Age rural landscape survive. If these lands were not particularly poor during the kinder climates of the Bronze Age, they were certainly not the main heartlands of farming. So the moors of the Peak and Pennines, Devon and Cornwall and the Western Isles offer visions of backwater life which may not be at all typical of the farming and settlement traditions of the much richer English plains and vales. In Chapter 8 we described the remarkable reave-girt Bronze Age territories which existed on Dartmoor, and the moor is also littered with the remains of the settlements of the period. They show that the dwellings, with their low stone walls and conical thatched roofs, were generally quite similar, but that a considerable variety of different settlement forms existed.

First there were village-like forms, mainly small, in which a few or a dozen or so huts were scattered within an encircling rubble-walled compound. Grimspound is the most visitworthy example, and still displays the paved area around the compound entrance portals which suggests that beasts were regularly driven in and out so that their hoofs would have churned the ground had paving stones not been provided. Inside the compound, small stock pens were built, while the village was sited close to a stream so that cattle may have been watered there and then penned in the village overnight, secure from rustlers. Several similar village compounds existed and at some examples the traces of small garden plots can be recognized.

Secondly, there were the open or unenclosed settlements, of which perhaps the best example lies beyond the Devon boundary, at Stannon Down on Bodmin Moor. Here, the traces of some sixty-eight circular huts have been counted and they form an apparently random scatter which contains some small hut clusters which are linked by low walls, like beads on a bangle, to embrace small enclosures. In addition to the village-like groupings, the south-western moors contained loose, unenclosed, hamlet-sized clusters of huts and also isolated farmsteads, some with huts that stood inside low-walled pounds and others that were freestanding.

Despite their diverse forms, all these settlements seem to have been associated with livestock farming which was supplemented by vegetables grown in small garden plots. On the drier, eastern slopes of Dartmoor mixed farming settlements were more common. In the case of the example at Horridge Common, four dwellings formed a loose cluster and another farmstead lay about 100 metres from the group. The sur-rounding area of around eight acres (three hectares) was divided into small, oblong arable fields, some with their boundaries marked by low scarps or lynchets. At places such as this, peripheral though it may have been to the mainstreams of Bronze Age agriculture, one can see the bare skeleton of a Bronze Age farming settlement and then imagination can add flesh to the half-buried bones.

The Horringer Common settlement has a date of around 1300 BC and will have been a little younger than the farmstead at Gwithian near St. Ives in Cornwall, which stood on a sandy coastal site that was periodically rendered uninhabitable by sand blows. It stood in a ditched enclosure overlooking its group of small, rectangular arable fields, some ditched, some defined by walls built from stones gathered from the fields and some marked by lynchets produced by the scouring and dumping action of the plough as it gradually carved hillside terraces. When excavated, the fields revealed the criss-cross scratch marks in the sub-soil which showed the cross or double-ploughing practice that was universal in the Bronze Age, when small fields were tilled by a man dragging a bent branch or 'crook ard', or by light two-ox ploughs.

Most of the prehistoric fields and settlements that survive as recognizable monuments were the victims of environmental catastrophes which rendered their settings virtually uninhabitable, so saving them from destruction by later generations of farmers. In the later part of the Bronze Age, the gradual deterioration of farming environments, which the removal of trees and the over-cropping of soils and overgrazing of pastures had initiated, was intensified by climatic changes in the direction of cooler damper conditions. Valuable mineral salts were washed down from the upper levels of the soil and then surface layers of sour peat began to form. Slowly, the farmers were forced to abandon the moorland plateaus, while in the lowlands and downlands it seems that wholesale reorganization of field patterns took place. Chalky soils remained well drained and in parts of the Wessex downlands one can still recognize the traces of vast networks of small rectangular 'Celtic' fields which seem to have been superimposed on the landscape in a planned and deliberate manner. Whether this lowland revolution was partly caused by increasing pressure on farming resources as thousands of broken peasant families abandoned their upland farmsteads, one cannot say.

The fields and settlements of the Iron Age had much in common with those of the Bronze Age, although the increasing emphasis upon defence also underlines the tensions which resulted from the shortage of agricultural resources. We can still visualize a countryside which was liberally sprinkled with farmsteads and hamlets and had a much thinner stipple of village-sized settlements. The arable fields remained quite small and were of a roughly rectangular form, which shows the continuing importance of cross-ploughing. Small paddocks and garden plots still tended to cluster around the peasant dwellings, reflecting the age-old logic of organizing activities like gardening and caring for young animals, which demanded the most intensive inputs of time and care, closest to the homestead.

Despite the traditional conservatism of country life, it would be wrong to suppose that change was a stranger to the rural landscape. The changes that were enacted in the latter part of the Bronze Age did not represent the first change of direction in British agriculture, for even in the Neolithic period, around 3200 BC, a partial shift from arable to livestock farming seems to have taken place at a time when many long-worked lands were exhausted and some of the worn-out ploughlands were allowed to revert to forest. In some places archaeology has revealed local changes in farming practices. At Ogborne Mazey in Wiltshire, for example, a Bronze Age settlement was built across a redundant field bank, while at Winterborne Abbas in Dorset a group of round barrows stand on an older field boundary. Particularly in the past, a very large proportion of archaeological effort was concentrated upon the chalk downlands of Wessex, where the farming sequences tended to be quite complex. Being easily worked and initially productive, such downlands must have attracted the earlier generations of Neolithic farmers, but the thin dry soils will have easily become exhausted and then converted to pastoral farming. Several long barrows of the fourth millenium have been shown to stand upon pasture or waste land. At various other times, the exhaustion of soils in neighbouring environments will have provided an inducement to the re-establishment of downland ploughland; at others, climatic changes in the direction of damper conditions will have offered the prospect of lusher grazings and prompted another shift in emphasis. The evidence of one such switch is apparent at Martin Down in Hampshire, where, towards the end of the second millennium BC, a long bank, regarded as part of a ranch boundary, was driven across a network of small rectangular Bronze Age arable fields. This was not just a local switch, for as well as the establishment of the vast networks of smaller planned fields in the latter part of the Bronze Age there is also quite widespread evidence that large tracts of downland were repartitioned by ranch boundaries, suggesting the conversion of lands that were divided between many mixed farming communities into extensive livestock ranges; the ranch boundaries seem to mark the territorial divisions between large stock-rearing empires.

By the close of the Bronze Age, the countrysides of Britain seem to have been carrying the maximum population that their agricultural resources could support—a population level probably quite comparable to that which existed in Domesday England around 1800 years later. As we have described, the scarcity of free land created tensions which were expressed in the new emphasis on fortifications—even if the resultant farmsteads and village earthworks and palisades were far less formidable than the hillforts and only sufficient to deter the smallest bands of rustlers and raiders. Not all villages were fortified, and at the Iron Age settlement of Kestor on Dartmoor—which was sited on a valley slope below the level of the upland peat blanket which had spread across areas of Bronze Age settlement—one can see the remains of a loose open village which appears to date to around 700–600 BC. The ruins of about twenty-five circular stone-walled huts are scattered across the slope in a seemingly haphazard pattern. One hut is significantly larger than the rest and stands within its own circular compound. It is tempting to regard it as the superior dwelling of the local chieftain and a reflection of the increasingly hierarchical nature of Iron Age society, although it could have been a more specialized building, for it housed a small smelter and forge. Kestor is particularly interesting because it is linked to a field system which perhaps developed over several stages, and the great slabby boulders which were used to build the field boundaries still stand in line. Hoof-hollowed droveways along which the village cattle were driven from pasture to water can also still be recognized.

The prehistoric tradition in rural settlement ran right through into the Roman period and even in the English lowland areas where villa-based farming was introduced, the traditional field systems frequently remained in use. As with previous periods, the best-preserved remains have survived in marginal and peripheral upland areas, although air photograph evidence shows that the lowland countrysides of the Iron and Roman Iron Ages were heavily stippled by the patterns of farmsteads, hamlets and small

191

villages. It seems that the Romans were responsible for introducing a heavier iron-shod plough that was equipped with a knife-like coulter to slice the sod and a share and mould board to sever and turn it. One cannot know how widely such costly machines were adopted, but they did offer the potential for the creation of much larger and longer fields than had been demanded by the old technique of cross-tilling with the light prehistoric plough.

Of the various Romano-British settlements which survive, Ewe Close in Cumbria is as good an example as any of the 'paddocky' appearance of the typical village. The huts were still circular, with very thick stone walls and they were arranged in three tight clusters; each cluster was associated with a group of small, rather rectangular walled paddocks, while each hut and paddock group lay in a walled or embanked enclosure which was stock-proof rather than defensive. The relics here could never be mistaken for those of a deserted medieval village and present the impression of a jumble of dwellings and stores bound together by a stony web of paddock walls. To the extent that one can read the social lives and farming practices from these remains, we tend to imagine a tight little community composed of three tighter family groupings, and while one might guess that rough grazing land on the surrounding fells was held in common, the association between paddock groups and hut clusters seems to suggest the private ownership of livestock.

Late Iron Age and Romano-British settlements composed of courtyard houses (circular dwellings in which the domestic cells, stores and workshops are set in the walls around a central courtyard) existed in Cornwall and were much less common in other parts of western Britain. They ranged in size from villages like Chysauster and Carn Euny through hamlets like Bosullow Trehyllys, with its three courtyard houses and a complex of smaller simpler interlocking round huts, to isolated farmsteads. Garden plots, stock pens and 'Celtic' fields are often clearly associated with these settlements and there are now good archaeological grounds for believing that many of the living rectangular fields of Penwith were originally worked from such places. And so, in Cornwall at least, the Romano-British landscape is only partly fossilized and the splendid panoramas which can be enjoyed from the track leading to Zennor Quoit or from the ramparts of Trencrom hillfort display relics of field systems 2000 years old.

In this way, the transition zone between the prehistoric and historical periods seems also to mark the transition between those elements of the rural landscape which exist only as archaeological features and others which endure in some living countrysides, if only in fragmentary forms. This then is a suitable point at which to evaluate the achievements of five millennia of prehistoric farming and also the differences between prehistoric and later settlement forms. It has been conventional practice to regard all prehistoric landscapes as being very thinly peopled and to assume that the population increased very slowly, but steadily in the course of prehistoric time.

Such visions of the past can no longer be supported. We have noted that in many different areas land shortage and the over use of resources may have been encountered around 3200 BC; Domesday levels of population may have first been reached around 1000 BC, while the population of Roman Britain was probably considerably larger. Also, rather than rising at a steady rate, prehistoric levels of population seem to have

64. *The entrance to one of the courtyard houses in the Romano-British village of Chysauster, Cornwall.*

fluctuated as phases of agricultural advance and rising population levels were super-seded by periods when the over use of ploughlands and pastures and climatic deteriora-tions caused large-scale retreats of the frontiers of farming and changes of use within the agricultural arenas. While the medieval peasant farmer, who had the use of the heavy six and eight-ox plough, had some advantages over his prehistoric forbears, the farming methods that were current around 1000 BC were able to support nearly comparable levels of population—so they represented an alternative method of organizing the resources of the countryside rather than a method which was utterly primitive.

The differences between the prehistoric and the medieval traditions of rural settlement were very marked. Even where the surface or air photograph evidence is fragmentary, an archaeologist should always be able to distinguish between settlement relics that are medieval and those that are prehistoric or Romano-British, although a full-scale excavation might be necessary to decide whether such latter remains belonged to the Bronze Age or the Roman era. The prehistoric and Romano-British landscapes were dominated by farmsteads and hamlets while villages were always in a small minority. This seems to suggest that the land was worked by individual families and extended families rather than by intricate communal arrangements. Even so, free

65. *A landscape of dispersed settlement on the Pennine slopes above Darley, Nidderdale. Comparable densities of dispersed farmsteads existed in many parts of Britain during the later prehistoric and Roman periods. Most of these dwellings are farmsteads, although an old mill can be seen, centre right.*

farmers may have been a rarity and the successive generations of peasants probably rendered rents and tributes to the dynasties whose members were buried in the prestigious Neolithic tombs, to the Bronze Age chieftains whose exquisite gold and bronze ornaments and weapons are periodically discovered, and then to the hillfort barons of the Iron Age. The details of land tenure may have been as complex as those that we know to have operated in the medieval period, while many estates or territories probably included an area of common land.

Almost all prehistoric settlements were, to a greater or lesser extent, ephemeral. At one extreme we have the case of the Arran hut that we have mentioned which passed through so many rebuildings that it endured in one form or another throughout most of the Bronze Age, while a few of the Cornish courtyard house settlements might have been continuously occupied for around 500 years. Most prehistoric settlements however were only occupied for a few years, a few decades or a couple of centuries. Some very substantial round houses of timber or stone were built in the Iron Age and may have been the 'manor houses' of the period. Generally prehistoric dwellings were simple constructions which could easily be replaced. Often, a period of occupation may have ended when the dwellings became decrepit. The life of a modern thatched roof is

194

around twenty-five years, while excavations at the deserted medieval village of Wharram Percy in Yorkshire show that the peasant huts there had comparable lifespans, and prehistoric dwellings were probably similarly short-lived. Medieval villages and hamlets however were generally much more permanent features of the landscape. Although their homes would swiftly decay, each dwelling tended to stand in a fixed property plot, so that while house sites would migrate slightly with rebuilding, each successive dwelling was rooted within the bounds of the permanent plot. In the case of prehistoric settlements, however, it is generally impossible to recognize such plots and the choice of rebuilding sites seems to have been quite flexible. At an imaginary prehistoric settlement site displaying the traces of (say) ten huts, it might be reasonable to guess that at any particular time no more than three or four of the huts would have been serviceable and occupied, while after two or three episodes of house replacement, the settlement would have been abandoned. In contrast, a still-standing village house that was built in AD 1600 might lie within a property plot that was first marked out in AD 1100 and which had held up to twenty generations of dwellings until a really durable house was built at the end of the sixteenth century.

The romantic notion that the villages of England are often a legacy of the prehistoric period seems to be quite unfounded. Many villages must stand on the same sites that were occupied by prehistoric settlements, if only because, having been both numerous and short lived, a prehistoric settlement will have existed at or close to almost any randomly-chosen spot on the map. However, in order to prove a continuity of settlement in any place, one must be able to demonstrate that the history of settlement is unbroken by any episode of desertion. From time to time, excavation shows that settlements of different periods coincide. Examples include the surprising discovery of a Neolithic settlement during the excavation of a deserted medieval village at Tatton Park in Cheshire; the ruined medieval farmstead whose excavated remains provide a strange contrast to the courtyard houses at Carn Euny or the Bronze Age remains which underlie the deserted medieval village of Houndtor in Devon, while the souterrain at Rennibister on Orkney was only discovered when a section of the modern farmyard which overlay it collapsed. In the case of almost every such juxtaposition, however, the periods of settlement are separated by others when the sites were completely abandoned.

The examples of superimposed settlements would surely be much more numerous if it could be shown that prehistoric and medieval settlers chose their building sites with great care and deliberation. One need only look closely at the settings of a selection of living villages to realize that the majority seem to have arbitrary and indifferent sites. Two simple and widely-available factors seem to have exerted an influence: the nature of the contemporary road network and the availability of some form of water supply. Otherwise, while avoiding the soggiest marshes or the most wind-blasted situations, both prehistoric and medieval villages and hamlets offer little evidence of discerning and meticulous founding fathers. The best evidence for sensitivity and deliberation in the choice of sites can be found in the case of many of the older upland farmsteads, where the buildings are often built on south-facing slopes and in sheltered niches which offer some protection from the prevailing westerly winds and within easy reach of a stream or spring. Isolated farmsteads also offer the best examples of continuity in settlement, and Professor W. G. Hoskins has demonstrated that a high proportion of Devon farms stand on the sites of Saxon predecessors.

It seems that medieval settlements were created with some sort of intention that they would be permanent. Thousands of such places were destined to perish, but all seem to have been abandoned as the result of some distinct misfortune. The prehistoric settlements, on the other hand, were abandoned as a matter of course; although we still do not know the causes for this tradition of settlement drift and the desertion habit. In some cases, the abandonment may have been prompted by the death of a member of the community or, perhaps more frequently, by the contamination of the underground storage pits which were features of most ancient settlements. Whatever the causes, it is plain that prehistoric and medieval communities perceived their settlements in different ways and while the ancient peasants may have been bound to a particular farming territory or system of fields, the ties to a particular settlement could easily be cast aside.

Although a minority of the hillfort settlements mentioned in Chapter 11 seem to have been set out according to an orderly plan, the striking feature of the prehistoric village or hamlet was its apparent lack of coherence in the layout of dwellings, paddocks and storage pits. This is in complete contrast to the pattern of relics that can be seen at most deserted medieval village sites, where houses are generally aligned along streets and where one can often recognize the traces of components like greens, sections of planned expansion or redevelopment, church sites, peripheral manor houses and so on. In the ancient villages the round hut ruins generally seem to be scattered at random, like doughnuts dropped on a baker's floor. While some specialized planned villages were built under Roman influence or supervision, only the very loosest hints of planning seem to have affected the native settlement tradition during the Romano-British period. Chysauster is not as formless as most older villages, and although not apparently a planned village, the dwellings do seem to be arranged in four pairs, each pair sited on either side of the village street; but the village is also archaic in the way that semi-isolated farmsteads were dotted around the outer margin of the settlement.

More convincing hints that planning and coherence began to influence the layout of settlements during the Romano-British period have come from excavations of a settlement at Claydon Pike in Gloucestershire. Here, beside a straight and partly metalled road which formed the main street of the village, a settlement was laid out in the second half of the first century AD. It consisted of at least six rectangular blocks whose sides were defined by side streets. At the heart of the village was an open area measuring 152 by 90 feet (46 by 27 metres); domestic buildings lined the sides of this area and behind them was a yard with an oven, stacking areas and at the back of this area, a barn. The village seems to have been superimposed upon an area of Iron Age settlement and the evidence available so far does not allow a detailed interpretation of its buildings and function, but one can be sure that, with its regular layout and rectangular buildings, it will have been in striking contrast to the traditional settlements of the area.

Finally in this brief survey of ancient settlements we come to the question of why, when hamlets or farmsteads were the norm, villages should have existed at all? In a few specialized cases like Kestor or the Romano-British village at Din Lligwy on Anglesey, the settlement was associated with iron working, but in most cases the dwellings and activities of prehistoric village peasants seem to have been identical to those of the hamlet and farmstead dwelling majority. Otherwise, one cannot tell whether some peasants opted for village life because communal working activities were locally important, because the village offered social or defensive advantages, or because a chieftain might choose to concentrate some of his peasant subjects in a village.

Turning to the early Saxon era, it now seems that the much-vaunted colonization of the English landscape by village-centred open field farming was a non-event. Fields and settlement patterns seem to have remained much as they were, and the main archaeological evidence for change in the countryside relates to the introduction and adoption of small, rectangular, sunken-floored 'grub huts'. Larger timber-framed buildings had appeared in the Romano-British period and it is still not clear whether the Saxon grub huts were really dwellings or simply workshops and stores. But at least they do seem to have been a Saxon innovation—although hardly a revolutionary advance. Dispersed settlements of various sizes and the occasional village were still the

66. *The process of reconstruction continues at the remarkable early Saxon village site at West Stow, Suffolk.*

norm, with settlement drift and the desertion habit perpetuating the prehistoric tradition. The villages remained as rather incoherent places and, to the extent that one can picture a typical Saxon village, we imagine a rather sprawling, paddocky settlement consisting of various clusters each composed of a farmstead and its subservient stores, workshop and barns. At West Stow in Suffolk, a village founded by Saxon settlers in late Roman times, there seems to have been a loose organization of the buildings with one or more smaller sunken-floored buildings being grouped around each of the six more substantial houses, which the excavators termed 'halls'.

In the lowland areas affected by the Saxon immigration, the scatters of undefended farmsteads, hamlets and small villages seem to have existed within the surviving frameworks of Roman estates, while in the uplands of Britain basically Iron Age settlement patterns persisted. The evidence contained in early medieval Welsh documents can probably be projected back in time to describe a very elaborate system of land tenure, involving the payment of tribute to the estate-owning aristocrats, the grouping of hamlets into manors (*maenors*), their designation as specialized arable, pastoral, administrative or hunting centres and the distinction between settlements of free tenants and those inhabited by bondsmen. Although a detailed understanding of the countrysides of both upland and lowland Britain in the earlier centuries of the Dark Ages is still lacking, we can be sure that it had much more in common with the patterns existing in the Iron Age than with those which developed in the late Saxon and early medieval centuries and it probably involved very complicated systems of tenancy and estate organization.

17

The Remaking of the English Landscape

As Brian Roberts remarks: 'Few well-travelled topics offer more pitfalls for the unwary than the creation of Saxon England.' Rather than dwelling upon the many controversies associated with the remaking of the English landscape, we will attempt to pick a pathway through the groundmist of the Saxon scene, describe what we think we see, and hope to avoid the more cavernous pits.

During the Roman era—when, as we have said, an essentially Iron Age framework of rural settlements and field systems persisted—rising levels of population, prosperity and commerce encouraged the development of a heavily-settled and productively-worked countryside which was closely stippled with a wide variety of settlement forms. These ranged from the traditional farmstead, hamlet and village forms, some still supported by self-sufficient farming systems and others specializing in commercial production, through the new agricultural villas, to a diverse collection of industrial, administrative and market villages, some planned and others not, which were created under Roman influence or direction. So long as the countryside was peaceful and the burdens of taxation not too severe, these settlements flourished, but in the closing decades of the Roman era the conditions which had supported the prosperous and populous rural settlements began to crumble and their inhabitants turned increasingly towards self-sufficiency and survival.

When Roman rule collapsed around AD 410, attempts were made to perpetuate the old order, but they gradually withered as provincial dynasties competed for power and stability and unity disintegrated. Many lands which had previously supported farming reverted to woodland, and the decline and contraction of settlements seems to have been so marked that it might more easily be attributed to great plagues rather than to warfare. Meanwhile, Saxons, who had originally been imported as mercenaries—in attempts to counter barbarian raiders and who were already settled in various villages and suburbs interspersed with those of the indigenous people—were joined by other Saxon warriors and settlers immigrating from the continent during the fifth and sixth centuries. There was no organized Saxon invasion, but rather an intermittent trickle of new arrivals. Gradually, in some lowland regions, Saxon nobles gained control of the existing estates or assumed political power within a province, although the upland zones were little affected by the changes. In a few localities, the Saxon settlement appears to have been sufficiently forceful to displace some of the native peasant communities, but in general, the newcomers seem to have found niches in a disrupted and declining countryside. While small warbands roamed back and forth across the troubled face of England, British and Saxon peasants toiled, as peasants have always toiled, to support their families and enrich their masters. Slowly, and according to a process which remains unknown, simplified Saxon dialects became the language of England. Meanwhile, the old estates, fieldbanks, hedgerows and walls and the essential features of rural settlement endured.

Perhaps around the ninth century, there was the beginning of a prolonged revolution in the countryside which continued into the early centuries of the medieval era. In most parts of the English lowlands, villages, mostly small, appeared and gradually assumed a predominance over the traditional farmsteads and hamlets. At the same time, on most estates there was a wholesale reorganization of fields and farming practices which eventually produced an extremely complicated and sophisticated system of open field farming.

Old field divisions and old systems of tenancy were, at least in part, swept away to create a form of farming which depended upon intricate arrangements for communal labour. Arable land was divided into two, three or more vast fields; these fields were subdivided into rectangular blocks or 'furlongs'; the furlongs were divided into strips or 'selions', and the selions allocated to peasant tenants. Some of these tenants were free, but most were bondsmen of different grades. On average, a tenant might have held around thirty such strips, amounting to a thirty-acre (12-hectare) holding of strips scattered far and wide among the different open fields. Whether the holdings were

67. *Members of the Society for Landscape Studies exploring a system of medieval field strips which survive around Soham, Cambridgeshire. The vanguard walk across an old headland while a characteristically curving strip margin sweeps diagonally upwards from the centre-left edge.*

originally as dispersed and fragmented, or whether they became so as a result of inheritance and the division of original tenancies, is very hard to tell. In the case of some early medieval planned villages in the north east of England, the strips seem to have been allocated on the basis of 'sun division' or *Solskifte*. Tenement plots in the village were proportionate to the assessment figures for the agricultural tenancies borne by each tenant family; often the house plots were organized in two rows which faced each other across the village High Street or green. It seems to have been judged that the plots could be ordered in a clockwise direction moving sun-like around the village. In the surrounding open fields this sun division was continued, so that one tenant's strips always lay between those of his two neighbours in the village. (Despite the oppression and stifling influence of the feudal system, medieval village society seems to have been composed of a bubbling brew of lively little entrepreneurs who were forever selling, swopping, dividing and amalgamating lands and so it is almost impossible to know whether the *Solskifte* system of land allocation had great currency outside Scandinavia and the planned northern settlements although it has been noted at Hardingstone in Northamptonshire.) Outside the open fields, hay meadows were divided and allocated, woodlands designated and protected, while the common grazings and waste—vital elements in the mixed farming system—may have been very ancient components of the rural landscape which were absorbed into the new village farming system.

When this revolution had run its course, the countryside was transformed and the rural landscape was now organized from a scatter-pattern of villages, each village looking out across its little empire of open fields, paddocks and hay meadows to the woods, pastures and waste beyond ; a few hamlets controlled island holdings within the village-centred field systems (many villages were scarcely more than hamlets), while some farmsteads occupied niches within the broader patterns of village farming.

This transformation did not occur at a stroke and the character of the new system varied from region to region and from manor to manor. One cannot imagine that the thousands of new villages were peopled by immigrants, for the Saxon settlement, such as it was, lay in the scarcely remembered past. And so, the new organization of rural settlement can only have been produced by an implosion as, willingly or reluctantly, peasants abandoned the traditional farmsteads and hamlets and were established in new nucleated villages. It is possible that fragments of the landscape as it existed before the village revolution still survive, even in some lowland heartlands. In counties such as Essex, Norfolk and Bedfordshire, villages are often ringed by tiny villages, hamlets and farmstead clusters which are known variously as 'greens' or 'ends'. Some of these can be shown to be of a medieval vintage and were probably hived off as daughter settlements of the larger village. Others, however, predated the village revolution, for Saxon pottery has been found at some Bedfordshire examples, while both Romano-British and Saxon sherds have recently been recognized at the sites of some Essex ends that were occupied until the medieval period or later.

The twin revolutions of settlement nucleation and open field farming seem to have occurred at the same time and it is impossible to believe that they were not the two main facets of the same process. It is almost as hard to imagine that in each locality the reorganization was not largely masterminded by the individual estate owner. Given the

68. Melting snow lingers longest in the furrows to reveal a pattern of medieval ridge and furrow near Richmond, Yorkshire.

political conditions of the centuries concerned, the revolutions could not have been centrally directed by any monarch and so it probably spread by a process of imitation, as each landowner copied the initiatives taken by neighbours and aspired to profit from the improvements which the reorganization of the countryside offered. From the point of view of the landlord, the new system offered a tightly integrated and more productive method of farming, while it was easier to oversee the affairs of tenants who were concentrated in a few villages rather than scattered across the countryside. Population levels will have been rising to produce new problems of land shortage and so it is easy to see that society as a whole stood to benefit from the new arrangements. Even so, given that rather than being good collectivists, peasant farmers the world over tend to be ardent materialists, it is hard to see how the reorganization was sold to the more influential tenants. But because open field farming was unremitting in its demands for co-operation at the most detailed levels, it would have been difficult to operate the system without the goodwill of at least the leading lights in the new village societies.

Although the remaking of the English landscape must have been approved and indeed enforced by the local estate owners, it could have been partly rooted in a more spontaneous form of peasant co-operation at the grassroots level. Perhaps, as Brian Roberts has suggested, the precursor of the nucleated village was a little settlement which might be called a 'linked farm cluster' in which the neighbouring tenant households enjoyed the advantages of performing certain demanding tasks—like ploughing and the pooling of oxen to form plough teams—in common.

Even so, the age-old dominance of the land-owning class must never be forgotten. The later prehistoric and Roman periods left a legacy of large 'multiple estates' which seem to have been federations of townships in which the different units tended to specialize in different areas of estate production. In contrast, in its original form, village-based open field farming was essentially a localized mixed-farming system which offered self-sufficiency within a small and compact area so that in each little land cell, every effort was made to achieve a balance between ploughland, hay meadow, common pasture and woodland resources. Perhaps then, the open field system arose partly from the fragmentation of the extensive multiple estates into many smaller manorial units such as might be held by lesser thanes or knights?

It may also be significant that the revolution occurred at a time when large numbers of field churches were being built to assume the religious duties which had previously been centralized in, and operated from the older Minster churches as described in Chapter 3. Once established, a local church would act as a magnet to footloose settlement, while a reorganization of the settlement pattern could have been part and parcel of an estate-owner's church-building activities.

While this remaking of the English landscape established the outlines of countrysides which survived for a millennium in some areas, it is also very likely that fragments of older countrysides were absorbed into the new organization. Since they were the units upon which crop rotations were normally operated, the furlong divisions were much more important than the vast fields in which they lay, and in a few cases it has been shown that open field furlongs existed as independent fields in the Roman period. Also, it is likely that Dark Age farmers had often operated a version of the infield–outfield system of farming. This involved the designation of an expanse of superior ploughland as the 'infield' and it was kept in constant production by generous applications of farmyard muck. The infield was surrounded by a network of 'outfields', parts of which were periodically ploughed and cropped to exhaustion and then allowed to revert to a long fallow under pasture. The fully-fledged open field farming systems of England could only be operated in areas that were sufficiently fertile to support substantial village communities. In the upland areas, the size of settlements was limited by the scarcity of good ploughland; there the older system survived intact and, within many now-independent farms, elements of the system still endure.

Despite their limited assets of good arable land, the upland farming communities enjoyed a higher level of flexibility, for the general availability of poor to mediocre land meant that the outfield zone of occasionally ploughed fields could always be extended simply by taking in new areas from the commons and waste. On the heavily-populated lowlands, however, there was no such escape valve; new ploughland could only be won at the cost of severely disrupting the balance between crops, pasture and fodder. Therefore, we can imagine that village-centred open field farming superseded infield–outfield farming in the lowlands by a process which involved a merging of infields and outfields to produce a set of vast open fields, after which farmyard muck was spread across the entire arable area rather than being the monopoly of the infield. The reduction in the amount of fertiliser that resulted when the muck was spread more thinly was compensated by the fact that the introduction of a three-course rotation allowed land to be rested every third year, when a furlong was fallowed and grazed. This is a rather complicated notion, but the effect of the change can be conceptualized as an expansion of the infield across most of the outfield area, the division of the vast expanse of ploughland which resulted in fields, furlongs and strips, accompanied by an effort to obtain the right equilibrium between ploughland, pasture, meadow and waste in every land cell where the new system operated. In the event, the main advantage of the new arrangement may not have been the creation of more ploughland, but the provision of more pastures as the more productive crop-growing method released temporary ploughland for use as permanent pasture.

Finally, it must be realized that systems of open field farming varied considerably from region to region and from manor to manor. It is also clear that in each area the system evolved through different stages, so that the field and settlement patterns that confronted the Parliamentary Enclosure commissioners of the eighteenth and nineteenth centuries will have been several evolutionary stages removed from the patterns as they were originally laid out. There is mounting evidence that some extremely attenuated 'long furlongs', which were several hundreds of yards in length, were broken up to form conventional furlongs early in the medieval period, while at the end of the Middle Ages, perhaps as a result of the adoption of horse-drawn ploughs, the headlands separating some furlongs were over-ploughed so that strips were lengthened and furlongs amalgamated. Meanwhile, local enclosures by private agreements between tenants often removed lands from the arena of communal open field farming.

Throughout the period a lively peasant land market operated, so that the patterns of land holdings were in a constant state of flux, making it nigh impossible to discover the

69. *Stone walls in parallel rows trace medieval field divisions running back from the roadside houses at Chelmorton, Derbyshire.*

original appearance and layout of holdings. Also, while the system was originally one of mixed farming and local self-sufficiency, open field farming was very flexible; by the later part of the Middle Ages, many village communities were specializing in particular areas of commercial production. By virtue of its very flexibility, and contrary to many of the criticisms levelled against it by eighteenth-century agricultural improvers, this was an efficient and productive system of farming providing tenants were prepared to submit to the massive administrative and organizational burdens which it imposed.

It is a common feature of landscape history that the more that we learn about a subject, the more complicated it tends to become. We have tried to present all the various factors relating to the remaking of the English landscape in as straightforward a manner as possible. Even so, the reader should not feel embarrassed if left a little muddled and perplexed by all the different questions which must be taken into account. Yet anyone who really wants to understand the medieval landscape and its legacies cannot bypass this morass of competing and conflicting theories, fragmentary evidence and challenging relics. It is also rather daunting to think that, if ever an accurate picture of the forces which moulded the countrysides of medieval England does emerge, it is likely to be even more complicated than one imagines! At present, we cannot discover the logic which surely underpinned some of the features of open field farming.

One of these blind spots in our visions of the past concerns the fact that we cannot see why co-operative strip farming could not have been operated while at the same time retaining the older pattern of enclosed fields. Neither is it clear why peasant holdings seem to have consisted of strips which were widely scattered across the open fields, ensuring that peasants and plough beasts used much time and energy in long treks to remote corners of the village open fields. Indeed, if we follow each thread of logic through to its apparent conclusion we dismember the entire system, just as Parliamentary Enclosure did in areas where it still endured. And yet, open field farming was retained for up to a millennium and so it must have offered distinct and positive advantages to a large proportion of the village community.

18

Medieval Villages and Fields

We now know enough about medieval villages to appreciate that most of what was thought to be known about them was wrong. They were not stable; generally did not stand singly and regally within their parishes, and cannot be classified in simple categories according to their shapes and layout. Indeed, when we look at the village in terms of the whole spectrum of history and prehistory, we find that villages are not inevitable or even typical features of the lowland landscape. Before the remaking of the landscape described above, villages were relatively uncommon. They might also be uncommon today had not the village discovered new roles after the dismemberment of open field farming.

Much ink has been spilled by guidebook writers in describing the rambling, relaxed appearance of villages which are offered as the antithesis of formal planning. Those who look more closely at villages will soon realize that in fact many villages are wholly planned, and others include planned additions or areas of planned redevelopment. Indeed, one might go further, for if we are right in thinking that the deliberate creation of villages was a vital component in the remaking of the English landscape, then the vast majority of English villages must be planned, whether or not they display the straight streets, right-angled road junctions and geometrical greens which are normally associated with planning. Having reorganized his estate according to the dictates of open field farming, the landlord might not have cared very much whether his tenants were continually changing the details of the landscape, for each piece of land continued to yield its prescribed quota of rents and services. Similarly, once created, villages were often free to wander, shrink or grow, and this did not matter to the landlord so long as a dormitory for tenants existed for as long as tenants were needed.

Much has also been written about the 'typical' village and one is often offered an image of a settlement which has stood supreme at the heart of its parish since 500 years

70. *The shrunken village of Little Minting, Lincolnshire. Air photography reveals the corduroy patterns of ridge and furrow above the village, while the earthworks of a once much larger village appear particularly well in the lower left quadrant.*

before its name and people were recorded in Domesday Book. Yet it is quite clear that there was no such thing as a typical village. Within their parishes and manors (which very often had different boundaries) a minority of villages may have stood alone, but usually a parish or an estate was shared with other smaller villages, hamlets or little farm clusters. These lesser settlements often tended to decay or to be absorbed by an expanding neighbour, so creating an illusion of solitary settlement in parishes which had once supported 'multiple settlement'. Many villages are 'polyfocal', a term coined by one of the authors to describe an apparently single settlement which really consists of several originally distinct components. Usually, the origins of the polyfocal village are lost in the medieval mists, but occasionally it is possible to recover an explanation.

Piddletrenthide in Dorset is one such case. It is an elongated, straggling village which would, in less discerning times, have been classed as a 'linear' or 'street' village—but such simple labels can seldom describe anything as complicated as an English village. The name (as quaint as any in this county whose villages seem to be named by comedians or after Shakespearean actors) means 'the settlement on the River Piddle which pays tax on thirty hides of land'. Charters of 891, 996 and 1019 fix various of the village boundaries and the documents also show that originally the 'village' was three separate settlements, each with its own field system and each controlling a land area of about ten hides. These three settlements were lumped together within the same parish, and gradually they grew together to form a single elongated village in which the three original components can just be recognized.

Welton in Lincolnshire is polyfocal, but for a different reason. When it was recently surveyed for the RCHM it was realized that the present rather disjointed village in fact consisted of five distinct settlements. It emerges that the parish must have been granted to the Bishop of Lincoln and was then divided into 'prebendal manors', each of which was allocated to a canon of Lincoln Cathedral and managed separately. The modern village results from the merging of the former manorial settlements.

The medieval English landscape held many more villages than can be seen in the modern countryside, and the study of deserted medieval settlement underlines the way in which the link between the village and its lands was not a tie so much as a lifeline. When villages grew, as most did during the eleventh, twelfth and thirteenth centuries, so the hunger for land increased. In the chalk downlands and in the northern dales, plough terraces or 'strip lynchets' were engraved into steep hillsides in urgent efforts to win some extra ploughland. In most places, daughter settlements were hived off from

71. *The deserted medieval village of Argam, Yorkshire. Although the rectangular house sites are clearly visible, the village appears to have had a complicated history of growth and contraction. It was built to nestle close to the older linear earthwork of the Argam Dyke, which can be seen faintly running across the upper right corner of the photograph.*

the existing villages and were often established on thinly-soiled uplands, peaty moors, sandy places or the cold damp clays of the vales. Often, such small and vulnerable villages which had been planted in uninviting settings began to fail when their over-worked ploughlands and over-grazed pastures could no longer respond to the demands of their farmers. Then they perished in their hundreds when the climate deteriorated in the thirteenth, fourteenth and fifteenth centuries.

Thousands of other villages perished not because their lands were frail or worked out, but because the masters of the countryside coveted these lands for other uses. The first onslaughts on village England were localized and the victims were settlements which had the misfortune to lie on lands where Cistercian communities sought to establish monastic houses or, more commonly, monastic farms or 'granges'. The Cistercian Rule frowned on contacts between monks and lay communities and so scores of innocent communities were evicted. The next assault, occurring mainly in the late fourteenth, fifteenth and early sixteenth centuries was catastrophic, devastating scores of Midland parishes and cutting great depopulated swathes through other areas like Wessex and the Yorkshire Wolds. Its causes were both economic and political: the Great Pestilence of the mid fourteenth century had removed at least one third of the English population and had transformed a situation of land hunger and cheap over-abundant labour into one in which labour was scarce, militant and costly. Scores of landlords realized that by clearing villages, evicting tenants and converting the old village fields into sheep pastures, their estates would yield higher profits while the nagging disputes between the landlord and his tenants and labourers would be removed.

72. *Austwick near Settle, Yorkshire, has expanded along a pattern of medieval strip lynchets, seen here as terraces running horizontally across the centre section of the photograph.*

Often, the conversion of open field land to sheep pasture brought a change in the field patterns, as at Wormleighton in Warwickshire where the *nouveau riche* Spencer dynasty began its prolonged rise to fame and glory by evicting the villagers in the years around 1500. An estate map of 1634 shows the parish divided into four great 'charges' or leases, each one a balanced sheep-rearing unit with pasture, meadow and water. Each of these charges may originally have been one of the unfortunate village's open fields. Old village closes were converted into stock pens and new hedged and banked enclosures were created, while the main grazings were partitioned by great double hedgerows, with the spaces between the hedges and ditches being planted with oak timber, hitherto in short supply.

By Elizabethan times, when the sheep clearances were almost over, a new threat to village England arose from the emerging fashion for landscaped parks which we described in Chapter 29. Not only were old village lands coveted—fields which had produced the very wealth allowing the landlords to contemplate their destruction—but also the traditional ramshackle villages were judged unsightly and banished from the landscaped scene. In the post-medieval period, the process of 'engrossment', whereby successful farmers steadily bought up the holdings of their neighbours, also condemned many a small village to a wasting death as one farming household after another departed.

And so, while it is true that the framework of the English rural settlement pattern was remodelled in the centuries which bracket the Norman Conquest, many of the little components of the medieval settlement scene have disappeared. Plantagenet England contained far more small villages than we see today, while other villages have become much enlarged through the gradual merging of formerly distinct settlements; as a result of small-scale successes in medieval trading or manufacturing, or, most recently, by attracting large numbers of middle-class commuters.

Despite the babblings of the glossy guidebooks, there is not a village in the realm which looks even remotely as it did in the High Middle Ages. By a detailed scrutiny of old maps, the oldest surviving buildings, street names and road alignments it is often possible to chart the post-medieval evolution of a village. But to do this is rather like seeing a chicken grow into a hen while staying blind to all the fascinating changes which took place in the seclusion of the eggshell.

We do know that medieval villages underwent many changes of form as greens were inserted into older patterns, derelict streets were sloughed off and abandoned, new streets were forged, planned areas of development were grafted on to old layouts and new layouts created by demolition and redevelopment. Sometimes a glimpse of some of these lively changes can be gained from a careful study of the subtle earthwork patterns on the fringes of a village, but a real understanding can only be gained by excavation of a very detailed and widespread nature. Just such an excavation has been in progress at the deserted medieval village of Wharram Percy in Yorkshire for a quarter of a century and most of the village area is still to be explored. The information from Wharram Percy has transformed our understanding of the medieval village, underlined the complexity of village development and opened new portholes on the medieval world.

Not only did medieval villages turn and turn about upon their original sites, they also

73. *Castleton, like many other medieval castle villages, is a planned creation. The church stands in one rectangular plot and the market area lies just below the churchyard. Fragments of the medieval field system survive nearby. Note too the dispersed farmsteads appearing as white dots on the distant hillside.*

frequently hopped or drifted across their fields to exploit new situations. The causes for migration were varied and they are usually impossible to discover. Sometimes, the existence of an area of common pasture seems to have acted like a magnet to drifting settlement in areas where such grazings were in short supply; in other cases, changes in road priorities seem to have drawn villages to newly bustling highways, particularly when there was the opportunity to establish a village market; in others estate reorganization must have been the cause.

74. *The shifted medieval village of Castle Camps, Cambridgeshire. The medieval church still stands in the outer bailey of the old castle, but for reasons that are not known its village has drifted away to a new site several hundreds of yards away.*

19

After the Middle Ages

Villages emerged from the Middle Ages with their original numbers much reduced, their essential forms mostly established and with the surviving villages being on the whole considerably larger than they had been at the start of the period. After the medieval period, the tendency for villages to shift or change their layouts was much less than before. This was partly due to the effects of the 'Great Rebuilding' movement which slowly rolled across the country from the south east during the sixteenth, seventeenth and eighteenth centuries. It resulted in the construction of houses which were much more spacious and far more durable than hitherto—and which were much less likely to be abandoned to the whims of settlement drift.

Fields, like villages, had evolved through the Middle Ages, yet while the essential patterns of late sixteenth-century village settlement have tended to endure, the old field patterns have been radically transformed. In many areas however the open field arrangements of the early medieval period had been dismantled piecemeal as a result of successive enclosures of the communally-worked lands by agreements between the village farmers. In other parishes, the pattern was more complicated with enclosed strips or blocks of strips standing among the surviving areas of open field land, while in others peripheral packages of privately-farmed land marked local enclosures of woodland and waste. These processes of enclosure by agreement continued in the seventeenth and eighteenth centuries, so that around 1700 about half of the ploughland in England and Wales lay in open field strips, and the other half in private enclosures.

Then, mainly in the Georgian period, Acts of Parliamentary Enclosure changed the field patterns in almost 3000 English parishes, either by reorganizing the surviving fragments of open field and common land or, more frequently, by dismantling complete systems of open fields, meadows, commons and waste. In such places, as W. G. Hoskins has described, 'hardly a landmark of the old parish would have remained.' First the leading land owners in a particular parish petitioned Parliament for an Enclosure Act and then commissioners and surveyors were appointed to draft the outlines of the brave new parochial world. The open fields, meadows and commons were partitioned and each yeoman and copyholder was allocated a compacted holding of land which was deemed to equate with the formerly fragmented holding. The Enclosure provisions included a rationalization of the ancient road and track networks, and new straight roads were often prescribed, while the hedging or walling of the newly-allocated fields was an important obligation of the land holder.

75. A particularly fine and well-maintained system of Enclosure hedgerows surviving near Holkham Hall, Norfolk, home of the eighteenth-century agricultural reformer Coke of Holkham.

76. Moorland enclosure on Blubberhouse Moor near Harrogate, probably dating from about 1780. Note the uncompromising geometry of the field walls and how the narrow ridge and furrow patterns in the large field below centre fit the outlines of the field and must post-date the Enclosure.

The changes created a fresh and quite unprecedented form of English scenery in each of the parishes affected. It was a geometrical countryside, with straight-hedged rectangular fields, sometimes punctuated with spinneys, fringed by shelter belts or gashed by short, straight Enclosure roads and tracks. Society as well as scenery was affected. Enclosure was generally supported by agricultural reformers, leading landowners and most of the larger freeholders and copyholders. Even so, it completely undermined the livelihoods of commoners, cottagers, those without clear title to their lands and many smaller tenants who depended heavily upon the resources of the commons: it was justly loathed and feared by them. Few were able to remain as small farmers for very long after the implementation of an Act and many became labourers employed by more fortunate neighbours. In these ways, the changes marked the end of the English peasant.

They also had important implications for the rural patterns of settlement. Previously most farmsteads had flanked the streets and back lanes of villages—as they still do at the polyfocal village of Laxton in Nottinghamshire, where relics of open field farming still survive. After Enclosure, the farming household had good incentives to move from their old village-based farmstead into a purpose-built home and work-base situated at the heart of the new compact holding. Such eighteenth and early nineteenth-century

213

farmsteads—their architecture a dour celebration of the good fortune and opportunities which the Enclosure revolution had bestowed—are common features in the countrysides affected.

Although farmsteads large and small had been the commonest buildings in the English village, this exodus of the more prosperous elements in the community did not tend to cause the collapse and disintegration of the settlement. Unmechanized and lightly-mechanized farming still demanded massive rural labour forces. Old farmsteads could be sub-divided into labourer's cottages or converted into pubs, stores or workshops and the growth in service industries, patronage and democratic values spawned village shops, post offices, pumps and other amenities and schools. Thus, in the course of the nineteenth century, the village was slowly remodelled from being the work-base of self-sufficient peasant families to becoming a dormitory for farm labourers and tradesmen and a service centre dispensing many little goods and services which its inhabitants would previously have done without or produced at home. The village with its store, post office, pump and workshops which features in popular visions of the past was really a quite recent creation of the nineteenth century.

While it almost invariably survived the traumas of Parliamentary Enclosure, the village came face to face with the threat of disintegration in the decades between about 1880 and the Great Depression. The mechanization of farming, which succeeded where Enclosure had failed in clearing the crowded fields of the ant-like armies of labourers, the economic and genocidal effects of the Great War and successive farm price crises all took their toll; villages seemed fated to bleed to death as one family after another sought new opportunities in the town. The village tended often to be left in the care of aged guardians, too stubborn or too poverty-stricken to desert their homes.

The revitalization of the village was, in large part, the result of the new commuting habit which the railways and, more importantly, the rise in private car ownership had made possible. Typically, the modern English village is a settlement that is polyfocal in a new social and economic way. It tends to contain the fragments of a dwindling indigenous working-class community and a growing articulate, mobile and sometimes a little domineering population of middle-class commuters. As the older cottages are sold, renovated and commandeered by affluent newcomers, the remnants of the old population tend to be found in charity cottages, council estates or else they may move to live with children who have left the village to seek employment.

When the new machines cleared the crowded fields, the ancient lifeline between the village and its fields was severed forever. Many newcomers, attracted by visions of village life so assiduously cultivated by the glossy guidebooks found that the surrounding fields were a no-go area, guarded by loathsome little signs, while the networks of footpaths that had once existed were ploughed into oblivion. Yet while they might wring no changes from the masters of the countrysides, at least the new village middle classes can hope to win other campaigns which the indigenous population, with its interminable history of being kicked around by authority, could never contemplate, let alone win.

The study of rural settlement history shows that villages only appear and are only sustained by special, favourable circumstances. Rather than being permanent and inevitable, they are both vital and vulnerable. Many a modern village is sustained by the commuting habit. But with its school closed, its old community senile, unemployed or in flight, its shop, pubs and little industries as victims of the economic situation, its bus service withering and its rights of access to the surrounding countryside stolen, the village ceases to be an attractive place in which to live and becomes just an inconveniently remote dormitory. Villages often only survive because they have discovered a useful new role to play. If this role should disintegrate, then an invaluable symbol in the national sentiment will not exist outside the pages of the popular countryside books.

In describing the broad themes of rural development in the post-medieval centuries, some detailed or more local factors have been overlooked. The dismantling of open fields was not the only important change, for as well as reorganizing the existing lands and fields, the period also witnessed the winning of some new lands. Prehistoric, Dark Age and medieval communities had many agricultural triumphs, but they tended to be daunted by the challenges of large-scale land drainage, the problems being not so much technological as organizational. The story of the seventeenth and eighteenth-century drainage of the Fens has been told many times, but important land reclamation projects were pursued elsewhere. The Dissolution of the Monasteries had left the Crown with a claim to ownership of the King's Sedgemoor in Somerset, but attempts to launch reclamation projects by the Stuart kings amounted to little more than a comedy of errors, spiced by episodes of corruption and speculation and opposed by legions of peasants and small landowners. In the latter part of the eighteenth century, the rising

77. Field patterns produced by the enclosure of the Somerset Levels. Note the curving hedgerows on the distant ridge of higher land, suggesting that this better-drained area was cultivated in the medieval period. This view is obtained from the ruined medieval church site on Burrow Mump near Bridgewater.

fashion for agricultural improvement created a climate in which plans for land drainage could flourish and in which the seasonal inundation of potentially good grazing lands could be regarded generally as what Arthur Young had called 'a disgrace to the whole Nation'. In 1775 a Bill for the draining of Sedgemoor was defeated because of the blatant malpractices of its leading proponent, who sought to profit from the scheme and so settle his gambling debts. The argument was finally settled by an Act of 1791, after which the River Cary was diverted away from the River Parret into a new channel cut across Sedgemoor. Some 4,063 claims to land holdings in the newly-drained areas were raised and 1,796 of them were allowed. In the course of the following years the newly-drained land was first partitioned by surveyors according to the now-familiar rectangular patterns and then, gradually, a landscape of fields bordered by deep ditches or 'rhines' developed, the rhines being five feet (1.5 metres) deep, eight feet (2.4 metres) wide at their banks and four feet (1.2 metres) wide at their bottoms and graced on either side by rows of willows.

In the uplands one can sometimes see field patterns which also result from land reclamation programmes. Exmoor was an ancient royal forest and at the start of the nineteenth century it was grazed in summer by some 25,000 sheep which were driven up onto the moor from around fifty lowland parishes. In 1815 an Act of Parliamentary Enclosure was passed and in 1818 around 15,000 acres of moorland were sold to an ironmaster from the Midlands, John Knight. The whole property was walled and then partitioned between fifteen new farms, the farms sub-divided by high earthen field banks and the field packages protected by shelter belts. Other large blocks of moorland were sold off in the decades which followed, and another English landscape was completely transformed. In other parts of the country one can see the effects of recent enclosures on a much smaller scale. Ramblers on the track that leads to the curious Men-an-tol monument in Cornwall will not fail to notice the sturdy field walls in the forbidden fields beside the track. Although they are built of massive moorstone blocks, they are perfectly straight and in striking contrast to the curving walls of the ancient fields which pattern the distant scene. The fields belong to Coronation Farm, named and founded at the time of the Coronation of Edward VII when this small section of moor was reclaimed.

The study of field patterns reveals long episodes of slow evolution which are periodically breached by outbreaks of wholesale revolutionary change which may be experienced at the local or national level. The countryside was never an Eden. Periodically ecological crises would erupt as a result of over-cropping or over-grazing or climatic changes and they were solved in a brutal manner as Nature took her revenge, areas were abandoned and fertility slowly restored. For as far back in time as we can see, the masters of the countryside have flourished on the rents, tribute and efforts of peasants and tenants who they accepted or evicted as circumstances required. Yet outside the designated hunting forests, the issues of access and recreation were seldom important so that the most cruelly exploited medieval peasant enjoyed far better rights of access to the countryside than does the modern rambler. With the passage of time, one type of countryside that was glorious, brimful of character, teeming with wildlife and spangled with communities of wild plants yielded to another. For many a half-starved peasant family the joys of living in such countrysides must have been their only consolation. There are some erudite and educated commentators who suggest that men who were sufficiently erudite and educated as to appreciate the British landscape only appeared in the eighteenth century. But if we go back to the oldest literature which exists north of the Alps, to the semi-pagan Celtic myths of Ireland, we find a tradition which is most strongly characterized by its keenly observed descriptions of the countryside, its moods and the ways of its wildlife.

Now a new revolution is sweeping across the fieldscapes of Britain. It differs from all the previous revolutions in that while old patterns of wildlife and beauty are being extinguished, no new beauty or interest is being created. Wetlands are drained, moorlands ploughed-up and seeded with a grass monoculture, ancient woodlands are ripped-out, but the most devastating changes result from the grubbing out of the hedgerows which have been the most glorious and characteristic features of the British countryside. Old battles and revolutions in the countryside were fought on the issues of profits and progress and sooner or later victory would be won by whatever changes were considered advantageous by the larger landowners. As a result of medieval sheep enclosures, engrossment, Parliamentary Enclosure and land reclamation schemes, countless households of poor peasants and commoners were sacrificed on the altars of progress and evicted or left destitute. But they were never expected to pay the robber in the way that, as Miriam Shoard has detailed, the modern taxpayer is subsidising the theft and destruction of the landscape. Sectional interpretations of profit and progress are ripping the heart out of the countrysides of lowland England wherever it still beats; Devon, Herefordshire and the northern dales are beginning to shiver in the winds of change and no countrysides are secure. Yet so long as petty local concessions are heralded as victories for conservation, the battle to preserve the landscape heritage will never be fought, let alone be won.

Turning now to the more cheerful topic of rural settlement, it can be seen that although the post-medieval village became less footloose and lively as the Great Rebuilding cemented its layout, wherever the link with the surrounding fields endured, the village could still respond to changes. This is beautifully illustrated in the case of the village of Killinghall near Harrogate. In the latter part of the eighteenth century it existed as a string of small farmsteads which hemmed the edge of a Forest of Knaresborough common, while the village ploughlands and pastures to the north west of the farmsteads had been enclosed by agreements towards the end of the Middle Ages. Two important changes affected the community in the 1770s: the Enclosure of the common and the turnpiking of two trackways which ran across it to converge at the northern tip of the settlement. The common-edge situation was now redundant, while the much improved roads began to bustle with through traffic. Killinghall responded by slowly migrating to take up a new position astride the turnpikes so that by the 1850s the move was well advanced, but history not yet forgotten and the more conservative and less mobile farmsteads were known as 'Old Town Houses'.

Elsewhere some new villages appeared. Previously the masters of the countryside had moved villages which intruded upon their plans for parks and had built prettified replacement villages or had titivated existing villages. Blaise Hamlet near Bristol was rather different and was built in 1810–12 for J. S. Hartford and designed by John Nash and George Repton as a home for the elderly retainers on Blaise Castle estate. Here, for the first time, we find a village which was a completely artificial creation and which, instead of being an organic or necessary part of the countryside, was a manifestation in brick, thatch and mortar of a picturesque vision of what a village could and should be. In this way, Blaise Hamlet is the direct forbear of all the hundreds of contrived village landscapes that are being created today, complete with their twee carved village signs, exposed timber frames, well-mown greens and recently-acquired 'Georgian' bow windows. Which all goes to show that some mistaken visions of the past can be so powerful that they result in the creation of landscapes which had no previous existence outside the imagination and popular whimsy.

Blaise Hamlet inspired several other model villages while industrialization was an important factor in the process of post-medieval village creation or 'late nucleation'. About three miles to the west of Killinghall is the village of Birstwith. When this part of Nidderdale was mapped in 1772 no village existed. Some coal pits lay close to the river but there was very little settlement in the valley, although on the plateau to the south there was a quite heavy scatter of dwellings occupied mainly by small farmers who supplemented farming by cottage-based textile industries. Around the turn of the century, a water-powered cotton mill was established near the river by the Greenwood family and the transition from cottage crafts to the factory industry and the establishment of some estate cottages, a church and school under the Greenwood patronage created a village where none had previously existed. Some industrial villages, like Arkwright's Cromford in Derbyshire or Titus Salt's Saltaire in West Yorkshire were carefully planned and provided superior working-class accommodation, while others grew in a more gradual and chaotic manner as workers were drawn to the new industrial, mining and quarrying sites.

In describing the saga of the village and its fields we have focused attention upon the English lowlands. The feudal process of village creation reached out beyond England into some lowland areas of Scotland and Wales, while Normans and other alien medieval landlords often attempted to establish villages in Ireland. On the whole though, the more ancient tradition of farmstead and hamlet settlement was better adapted to the stock-rearing lifestyles and lighter population densities of the northern and western uplands; where small villages did exist, they tended to display the loose formless appearance and footloose habits which were typical of ancient settlements. Arnol on Lewis is a good example. The original village was on a site overlooking Mol a' Chladaich beach, where the archaeological evidence shows that settlements had drifted up and down the sands since at least the first century AD. In the course of time, the villagers gradually used up the nearby supplies of peat, while winter storms caused boulders to be piled-up on the foreshore where they impeded drainage. Around 1880, the village migrated from the seashore and took up a new position about half a mile inland. In the 1890s, improved roads were constructed in the township and they exerted a magnetic effect on footloose settlement, so that as the village crystallized it developed a rather straggling linear appearance as new blackhouses were built beside the road. The surrounding lands were divided into strip-like holdings which radiated

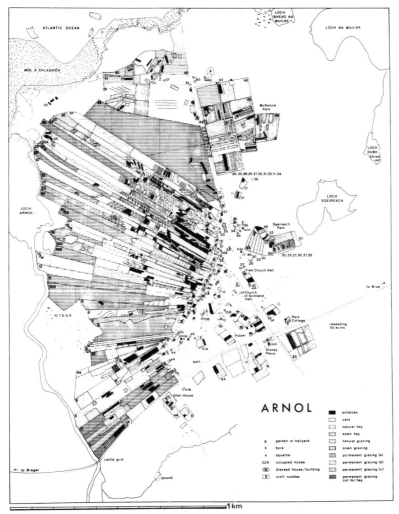

Fig. 5. *Layout of the village of Arnol, based on a survey by the Dept. of Geography, University of Glasgow (from* The Arnol Blackhouse Villages section, *HMSO).*

outwards from each blackhouse towards the shore. The result of these changes was the development of a village of single-storey thatched dwellings, many shared by the crofters and their livestock, which had a loose, rather disorderly appearance and which was bordered by strip-like fields. The effect was medieval or older, and the vintage, late Victorian. Arnol was built at a time of population growth which placed great pressure on its farming resources. In the 1880s it was home to forty-five tenant families and ten other families who were landless. Such is the nature of the modern economic miracle that in 1960 only nine village houses remained in occupation.

Reflections

Our understanding of the village has suffered because we have confused romance and sentiment with historical fact. Life in clamourous urban worlds and a sequence of twentieth-century disasters and political uncertainties have created a psychological and emotional need for islands of permanence, stability and traditional values; the village has become a focus for all these sentiments.

So the village came to symbolize a range of qualities which it never really possessed. As a psychological symbol it could live an independent life in the minds of all those who needed to believe that the countryside was stippled with steadfast and picturesque small settlements which had survived little changed through all the historical centuries of tribulation and conflict. This romantic and unreal world of village England was studiously cultivated by the glossy gazetteers and guidebooks which steered the day-trippers away from the more typical and often more interesting villages towards the twee nooks where the vistas of rosehung walls, babbling millstreams and timber-framed teashops beckoned. Photographs were selected with such concern for the *bijou* cameo that one might never know that cars, telegraph poles, road markings or rain ever afflicted the deodourized world of the village. As a result, the most interesting historical features and challenges were overlooked and the village is fair game for any writer who can cobble together a few taproom anecdotes, eulogize the scene around the green and describe the village vistas in honeyed prose which is unsullied by any understanding of real landscape history.

In fact, villages offer a great deal more fascination although instead of being living legacies from the Iron Age, early-Saxon or Roman worlds, they are mainly the products of a still-mysterious reorganization of the countryside which occurred in the centuries around the Norman Conquest.

The first key to an appreciation of the village is the ability to see the settlement in relation to the package of lands which supported it and gave it a reason for being throughout most of its life. Next, one must learn to see the village as a volatile and vulnerable place which could engage in surges of growth when held by an ambitious and interested landlord, yet just as swiftly subside when fortune and new designs conspired against it. In most villages, the post-medieval phases of development have obliterated much of the evidence of the medieval sequences of expansion and shrinkage, although the earthworks at deserted village sites show layouts frozen at the time of destruction or abandonment. Often, the evidence that they offer is far more complicated than one might imagine and recent work by RCHM investigators in Lincolnshire has resulted in the mapping of earthworks at some almost incredibly extensive and complex shrunken and deserted settlements.

Much more work will be needed before we can generalize with any certainty about village origins, but almost any enduring village offers the determined local historian a fine, if often perplexing subject for study. All those who make the effort will find that real villages are far more gutsy and interesting than the sweetly insipid places which nestle coyly in the pages of the guidebooks.

PART V

Towns: The Wild Cards of Landscape History

20

Introduction: Man the Town-maker

The British are an urban people renowned as a nation of country-lovers. This attachment to the countryside has more to do with nostalgia than experience, for three out of every four of us are town-dwellers. In the nineteenth century millions of destitute or jobless rural peasants and hirelings were pleased to desert the scenes of their exploitation in village England for the better wages, security and dwellings available in the rapidly-growing industrial towns. There they jostled and mixed with the hordes of broken tenants arriving in rivers and convoys from Scotland and Ireland. But as the Industrial Revolution converted a rural patchwork of provincial peasantries into an urban society, so memories of the searing hardships and injustices of country life faded. Gradually, the countryside was perceived as a place of tranquility and simple, solid values. Meanwhile, the initial glamour of the saviour town was forgotten in the drab but frenzied monotony of urban life and work. And so the town was taken for granted.

The perceived banality of towns like Wigan, Scunthorpe, Ongar and, more latterly, Neasden make such places symbolic targets for comedians and satirists, but the industrial towns and the metropolitan backwaters were seldom deemed deserving of serious study. Even today, there is no coherent study of 'urbanology'; in the quite recent past archaeologists tended only to be interested in Roman relics; historians might draw the line of respectability in urban studies at the close of the Middle Ages; it was left to the geographers to develop a rather lop-sided perception of urban whys and wherefores. In the earlier part of this century they were guided by the philosophy of 'environmental determinism', a sort of geographical Darwinism, re-imported from influential German sources.

According to the general premises of this approach, the town was the product of its geographical setting and so towns were judged to appear at geographically strategic sites like bridging points on rivers, natural harbours, coalfields and road junctions. Of course, one can always find examples of towns which benefit from such locations, but the search for classical examples of bridge towns like London, ports like Plymouth or local resource-exploiters like Bath can lead one to overlook the scores of towns which have indifferent or arbitrary sites and yet flourish oblivious to the dictates of environmental determinism.

The key point in all this is that towns do *not* make themselves, erupting like mushrooms wherever the geographical climate is most balmy: towns are made by men. Each and every one is the product of human decisions and choices. Some can be traced back through time to a single founding father, while others represent an accumulation of different decisions taken at different times. No town ever appeared without being kicked into life by an ambitious or visionary man, woman or clique, and then sustained by latterday entrepreneurs and townsfolk. Sometimes the founder is anonymous and the original vision blurred or forgotten. In other cases, a dusty image of the mini-Moses gazes down upon the echoing recesses of public buildings in towns where not one resident in a hundred has the remotest notion of how or why the hometown was created.

Each town, then, is the embodiment of the ideas and will-power of individuals as well as unique sequences of historical accidents. Bath has already been cited as an exploiter of a local resource and it is quite true that without the mineral springs, which have been famed since at least Roman times, there might be no Bath. Still, springs do not make towns—but human visions of their potential may. In this case, the eighteenth-century revival of the spa and declined medieval wool town as a Mecca for self-indulgent fashionable society was guided by human factors. There was the trend-setting visit to test the curative powers of the waters made by Queen Anne in 1702–3; the subsequent patronage and promotion of the town by Beau Nash and, particularly, the vision and determination of John Wood (1705–54). The son of a humble local builder, he designed the lavish and elegant core of the spa and then raised the speculative capital essential to the fruition of the project after the Corporation had shied away from the ambitious scheme.

At least in the case of Bath, the local resources prodded the imagination with strong hints about the potential for an urban revival, but there are plenty of other towns which defy the logic of economic geography. The defiance of Thaxted in Essex ended long ago, but the splendid medieval guildhall endures as a legacy of the town's former glories as a centre of the English cutlery industry. Just why a cutlery industry should have developed at Thaxted is rather a mystery, but surely reflects a quirk of human choice and an accident of history since the town had no special resource base or qualification for its role. The industry seems to have been introduced by the Earls of Clare. During the fourteenth century it grew to considerable importance, with some of the wealth that it generated being preserved in the church, begun in 1340, and the guildhall of 1390. By the end of the fifteenth century it was in decline.

Thaxted also reminds us that the continuing existence of a town may not reflect the benign influences of its geographical setting, but rather the doggedness and ingenuity which individuals and communities display in the face of adversity. When faced by the decline of the cutlery industry, the people of Thaxted responded by petitioning for a borough charter, which was won in 1556, with provisions for the institution of a mayor and council, a school and, most importantly, a weekly market and four fairs. The charter was extinguished in 1686. Small industries have come and gone, but Thaxted meanwhile secured a niche as a rural service centre, allowing its survival as a noble townlet in a landscape of villages.

The case of Harrogate in Yorkshire shows that the battle between the natural forces for urban decline and the communal instinct for survival is still a feature of the urban story. Like Bath, Harrogate's fame is based upon local mineral springs, but the emergence and rapid expansion of the town was as much a tribute to human decisions, fancies and efforts. These included the early promotional achievements of pioneer

78. *The Roman baths, Bath.*

publicists like the sixteenth-century local William Slingsby who paved and walled one of the boggy wells and announced that it waters 'did excell the tart fountains beyond the seas'. By the 1630s, a small Harrogate season had become established and scores of visitors were attracted to the new social ritual of 'taking the waters'. Seventeenth-century travel writers vied with each other to encapsulate the character of the springs

79. *The medieval guildhall, Thaxted, stands in the road island on the left and the other buildings could represent later infilling behind the guildhall.*

and in one of the more restrained appraisals, John Ray proclaimed that Harrogate water 'stinks noisesomely, like rotten eggs'. As often, any publicity seems to have been welcome, and, as the aristocratic fashion for spa seasons gathered momentum, the fortunes of Harrogate steadily rose. A town developed around the wells and its growth was boosted by the construction of turnpike roads in the second half of the eighteenth century. More turnpikes followed in the early nineteenth century and the arrival of a direct railway link in 1848 seemed to guarantee the future of Harrogate, which was receiving around 12,000 visitors each year.

However, fashions are man-made and fickle; while the gluttony and wealth which had provided the pretext and the means for the spa season fell victims to social changes, medical opinion began to cast doubts upon the magical efficacy of spa waters. The Spa Rooms were pulled down in 1939 and the Pump Rooms closed shortly after. Harrogate was rapidly losing its *raison d'être*, but during World War II fate was postponed when the town's ample hotel accommodation was requisitioned for military administrative uses. After the war, Harrogate faced a descent into dowdiness. Diminishing numbers of genteel and ageing hotels had futures as insecure as those of their genteel, ageing and diminishing residents, but the town's administrators realized that the conference industry might offer salvation to Harrogate and its top-heavy superstructure of hotels.

The heyday of the spa had left a legacy of parks, gardens, theatres and other amenities which were major assets as the town entered the competitive arena of the conference industry. Then, in the late 1970s, the authorities took one of the most adventurous gambles in any urban survival strategy by launching a multi-million-pound conference centre scheme at an almost crippling cost. Should it succeed, the continuing prosperity of Harrogate will have little to do with natural geographical advantage, but be a tribute to human initiative and the communal instinct for survival.

80. *The old pump room at Harrogate.*

Harrogate and Thaxted are relevant examples, for at some stage in its career, the typical town will face a crossroads. Some towns have been guided along so many promising avenues that the original urban vision has been forgotten, or seems to have little relevance to the sprawling metropolis which it spawned. Birmingham shares with Harrogate a stake in the conference industry, but they have little else in common. It appeared in Domesday Book of 1086 as a miniscule estate, dwarfed by the adjacent manors of Aston, Selly Oak and Erdington. The first step on the long road to metropolitan grandeur was represented by an unremarkable market charter won by the Birmingham family in 1166. This provided the means by which the village gradually captured the surrounding market trade, so that by the fifteenth century it had outgrown its neighbours and entered the lower ranks of the provincial market towns. By 1540, John Leland tells us that the town had a single main street a quarter of a mile in length, and just one church. However, it seems that the moderate success of the market had attracted a small industrial community: 'There be many smithes in the towne that use to make knives and all manner of cuttynge tooles, and many lorimars that make byts (harness-makers), and a greate many naylors.' From the acorn of the twelfth-century market charter an exceptional conurbation was to develop, but even four centuries after the town had been nudged into life one would have needed great powers of prediction to imagine the industrial consequences of the humdrum market grant.

Many other towns originated from seemingly inconsequential market charters, but there were also scores which lacked the accidents of fate, the home-grown visionaries and entrepreneurs or the communal will necessary to sustain a hopeful borough along the metropolitan road. Stillborn or stunted townlets like New Buckenham in Norfolk are fascinating places, where the hallmark of broken dreams is exposed in the survival of little urban layouts which may be six, seven or eight centuries in age. All manner of flights of fancy can create towns and, in the case of New Buckenham the town seems to have been born in William de Albany's disenchantment with the castle that he held at nearby Old Buckenham. In the middle of the twelfth century he bought a castle site beyond the boundary of his manor from the Bishop of Norwich. It lay on the edge of a low spur but the terrain allowed the construction of a wet moat. William's round keep of flint was then built on the edge of the sunken centre of a formidable earthen motte and the town of New Buckenham which developed 200 yards (183 m) away was a later

81. *Harrogate's new conference centre.*

82. The market house on the planned green at New Buckenham.

addition, perhaps a successor to whatever settlement may have existed atop the motte. Its origins are uncertain, but the market charter which was the legal prerequisite for urban growth was obtained in 1285.

The town was set out on open land according to a regular plan defined by a town ditch and consisting of a gridwork of streets which divided the site into rectangular development plots or '*insulae*' (islands), while the market square filled the space between the two parallel main streets. As with so many other feudal market foundations, New Buckenham failed either to grow or contract very much and so it remained penned in the marchlands between the rural village and the thriving market town. 'Forestallers' who traded outside the protected market caused problems but townlets with less attractive situations have been known to flourish and so one can only guess that New Buckenham simply failed to produce the entrepreneurs and ideas needed to put the motors of urban growth in gear. As a result, it is one of the most suitable testing grounds for the learner drivers of landscape history, displaying excellent examples of a planned medieval layout, subsequent encroachments of dwellings on the market area, a town ditch and many clear-cut if hideous adaptations of medieval buildings.

New Buckenham originated not because it had any particular natural advantages as a market town, but because it happened to lie close to a reasonable but unexceptional castle site. There were other towns that flaunted the human capacity for choosing sites and were unequivocally awful—several of them still flourish in defiance of the laws of geography and civil engineering. They include Yarmouth, which originated on unstable sand dunes; Salisbury, on flood-prone river meadows; Cambridge, on a patchwork of marshes and gravel islands; Edinburgh, whose medieval and post-medieval components were separated by a swampy loch, and King's Lynn, built on soggy estuarine lagoons.

The example of Salisbury is outstanding because it involved the desertion of one unsuitable site for another which was little better. The precursor of Salisbury was Old Sarum, an early borough situated inside and outside the oval ramparts of a truly phenomenal Iron Age hillfort. In the Roman period the town of *Sorbiodunum* was built near the hillfort at an important confluence of routeways, while Saxons subsequently recolonized and enhanced the Iron Age ramparts, establishing the important town of *Seares byrig*. Four years after the battle of Hastings, the Conqueror disbanded his army at Old Sarum and a royal castle was erected upon a massive motte sited at the centre of the ancient ramparts. The greatest boost to Old Sarum came in 1075, with the enactment that rural sees should be transferred to urban foci—one consequence being the transfer of the diocese of Sherborne and Ramsbury, held in plurality by Bishop Herman, to the hilltop town.

As a result, two headstrong communities, the royal castle garrison and the clerics attached to the new cathedral, were penned cheek by jowl and habit by hauberk within the cramped confines of the Iron Age ramparts, although part of the civil settlement and the canon's dwellings lay outside. In 1130, the bishop's authority over the garrison was superseded by that of the castellan and, soldiers not always being noted for their respect for civilian personages, it was not long before the churchmen were complaining of interference with their religious observances. Garrison and clergy competed for building sites, the wind blasted the chalk summit 'so that the clerks can hardly hear each other sing', while the churchmen came to realize why both the Roman and Saxon place-names referred to the 'dry fortress'. In 1217, Bishop Richard Poore petitioned the Pope for leave to relocate the cathedral.

The new city of Salisbury, which was established two miles from Old Sarum, was the product of these tribulations and it provides a superb example of the way in which the accidents of history can spawn a great city. With some discrimination, the bishop appealed to the abbess for a building site at Wilton, three miles to the south west of Old Sarum. But his request was refused and, as a result, he was forced to build upon lands of his own to the south east, in the uninviting floodplain of the Avon. And so, the

83. *The plan of the original cathedral outlined on the turf at Old Sarum.*

grid-planned cathedral centre which developed in the years after 1220 had exchanged a site which was glaringly deficient in water supplies for another, where water was embarrassingly abundant. The grid plan was not perfectly regular and it has recently been shown that streets were kinked to conform to the requirements of the street drainage pattern.

The combination of old roots, a bad site and the fortuitous accidents of history is repeated in the case of Cambridge. A Roman fort was established on a dry and locally commanding ridge overlooking the northern bank of the River Cam near Castle Hill, where several important routeways merged by a river crossing. Saxons were settled here before the collapse of Roman control, but at the end of the seventh century Bede records that Cambridge was a 'desolate little city'. Later it seems that a planned Danish trading centre was built across the river and St. Clement's church has a typical Danish dedication. In the late Saxon period there was a further revival and Domesday Book shows a respectable settlement consisting of ten wards and 373 dwellings. The Norman town lay around the chalk outcrop of Castle Hill, where twenty-seven dwellings were removed in the building of the castle mound, and it extended on to gravel terraces beside the river and to the sodden low-lying ground beside the river wharfes and inlets or 'hythes'. The market area which was to form the core of the modern town lay some distance from the main mass of the Norman town, and beyond the Danish component, on a drier island to the south of the river, separated from it by an expanse of uncolonized marsh. Running across these river marshes towards the castle and crossing was Bridge Street, which carried the roads from Colchester and from London from their convergence in the church-studded southern outlier of Cambridge to the ancient town nucleus north of the river and thence towards the fen towns of Huntingdon and St. Neots.

Subsequent growth emphasized the shift in the centre of gravity of Cambridge from the Roman and Saxon nucleus to the north of the river, to the university, church and

230

market complex to the south; it involved the development of the medieval town along the spine represented by Bridge Street and its southward extension along the Colchester road. It also involved the colonization of, and competition for tracts of marsh and river meadow. Of course, the main impetus resulted from the establishment of Cambridge as a centre for medieval learning. But just why Cambridge should have secured such a special niche remains largely mysterious. Certainly there was nothing in the geography or the history of Cambridge which signalled its destiny and we are surely meeting one of history's many accidents.

To its credit, Cambridge had a castle commanding a crossing on a bustling trading river, but on the debit side of its balance sheet inviting sites for urban expansion were singularly rare and so any objective early medieval assessment would have predicted an unspectacular future. The first college, Peterhouse, was founded by the Bishop of Ely in 1280, but the university had older roots for students are known to have been established in hostels throughout most of the thirteenth century and a migration of dissident scholars from Oxford was recorded in 1209. Perhaps the market provided the seedbed for the university; it was not mentioned in Domesday, but had surely existed in late Saxon times. An arc of Norman abbeys dotted the fenland to the north; monks will have frequently visited the market in Cambridge, while other monks and friars will have passed through the town, perhaps pausing to preach at one of the several churches near the market. Some must have lingered, gaining reputations as teachers, attracting small student flocks and encouraging other clerics to settle in Cambridge until the formal establishment of Peterhouse virtually ensured that other colleges would follow.

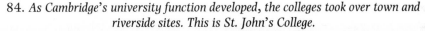

84. *As Cambridge's university function developed, the colleges took over town and riverside sites. This is St. John's College.*

85. *The market at Cambridge has probably been sited here since Norman times, although the Saxon market may have been elsewhere in the town.*

Even so, there were scores of other towns with markets, churches, and nearby abbeys and most of them had better facilities for expansion, while several had much stronger links with the myths and traditions of Christian scholarship. The establishment of new colleges in the fifteenth and sixteenth centuries resulted in colleges like Emmanuel and Pembroke following the lead of Peterhouse and exploiting peripheral gravel islands, colonizing unattractive sites beside the Bridge Street axis, as with St. John's or elbowing aside dwellings and commercial hythes and warehouses to exploit sites near to the river, as in the cases of Trinity, Clare, Gonville and King's. The encroachments of such colleges actually intensified a more complex decline in the town's population and when King's was built in the 1440s, houses and hostels, a church and important hythes were lost while a street was truncated. It was not until the Parliamentary Enclosure of the town fields in the early nineteenth century that well-drained building sites on gravel were released from agriculture for urban expansion. Thus one cannot help but think that, whatever the germinal reasons for Cambridge's academic stardom, almost any other medieval town would have offered a more convenient choice.

An exceptional blindness to the merits of terrain was also evident in the early development of King's Lynn. The pre-urban ancestry of the town can be traced to late Saxon village settlements, but in the 1090s, a new town equipped with a market was established on the banks of estuarine lagoons. It had two distinct and separate cores—Bishop's Lynn and South Lynn—which did not merge until the mid sixteenth century

232

and there were two markets. The first attempt at urban expansion occurred in the eleventh century and involved an exceptionally ill-chosen site at Bishop's Lynn. It was the second attempted expansion at South Lynn in the mid twelfth century which set the town in motion.

In the cases both of Cambridge and Lynn we have met examples of two-centred (bifocal?) towns and a shift in the centre of gravity from one nucleus to another. In the cases of several of the larger towns, urbanization around two or more cores and changes in the relative importance of the different nuclei can be discovered.

It is particularly well represented in the case of Aberdeen which now sprawls across the estuaries of the large northern rivers, the Dee and the Don. The medieval Royal Burgh and ecclesiastical town developed around the gorge and estuary of the Don, while the New Town and commercial port were sited more than a mile away, near the mouth of the Dee. Aberdeen graduates are wont to boast that the city had two universities at a time when only two universities existed in England. King's College was begun in Old Aberdeen in 1500, but because of a lingering affinity between King's, its patron the Earl of Huntly and the Catholic faith, a Protestant rival in the form of Marischal College was founded in the New Town in 1593. Post-medieval industrial development favoured the extensive harbour and its environs at the New Town and although suburban development has expanded the city northwards far beyond the Old Town, Old Aberdeen survives as an island with a distinctive medieval personality.

There are other towns still whose prospects and patterns of growth did not involve an oscillation of fortunes between internal urban cores, but were tied to the fortunes of other towns. Some of these towns have failed, and although one can usually find an objective cause for their decline, the psychology of desertion seems to be a crucial though neglected factor, for our examples have already shown that local talent and determination can outweigh the forces of misfortune and environmental hostility. During the Middle Ages the trading towns around the Humber estuary competed vigorously for their stakes in North Sea and coastal commerce. The twin Raven towns near Spurn Head—Ravenser and Ravenserodd—were making unwelcome inroads into Grimsby's trade, but in their case no amount of psychotherapy could have salvaged their prospects for they were obliterated by the sea in the fourteenth century. The twelfth-century planned port of Hedon had been competing with the Raven towns, and also with the royal port of Kingston-upon-Hull. However, in 1280 it was reported that taxes and the competition were inducing the tradesmen of Hedon to migrate to the 'two good ports increasing daily' (Hull and Ravenserodd). The problems were worsened by the silting of the River Hedon and although some of the population responded to adversity by relocating the nearby village of Paull to serve as a river mouth outport and Nature eliminated the challenge of the Raven towns, by the end of the Middle Ages Hull had emerged triumphant and the fossilization which preserves so many of the medieval features in the Hedon plan had begun.

Such examples remind us that, rather than being the predictable expressions of organic growth according to simple geographical formulae, towns are truly the wild cards of landscape history, embodying human whims and foibles, historical accidents, influences exerted by quite distant competitors and the unforetold consequences of environmental change. The relationship between towns could be symbiotic as well as competitive: the ancient lost town of Torksey served Lincoln as a river outport on the Trent, but when the new port of Boston at the mouth of the River Witham captured Lincoln's role as a staple market for wool, Lincoln's chill seems to have proved a terminal ailment for Torksey. We are left to ponder the psychology of failure as it affected Torksey; other towns have recovered from worse setbacks but Torksey does not even survive as a fossilized townlet like New Buckenham, Hedon or Thaxted but has vanished utterly, apart from a hamlet-sized fag-end of settlement which preserves little of the medieval layout of a once substantial town. There are also modern examples which show how quite distant forces can shape the destiny of settlement. Thus modern New Towns like Cumbernauld near Glasgow or Milton Keynes in Buckinghamshire and overspill towns like Thetford and Peterborough owe their modern roles not so much to local conditions as to national planning policies and the internal traumas of giant conurbations like Glasgow and London.

In all areas of landscape history one looks for valid generalizations. Where features like fields or roads or castles are concerned, they can often be found. In the cases of villages the generalizations are more difficult to detect although they are probably there to be discovered. In the case of the town however, quirkiness and unpredictability almost appear as the only general factors. The notion of the 'organic' town, spawned by a combination of geographical favours and developed by 'rational' human decisions is often assumed but then found threadbare. Towns are the creations of people and people do not tend to be particularly rational, except in subtle and convoluted ways. And so, a flourishing legacy of towns reminds us that human resolution, ingenuity and often bloody-mindedness can wring success from a tangle of bad choices and indifferent settings. Meanwhile, the accidents of history are ever lurking in the wings to divert the path to urban stardom along new and unexpected by-roads.

21

Towns through Time

We have seen the defiant individualism of the town, but it is still possible to recognize the existence of different sorts of towns at different periods in history. We have also said that towns have been taken for granted and so it is easy to overlook the most fundamental question: Why should there be towns? Towns are certainly not essential to communal defence, and while some older towns were created as forts or grew in the protective shadow of a citadel, in the age of a propertied democracy towns are liabilities because they have to be defended, or appear to be so—tasks fraught with costs and difficulties. Towns are not essential for sophisticated religious observances and indeed the European monastic tradition was partly born in Ireland, where the very absence of towns resulted in the development of the monastic alternative to diocesan Christianity. The town may, or may not be a prerequisite for advanced and comprehensive administration, but the example of the Early and Middle Saxon periods show that at least a rough and ready form of administration can be operated from rural estate centres and palaces.

The main role of the town is as a trading centre where buyers, sellers and manufacturers enact the detailed interplay essential to the operation of a reasonably sophisticated economy. The more active the trading and the more intricate the exchanges between suppliers, combiners and distributors of goods, the greater the need for bigger and better towns. Thus the town is a place of coming together, where the practitioners of inter-dependent activities can maximize the convenience of their contacts. However, once the urban idea has taken root, specialized types of ecclesiastical, defensive or administrative towns may develop within the general framework of economic urban activities.

The answer to the question of why the prehistoric societies of Britain failed to create fully-fledged towns may not be that the people were too 'primitive', but that towns were surplus to the requirements of societies whose economic activities operated at relatively modest and simple levels. The next question that one might ask is: How close did these societies come to creating genuine towns?

The answer is: Probably within two or three centuries. By the time of the Roman conquest, the indigenous peoples of Britain had created a number of extensive settlements or *oppida* which were town-like in their areas and populations, but which would fall below most conventional urban standards in terms of their layouts, buildings and coherence. The roots of these late pre-Roman Iron Age proto-towns extend more deeply; just how deeply, we cannot be sure, but the existence of several Bronze Age river trading ports with hundreds of inhabitants, bustling wharves and markets is, at least, a possibility—one has been discovered at Runnymede in Surrey.

Rather different urban prototypes are represented by the substantial Iron Age hillfort settlements of which numerous examples have been recognized in recent years. Depending upon the hillfort concerned, the settlements could be large, small or absent; temporary or semi-permanent; planned or jumbled and formless. A few, like Hod Hill in Dorset (see p. 147), or Tre'r Ceiri on the Lleyn Peninsula might be compared in size to respectable medieval market towns, although the functions of these lofty windswept hut agglomerations remains rather mysterious. As visitors to such places will know, the ascent can be short and sharp or positively exhausting and in order to enjoy the security and, perhaps, the prestige associated with hillfort life, much comfort and convenience will have been sacrificed. Having done our share of hillfort ascents we have a profound respect for the fitness and vigour of their ancient inhabitants.

The evidence from hillfort settlement excavations does not seem to show that the fort dwellers were a special élite or caste. The majority seem to have been peasants like the people of the plains and valleys below. Perhaps the most intriguing evidence comes in the form of the abundance of grain storage pits or raised timber granaries which are so commonly revealed. As we have said, they suggest that the hillfort proto-towns might have served in part as centres for the assembly and redistribution of the harvest—at least in the drier areas where arable farming was important. The settlements were quite probably also the capitals and sub-centres of tribal territories and an ability to marshal the system of food supply would have enhanced the power of the chiefs and the status of their centres of control.

Towards the end of the pre-Roman Iron Age, the power foci of several English tribal territories seems to have been centralized and relocated in sprawling defended lowland capitals. We know less about these *oppida* than we do about the hillfort settlements; a few are only known from their rampart outworks and others were replaced by Roman towns, but they certainly seem to have been varied, ranging from walled hill settlements like Traprain Law in the former county of East Lothian to complex political and manufacturing foci like Camulodunum near Colchester. If we can reconstruct a composite model of the typical *oppidum* from the limited English evidence, we envisage a sizeable but incoherent settlement, shielded by earthen ramparts and ditches which control its approaches. It contains the mint of the tribal chieftain producing a crude coinage and clusters of iron, pottery or other workshops. There are shanty agglomerations of huts which resemble those of the rural peasants and, set apart within one or more enclosures and surrounded by paddocks, the more imposing huts of the chief, his family and retainers. A large part of the complex might consist of a virtually rural estate, perhaps serving as a royal hunting park.

Such a settlement will have lacked the formality and sophistication of the typical Roman provincial centre and it is interesting to reflect that, although the chieftains must have had at least an inkling of knowledge of the towns which Roman imperialism had stamped upon the continental landscape, the towns which they sought to create were expressions of the indigenous culture and bore little if any resemblance to the Roman stereotypes. Although the *oppida* were several evolutionary stages removed from the refined and articulate cities of the Romans, there is no doubt that, had there been no Roman invasion, the *oppida* would have developed into coherent urban capitals.

The town and the road were the key physical expressions of Roman civilization—a civilization which adopted ideas from other cultures like a discerning magpie. Even so, the Romans had nothing to learn about town-making from the British and the only contribution of the *oppida* to Roman urbanization involved the reuse of proto-town sites or the choice of nearby successor sites. Thus, following the burning of its Roman *colonia* addition in the Boudicca revolt, Camulodunum was superseded by nearby Colchester; Silchester was superimposed upon the Artrebrate capital, and Dorchester accommodated natives resettled from the broken hillfort capital of Maiden Castle.

Where the Roman town was not a fairly direct successor to a nearby native capital, and sometimes where it was, the key factor in its siting generally involved military rather than trading considerations and towns frequently developed from or beside forts and camps. In lowland Britain, the scope and pace of the urban transformation was remarkable. Within a century of the conquest, a land which had boasted only a few loosely sprawling tribal capitals had become studded with towns and townlets of many types, a proportion of them being meticulously planned and a few were distinctly elegant and imposing.

Most schoolchildren can sketch a 'typical' Roman town plan, with its polygonal outline, originally undefended but later defined by earthworks, then walls and later by walls with artillery bastions; the four gates to the north, south, east and west which leave the walls through gateways which became increasingly monumental; the division of the urban interior into rectangular *insulae* by the geometrical gridwork of streets; the central *insula* which accommodates the *forum* with the market area as a square flanked on three sides by shops or offices and on the fourth by the town hall or *basillica*; other important public buildings such as the bath house complex and the *mansio* (an official hotel) occupying other *insulae*, while the theatre might stand within or outside the defended perimeter. Such towns had been developed and refined within the Classical heartlands, exported as the empire expanded and then transplanted to Britain without any special concessions to the island milieu. To the extent that the town of Roman Britain might differ from its equivalent in areas closer to the Mediterranean core of the Empire, the contrast might be reflected in the greater abundance of cheap building land in Britain which allowed a looser development of the *insula* building plots with more space available for ornamental gardens.

Imperialists generally tend to attempt to recreate a vision of the motherland in their colonies, exporting the beliefs, habits and structures which they cherish and superimposing them upon the peoples and landscapes of the captive setting. The Roman town performed many essential military, economic and administrative roles, but its political and psychological impact was also profound. The leading lights in British society can only have been staggered by the disciplined organization, monumental masonry and carefully-engineered heating, water distribution and sewage disposal systems displayed in the grander Roman towns. The elegance and studied debauchery of Roman town life were soon available to the native aristocrats and their Romanization must have transformed the outlooks and aspirations of the lower levels of native society, whose members had traditionally followed the lead of their nobles.

The classroom model of the Roman town is only acceptable so long as we remember that there were several other types of town in Roman Britain, while each town evolved through time. The effects of changing circumstances were apparent at the urban perimeters in the transition from the open town to ramparted, walled and bastioned modes. In part, these changes reflected the growing frequency and severity of barbarian attacks during the course of the Roman occupation, but they also expressed the value of a town wall as an urban status symbol, with the developing fashion for monumental gateways serving to announce the prestige of the centre to travellers and tradesmen as they arrived and departed. The town houses and shops which flanked the *insulae* also evolved as original timber buildings which tended to be replaced by ones of stone; shops amalgamated and the development islands became packed with dwellings, shops and workshops or gap-toothed and shabby according to fluctuations in urban fortunes.

The 'typical' town model applied to major administrative centres like Silchester or St. Alban's but was less appropriate where many of the lesser towns were concerned.

86. *Relics of the Roman town at Corbridge ; the view along a colonnade running along the end of the granaries of this supply base.*

These included the *coloniae*, which became numerous during the early post-conquest period as military towns established at the sites of conquest forts and camps and populated by time-elapsed soldiers. As the political climate mellowed, so several *coloniae*, like Lincoln and Gloucester, developed administrative and commercial roles and became more 'typical' in appearance, although in these two cases, the towns adopted the ramparts of the original forts.

As Imperial rule became entrenched and the new-found stability and organization of lowland England stimulated the development of trade, so there was a more organic or spontaneous expansion of roadside villages or military posts. Many such places acquired the massive walls which became the essential hallmarks of the Roman town, although within rambling unplanned layouts were often preserved. Hovering in the borderlands between true towns and villages were the roadside townlets or *vici*, a mixed bag of settlements with special commercial, military or administrative roles which elevated them above the ranks of the larger native villages. They ranged from places like

Kenchester in Herefordshire, with a twenty-two acre site defined by a lozenge of walls and with both refined and prosaic buildings beside its through-road, to unwalled and nondescript trading settlements.

Another category of settlement—recently recognized as a result of work at Neatham in Hampshire, Hacheston in Suffolk and a number of sites in Northamptonshire, such as Ashton—contains very large but jumbled settlements. Though more extensive than many of the 'typical' towns of Roman Britain, the places in this group lacked walls, paved streets, refined layouts and some had a mixture of stone and timber buildings, while others had only wooden huts. Perhaps they represent an indigenous response to the Roman idea of urbanization, but without the considered sophistications of Roman design and planning.

There were also towns which occupied specialized niches: ports of many sizes; discrete manufacturing settlements, and also, what might be regarded as loose industrial conurbations like the pottery-making complex of kilns, wharves, workshops and settlement clusters which punctuated the banks of the River Nene for a distance of ten miles westwards from Peterborough.

As we have said, the Romans had nothing to learn about town design from the people of Britain, but the gawky indigenous urban tradition did not entirely end when the evolution of the *oppida* was overtaken by the Roman conquest. Imperial rule imposed unprecedented levels of organization, integration and stability on a hitherto turbulent and fragmented land. All forms of production and trading benefitted, and as individuals and communities responded to the new opportunities, so native and Classical concepts merged in the creation of a varied array of townlets, shanty boom-towns and manufacturing complexes. Also, it is worth reflecting that while the conventional Roman town represented the epitome of town planning, many of the greater foci of Roman Britain were not sited according to the geographical rule book, but owed their situations to the accidents of history and might arise at the spots where a weary cohort dug the ramparts of a night encampment or where a fort was erected to control a stillborn threat of guerrilla advance.

We know much less about the towns of the Dark Ages. There has been much scholarly jousting between those who believe that urban life survived the epidemics, skirmishes and political chaos of the later fifth and sixth centuries and those who visualize a complete collapse of life in towns. As we now see it, the truth seems to be more complex and to lie within these extremes.

The evidence from Canterbury was at first thought to support the continuity thesis, for the traces of early Saxon 'grub huts' were found in the heart of the formerly Roman city. However, more recent excavations by the Canterbury Archaeological Trust have shown that there was a breakdown in the management of the town around 350, when the sewage system seized up and public and private baths were polluted. Early in the fifth century, there was a more serious collapse. For at least a century, Canterbury seems to have been deserted or, at best, to have degenerated into a squalid village, until the Saxon huts were built, probably in the second half of the sixth century. The decay of the city is evidenced by a black humus layer which seals the Roman remains and shows that the town had become field plots or even a wilderness. The picture which emerges from Cambridge, Carlisle, Chelmsford and Gloucester is not dissimilar, but at all these places the fifth-century occupation of the towns by people who lived in relatively crude timber huts was followed by a more complete abandonment. These towns were to be resettled later in the Saxon period and regain importance, while others like Silchester and Irchester were doomed. At Dorchester-on-Thames in Oxfordshire, however, a different picture emerges, and occupation in different forms persisted through the troubled centuries.

In very general terms it was the restoration of centralized control, and relative stability, allowing the re-establishment of commerce, which in turn allowed a partial urban revival in the late Saxon period. With towns, however, there are crucial exceptions to any rule, represented in this case by the royal establishment of a series of fortified settlements or *burhs* as the key components in Alfred's strategy to secure territory from Danish invasion and control. The military aspects of these *burhs* are discussed in Chapter 13, but it is important to note that several *burhs* swiftly gained economic activities to underwrite their survival.

Although it remains shrouded in mysteries, the urbanization of Saxon England involved much more than the establishment of *burhs* and the reoccupation of derelict and degenerate Roman centres. As ever when new evidence becomes available it tends to increase the complexity of the subject. This is demonstrated by recent work accomplished by the Archaeological Unit of the Northampton Development Corporation.

Societies of many different ages considered the locality an important one, as evidenced by the great Briar Hill causewayed enclosure of the Neolithic period, the Iron Age hillfort of Hunsbury and the Romano-British townlet at Duston, all grouped within a few square miles of countryside close to Northampton. It is possible that Duston was occupied throughout the transition from Roman to Saxon control and it seems that St. Peter's church in nearby Northampton was preceded by an early eighth-century minster. The bulk of modern Northampton lies to the east, and at this time the settlement may not have existed as a town but as the 'caput' or administrative centre of a large royal estate, with the minster being erected on royal land nearby. Perhaps significantly, the traces of a large timber building, possibly an important Dark Age hall are currently being explored beside the church. It was during the tenth and eleventh centuries that Northampton expanded as a notable commercial and administrative centre. The impetus may have come firstly from a planned defensive or commercial Danish settlement established around the pre-existing Saxon focus and the town expanded its trading and administrative functions during the centuries preceding 1086, when the Domesday Book reveals a town of some 300 houses. The Normans added a castle and expanded the administrative functions, with Northampton emerging as an important provincial focus.

It is now being recognized that a number of other Saxon towns originated as the non-urban caputs of estates and at royal palace sites. Tamworth in Staffordshire was preceded by a palace of King Offa of Mercia (757–96), while Winchester seems to have been a ruinous and largely deserted legacy of the Roman Empire when, about 650, a West Saxon king established a church there and shortly afterwards Winchester was both a royal residence and the focus of a diocese. However, it may only have emerged as a fully-fledged town in the late ninth century, under King Alfred, when the street patterns of a planned town were superimposed across the alignments of the buried Roman settlement. Similarly, a number of the contemporary *burhs* appear to have been directly preceded by royal administrative centres. Frequently, there are good reasons to suspect that these Saxon caputs were controlling estates which had previously existed as coherent administrative or tenurial divisions of the Roman landscape. And so, the continuity between Roman and Saxon England may not be found so much in the persistence of towns through the turbulent centuries of the Dark Ages as in the creation of towns around older Saxon caputs which were dominating essentially Roman land divisions.

So far as one can summarize the frugal evidence, it seems that following the collapse of Roman political control in the early years of the fifth century, the towns which were not already in decline entered a phase of contraction during which their Roman amenities decayed, while newcomers, who may have been Saxons, established their wooden dwellings in open or derelict spaces within the walls. A period of more complete abandonment followed, during which towns perished utterly or hibernated as unimposing villages. In the late ninth, tenth and eleventh centuries there was a gradual but sustained urban revival. As a result, by the time of the Norman Conquest England was generously sprinkled with flourishing towns, most of them small and with populations numbered only in hundreds, but some of them like London, York and Thetford were very substantial.

The outstanding characteristic, shared by virtually all these towns, was that of newness—for very few were really more than a couple of centuries old. They had a wide variety of origins: there will have been a tiny proportion of centres occupied continuously since Roman times; several more Roman towns which had been recolonized after centuries of decay; others, probably quite numerous, which had developed from older royal caputs, and some which may have grown organically or without individual direction or planning from successful villages. These organic towns, of which Thetford may be an example, will have been greatly outnumbered by the planned new towns of Saxon England. These in turn were numerous and diverse, including not only the *burhs*, but also other royal foundations and a number of towns which were created and laid out by churchmen. These include St. Albans and Bury St. Edmunds. At St. Albans, Abbot Wulsin realigned the old Roman Watling Street so that it passed the abbey gate, where a large triangular market place was created; tradesmen were bribed with free building materials to establish stalls and dwellings. Much more direct than the link with Roman *Verulamium* was the overlap with the small Saxon *burh* of Kingsbury, lying between the cathedral market nucleus and the decaying Roman town. At Bury, the Saxon monastery was abandoned and the relics of St. Edmund removed to London in 1010, in the face of Danish attacks. The town was founded in 1013 with a spacious market place and a gridwork of streets which remain striking features of the modern townscape. Most Saxon towns could therefore look back across their short histories to a powerful founder and a similar pattern of sponsorship persisted during the Middle Ages.

Before exploring the towns of the medieval period, we should turn briefly to the non-

241

towns and proto-towns of the Celtic North. The non-town category seems to include places which Dark Age writers had described by terms such as *civitas* or *caput regionis*, words which may roughly be translated as 'capital' and which later historians presumed to indicate towns. However, a recent exploration of a number of these places by Leslie Alcock, including Castle Rock, Dumbarton, the Scottic 'capital' of Dunadd and Pictish Dundurn, has suggested that the northern capitals were defended places belonging more to the ancestry of the medieval castle than that of the town. He believes that we should see these non-towns as defensive sites 'periodically visited, on circuit, by the ruler, his court and his war band; permanently occupied by a small garrison'. The

87. Lichfield, a comprehensively planned medieval town.

88. *The neat rectangular patterns of medieval planning are plainly evident in the streets of Rye.*

proto-towns are even more hypothetical, but there is a case to be argued for the Dark Age existence of substantial settlements rooted in the traditions of Iron Age *oppida*. The evidence for one example probably lay on the Burghead promontory on the Moray shore until the partial destruction of the site in 1808, when the proprietors constructed a planned fishing townlet which superseded an older fishing village.

In Ireland, the situation was different again. As a result of the glittering achievements of monastic Christianity, Ireland was unusual in emerging from the Dark Ages with its reputation for civilization greatly enhanced. But there were no indigenous towns. The first Irish towns were Norse Viking trading settlements like the impressive entrepôt of Dublin (fortified in 841), Limerick, Waterford and Wexford. Even so, towns did not become numerous until after the arrival of Anglo-Norman feudalism in the twelfth and thirteenth centuries, and while charters were liberally dished out and efforts made to attract merchants and artisans, many of the urban creations were artificial, stunted or stillborn.

89. *The medieval market cross and stocks at Ripley near Harrogate. Many hopeful villages were thwarted in their bids for urban stardom by the stagnation of their markets. Behind the early nineteenth-century mock Tudor cottages lies the medieval castle.*

Although the popular imagination tends to suffer a black-out where Dark Age towns are concerned there are popular stereotypes of the 'typical' Roman and medieval towns. The town of the Middle Ages is perceived as a raucous and smelly jungle of narrow twisting streets and the very antithesis of town-planning—a perception which probably derives from visits to fragments of medieval townscape surviving in the cores of large modern towns like York or the Old Town quarter of Edinburgh. The evidence which survives at Baldock, Caernarfon or New Buckenham, or most clearly at the stunted town of New Winchelsea although no less typical is quite different: it reveals comprehensively planned foundations. Raucous and smelly the medieval towns may have been, but the majority of them were deliberate creations and many were partly or wholly planned.

The centuries following the Norman Conquest witnessed an intensification of many of the processes which had created towns in late Saxon England. The winning of a market charter was the conventional prerequisite for urban growth, and as a result the location of medieval towns could be either the results of accidents or design. (Market charters did not make towns however, and it was the attainment of legal burgage tenure which promised membership of the élite urban club.)

244

The accidents mentioned might concern the coming to power or otherwise of a feudal lord with sufficient perspicacity, ambition or greed to recognize the potential revenues which might accrue from market tolls. And having obtained his charter, the lord might locate the market, 'accidentally', in a village which had no particular qualification as a trading centre. He might only control one village and in any event, the emergence of a market town usually owed much to the enterprise of the feudal lord, the disposition of his estates and at least a token effort to locate new markets away from existing competitors. But entrepreneurship was sometimes complemented by superior levels of insight and design. This seems to have been the case at Royston in Hertfordshire. The site, lying at the intersection of two major highways, was empty when a house of Augustinian Canons was founded there in the late twelfth century. The trading potential was swiftly recognized and in 1189 the prior won the right to a market and fair. A planned new town was the result and it grew rapidly, to the extent that the original road island market place became smothered in shops and a new triangular market was installed.

The growth of towns as a result of market creations was an established pattern in late Saxon England, but the defensive town or *burh* did not really have many equivalents in Norman England. There were, of course, many towns which flourished in the protective shadow of a feudal stronghold or even in the bailey of a castle, but the towns themselves were not defensive. Sometimes, the town, market and castle were components in a single package of feudal creation, while at others the creation and planning of a market town were supervised by the lord from his nearby keep. The hardbitten landscape historian will automatically expect and look for the traces of medieval planning in any town or village which slumbers beside a medieval castle. The planning may be blatantly obvious in a rectangular gridwork of streets—as at Castleton in Derbyshire, Castle Rising in Norfolk or Castle Hedingham in Essex—or more subtle— as at Clun in Shropshire where the idyllic old village around the church was complemented by a new planned town located across the river with its High Street and market place aligned towards the massive castle earthworks.

What then did the towns of medieval England look like? In many ways it is easier to generalize about the smaller and less-successful creations than about the urban super-stars, where clues may survive in street patterns but where detailed proof can only be obtained through excavation. Some of the medieval new towns were thoroughly and comprehensively planned according to the rather Romanesque model of a rectangular gridwork of streets; Hedon near Hull can be added to the various examples already given. Others, many of them the products of a more organic pattern of growth, had more of a resemblance to the village writ large. This is to say that they often consisted of dwellings aligned along each side of a through-road, with elongated ribbons of toft land extending back behind the dwellings to back-lanes which delimited the urban package. The most obvious differences from villages concerned size and the modifica-tions to the through-road, which might be broadened either gradually or suddenly to create a cigar-shaped, triangular or rectangular market place.

A fairly clear example of this sort of layout is preserved in Chipping Campden in Gloucestershire, although buildings have encroached upon the central area of the

90. *These industrial terraces at Skipton run back at right angles to the town's main street, filling the medieval closes of the street-side buildings.*

cigar-shaped market place to create an island of buildings. At Skipton in Yorkshire the simple medieval pattern has been partly masked by the effects of growth which followed the arrival of the Leeds and Liverpool Canal in 1774, but with a little poking and prying the old patterns emerge. The small agricultural village was singled out for future growth in the late eleventh century, when a Norman castle was built to serve as the caput of the extensive Honour of Skipton and was sited on a rock which overlooks the present settlement. A market developed at the head of the present High Street, between the castle and the church which was built nearby. As the medieval town developed, its form was governed by an 'H'-shaped layout of roads, with most of the development taking place on the flanks of the bar of the H, along the High Street which linked two parallel east-west routeways, the lower of which was the old Roman Road from Aldborough to Ribchester. The broad High Street, with the church and castle at its head and the Roman Road at its foot accommodated the medieval market. It still serves as a market place although it has slightly narrowed as the shop frontages have advanced while an island line of properties known as Middle Row in the lower part of High Street may also be encroachments. Perhaps most interesting are the alignments of terraced housing which have developed behind the shop frontages at right angles to the High Street, for each terrace represents an infilling of a long toft attached to a particular High Street property.

The larger medieval towns may always have been more complex. Recent work, notably in East Anglia, suggests that the 'polyfocal' concept developed by one of the authors in relation to villages, can also be applied to larger medieval towns. Some which seem to have originated as planned additions were grafted on to separate rural villages, the agglomerations of artificial developments and unplanned settlements later being embraced by medieval walls, while the urban core area might migrate from one component to another until more permanent building developments and the process of trial and error stabilized the pattern.

This stabilization of the basic town layout tended to occur before town maps became available at the end of the Middle Ages, and since only the main streets of towns tend to endure while lanes and courtyards are often truncated or built over, the earlier centuries of the development of large towns are generally only revealed by excavations. Work in East Anglia, notably in Norwich, shows that the more important dwellings did not tend to have their frontages aligned along the main streets, but were set back in lanes at the ends of the main streets, while the poorer dwellings tended to be set along the main streets, but later were built around yards.

Outer walls became a feature of most greater medieval towns. Often they were first built to encircle the loose agglomerations of settlements which combined to form these towns, and areas of open land might also be included. As the towns grew, however, the rigid corset of walls and the pattern of gateways admitting the main access roads could closely govern the form of the town. The Saxon *burhs* apart, the main period for the construction of town walls seems to have been the thirteenth century, although some walls and many gateways were earlier. As development spread over the legally-defined urban area, so extra-mural suburbs developed, often as roadside shanty towns for the poorer classes, but sometimes as prosperous neighbourhoods as at Redcliffe in Bristol.

Fragments of medieval town walls are now often conserved as symbols of civic pride; in medieval times, when each townsman had a responsibility to work on their maintenance, town walls were also symbols of civic prestige and status. Most walls were not primarily provided to defend the community as such, but to protect the trade and privileges which were its *raison d'être*. In this way, the walls served to define the area of the town; to control access through the limited provision of gateways where trading tolls could be collected, and to demarcate and protect the urban areas where residents enjoyed special privileges and immunities from the feudal lords outside.

As a town flourished, so the area within the walls became packed with dwellings and enterprises. Prestigious new developments cut across old side streets, gardens were sub-divided to provide new building plots and rows were demolished to create new trading areas. Eventually, new residential developments had to spill out to fill open spaces outside the walls, and in some cases salients or great new loops of walls or earthbanks were built to defend the extensions, as at Carmarthen where the eastern planned extension to the town was walled in 1415 to produce a two-fold increase in the urban area. More often, the challenge of embracing the growing suburban sprawl with new masonry or earthbanks was not accepted, and by the close of the Middle Ages most successful towns had outgrown their walls and these were often ill-maintained and furtively robbed for building stone. A flurried construction of perimeter earthworks was attempted in some places like Kings Lynn, Reading and Newark at the time of the Civil War, but town walls as such had long been outmoded.

At least over most of England, town walls were military in appearance rather than function, but they had an important political symbolism. They defined alien islands in a landscape which was otherwise dominated by the feudal powers of aristocratic landowners and as such, they marked the frontiers between the ultra-conservatism of

91. *A medieval town gate at Carmarthen.*

the countryside and the world of the ambitious entrepreneur. They also delimited a sanctuary where the peasant refugee could escape from bondage if he was lucky enough to become established as a townsman by residing uncaptured for a year and a day. Not surprisingly then, borough status was the ambition of every hopeful and successful urban community. Such status gave the burgesses the right to appoint a corporation which had control within the urban area, the freedom to collect and pay their own taxes to the Crown and the right to their own law court. Fortunately for the aspiring burgesses, the kings of England were usually hard up and the selling of charters was a prime means of raising revenue. Around 250 borough charters survive from the reigns of Richard I and John alone.

Outside England, the political importance of the town had other dimensions. In Scotland a succession of medieval kings attempted to rule a kingdom in which the effectiveness of central control tended to diminish with distance from the capital and proximity to the Highlands, where Celtic traditions and clan loyalties rivalled allegiance to the Crown. From the reign of Malcolm Ceannmor (1057–93) onwards, the medieval kings of Scotland attempted to exploit and export feudalism as a device for securing the homage and obedience of the provincial potentates. The export of towns became an important facet of the strategy of infeudation, introduced in the reign of David I (1124–53) when a number of Royal Burghs with extensive trading monopolies were established, some with alien communities of merchants and artisans. During this reign a union of four burghs—Edinburgh, Stirling, Roxburgh and Berwick-on-Tweed—was formed and these towns sent delegates to meetings at Haddington, where rules concerning trading, lay enforcement and justice were drawn up. These rules were often imitated in English towns, although the Scottish towns were slower in being able to purchase rights to collect their own taxes. Although the meanness of Aberdonians is enshrined in legend, it is worth noting that Aberdeen set the precedent for such rights in 1319 and paid £213, while Edinburgh managed to secure the privilege at the knock-down rate of £35 per annum. The Royal Burghs tended to be the larger and more prestigious places, while the Burghs of Barony which were created by provincial lords tended to be and often to remain quite small, although there were a few larger towns in this category, like Dunbar. The emaciated condition of many Burghs of Barony had more to do with policy than with geography, for the baronial towns had no trading rights beyond the urban bounds and their natural hinterlands were often monopolized by Royal Burghs. Thus the medieval growth of Glasgow, a Burgh of Barony created by the Bishop, was retarded by the trading monopoly exploited by the Royal Burgh of Rutherglen.

In Wales too, the medieval town was often a political instrument, but there it tended to be introduced by alien intruders and partly peopled by English merchants and tradesmen. Some of the earlier medieval towns were erected by independent Norman lords and their descendants. A Norman castle was established at Old Radnor in Powys and a village and church huddled in its shadow, but in the mid thirteenth century a fortified planned town was planted a couple of miles to the west. An old road became New Radnor's High Street, a substantial castle was built on the northern side of the road while the land to the south was divided by a grid of streets to form roughly rectangular development plots, while earthen ramparts looped out from the castle to defend the entire urban package. The main street was also New Radnor's market place, but the feudal innovations never really bore fruit and today some of the streets are marked only by hedges and field tracks.

The use of the castle-guarded town with an immigrant community of English burgesses by Edward I, in his subjugation of Wales, proved far more effective and purposeful, although the financial costs were astronomical. At places like Conwy and Caernarfon the walls which shielded the immigrants were truly defensive in function and at Caernarfon the town wall and ditch were built before the castle was begun. The burgesses of Flint had to rely upon an encircling ditch and earthbank, with the castle as

249

a final refuge; but all these Edwardian towns were precisely planned components of a coherent policy for the pacification of Wales.

Politics rather than geography guided the medieval fortunes of the Welsh towns. They were sited according to military rather than economic principles and adopted colonial trading practices, with the guilds of English merchants trading manufactured goods for countryside produce and monopolizing commerce. Welsh resentment of this monopoly fuelled the Glendower uprising of the fifteenth century. Contrary to normal experience, the Edwardian towns tended to decline in the stable conditions which followed the Union of 1536. The fortresses became redundant while the artificial economic advantages which the burgesses had enjoyed through their trading monopolies were withdrawn and Welsh tradesmen, operating from other centres, emerged as successful competitors.

In Ireland, where Anglo-Norman feudal lords had created a shoal of hopeful feudal townlets which were blessed with generous trading privileges, the conditions were similar, with politics guiding the destinies of the rural boroughs. These castle-guarded places had played important roles in earlier attempts to pacify Ireland and consolidate English interests. After the Elizabethan reconquest of Ireland, the castle garrisons were no longer needed and the rights which grateful English monarchs had bestowed upon the towns and townlets were resented. As English policy eroded the independent status of these places, with revisions of charters and curtailments of municipal rights and liberties, so the boroughs tended to decline. They had been created to buttress feudalism and many were unable to survive the decay of feudal practices. In many an Irish field, a castle mound and a ruined church stand among the overgrown holloways of a failed townlet, epitaphs to the artificiality of the town-making process.

In the course of the Middle Ages there was a fairly steady increase in the numbers of English towns and the majority of towns experienced considerable but unspectacular growth. Less than fifty boroughs existed in 1086 while there were more than a hundred of them by the thirteenth century. Estimates of population for periods before the nineteenth century are notoriously difficult to calculate, but at the close of the Middle Ages, during the reign of Henry VIII, the population of England may have been around four and a half million. By this time London had emerged as a dominating metropolis, with a population perhaps as high as 300,000 and greater than that of the whole of Wales. Towns in the next rank were far smaller and in order of size they were probably Norwich, Bristol, (Edinburgh), Newcastle, York, Exeter and Gloucester, with populations ranging from around 15,000 to 8,000.

By the Tudor period the elevation of villages into the urban ranks and the creation of a large flock of planned new towns had virtually completed the distribution pattern of provincial market centres and the dynamic for new town creation was lost until the headlong rush into urbanization which followed the Industrial Revolution—except in Ireland where many colonial plantation towns were created in the late sixteenth and seventeenth centuries. Created both by official policy and by landlords, these towns were planned according to the simple themes of the High Street and market square, and as in medieval Wales they were political creations with 'safe' and substantially alien populations.

Only one Englishman in every eight or ten would have been a townsman at the end of the Middle Ages. It was only around the middle of the nineteenth century that the population balance began to tip on the urban side. The last 130 years have witnessed an almost incredible urban transformation of the landscape creating a population which is eighty per cent urban and only in very recent years has a slight drift towards commuting from rural homes begun to affect the balance.

The urbanization of the last century or so has been like a maelstrom, sucking in countryfolk and immigrants and so, given its revolutionary impact on the landscape and society, it is easy to forget that some seventeenth and eighteenth-century commentators regarded the urbanization of their times as startling and unprecedented. One feature of the accelerating growth of towns was the expansion of working-class slum quarters. Meanwhile, at the other end of the social scale, the decay of feudalism and the rise of capitalism tended to make the fortunes of a town even more dependent upon the ambitions, drive and idiosyncracies of the native entrepreneur. In some quite large towns, prosperity and growth depended upon the decisions of a small handful of merchant, manufacturing or retailing families, while several smaller towns were entirely dependent upon a single commercial dynasty.

The seventeenth and eighteenth centuries witnessed a revival of interest in the Classical world and the fashionable quest to create orderly symmetrical landscapes, which we described in relation to houses and gardens, also conditioned the urban visions. However, since medieval enterprise had filled most of the urban niches in the landscape, few new towns were created and the Neo-Classical planned developments tended to consist of extensions or insertions affecting existing towns. Three decades before the Great Fire of London of 1666, Inigo Jones had been employed to mastermind the redevelopment of Covent Garden as a fashionable residential area, but this and other mid-seventeenth century schemes were dwarfed by the sweeping pageant of rebuilding which Christopher Wren created on the charred canvas of the city. Much of the outline is preserved in the modern street plan, but the rebuilt city was a considerable departure from Wren's original vision. This had included juxtapositions of spider's web and grid-iron street plans, parks and open spaces and avenues aimed on distant churches which were provided as much as eyecatchers as for religious purposes. Most of the medieval street pattern survived the changes, although new regulations and fashions produced a gracious Baroque townscape of imposing brick and stone buildings punctuated by elegant white churches.

The changes which fashion and necessity wrought at Edinburgh are much more impressive. The medieval city, lying to the south of the quagmires and waters of the Nor Loch, was a jumble of both imposing and squalid buildings, lanes and market streets grouped beside the Land Market and Canon Gate streets which ran from the castle gates eastwards to the Abbey. The growth of the city was restricted by a corset of bogs, lake and crag, but after eighty-nine years of vacillation a proposal to leapfrog the Nor Loch (bridged in 1763) and build a modern extension to the city on good ground to its north was put into effect in 1770. James Craig designed a dignified but exciting New Town with a basic grid-iron plan of broad avenues which was diversified by the inclusion of open spaces and circular circuses. Although speculative developers marred the integrity of the plans, the New Town was built as a coherent unit, and this resulted in problems when the success of the venture produced a need for expansion; but plans by Robert Reid in 1804 and William Playfair in 1814 successfully extended the New Town northwards and eastwards respectively. Early nineteenth-century Edinburgh thus consisted of distinctive medieval and modern components which were separated by the former marshes of the Nor Loch. The drainage of this trough had provided an open channel allowing the railway to enter the heart of the city where it still marks the divide between two completely different but attractive townscapes.

Elsewhere, the impact of Georgian and Regency notions of town planning are encapsulated in the urban landscapes of the fashionable and rapidly expanded spa towns like Bath, Cheltenham and Leamington. Popular planning motifs included the crescent, the square, the circular or oval circus and the rectangular gridwork of broad avenues and streets. All these elements are magnificently displayed in the early eighteenth-century spa developments in Bath; the West End of London still displays a series of gracious squares; Wisbech has an unusual form of circus which is formed of two linked crescents embracing an oval area which was the old castle site, while both Brighton and Hove display elegant compilations of squares and crescents.

Such imposing creations were associated with upper and middle-class residential developments, but meanwhile, although some unfortunate centres like the old port of Porlock or the failed market town of Stogursey, both in Somerset, were in decline, most towns were expanding in time with a quickening commercial heartbeat. A few new towns were built, such as the river port of Stourport, while elsewhere local industrial enterprises produced towns from villages and established towns advanced far beyond their medieval confines. Much of this growth produced landscapes completely different from the planned splendour of the large scale residential developments in Edinburgh or Bath, with squalid slum buildings packing medieval lanes, yards and gardens or processions of discordant buildings straggling outwards along the roads serving old market centres.

No reconnaissance of the eighteenth-century landscape of Britain could be complete without a journey to the north east of Scotland. Here, the construction of a multitude of neatly planned townlets and hopeful villages was part of a campaign of improvements accomplished by enterprising landlords and aristocrats who realized that the English victory at Culloden in 1746 signalled a complete break with old traditions. While the ghastly Clearances were being enacted in the Highlands, in the north east the emphasis was upon a reorganization of the countryside. Many tenants were evicted from the scores of small and squalid agricultural 'fermtouns', but the hard-nosed attitudes of the landlords were often accompanied by extremes of optimism. Thus, as drainage, enclosure, new methods of husbandry and the reorganization of tenancies transformed the countryside, the landscape became stippled with new settlements which were provided to improve the living conditions of the remaining tenants and, hopefully, to provide industrial alternatives to the drudgery of life in a still overpopulated country-side.

Because Neo-Classical ideals of a formal geometrically-organized landscape were fashionable, and also because grid-plan layouts could easily be extended in the event of success and growth, simple formats based on straight roads, squares or rectangular greens and right-angled intersections were almost universal. Such disciplined layouts can be seen at the new fishing village at Burghead; Lord Findlater's New Keith of 1750; Cuminestown, where the improving landlord Cumine of Auchry tried to establish a cottage linen industry, and more pathetically at New Leeds where the village of 1787 had failed to fill its original street grid. Frequently swathed in sea mists and with stones, skies and seas so often grey, the north east needs some splashes of colour. Sadly, the stereotyped severity of the eighteenth-century village and townlet architecture adds to the dourness of the scene, redolent though it is of the brave new visions of the eighteenth century.

At the beginning of Victoria's reign the population of the United Kingdom was twenty-six million; by the time of her death it was forty-two million. In 1851 the ratio of town to country dwellers was almost even, but by 1901 three people in four were townsfolk and in the course of the preceding century about eighty towns had grown to exceed the 50,000 population mark. In the landscape this phenomenal growth was expressed in vast acreages of urban sprawl which spread uncontrollably, like ink across the blotting paper of rural Britain. For many of the people who had been sucked into the urban maelstrom, the houses and amenities available were deplorable: in 1840 Liverpool alone included about 30,000 cellar-dwellers in its population. By 1889, Liverpool—by this time regarded as the world's richest city—had 1,200,000, equal to one third of its citizens, earning insufficient wages to support a tolerable standard of nutrition, clothing and shelter. Even so, millions of destitute countryfolk regarded the town as a sanctuary from rural deprivation.

The credit and the blame for these almost incredible developments lie largely with industrialization. Much of the early action in the Industrial Revolution was enacted at remote manufacturing sites which were tied to water-power supplies and devoid of the suitable level building sites and communications essential to urban growth, while a high proportion of production flowed from dispersed cottage-based industries. Two developments in particular allowed the Industrial Revolution to release its latent potential for urbanization. These were the improvements in the design of steam engines, which allowed industry to migrate from the water-power sources to urban factories, often in new coalfield towns; secondly, the successful application of steam power to the railway. Although urban expansion had taken place at unprecedented levels in the first half of the nineteenth century, it was the arrival of the railway that could be expected to put the motors of urban growth into overdrive.

The Industrial Revolution is generally said to have started around 1760. As the waves of industrialization rolled across Britain, quite different types of urban landscapes were produced according to the stage of development reached and the character of the pre-Industrial landscape. This can clearly be seen in a short stretch of the Calder Valley between Heptonstall and Halifax. Heptonstall preserves its appearance of a pre-Revolutionary industrial village, with the short rows of weavers' cottages interspersed with old farmsteads and grouped tightly around the now ruined medieval church and village cloth hall. It perches on a lofty knoll overlooking the valley. The relics of the old cottage-based hand-weaving industry survive as a result of changes in the technology of textile manufacturing. With the development of the water-frame spinning machine in 1769 and the carding machine in 1775, manufacturing processes drifted first to small mills which drew their power from nearby streams, and then to larger mills established by the main river where fulling mills had long existed. Then weaving itself migrated to new mills sited beside navigable waterways among the carding, spinning and fulling plants.

This phase in the industrial cycle gave rise to the mean congested industrial landscapes which are popularly associated with the Revolution. From Heptonstall one can look down on Hebden Bridge, where the mills jostled for riverside sites and the first generations of factory workers were crammed in tall terraced blocks which snake and teeter on the steep surrounding slopes. Such pairings of old and newer industrial settlements are quite frequent in Pennine manufacturing areas, with Baildon being superseded by Baildon Bridge and Sowerby passing the industrial baton to Sowerby Bridge below. Although Hebden Bridge survives as a microcosm of unplanned nineteenth-century urban chaos, the town was not destined for spectacular growth: to see a landscape of rampant industrialization one must travel a little further down the valley to Halifax.

Halifax had emerged as a prominent centre of the textile industry by the sixteenth century, with corn, wool and cloth markets. Corn mills and fulling mills were established along a stretch of the Hebble Brook running from the old town centre to the confluence with the Calder. The introduction of steam power in the years around and after 1800 saw the establishment of large numbers of worsted mills along the Brook. The stream became flanked by a chaotic succession of mills as industrialists competed for footholds on its shores. The rapidly expanding urban landscape was equally undisciplined, with terraces of industrial housing being crammed into such spaces as were available until, in the 1860s, the scope for infilling was exhausted and the town burst through its old boundaries. Halifax expanded westwards, the eastern slopes of the Hebble valley being too steep for building even in this age of rampant and unchecked urbanization. In the ten years following the Census of 1861 the population of Halifax grew from 37,000 to 65,000.

Largely unplanned jungles of speculative industrial and residential development like Halifax bred pollution and deprivation, but they were also the seedbeds for a remarkably gutsy form of civic pride which, with the backing of local patrons, often produced the redevelopment of parts of the urban core for prestigious building works. In Halifax this mood is expressed in the Town Hall of 1860–2 and the Borough Market of 1892. In Birmingham the impact of civic pride on the tangled industrial landscape was much more profound, with the enormously influential Chamberlain family spearheading the Corporation Street plan and driving an imposing new avenue of shops and municipal buildings across a wasteland of slum housing between 1878 and 1882.

Although late nineteenth-century civic pride and local patronage often achieved a remodelling of parts of a congested town centre, more sweeping assaults upon the inner acreages of worn-out housing and backyard industries were generally postponed. Despite the vast scale of nineteenth-century urbanization, each conurbation tended to grow as a mosaic of small and piecemeal speculative developments. As a result, small pockets of land became engulfed in the urban sprawl as and when they became available. Thus, in the case of Leeds Professor M. W. Beresford has shown that when old open field land was released for sale following the Enclosure of lands on the town margins, the new terrace and factory patterns reflected the outlines of the fields in which they had been built. A medieval 'reversed S' field boundary survived when the geometrical Enclosure network of new fields was superimposed across most of the farmland, and it continued to endure through the urban development emerging as a slightly curving lane between houses fronting on Oxford Road and others lining Cambridge Road.

Not all the nineteenth-century industrial towns danced to the discordant tunes of unchecked private capitalism. A short journey across the watershed which overlooks the industrial chaos of Halifax will take one to Saltaire. This living monument is, in its way, as visitworthy as Stonehenge or any castle or mansion. The village was founded in 1850 by the industrialist Sir Titus Salt who was guided by benevolent visions of an industrial community quite different from those which suffered in Halifax or Bradford. Saltaire was not only meticulously planned according to the time-honoured grid-iron principle; it was also titivated with Italianate trimmings, subtly stated in the terraced houses, more obvious in the almshouses and massive textile factory and boldly flourished in the church and numerous public buildings.

The mill at Saltaire is still operating and the townlet provides us with a winsome and coherent image of industrial landscapes as they might have been had the entrepreneurs been more concerned to blend ambition with humanity. Saltaire appeared at a late stage in the Industrial Revolution as a reaction against the hardship and chaos that it had produced. But there were other alternative industrial prototypes, like Gatehouse of Fleet in the former county of Kircudbright, whose industrial development in the decades around 1800 was masterminded by enlightened landlords of the Murray of Cally family, or Morriston near Swansea. Morriston was the creation of a metal master, John Morris, and was built in 1790–6. As at Gatehouse of Fleet, a simple grid plan was adopted, but here the streets enclosed an area which was divided into plots on which the industrial workers could raise vegetables and graze a cow. Sadly, places like Saltaire and Morriston were the exceptions in the landscapes of nineteenth-century urbanization, and so we are left to pick up the pieces.

The modern town is, in part, an attempt to avoid the worst consequences of unplanned development through the imposition of regulations concerning sanitation, house construction and land use. While the worst excesses of unbridled entrepreneurship are generally avoided in the modern developments, many deprived and squalid areas cry vainly for redevelopment and hundreds of thousands of people await housing or rehousing. At the same time, the twentieth century has produced problems of its own, as the civilizing influence of the railway has been superseded by the tyranny of the motor car and lorry. Many a fine old city centre and elegant suburb has been sacrificed on the altar of the internal combustion engine. And many a dimwitted corporation has surrendered its heritage of historic municipal buildings for the baubles of redevelopment offered by development companies and their attendant fad-merchants. Old and noble towns are beginning to look depressingly alike.

92. *Almshouses at Saltaire near Bingley where the town is the creation of the Victorian industrialist, Sir Titus Salt.*

Modern towns have several distinctive facets, but the outstanding feature of twentieth-century urbanization is the residential suburb. The influence of the speculative builder, who has expanded the town outwards across the surrounding countryside through its accretion of little suburban developments or has grafted housing estates on to the edges of villages until they have become dormitory towns, or have merged their growth with that of a nearby town, has been profound. So profound, that the majority of our readers are probably residing in spec-built suburban estates. It is easy to mock the supposed banality of such places, but theirs are the characteristic landscapes of our age. Suburban readers who are keen to explore landscape history have no need to focus their attention on some idyllic and distant village, for the story of the suburb is one of the most neglected areas in the field of landscape study. Every suburb has been superimposed on an area of old countryside and it is often the case that more evidence of the features and layout of the old landscape will be preserved in the street names, property and housing-estate boundaries and lanes of the suburb than survives in the surrounding agricultural wastelands of modern farming. Also, since most suburbs have appeared in the last century or so, the different chapters in their history are recorded in successive maps, building accounts and municipal records and the relevant information is much more plentiful and accessible than the terse documents which relate to medieval village history. Jack Ravensdale's recovery of the history of Ealing provides a fascinating guide and example.

One can easily be dazzled by the modernity of recent town developments, but the study of urban history seems to tell us that nothing is new while nothing is ever exactly duplicated. The Peterlees and Cumbernaulds of our time have their equivalents in the planned new towns of the Roman, Dark Age and medieval eras; medieval people knew all about the problems of inner-city decay, constricting town boundaries and unbridled suburban sprawl, while each urban age has produced both precisely planned model settlements and the rambling products of piecemeal and spontaneous growth. Even so, each town has had its own distinctive individuality, its own reason for being and a destiny shaped by the ambitions, initiatives and foibles of home-grown entrepreneurs and administrators.

Even today, when urban development is guided by an essential framework of planning controls and when one city centre after another surrenders to the stereotyped anonymity of the Development Plan, we can predict that the towns of the future will be the products of historical accidents, quirky decisions and dynamic individuals. The

93. Industrial expansion at Skipton, where the rows of terraced houses advanced towards the surrounding moors.

modern New Towns might seem to epitomize the era of meticulous planning and objective decision-making, yet P. H. Levin has shown that several are the result of the inflexibility in human attitudes which resulted from an over-commitment to narrow courses of action at an early stage in the planning process. Many of the decision-makers had staked their reputations, pride and loyalties on particular policies and would not accept the loss of face and credibility which would have been incurred by a major change of plan. And so it seems that Man the Town-Maker is alive and well.

Reflections

If history could begin again, we wonder how often the town-makers would be drawn to the same sites which support towns today? The settings of places like London, Dublin or Plymouth would surely prove irresistibly attractive, but many other features of the urban pattern would probably not be replicated. So often the towns of Britain were born in the minds of local landlords, entrepreneurs and visionaries and then sustained by subsequent generations of townsfolk who resourcefully explored new avenues of opportunity once the original attractions had been exhausted. The logic of the economic or terrain endowment often had little say in the matter or else served only to cast obstacles in the path of human resolve.

Because towns are important and relatively recent features of the British landscape, their histories tend to be tolerably well documented. And so it is possible to catch glimpses of the individuals whose visions became manifest in the form of a brave new town. But thrusting individualism which ploughs a path through all the barriers of logic and natural disadvantage is surely much older than recorded history. And so we are left to wonder how many of the remarkable prehistoric monuments like Silbury Hill, the Ring of Brodgar or Maes Howe are also monuments to the quirky ambitions of a powerful and single-minded visionary?

While so many towns had their beginnings in a market charter won by an ambitious landowner, and then expanded as the burgesses obtained the coveted borough status, thereafter the urban history could advance in a host of possible directions. Individual initiatives, historical accidents and civic pride and ambitions combined with local building traditions to produce a wonderful legacy of varied and personable local or regional centres, the stages in their growth subtly marked in the townscape by road alignments, property boundaries and street names. But so often, the results of the last two or three decades of 'progress' have been the erasure of all the features which gave a town its character and the superimposition of a concrete superstructure of bland, tacky and anonymous redevelopment. The same classes of civic leaders which had once served the town so well with their visions and initiatives can now often see no further than the unworkable fantasy worlds modelled in cardboard and plywood by the development corporations.

PART VI

Visions of Home

Introduction

> As each new work proceeds, the newspapers and magazines are furnished
> with commendatory notices by *dilettanti* of a literary turn, who indicate, in
> scholarly detail, and with a tone of wondering admiration, what they call
> the merits of the architect's design. The public listen vaguely, and accept. Of
> building art they have no practical or sympathetic knowledge; and, though
> architecture in abundant ugliness surrounds them, and in absurd unfitness
> harasses their lives, they rest content with, and are possibly a little proud of,
> their sad ignorance.

These words flowed from the waspish pen of John T. Emmett in 1881, but might they
not be applied to modern attitudes to buildings? He described a public afflicted by the
latest architectural creations yet rather mystified by the architectural pronouncements
of the self-appointed arbiters of taste. When perceived from the perspective of Fine Art,
houses can be rather confusing and formidable subjects. Their parts and portions are
festooned with fancy names like 'squinch' and 'soffit', 'triglyphs' and 'trumeau'. At the
same time, one is instructed that certain pieces of architecture are 'important' or
'commendable' while others are 'deplorable' or 'gauche'—and it is not always easy to
see why. A measure of expert comment can be quite helpful, but the reader or listener is
seldom reminded that liking what you like, for no other reason than because you like it,
is quite OK.

Here we offer a rather unfamiliar approach to houses, for we explore the house in its
most important role: as a home. All our readers will be familiar with at least one home,
its layout, suitability and influence on domestic life and so we hope that all those who
are alienated or mystified by the more general approach to buildings may be able to find
some interest and many points of contact with the house, when it is presented as a
home.

'House' is a rather neutral word which is redolent of bricks and mortar, walls, roofs
and windows, but little more. 'Home', in contrast, is one of the most emotive words in
the English language, for it conveys a sense of security, territory, family, domesticity
and probably many other connotations which psychologists are wont to explore. As a
physical structure of compartments, boards and bricks, the house itself probably plays
second, third or fourth fiddle in most people's perception of home. But, of course, houses
are homes, and when we peel away the external architectural trappings we find that the
main stages in the development of the house were not accomplished to please or obey
architects, but to harmonize with the changing patterns of domestic life.

A place where offspring can be produced and protected is a basic requirement of most
creatures. Thus almost from the beginning of man's existence in Britain, he has sought
a home to shelter his family and serve as a base from which to undertake his various
economic activities. Over the millennia the perception of home has changed

considerably, partly as a result of technological advances, but more particularly because of social developments and changes.

From the outset of human history in Britain the home has been a physical expression of family, social conditions and norms. In this chapter we are concerned with the setting built for domestic life and when we look at homes we see great differences through time and space. They are not just the results of advancing technology, changing building materials, or architectural fashions—important though these may be.

There are other factors which have also played key parts. The 'look' of a house is the result of a number of major factors: the first concerns the availability of building materials, which may be wood, stone, mud, brick, concrete and so on. These controls may be simple—for example, there may be stone close by but no trees—or they may involve complex and changing economic factors such as the relative cost of imported brick versus local stone. Such economic factors may operate at different levels depending on whether the builder is concerned with the erection of a hundred houses for profit, or is an aspiring do-it-yourself home-maker.

The second major factor is the technology available to a given society. This might involve the ability to shape stone, produce bricks or mix concrete or, at a more complex level, the existence or otherwise of an industrial base which can provide steel girders or produce millions of bricks. There are also the obvious related economic considerations, particularly the cost of building in relation to the purse of the would-be home owner.

The third factor concerns the organization of contemporary society. Here we would consider the existence of a middle class and the power and political strength of the ruling classes, for class values and capabilities will certainly influence the type of house to be constructed. Social norms, perceptions and attitudes set standards which generally determine the form and nature of 'home'. Thus a society which is conditioned by a belief in extended families with wives, husbands, children, grandparents, cousins, aunts and uncles all living together, will visualize very different houses from one which sees wife, husband and two children as the 'ideal' unit.

The organization of the family group is also important: does the family want to carry out all its activities together or does it expect rooms adapted for special functions such as for eating, food preparation, sleeping and recreation? Another factor is the collective or individual nature of the fashionable status! Do people want to have homes that all look alike, or all look different? Do they wish to flaunt or mask their wealth or status? Do they wish to 'keep up with the Joneses' or are they content to live as their ancestors did? Are new ideas about materials, construction, technology, or architectural design able to move swiftly through contemporary society or filter more slowly?

All these functions—and many more—influence what houses looked like in the past and how they appear today. Perhaps the most important aspect of houses is that they have never remained the same, even though their basic structures may stay unaltered. In the course of work, one is constantly being asked: How old is my house? The questioner may be told 'It is sixteenth century in origin.' This is always regarded as much more satisfying and interesting than if he is told 'It is eighteenth century in date.' This antiquarian attitude seems to deflect from the whole interest of houses as homes.

One can understand far more about the history of man by studying a crude nineteenth-century cottage which has been constantly changed by its successive occupants than by examining a magnificent sixteenth-century house which has hardly been altered at all.

In these chapters then we shall not set our sights on the features that interest some owners or students of houses: details of peg-holes and trusses, ingle-nooks and chamfered beams are not our concern. Home is a total concept and our interest is to see the overall development of houses as homes and how man's ideal of a home has changed over the ages.

22

Prehistoric, Roman and Dark Age Houses

The earliest homes that we have any knowledge of in Britain were caves. Upper Palaeolithic man, who lived in this country between around 12,000 and about 8000 BC, certainly lived in caves at times—although he probably lived elsewhere as well. Caves were well suited to the contemporary way of life: not only providing convenient shelter, but also being usually spacious enough for the large family groups that almost certainly existed then.

But caves are merely natural features rather than human creations. It is not until the Mesolithic period between about 8000 and 5000 BC that man-made structures appeared in Britain—at least in forms that modern archaeologists can recognize. The excavated remains of these houses seem very primitive and insubstantial, and if we are not careful we may fall into the trap of believing that their builders and occupiers were also primitive simple people, living on the verge of starvation for most of their lives. It is true that the remains of the dwellings of this remote period are hardly impressive. In some cases only the small depressions where a semi-circle of thin branches or stakes were once driven into the ground have been discovered, associated with traces of a hearth and flint-tool fragments. Sometimes there is even less to discover: perhaps just a circle of stones lying near a hearth and tool fragments, or a crescentic scoop in the ground.

These remains have been interpreted, probably correctly, as the sites of tents or wigwam-like structures made of branches and hides. Yet because the traces are slight and living in tents seems somewhat primitive, we must not assume that the standard of living was pitiful or that the occupants starved or froze to death. Temporary, or rather portable hide structures can be extremely comfortable and warm and also elaborately decorated, as the wigwams of American Indians indicate. More important, these structures were admirably suited to the Mesolithic lifestyle for the people were hunters and gatherers. They followed herds of migratory animals from lowland to upland. They progressed up the river valleys living on fish, combed the forest for seasonal berries and nuts and trapped small animals. Thus lightly-built and easily-transportable tents were the most appropriate form of house for such nomads. Some of these temporary structures were quite large: members of a group discovered at Mount Sandel in Northern Ireland were seventeen feet in diameter covering an area much larger than most modern living-rooms. A small hunting group could have lived very comfortably within one.

There is no doubt that when it was necessary or desirable to build more substantial dwellings, Mesolithic people were quite capable of doing so. Excavations at Braishfield near Romsey in Hampshire have uncovered a group of roughly circular huts, each around fifteen feet in diameter, with vertical walls supported by stout earthfast posts. Such houses were either the winter quarters of a large family group or components of a permanent centre where elderly folk and infants might have lived throughout the year while other members of the group were away hunting and living in tents. Thus the evidence of Mesolithic houses does not show that their occupants were truly backward or primitive: they had dwellings that were well suited to their way of life.

Around 5000 BC Mesolithic people were either submerged by immigrants or adopted different lifestyles. Whichever of these alternatives occurred—archaeologists still argue which—there were radical changes in the nature of British life. Folk began to make pottery, to till the fields, to use domestic animals and, as we have seen, to construct elaborate tombs for their dead and huge 'temples' for their gods. Their tombs and temples prove that they had the ability to use stone and timber to build complex structures. Indeed, it has been suggested that the massive timber 'mortuary houses' found buried under long barrows, the great circles of timber posts found at the 'temples' of Durrington Walls, Marden and Woodhenge, all in Wiltshire, and at Mount Pleasant near Dorchester in Dorset, as well as the contemporary stone-chambered tombs, were at least partly inspired by existing houses.

The more sedentary life of the Neolithic peasant who was anchored to his fields meant that houses too had to be more durable and certainly more substantial than most of those of the Mesolithic period.

A major problem is associated with the recovery of evidence: where timber was easily available, as in most parts of Neolithic Britain, it was usual to build houses of wood. Simple wooden structures inevitably had short lives of perhaps no more than twenty-five years before they had to be replaced. Further, the traces that such structures may leave are minimal so that even the most skilful archaeologists will rarely find more than the holes which held the upright timbers of the walls; central post-holes to support the roof if the building was large; gullies cut below the eaves for drainage; doorways and hearths. Nothing usually survives to indicate the internal arrangements of the houses nor, except on rare occasions, the status of the occupants or the size of the family unit who lived there. So although we have a considerable amount of evidence of Neolithic houses, it is difficult to be sure that we understand quite how they were used.

During the Neolithic period we know that there were certainly circular, oval and rectangular houses, usually with upright posts supporting wattle walls and with thatched roofs. But, with some important exceptions, almost nothing is known of the internal arrangements. One important feature, however, does emerge: the quite considerable size of such huts. A rectangular one, at Haldon Hill near Exeter, Devon, was twenty-five feet long and fifteen feet wide (7.6 by 4.6 m). Another at Fengate near Peterborough, was twenty feet by eighteen feet (6 by 5.5 m) while one at Trelystan near Welshpool in mid Wales was again almost square and twelve feet (3.7 m) across. These dimensions may not seem very impressive, but when they are compared with a typical modern lounge, it can be appreciated that such huts were quite spacious. Given that the inhabitants preferred to live, eat and sleep together, it is clear that such houses could easily have held a family group in reasonable comfort and indeed they were perhaps intended as extended family homes for three generations numbering as many as eight or ten people.

For the whole of the prehistoric period houses that were built of stone provide the most telling and durable evidence. These have not only survived in much better condition than the timber ones, but they often contain evidence, also in stone, of internal arrangements that can throw more light on the numbers of occupants and their ways of life. Such stone-built Neolithic houses have been noted and excavated in Scotland and particularly on Orkney and on the Shetlands where wood was in shorter supply and stone, easily available. The recent work by A. Whittle on the Scord of Brouster, Shetland, shows this well. A group of circular to oval houses, with their associated fields, has been found, and two excavated. One was twenty feet by fourteen feet (6 by 4.3 m), the other only fourteen feet by ten feet (4.3 by 3 m), but both had recesses or alcoves arranged around the internal walls. We cannot be certain what these recesses were used for, but the larger ones are of such a size as to suggest that they were 'bedrooms' which could have held at least two people and their personal possessions quite comfortably. It is possible that the larger house could have provided a home for at least ten to twelve people while the smaller one might have held six to eight. Again the implications are that these houses were occupied by extended family groups living together, but with a certain degree of privacy.

Even more important are the complex stone structures excavated many years ago at Skara Brae and Rinyo on Orkney. These were substantial dwellings, and the use of flagstones as a substitute for wood meant that a host of minor details were preserved. The houses were stone-built, sub-rectangular, measuring twenty feet by eighteen feet (6 by 5.5 m), to fourteen feet by twelve feet (4.3 by 3.7 m), with central hearths. In the walls were bed-spaces enclosed by slabs with shelves set in the wall above them. There were even two-shelved dressers. Small cells, let into some walls, were probably for storage, although some dwellings had drains in them which may have been latrines. These huts were grouped into clusters, connected by paved and roofed passages, and Skara Brae was a village rather than a hamlet with one hut seemingly serving as a 'workshop'. It seems likely that such groups of huts formed the homes of more than just an extended family, for together they could have housed fifty or more people. None of the individual houses was notably better finished than others, although variations in their sizes might suggest subtle differences in status or wealth.

Nothing from the late prehistoric period can rival the Neolithic Orcadian houses in terms of surviving internal arrangements. Nevertheless, from the hundreds of house sites of the Bronze Age and Iron Age that have been excavated the same type of basic form of the simple, one-roomed, circular hut can be seen to be the most common. Sizes vary considerably as do the apparent technical structural details. However, the basic consistency of shape and form indicates that these buildings were admirably suited to the way of life of these remote times, otherwise they would have changed. Thus, people were contented to live in close proximity, in large family groups housed in one or several huts. The dwellings underline not only the physical advantage of warmth which close living proximity offered but also the social advantages of family cohesion, sharing and caring which must have been fundamental to prehistoric life.

Archaeology suggests that there were, however, divisions of status and/or wealth both within and between family groups. At the Bronze Age site at Black Patch in Sussex the occupied areas consisted of platforms cut into the hillside. One of these platforms was excavated and was shown to consist of five separate terraces each carrying the remains of a circular wooden hut about twelve feet in diameter. Two of the huts were obviously for storage, and three were houses. Of the latter, only one was set within its own yard and had its own pond. It also contained markedly richer material remains. The excavator suggested that this building was home of the head of the extended family whose members occupied the other huts.

Particularly in the Iron Age there was a wide variety of hut sizes which almost certainly indicates differences in status. At the hillfort of Hod Hill, Dorset, where around seventy of the possible total of 200 huts have been identified, they range from twenty-two feet to thirty-six feet (6.7 m to 10.9 m) in diameter, although the majority are around thirty feet (9.1 m); at a site at Little Waltham, Essex, the sixteen Iron Age huts found there were between twenty-eight and forty feet (8.5 m and 12.2 m) across. One of the largest Iron Age houses found was at Brandon, Durham. It was a solitary farmstead and was some forty-nine feet (14.9 m) in diameter. In floor area this is equivalent to a modern eight-roomed bungalow with each room fifteen feet (4.6 m) square: a substantial dwelling by any criteria.

As in the Neolithic period, in areas where stone was used for construction much more information can be discovered. At the late Iron Age village of Carn Euny in Cornwall, ten houses have been excavated. Three were large, around twenty-five feet (7.6 m) across, but the rest were much smaller, in the fifteen to eighteen-foot (4.6 m to 5.5 m) range. More important was the fact that the excavator was able to identify interior divisions whereby the huts were divided into separate compartments, probably to give separate sleeping and living areas although the function of the associated fogou remains largely mysterious.

Although the majority of Bronze Age and Iron Age houses were circular, this was not a universal shape. Rectangular houses often occurred, sometimes in considerable numbers. At the hillfort of Danebury near Stockbridge, Hampshire, in the third century BC new streets lined with rectangular houses nine to ten feet (2.7 m to 3 m) across were laid out. This suggests that some form of centralized authority conceived or supervised the work. Arrangements in some continental defended Iron Age settlements were even more striking, with people living in long buildings like barrack blocks.

Slim as it is, the archaeological evidence for prehistoric times indicates certain important aspects of the way that people occupied their abodes. The houses were usually admirably adapted to the lifestyles of their occupants. The houses also clearly indicate differences in status, whether based on wealth or power. Thus they support other archaeological evidence for complex social division and organization. There are also clear indications that the large extended family normally lived either in one structure or in grouped dwellings. The last, and perhaps most important, factor to emerge is that, despite the apparent simplicity of the structures, the actual way of life inside these houses was not by any means a primitive 'free-for-all'. Even in the larger, almost cavernous circular huts there was a division of 'territory' with sleeping, working and living areas clearly defined, and even perhaps what we might term 'controlled circulation'. Domestic life was probably less 'barbarous' and uncomfortable than the old books suggest, but, within the confines of the typical hut, there will have been little tolerance of riotous and undisciplined horseplay from the children!

As always when one examines the Roman period one encounters the impact of a civilized and highly sophisticated culture being imposed on an advanced but less refined one. Much of the interest lies in trying to establish the effect of the former on the latter. Nowhere is this more fascinating than in terms of houses. The best analogy is that of the nineteenth and twentieth-century colonial powers on the African continent. There, the native population lived in fairly simple structures, although these too covered a complex social organization and in parts of East Africa it was normal for villagers to set aside a working day in the course of which the whole community would build a serviceable and comfortable roundhouse for a family in need. Then, quite suddenly, colonial administrators, soldiers, missionaries, and traders arrived bringing their own ideas of what a house should be like. Gradually, but by no means completely, the native population accepted these ideas and slowly altered the appearance of their houses. Often social conventions from two contrasting cultures will meet and merge and an author's wife recalls an East African wattle and thatch roundhouse built complete with a flushing lavatory.

Cultural convergence on 'the home' is clear in Roman Britain. The Roman army, administrators and merchants arrived in Britain in AD 43 with a new, and for Britain, quite alien concept of the house. This was rectangular in form, built often of stone or brick, roofed with tiles and, most important of all, it was structurally sub-divided into a number of compartments which had specialized functions or uses. In addition there were other minor though important structural components or architectural features such as porticos or verandahs, mosaics or painted walls and heating systems. There were also specialized forms of buildings including shops and these too were of forms evolved in the Mediterranean metropolises. All these forms and features arrived suddenly and their impact on the native population of Britain was considerable. They were immediately presented with the new, and to their eyes, spectacular types of houses occupied by the conquerors. Almost immediately these new structures were imitated; with very different results. At the highest level is the Roman palace at Fishbourne near

Chichester, West Sussex. This was built about AD 75 almost certainly for Cogidubnus, a native king who had given the Romans considerable help during the conquest. He was allowed to retain his position and served as a client-king on behalf of Rome, continuing to rule his people within the framework of the new Roman province.

To emphasize his status, he seems to have had a palace built for him which was the height of fashion. It must certainly have been erected by a team of foreign craftsmen and designers, for the size, complexity, architectural elaboration and decorative detail were quite unknown in Britain at that time. In contrast, the much more conservative and provincial group of roundhouses and square enclosures recently discovered near Thetford, Norfolk, and provisionally identified as the 'palace' of the first-century Iceni Queen Boudicca, shows the persistence of old visions of the royal home. At the lower end of the scale, in the newly-created towns where some Iron Age people were persuaded or forced to live, lines of timber huts and shops appeared. These may have loosely resembled the shanty towns which have grown up beside some modern tropical cities. Yet the shops, though crudely built of timber, were usually rectangular, arranged end on to the street with open fronts to display wares, and living rooms and store rooms behind. All these features were direct imitations of those of Mediterranean city shops.

As the Roman period advanced, all levels of society in Britain continued to mimic the imported traditions, ideas and methods. The upper governing and land-owning classes, often directly descended from Iron Age chieftains, built themselves country villas, town houses or both. Such structures were often continuously enlarged or improved parallel to the increased wealth or status of their owners—but they also sometimes declined and contracted as their owners fell on difficult times. Although the imitations were sometimes crude when compared to the standards of the Classical world, many fashionable details were copied. Villas gradually developed from being simple rectangular ranges of rooms, through 'U'-shaped or 'winged-villas', into major houses lying around central courtyards. The well-known villas at Brading on the Isle of Wight, North Leigh in Oxfordshire, or Lullingstone in Kent all show this culmination. In each there was elaborate if somewhat gauche mimicing of Roman stereotypes with elaborate mosaic floors and painted walls. The numerous rooms each had specific functions; kitchens were separated from dining-rooms, bedrooms from sitting-rooms, while servants occupied the remoter corners.

The same development occurred in towns, where great courtyard mansions appeared, and lower down the social scale the smaller landowners or wealthy farmers attempted similar but less sophisticated imitations. The villa at Hailstone in Gloucestershire is a simple rectangular building measuring seventy-five feet by forty-five feet (22.9 m by 13.7 m) and is divided into seven separate rooms, but lacks mosaic floors or heating systems. Even some peasants often introduced the trappings of Roman ideas albeit at a very simple level. A number of traditional circular wooden huts have been excavated and found to differ from their prehistoric predecessors only in the adoption of painted wall plaster. And of course, there are many 'Roman' huts, occupied by the very lowest levels of native society, which are structurally and functionally no different from those of the pre-conquest Iron Age.

As with the great villas, the lesser buildings changed over time as their inmates learnt more of the Roman way of life. A good example is the Roman settlement excavated at Studland in Dorset. It began life shortly after the Roman conquest as a group of circular timber huts of the traditional type. These huts only lasted about twenty-five years and were then replaced by rectangular huts, also of timber but on stone foundations. These new structures then sufficed for the next 300 years. At Odell, in Bedfordshire, a similar group of circular wooden huts was erected just before the Roman conquest. They were occupied unaltered until AD 100 when they were replaced by another cluster of identical dwellings. These were rebuilt a number of times and it was not until the third century AD that a rectangular stone building containing five separate rooms appeared. A site near Northampton provided a variant on the same theme. There, two circular wooden huts were built in the late first century AD. They existed, with much rebuilding, until 280 when a circular stone building replaced them.

It is this great variety of house types that is a striking feature of the Roman period: there are the great villas or town houses; simpler villas; smaller urban dwellings; small rectangular stone or timber farm houses; rectangular stone two-roomed cottages, and circular huts of stone or timber—all experiencing substantial or detailed evolution during the occupation. There were also houses in which men and animals shared the same roof. At Studland the later rectangular huts were divided into two rooms, one used by the family as a communal dwelling-room and the other as a byre for their livestock. A variant of this type of occupation existed in the numerous 'aisled barns' or halls, which seem to have been spacious structures with the flanking side aisles divided from the main hall or 'nave' by posts or piers. Some were certainly built only for cattle and storage and were later partitioned for use as dwelling-houses. But others seem to have been shared by humans and animals from the outset.

There is still much to be learnt about the domestic social relationships of this period. By their sizes, the simple huts imply that the traditional extended family groups were still in existence. What is less obvious is whether the members of the upper social echelons who dwelt in the villas or town houses also preserved the extended family tradition. While it is possible to identify major living rooms, kitchens and even servants' quarters, it is archaeologically impossible to discover the relationship between the various smaller rooms and the people who used them.

The variety of the structures, the evidence of domestic changes for better or for worse, the expressions of wealth, status and fashion, as well as the occasional indications of family relationships, all vividly show the social and architectural complexity of Roman Britain. Beyond the boundaries of the Empire, as we might expect, the homes were less sophisticated. Most people continued to recreate the dwellings of their prehistoric ancestors. As we have seen, this also occurred within the Empire, and simple circular timber or stone structures were particularly common in Wales, northern England and southern Scotland. A large group of stone huts on the mountain behind Holyhead on Anglesey, known to have been occupied from the second to the fourth century AD, contains small stone roundhouses although there are also some little rectangular buildings which may have been used for manufacturing. There was also much local variation, for not far from Holyhead is the site at Din Lligwy, a fourth-century settlement. It consists of two massive circular stone huts, associated with several

94. *The last generation of circular dwellings in Britain is represented by this substantial house in the Romano-British village of Din Lligwy on Anglesey.*

rectangular ones which seem to be the workshops of a metalwork industry and this industrial hamlet-cum-local capital was surrounded by a polygonal stone rampart.

The removal of Roman military and political power and the slow disintegration of the Roman way of life in Britain produced major changes in house design. The stone villas and houses were gradually abandoned and there was a return to much simpler structures. In the north and west of Britain, where the Roman influence had been light, people continued to live in much the same way that they had always lived.

The best and most recent evidence of the houses of this period has come from a series of modern excavations on so-called Saxon villages and 'palace' sites. The villages include the sites at Catholme in Staffordshire, Chalton in Hampshire, Bishopstone in Sussex and West Stow in Suffolk. At all of them the characteristic dwellings were rectangular timber buildings of varying sizes which usually range from thirty feet by fifteen feet (9.1 m by 4.6 m) to twenty feet by ten feet (6 m by 3 m). The larger ones usually had 'opposed doorways', roughly in the centre of the long sides and many had partitions forming one large room and one that was much smaller. The smaller structures were usually only one room in extent and had a single door. Archaeologists tend to call the larger structures 'halls' and certainly the remains reveal a very substantial room which was much bigger than the average modern lounge and dining-room. It has been suggested that such large rooms did indeed function as a 'hall' in which the family unit lived and slept, perhaps with the smaller room being used as a bedroom for the senior members of the family. The smaller structures may have been the homes of lower status families whose members lived entirely within a single room. A curious feature of most smaller 'Saxon' halls and huts is a scooped-out sunken floor. The function of the floor pit is much debated, but it is likely to have been boarded over, in which case it might have served to provide drainage and thus preserve the floor boards.

Excavations at Cheddar in Somerset, and at Yeavering in Northumberland have revealed larger halls, but these were royal dwellings which provided clear pictures of the upper classes in Dark Age society. Apart from their great size (the ninth-century hall at Cheddar measured seventy-eight feet by twenty feet (23.7 m by 6 m)) and relatively minor sophistications such as the detached kitchen at Yeavering, they seem to reveal domestic lifestyles which were not vastly different from those of smaller halls. Certainly the large halls were designed to provide formal and informal accommodation for the numerous retainers who were the essence of lordly society, but like the lesser halls they essentially provided a single spacious living-room for all. The great occasions with feasting and story-telling so graphically described in *Beowulf* and other epics were enacted in great halls such as these, but the basic mode of living seems to have been quite similar at all levels of society.

23

Home in the Middle Ages

Our earliest houses which endure as standing structures date from the late eleventh and twelfth centuries. Their very existence, and the increasing tendency for dwellings to persist as the period progressed means that we have a better understanding of medieval than of older homes. Yet it must be stressed that the medieval houses that remain for us to see are those of the upper social classes. The homes of the great peasant mass of the population are only known to us as a result of archaeological excavations. This poses considerable problems for our understanding of medieval houses in general; we are dealing with two quite different types of historical evidence which are sometimes difficult to reconcile.

Nevertheless, certain trends are clear. Perhaps the most important of these is that at last we can begin to recognize the often subtle differences in lifestyle and thus in house types between the various social classes. There are the castles and palaces of the kings and major lords; the manor houses of the lesser nobility; the town houses and farmhouses of the merchant classes and richer independent farmers; and the cottages of peasants, all of which we will shortly examine. But superimposed on these differences was another important feature: for the greater part of the medieval period, all levels of society still clung to the norm of having a 'hall', one major room in which most domesticated activities took place.

The idea of the hall spanned the social spectrum even though the halls varied greatly in their sizes and appointments. In the great royal or baronial castles these were often vast and sumptuous. Some of the earliest were incorporated within the great stone keeps as at the royal castle at Dover, or the stronghold of the Earls of Oxford at Castle Hedingham in Essex. These great halls often had fireplaces, galleries and window seats which may still survive. Later halls were often erected in the bailies of castles for use by retainers and they were generally similar. But such halls did not stand alone, nor did they exist unchanged throughout medieval times. The development of the freestanding medieval house, though focused on the hall, involved much more.

Although halls may have originated as the sole communal living room of the family, at least by the twelfth century, the upper classes of society were demanding more elaborate domestic provisions. Even in the early Norman castles the halls in the keeps had other associated rooms: kitchens, for the preparation of food, existed usually in the basements, or as separate buildings on lower floors; private retiring rooms or 'solars' for the masters and their families were provided, either adjacent to the great hall or on upper floors; halls outside the confines of the castle keeps gradually acquired other structures, often added as separate wings or blocks while the hall itself was often altered to provide more convenient accommodation. The earliest halls were usually barn-like structures with lofty ceilingless rooms and central open hearths whose smoke filtered out through a hole in the roof or gable. This hole was later improved by the construction of complex shuttered louvres, sophisticated contrivances to assist the draught while giving protection against the weather.

In the eleventh and twelfth centuries some halls were actually built above a storage basement and so stood at first floor level. Those at Boothby Pagnell in Lincolnshire (c. 1200), Hemingford Grey Manor House, Cambridgeshire (c. 1150), and 'The Jew's Houses' at Lincoln (1170–80) are all good examples. It is possible that these were intended to provide at least an element of defence and certainly 'first floor halls' continued to be built in the Welsh Marches and the Scottish Borders into the fourteenth century. Even so, ground floor halls were always more common and the first floor halls may reflect passing fashion and personal fancies as much as, or more than, any coherent quest for protection.

The structure of the hall itself also changed throughout the medieval period. At first many were 'aisled'—that is to say, that they had a central nave flanked by side aisles, and defined by the piers or posts which supported the roof. The purpose of aisle-posts was to increase the possible room width. Good examples of such aisled halls which were built by a variety of owners, and sometimes much altered in later times, are at Oakham Castle (1190), the Bishop's Palace at Lincoln (c. 1224), and Little Chesterford Manor House, Essex (c. 1222–30). But in the thirteenth century experiments in supporting wide roofs without aisles had been successfully accomplished. An early example is that of the Old Deanery, Salisbury, Wiltshire, where a traditional roof structure is supported by braces set on stone corbels which project from the walls. Later, and becoming much more widespread, was the fourteenth-century development of arch-braced and

95. *Norman architecture displayed in the School of Pythagoras in Cambridge.*

hammer-beam roofs where the whole roof structure was self-supporting. Westminster Hall is perhaps the finest example of a hammer-beam roof and it clearly displays the way in which all such open roofs were often elaborately decorated to proclaim the status and wealth of the owners.

The internal arrangements of the halls also developed during the medieval period. One end became the site of the 'high table' which was often raised on a dais, where the family would sit for meals while the lower part of the hall was occupied by servants, relatives or guests. At the other end the hall was frequently extended, sometimes as a structurally separate block, to provide service apartments. These were usually a 'buttery', originally built for the storage and preparation of drink, and a 'pantry' to hold bread and cutlery. Running between the two there was often a passage leading to the kitchen which, because of the risk of fire until the fifteenth century, was generally an isolated detached building. Between the buttery, the pantry and the hall, there was usually a longitudinal passageway separated from the hall itself by a screen and linked to the outside by opposed doorways. This passage, for obvious reasons, was usually termed 'the screens'.

The solar was frequently built above the buttery and pantry block in early elaborations of the greater hall houses. Sometimes called the 'great chamber', examples provided with internal fireplaces and wall-chimneys existed from at least the late eleventh century. These rooms provided some privacy for the head of the household and his immediate family reflecting an early step in the gradual retreat from the norm of communal living. Soon afterwards, or perhaps as a parallel development, the 'great chamber' found a new location, being positioned at the opposite end of the hall adjacent to the high table. Such solars were usually separate structures often roofed transversely to the hall.

The block then acquired a ground floor room which became the private sitting room or 'parlour', with the solar or great chamber perhaps surviving more narrowly as a bedroom above. Access to the solar was now gained by a staircase set in the wall thickness or in an externally projecting tower, to avoid taking up space at the high table end of the hall. This projection was later often expanded, given external windows following the removal of the staircase, and thus it provided much-needed light to the high table while serving as a semi-private sitting-out bay. The room above the buttery and pantry then became the bedroom for the children or elderly of the family or for the guests or, in large and wealthy households, for the 'steward' or chief officer of the household.

So, by the fourteenth century the typical upper-class home adopted over most of England consisted of a central hall with two-storey blocks at each end, endowing the house with an 'H'-shaped plan. Further changes adopted from the late fourteenth century onwards included the attachment of the kitchen block to the rear of the pantry and buttery, to form a more compact arrangement. In addition, especially in the more prestigious homes, there was often a further extension of the building to cope with the problems of increasing numbers of retainers and guests, all of whom gradually expected improving standards of living. It was always difficult to obtain materials of sufficient length to expand structures beyond a one room width while social norms still accepted enclosed courtyards or cloisters as suitable structures for communal living.

In both religious houses and in the bailies of castles, additional accommodation often took the form of buildings arranged around a central courtyard. And so there emerged the classic medieval house with the hall on one side of this courtyard and with store-houses, perhaps a chapel, guest-rooms, servants' quarters, and a semi-defensive fortified gatehouse or entrance way lining the other three sides. Different variations on this theme can be seen at Stokesay in Shropshire and Markenfield near Ripon. Outer courts, with stabling barns, warehouses and further servants' quarters also appeared when an owner was very wealthy, the whole sometimes being surrounded by a moat to emphasize his status. Many examples of this form of house still exist, perhaps best exemplified—albeit for rather special purposes—in the older colleges at Oxford and Cambridge.

Few houses that survive from this period show all the features described above. Their existence depended heavily on the status and wealth of the owner. One interesting house which does show many of these aspects, largely because it was rebuilt at a relatively late medieval date is at Cotehele near Calstock in Cornwall. What remains today is mainly of the late fifteenth century, though there were some later structural alterations. The modest hall, only forty feet (12.2 m) long, is open to a roof which is supported by highly-carved arch-braces with moulded wind braces between the purlins providing an elaborate decorative effect. At one end, three doors give access into the kitchen, pantry and buttery, while at the other, there is a raised dais lit by a broad mullioned window. Beyond the dais is the parlour from which a small doorway gives access to a private chapel. The chapel forms part of one side of a square courtyard lined

96. *Good medieval timber-framing displayed in this shop at Ashwell, Hertfordshire.*

by narrow ranges of rooms, two with their own private staircases; these rooms were lodgings, originally for guests. The main entrance into the courtyard is by way of a massive gate-tower, suitably crenellated to impress visitors, although the armour of masonry was purely for show and had no defensive purpose. Attached to the main courtyard is a smaller one, also lined by ranges of buildings. Its name, 'Retainers Court', explains its purpose.

Cotehele is built of massive granite blocks hewn from the surrounding hills. Other houses, often constructed of quite different materials, show the same features. They include Penshurst Place in Kent, dating from the mid fourteenth century and Compton Wyngates in Warwickshire, of the early sixteenth century.

In fact, however, there are few houses which still display all their medieval features so well and hardly any which show a complete building all of one period. This is because, like all houses, those of the medieval period were constantly changed while only a small number were completely built anew. Extensive alterations and enlargements are not confined merely to modern houses: they have always occurred as the medieval upper and middle-class houses show. Such changes underline the rather perplexing descriptions which emerge from scholarly examinations of medieval buildings indicating types of timber jointing, blocked windows and straight joints. These technical details tend to mask the continuing process of change in medieval houses which were improved and altered to keep up with fashion, or declined as the owners fell on hard times. If the descriptions which mention fourteenth-century fireplaces, or sixteenth-century partitions make a house appear the product of distinct building phases, the truth is likely to be still more complicated for houses were in states of continuous modification and not all the changes are obvious or datable.

So far we have only looked at the homes of the top people of medieval society but the great bulk of the population lived in very different conditions and in houses that have not survived into the present. The details of these have to be obtained by patient and long-term excavation in areas where, for a variety of reasons, occupation was abandoned at a relatively early date. Most of our information on medieval peasant houses has come from excavations on the sites of deserted villages. Such excavations, invaluable as they are, are much less informative than a standing building and so, as with prehistoric and Roman houses, there is much about medieval peasant houses that we still do not know. We can certainly ascertain their shapes, sizes, numbers of rooms, types of foundations and, with reasonable certainty, suggest the structure of their walls. But the above-ground structures often remain mysterious and minor details are difficult to find while roof structures can only be guessed at.

Most early medieval peasants' houses were of timber, either of posts driven into the ground to support roofs and walls, or set on a horizontal timber 'sill'. In certain areas, notably in south-west England and the north, turf walls were common and in some other places 'cob'—a mixture of mud, lime and straw—formed low 'dwarf walls'. In the twelfth to thirteenth centuries there was a tendency to replace timber with stone in places where it was available.

More interesting than the materials used, is the room arrangement of the houses erected by medieval peasants. There seem to be three basic forms: for those at the bottom end of the social scale, home was often a tiny and basic 'cot', usually a one-roomed house rarely measuring more than fifteen feet by six feet (4.6 m by 1.5 m). Occasionally cots were larger with two rooms and measured up to thirty feet by twelve feet (9.1 m by 3.7 m). They were probably the homes of the poorest landless peasants

97. *The Hangleton Cottage at the open air museum at Singleton, West Sussex, is a reconstruction of a medieval peasant dwelling excavated at Hangleton village which was deserted in the fourteenth century.*

who worked for others. The wealthier villeins and the free peasants usually lived in 'long-houses'. These varied considerably in size, from thirty feet by twelve feet (9.1 m by 3.7 m), to sixty feet by twelve feet (18.2 m by 3.7 m). They were characterized by having a 'living end', usually of two rooms: one for communal living and the other a small end room for sleeping, while at the other end of the house was a cow shed or byre. The byre was separated from the living area by a 'cross passage' with opposed doorways serving as front and back doorways.

A third type of house, normally built towards the end of the medieval period, was the farmstead. It served as home to the most prosperous peasants, people who in the fourteenth and fifteenth centuries were emerging as the Yeomen farmers. These dwellings consisted of a rectangular structure thirty to forty feet (9.1 m to 12.2 m) long and ten to twelve feet (3 m to 3.7 m) wide which was divided into two or three rooms, while the farm out-buildings existed as separate structures and were often arranged around a square courtyard. Such house and out-building clusters are known as 'courtyard farms' and many post-medieval examples remain in use.

In many excavations the change from long-house to courtyard farm has been revealed. At the deserted medieval village of Gomeldon near Salisbury, Wiltshire, long-houses were abandoned in the thirteenth century and replaced on the same site by courtyard farms. At other places, however, the change never took place. At Wharram

98. *The long-house was the most widely adopted form of peasant dwelling in Britain throughout the medieval period. This modified example of a long-house lies near Chun Castle hillfort in the west of Cornwall.*

99. *A small single-storey Irish cottage in stone, plaster and thatch near Sligo.*

100. *In Wales, even in the nineteenth century, squatter rights could be won by the builder of a* ty-unnos, *a house of one night. Many resembled this tiny dwelling at Nevern near Fishguard.*

Percy, Yorkshire, all the houses were of the long-house type when the village was finally abandoned in the early sixteenth century. And, as we shall see, the idea of the long-house continued in many parts of Britain for centuries after this: some examples from the English and Celtic uplands date only from the sixteenth century, while Hebridean 'black houses' were still being built in the nineteenth century.

As we have said, the hall provided a bridge which spanned the different medieval dwelling and social levels. Though often small and cramped, the peasant hall was, in effect, a communal living-room with a central open hearth. The other rooms were apparently primarily for sleeping while all waking activities were carried out in the main 'hall' or living-room. These basic features were to continue for most of the lower levels of post-medieval society for some time to come. But higher up the class ladder, changes which were happening in the late medieval times were eventually to filter down to affect the domestic life of all classes.

24

Houses in the Fifteenth, Sixteenth and Seventeenth Centuries

During the fifteenth century there were major changes in the domestic arrangements of the greater houses which inspired radically new ideas about building. One of the most important of these changes was the gradual emergence of fireplaces within the large open halls.

These fireplaces were served by large external flues and chimney stacks and brought a notable improvement in physical conditions of domestic life. But they also engendered much greater changes for the way in which people lived: with the superseding of the open fire and its attendant smoke hole in the roof, there was no longer any need for a vast open hall. There was thus a tendency to convert the upper part of the hall into separate rooms by inserting a low ceiling in the hall and using the upper spaces for rooms which could be approached from staircases either in the solar or the kitchen end of the house. These rooms provided additional privacy, so that children and elderly relatives could have their own bedrooms, while important guests could be given private apartments. The new rooms were usually interconnected and side passages were rare, so that by modern standards privacy was still limited. Nevertheless, the use of the upper part of the hall for extra rooms marked a major advance in living conditions. Such lowering of the height of the hall also brought extra advantages in terms of warmth and comfort.

These changes can be seen both in great houses as well as lesser manor houses distributed all over the southern part of Britain at the end of the Middle Ages. A particularly good example is at Madingley Hall, Cambridge. The house was built by Sir John Hynde between 1540 and 1550. Although much altered in later times, it was built on a traditional plan with a central hall and an oriel window, a screens passage leading to the kitchen wing and also a splendidly elaborate solar wing at the opposite end. There is a fine fireplace in the hall but no vast roof-space. Instead, there is a low ceiling and above a magnificent eighteenth-century salon developed from an original 'upper hall', a private chamber for the Hynde family. The upper hall had a fine carved roof of a type known as a 'false hammer-beam' which now lies hidden above a later ceiling. This traditionally-built roof was for the appreciation of the Hyndes and their favoured guests, not for the users of the hall below.

Far more common than this is the interesting process of adaptation whereby an earlier open hall was converted for the new lifestyle by the insertion of an upper floor. Sometimes the change was accompanied by the addition of a massive chimney stack which not only improved the comfort of the hall but also provided a means of support for the new ceiling and upper floor. A perfect example of the process is found at the small manor house at Barrington in Cambridgeshire. The house was originally built in the fourteenth century as an open-aisled hall, with a kitchen or service wing at one end and a solar wing at the other. It was remodelled in the sixteenth century but still retained its original character. In the early seventeenth century a floor, partially supported by a new central chimney stack, was inserted into the upper part of the hall. This floor provided extra bedrooms while the new chimney not only heated the hall, but also provided the cooking facilities in the kitchen at the service end. At the same time, the service and solar wings were rebuilt, extended and given their own internal chimney stacks and fireplaces, so providing heating for all the main rooms. Thus, quite suddenly, an old and probably decidedly uncomfortable house was transformed into a cosy, well-appointed home with every modern amenity.

It should not, however, be assumed that these obvious advantages meant the demise of the open halls. Nothing could be further from the truth, especially at the upper levels of society where one might have expected that halls would have been considered outmoded and replaced by more convenient arrangements. By the sixteenth century, the open hall was a deeply-rooted concept and part of a tradition which stretched back at least a thousand years. More importantly it was, like the castle, a major symbol and structure of medieval feudal society for it provided the place where the lord met his vassals and retainers and where business and entertainments were performed. The hall thus had a deep and ancient social function as well as an emotional appeal. It was not a feature to be easily abandoned, even in the pursuit of greater comfort. Indeed, the very nature of Tudor society with its emphasis on splendid social gatherings and displays of status actually supported the need for an ostentatious room for social functions. The halls themselves could be made more comfortable and imposing with highly decorative fireplaces and fittings while private rooms for other purposes were added to the home. Thus the hall remained as the core of the great house throughout the sixteenth and early seventeenth centuries. Even at Madingley, as we have seen, the traditional perception of the hall remained powerful—to the extent that two were provided, one for the family and one for social purposes.

Another telling example is Kirby in Northamptonshire which was begun in 1570 by Sir Humphrey Stafford and completed by the time of his death in 1575. Here is the house of the great Elizabethan magnate in all its glory. Yet, if we look closely we see a very traditional home: there is a massive open hall with a kitchen range at one end and at the other a parlour with bedrooms above. This block forms one side of a courtyard which is bounded on the other three sides by elaborate ranges of lodgings for retainers and guests. Other great houses of the period also show the same basic features and Burghley House near Stamford, which was built by Lord Cecil the great Elizabethan statesman, is yet another example.

Yet major changes too were afoot. The growing demand for extra rooms for particular purposes was making the great hall an effectively redundant feature no matter how deeply the association between hall and home was rooted. As a result, although it was often retained as a very spacious chamber, its function began to degenerate into that of an imposing vestibule or entrance apartment while more and more 'modern' rooms were added all around. At Kirby Hall for instance, the second owner, Sir Christopher Hatton, added a sumptuous set of rooms in the wing at the rear of the solar or parlour end of the house between 1575 and 1600, and they were largely for family use.

More significant, in terms of the future, was the appearance in the late sixteenth and early seventeenth centuries of a group of great houses which are characterized by so-called 'transverse-halls'. The best of these is Hardwick Hall in Derbyshire, built in the 1590s for Elizabeth, Countess of Shrewsbury, better known as Bess of Hardwick. At Hardwick, the hall is turned at right angles to the traditional line and the screens end

101. *These photographs represent successive stages in the modification of a Wealden house.*
  (a) *a Wealden house restored to its original medieval appearance at the Singleton museum;*
   (b) *a tastefully modernized Wealden house (the RHS windows apart) at Eastry, Kent;*
   (c) *a Wealden house unsympathetically converted into three units at New Buckenham.*

becomes the main entrance to the house. The hall, which still rose to a two-storey height, had become an entrance hall. Service rooms, including kitchens, pantries, and sculleries lie on either side of it and stairs led upwards to a complete suite of first floor family rooms. These included a dining-room, drawing-rooms, and bedrooms. Above them was another suite of state rooms for visitors, with a further floor of bedrooms above that.

The state rooms also included what was to become an absolute necessity for all houses of any pretention—a long gallery. Such rooms, which extended the full length of the house and were often suitably lined with tapestries, could be used for exercise by ladies during inclement weather, for games and for other social activities. The arrival of the long gallery often led to considerable difficulties in the planning of a house for it was sometimes extremely awkward to include one without disturbing the plan, circulation and room arrangement. At Kirby Hall the problem was solved by making the upper floor of one of the ranges of lodgings into a long gallery, and the same feature may be seen at Lanhydrock House, Cornwall. Sometimes, as at Hatfield House, Herts, of 1607–12, it was built above an open 'loggia' or verandah which occupied the ground floor space.

A splendid example of the demand for, difficulty in providing, and the potentially disastrous results of the need for a long gallery may be seen at Little Moreton Hall, Cheshire. The original open hall with kitchen at one end and parlour and solar at the other, was built around 1480 by Ralph Moreton. In 1559 a ceiling was inserted into

102. *The courtyard at Kirby Hall, Northamptonshire.*

the hall and great bay windows were added. In addition, two new ranges of family rooms, a chapel and lodgings for guests were erected. Such a house then provided everything that an aspiring country-gentleman required. But by the 1570s long galleries were the fashion and desirable. There was no room for such an addition at Little Moreton so the gallery was built as a second floor, on top of the existing guest range. This construction immediately led to serious structural failure for the main tie-beams had been cut through; only the insertion of highly decorated but crude wooden corbels in the ceiling of the hall below averted the disaster.

So far we have looked at sixteenth and seventeenth-century great houses purely from the viewpoint of room arrangements. But the sixteenth century saw a new and important change in the appearance of a house which reaches into the present day. Broadly speaking, in medieval times, the external appearance of a house was a reflection of its internal layout. Certainly it had to be imposing, often decorative with showy jetties, costly timbers or battlements but the outward appearance of the larger medieval house simply mirrored its internal functions. One can still look at the exterior of a medieval house and recognize its hall, service wing and solar end from their shapes. Changes in the form of additions, new windows and doors and so on were made to improve the internal workings of the house without too much forethought being exercised over the resulting external appearance. The result, of course, is the delightful changes in height in irregular groupings of chimney stacks and in the variety of individual blocks and bays which give medieval houses such enduring and individual characters.

By the sixteenth century however, attitudes had changed. Largely as a result of the Renaissance and the introduction to the western outposts of Europe of Classical ideas, the exteriors of houses became as important as their interiors—indeed sometimes more important. One aspect of this trend was the growing desire for applied Classical decoration, often in the forms of columns and capitals. This decoration was however rarely truly Classical. It was imported via Italy and France, mixed with traditional ideas and motives and often translated into brick. The results were the elaborate and highly decorative façades that are such characteristic aspects of the houses of this period. Even more influential was the idea that houses should have symmetrical elevations with, for example, a central entrance door, matching windows on all floors and balancing wings. The outcome of this was the development of the typical Elizabethan 'E'-plan house, although in fact the form persisted well into the seventeenth century. This 'E'-plan to some extent mirrored the 'H'-shaped medieval house and often the central block was still the great hall while the projecting wings perpetuated the function of the service and solar ends of medieval houses. Thus the old traditions and the new ideas gradually merged.

This merger was not, in fact, achieved without some problems. By placing the entrance door, which was suitably screened by a porch, in the centre of the main elevation, difficulties emerged. Instead of the entrance being at one end of the hall, it was now in the centre of one side. This made the hall considerably less effective as a place for social gatherings and the development of the hall towards a mere vestibule was hastened. This in turn led naturally to the use of part of the hall as access to upper

103. *An unusual combination of timber-framing and a symmetrical façade at Rushbury, Shropshire.*

floors by filling it with an imposing structure. Gradually then the 'hall' began to take on its modern role.

This process was not always accepted. Many people still felt that they needed a traditional hall, as well as the fashionable central entrance door in a symmetrical elevation. One escape from the dilemma was to push the hall sideways so that the door still opened into one of its ends while the bulk of the hall lay to one side of the entrance. The other balancing part of the main block then had to be used for the traditional service rooms even though they now formed part of the principal façade.

Again we can see this problem and its solution at Kirby Hall. As noted above, the main range has the traditional hall with kitchen and solar ranges at each end but the elevation has perfect symmetry. The central entrance door leads into the service end of the hall which occupies the right hand end of the range with the solar range beyond. The left hand side of the entrance is taken up entirely by the kitchens, cellars and pantry, and their façade is identical to that of the great hall even repeating the lofty windows. Only the ceiling line of the buttery, which blocks one row of the glazing bars, gives the game away showing that this part of the range has rooms above the pantry, whereas the great hall rises through to the roof on the other side.

104. *Hatfield House in Hertfordshire of 1611 combining symmetry and Elizabethan influences.*

Sometimes the demands of fashion forced an inevitable compromise between function and appearance. This is well seen at Madingley Hall. As we saw earlier, the hall, albeit with a chamber above, was built to the traditional plan with service rooms and private rooms at either end. The main entrance porch led into a screens passage which, because the hall was in the centre of the range, was asymmetrical. To harmonize the elevation making it symmetrical, a traditional oriel window was built to balance the entrance porch and thus, together with suitably arranged windows, provided a symmetrical elevation. Yet this architectural stratagem failed completely for the Hyndes who lived here also required a fashionable long gallery. Some eighty-seven feet (26.5 m) long, this was set at the end of and at right angles to the solar end of the hall and projected forward from the main elevation, completely spoiling the overall symmetry. The long gallery wing has since been demolished, but a later, shorter wing which replaced it still shows the confusion of aims which confronted the house builders of this time.

These ideas so influential in the great houses of the Tudor and Jacobean periods did not find their way right down the social scale. Even so, there were important changes in the houses of small farmers and wealthy peasants which, in parts of southern Britain, at least produced an outburst of new building now described as 'The Great Rebuilding'. Countless new houses were built between 1550 and 1650, of which many still survive, while hundreds if not thousands more were altered and upgraded. The most important of the alterations concerned the abandonment of the open hall, the insertion of new ceilings with rooms above and the creation of new chimney stacks as we have described.

The new houses settled down to an almost standard arrangement although there were local modifications. Basically, these homes were still only one room in width and comprised three rooms on the ground floor, usually a kitchen, dining room and sitting-room, with three upper rooms. Sometimes one or both end rooms were built as separate wings producing an 'L'-, 'U'- or even 'T'-shape, but more normally the structure was a simple rectangular block. Chimneys and fireplaces became common, sometimes set against the end walls, sometimes set centrally within the building. In specific areas there were local variants and, for example, over many parts of East Anglia and south-east England there was an almost standard type of seventeenth-century house of three rooms with a large internal chimney stack between two of the rooms and

105. *Lilford Hall, Northamptonshire. The façade is of 1635 and the house was modified in the course of the seventeenth and early eighteenth centuries.*

with the main doorway positioned opposite the stack. The actual materials used to build such houses varied considerably : they were usually timber-framed but could be of clay bat, cob, stone or brick, as local sources determined.

Elsewhere, and especially in the north and west, the typical medieval peasant long-house form persisted, with some improvements. The most important of these was the division produced by an internal fireplace and chimney stack, usually built against the wall of the cross passage to heat the main living-rooms. A variant, common in northern England, is the so-called 'laithe-house' which consists of a combined dwelling house and barn—a 'laithe' under one roof. Here there were separate doorways into both house and laithe, but most still retained the basic three roomed plan for domestic accommodation.

Yet another type of the smaller house was that with the so-called 'through-passage' plan, where an axial passage divided the living room from the kitchen. This type seems to have had two origins. One was a development from the long-house whereby what had previously been byre or stable became a kitchen, the other is merely a lower class variant of the medieval screens passage separating the hall from the service wing. Most of these houses had internal fireplaces and chimneys to heat living-rooms, with end chimneys to heat the kitchen and provide the means for cooking.

Despite all these seemingly important variations, one important trend emerges: the gradually increasing demand for improved living standards. Physically it was reflected in an increasing number of rooms; the permanent separation of kitchens from dining rooms and parlours; the provision of a set of bedrooms instead of just one, and of fireplaces and chimneys to provide warmth in most rooms.

For the very lowest levels of society, the evidence is much scarcer. Most of the houses of this period have, understandably, disappeared and few of their remains have been excavated. Of the rare examples that survive, mainly in the southern part of Britain, most are crudely built and of only one storey. As always, the nature of their construction varied from region to region but they have many of the characteristics of the *cot* excavated on medieval villages. Most are open to the roof and comprise only two rooms: one for living and cooking, the other for sleeping. On the other hand a number are known which had internal or external fireplaces and chimney stacks. Thus, even at the lowest levels of society in England at least, improved standards of living are clearly evidenced.

The growing desire for better living conditions which is seen in the development of smaller houses in the sixteenth and early seventeenth centuries led to further changes. Often the parlour or solar area of a house was rebuilt to provide an increased number of rooms. Another common change was the provision of small rooms along the back of the house, under a lean-to roof—and such extensions are known as 'out-shots'. Out-shots were rare before the early seventeenth century but then became common providing extra storage, pantries, sculleries and washing facilities all conveniently within the house. Houses with out-shots have a plan which resembles that of a 'double-pile' house: a house which is two rooms deep and has the front and back at the same height. Yet though there may be an indirect connection, the origin of the double-pile house has to be sought elsewhere.

25

Houses of the later Seventeenth and Eighteenth Centuries

For all their elaborate decorations and symmetrical elevations most late medieval and early Jacobean houses still remained very firmly in the medieval tradition, reflecting the conservatism of domestic life in those times. Even so, in the late sixteenth century further changes took place which were to revolutionize the house. They can be seen in some of the grandest of the late sixteenth-century houses such as Hardwick Hall.

Here, with the turning of the hall at right angles and the setting of rooms on either side of it, the builders had effectively created a double-pile house: a building that was two rooms deep. It is difficult now to realize how revolutionary this concept was. Hitherto, with few exceptions, the houses were long and narrow with general access that was only possible by moving through successive rooms rather than into them. The double-pile house made it possible for rooms to be individually accessible, if necessary, from a single central circulating area. Again, Hardwick Hall illustrates this albeit on a lavish scale. The central hall allows the almost complete segregation of the service rooms and the living-rooms and, in this case, of the Countess's private suites from other private rooms. Thus individual rooms or whole areas of the house could be shut off for special or private usage. This change also emphasized the down grading of the great hall which tended even more to become the main circulating area from which doors, passages and staircases led to other rooms with specific purposes.

Such a plan, with the central hall and staircases, also harmonized with the demands for external symmetry which not only affected the main front elevation but the sides and back as well. The way was open for the development of a house-type which was eventually to change the way that almost everybody lived.

In spite of their more obvious advantages, these new arrangements were only slowly accepted. As we have seen, most of the seventeenth-century mansions perpetuated the traditional plan. It was not until the end of the century that double-pile houses became common, even for the élite. The first real house of this type was Coleshill in Berkshire of 1650 which, although altered internally, still stands. The architect, Roger Pratt, had been much influenced by development of houses on the continent and the external decoration and symmetry were certainly derived from abroad. But the internal arrangement was based more on developing English traditions rather than those of Europe. The great hall was still positioned in the centre of the façade with a great parlour beyond. But from the hall, passages led axially along the spine of the house giving access to separate suites of rooms, all of which had special functions. From the hall, a staircase rose to the first floor on which there was a Great Dining Chamber

106. *Wimpole Hall of the early eighteenth century, including a building of about 1640 in its central block.*

standing above the parlour and the same axial passages led to more suites of rooms.

This plan was a brilliant modification of the Hardwick Hall type of layout and allowed perfect symmetry to be maintained on all external elevations. But Coleshill also exhibits another, more important change. Achieving symmetry of arrangement in elevation left no place for a grand staircase set outside the hall as it had been since medieval times. Pratt solved the problem by placing it into the great hall itself where there was space for it to be constructed on a grand scale. By doing this, however, the hall finally lost its time-hallowed purpose as a dining-hall for retainers and servants. These people had to be given a separate dining-hall which was set in a basement, along with kitchens and other service rooms. The hall was thus reduced to a grandiose entrance or vestibule. More socially significant was the fact that all the occupants other than the dominant family and their guests were now isolated from the main part of the house. Henceforth, an increasing social divide between owners and servants developed, each now having their own apartments and consequently lifestyles. This unprecedented social arrangement was to dominate the planning of all types of houses until the twentieth century.

Plans introduced at houses such as Coleshill in the middle of the seventeenth century proved to be the ideals for most houses for over 150 years. Architectural fashions changed greatly, minor modifications were introduced and symmetry was enhanced by balancing wings or by linked pavilions. Yet whether one looks at a great palace such as Blenheim in Oxfordshire, of 1705–20, or fine but less pretentious houses such as Basildon Park in Berkshire, of 1776–1783, the same pattern of rooms is repeated together with symmetrical elevations.

The leaders of fashion altered the layout of great houses yet again in the eighteenth century as we shall describe. But the impact of what we have called the 'Coleshill plan' had a more widespread effect: as the eighteenth century advanced, the basic ideas of Coleshill and its prestigious contemporaries spread down the social scale. Local lords rebuilt their less extravagant houses to similar plans or altered their existing houses in attempts to achieve the comparable effects. Shugborough Hall, Staffordshire, begun in the 1690s for William Anson, was at first a modest house with an internal arrangement that in many respects mirrored Coleshill. It was later much extended in the 1740s but the extensions merely provided extra rooms for specific purposes.

Later, minor landowners, the wealthier clergy and then richer farmers all followed suit. By the end of the eighteenth century nobody with any pretensions to status or wealth would consider building anything but a symmetrical house of double depth, with a central door leading into a hall from which a staircase gave access to the rooms around. In those parts of Britain where, in the late eighteenth and early nineteenth centuries, the Parliamentary Enclosure Movement produced a new landscape of geometrical fields and farmhouses, all the Enclosure farmsteads conformed to this

107. *A series of fine houses with symmetrical brick façades lines the cathedral close at Salisbury.*

norm. The red brick farmhouses of the English Midlands, the white brick ones of East Anglia, the grey stone farmsteads of the northern hills, all echoed this basic appearance and internal arrangement. Of course there were minor differences in detail, but the similarities are more striking. Quite by chance, a form of house was devised in the middle of the seventeenth century which proved admirably suited to the ways of life and aspirations of almost all classes of English society.

By the nineteenth century, in rural areas at least, all but the poorest classes were housed in double-pile symmetrical houses which were either built to this design or achieved by massive modifications or additions to older houses. One fine example of the latter process is Rectory Farm at Barrington, Cambridgeshire. The house began as a fifteenth-century structure with an open hall with a service wing at one end and a solar range at the other. In the mid sixteenth century, a ceiling was built in the open hall, a central chimney inserted and the service wings reconstructed. Then, in 1772, the older solar wing was torn down and replaced by a neat brick structure with a symmetrical front, a central door and an entrance hall which had a room on each side. Instead of further rooms being installed beyond, the passage hall led into the old medieval range, which was relegated to the status of a service end and kitchens with servants' rooms above.

The lesser people of the eighteenth century were, on the whole, content or obliged to live in more traditional houses. The increasing use of cheap brick, particularly in southern Britain, enabled some changes in design to take place, one of the most significant being the replacement of a large internal multiple chimney by external stacks. These allowed all rooms to be heated easily, a much needed improvement. The commonest form of rural dwelling in many places consisted of a two or three-roomed house arranged in an elongated structure or perhaps in an 'L'-shape. The earliest of these tended to have internal chimneys, while later ones had end chimneys. The simple two-roomed dwelling with end chimneys enabled the builders to provide a central passage entrance between the rooms with access via a central door. This design allowed a symmetrical external elevation and so allowed at least a nod in the direction of contemporary fashion.

Despite all these changes poverty, conservatism and climate ensured that traditional concepts and methods persisted in many parts of Britain. In the uplands of northern England, for example, the long-houses or laithe-houses not only often existed unchanged but were also sometimes newly built in the traditional style. Here, the climate and traditional pastoral farming habits made it convenient, if not necessary, to perpetuate the old house form. Even so, national trends did have an effect: often the byre end of the long house was unchanged while the house end was demolished and rebuilt with a symmetrical front and central door. This type of modification continued until the end of the nineteenth century.

In Wales, Scotland and Ireland, while the upper classes gradually acquired houses which were identical in most repects to those of prestigious houses in England, the lesser lords and minor gentry generally lived in houses resembling types occupied by people of much lower status in England. Thus, Cara House on the Island of Cara, off Kintyre, in Argyll, built in 1773 by the main tenant or tacksman of the island, is a simple two-roomed structure with end chimneys and more or less symmetrical elevation. The same picture can be seen in Wales, where minor tenant farmers and freeholders lived from the late sixteenth century onwards in plain ranges which were divided into two or three rooms heated by end chimneys, and generally having access through a central doorway.

Again, less is known about the very lowest levels of society as the houses of these people have not survived. In the upland parts of Britain there are many thousands of abandoned cottages dating from the eighteenth or early nineteenth century which were deserted as a result of the Highland Clearances or Irish famines and emigrations. A few did survive into the present century and have been restored, although all were probably altered in detail towards the end of their lives. One excellent example is the Blackhouse at Arnol, on the Isle of Lewis, Scotland. Basically it is a 'long-house' in the medieval tradition. At one end is a large byre with cattle stalls. Then beyond a cross passage, the rest of the building is divided into two rooms, the nearer one called 'The Fire Room' with an open central hearth, and the further one known as 'The Sleeping Room'. The Arnol House also had a long barn attached to one of the long walls and entered via a door in the cross passage as well as by an external door on its other long side. Though the Arnol Blackhouse has relatively recent origins, it follows a long tradition of Highland houses. Eighteenth-century examples, now ruins, show similar plans, although some have porches or extra rooms built on the side of the house opposite to the barn. Elsewhere in northern Scotland, other examples of long-houses remain, often much simpler. The same kind of variations exist in Ireland to show that in the Celtic north and west change and improvements in houses were slow or non-existent for most people from medieval times until the nineteenth century or, in some localities, even later.

Returning to the eighteenth-century mansions we found that although a standard arrangement had emerged by 1700 and, as we have seen, this standard was gradually accepted and adapted by the lower orders of society, at the highest levels the houses continued to evolve to reflect alterations in the fashionable way of life. The eighteenth century saw the emergence of the 'polite society'. Aristocrats and wealthy people became more mobile, travelling between their country estates, London and the fashionable spa towns such as Bath and Buxton. As they perambulated round the country they stayed with friends or even strangers and at these gatherings the house was thrown open for parties, balls and other lavish entertainments. But the great house with its entrance hall, axial passages and discrete suites of rooms was not equipped for such a social whirl. Gradually houses were adapted to suit the new conditions. This was done by constructing, sometimes on the ground but often at first-floor level, an approach by a lavish staircase. From the entrance hall the staircase led to a suite of rooms which were interconnected and which were arranged at the head of the stairs to encircle the hall. The new houses were built with this arrangement in mind, while at older houses walls were demolished, interiors gutted and the new arrangements fitted in.

Hagley Hall in Worcestershire, which was built in 1752, shows the new ideas at work while combining the best of the old tradition as well as the new. It has an entrance hall or vestibule from which it was possible to circulate to the dining-room and then to the gallery, drawing-room, saloon and library and thence back into the hall. It also contained a sub-hall to one side which gave access only to the private apartments of the family.

26

The Development of the Modern House

The years between 1780 and 1900 saw no slackening in the development of the home. At the country house level practical challenges, fashion and new ideas all combined to produce new forms of structures. As the rich became richer, the number of retainers and servants needed to run mansions which were almost becoming labour-intensive industrial units began to pose problems. Maids were crammed in attics, footmen pushed into basements and butlers and housekeepers installed in small flatlets or apartments. Technical advances accruing from the Industrial Revolution were rapidly acquired by a society which was increasingly intrigued by mechanical devices.

Meanwhile, a steadily growing demand for improved standards of day-to-day living and regular lavish entertainments caused the installation of bathrooms, lavatories, laundries, and gigantic kitchens. Changes in fashion, habits and entertainments produced a need for conservatories, smoking-rooms, billiard-rooms, boudoirs, nurseries, breakfast-rooms, morning-rooms and studies as well as the more traditional dining-rooms, drawing-rooms and bedrooms. The neatly planned house, symmetrical outside and regularly arranged inside became impossible to achieve. In structural terms, wings often of considerable size had to be added to old houses, or incorporated in the designs of new ones. The wings accommodated the increasing numbers of service rooms as well as much needed servants' quarters. Sometimes other wings were designed entirely for the principal family's private use, so that the main house was almost relegated to the role of an entertainment complex. Of course, houses in the past had wings but these had usually been provided to produce the necessary symmetrical balance—but now symmetry fell out of fashion.

Romanticism, in its many aspects also effected revolution in the ordered world of the eighteenth century. Every facet of life had to pursue the 'natural' deal—no matter how contrived the results might seem. In this naturalistic new world the symmetrical house was literally a square peg. Once so ardently sought, it was rejected and asymmetry appeared as the new ideal. At first mere whimsical decoration, often in the 'Gothic'

108. *When the Industrial Revolution dawned in Britain there was some uncertainty as to the proper appearance for factories and many were built according to the precepts of domestic architecture. This is Arkwright's Mill at Cromford where water was used to power cotton manufacture in 1771.*

manner, was frequently applied to basically Classical houses, as at Great Missenden Abbey, Buckinghamshire. Soon, however, the regular formal elevations of houses surrendered to ranges of towers, pinnacles and spires, wings and extensions—all clustered in spiky and angular profusion. The Gothic style was admirably suited to romantic taste, but as the nineteenth century advanced and style followed style, Elizabethan, Italianate, French and even Classical and oriental forms were entangled in the designs of houses which only superficially resembled the sources of their inspiration. Knebworth House in Hertfordshire, built between 1843 and 1870, is a wildly medieval extravaganza, both inside and without, with towers, turrets, crenellations and baronial hall! Exactly as no medieval house ever was, it is a splendid safari through

109. *Papworth Hall, Cambridgeshire, a small country seat of c. 1815 which incorporates a mixture of Classical styles including the Ionic portico.*

110. *Knebworth House, Hertfordshire, a delicious Neo-Gothic fantasy produced by the remodelling of an older house in 1843.*

the Neo-Gothic world, while Waddesdon Manor, in Buckinghamshire, built in 1880 to 1889 as the home of the Rothschilds is an entertaining adventure in the French style.

The late nineteenth century marked the height of country house development. The early twentieth century saw its end as social and economic conditions that had supported it came to an end. Progress in social democracy meant that the authority which the great country house stood for was gradually eroded, while vast sums of money to maintain the mansions dried up. The uncertainties facing owners inevitably influenced the appearance of the few new houses that were built. Some remained grand and imposing and there was also a return to Classical symmetry, a form of architecture associated with the imperialism of Greece and Rome. An example is Bryanston House in Dorset, of 1895, which was constructed in a monumental and overbearing early eighteenth-century style. Other houses were huge but asymmetrical, often harking back to a medieval past which existed only in the romantic mind but which is well expressed at Castle Drogo in Devon, of 1910 to 1925. But houses became smaller, lower and built in ways which aped the old vernacular tradition with imitation timber-framing, mullioned windows and plans incorporating numerous separate blocks, so that the custom-built houses appeared to have grown up over time. Ashby St. Ledger House in Northamptonshire, of 1903, shows this well.

By the beginning of World War II, the era of the great house had ended. Since then none have been built, and indeed many have been demolished as the society which created them has been eroded.

Smaller houses of the nineteenth century and Edwardian periods developed in much the same way as the great ones, though more slowly, handed down to lower levels of society so that the standard farm house of the mid and even the late nineteenth century still had a symmetrical front with a central door leading to a staircase and hall on to which all rooms opened. The more important members of the middle classes, notably the clergy, took their lead from the aristocrats, and rectories, vicarages and minor manor houses often appeared in a variety of styles from a quirky Gothic to a formal Italianate. Inside, servants' quarters, studies and smoking-rooms appeared to produce what was often an incoherent arrangement which could only be countenanced because of the ready supply of servants.

As with great halls, by 1900 there was a return to less imposing structures with an emphasis on 'traditional' appearance and less lavish interiors. But even at the less affluent level, economic and social changes produced an end to the development of these types of houses. What followed was the development of housing for the democratic society.

The development of town and suburban houses is a rather different story from those relating to great country houses and other rural dwellings. Even so, the same interplays of change and conservatism were applicable, but with the addition of some notable new features. From the medieval towns, little survives except some examples of the homes of wealthier merchants and leading townsfolk. The homes of the great mass of urban dwellers do not survive in any great numbers from periods earlier than the seventeenth century. And indeed, there is not very much difference between a medieval manor house and a medieval town house except for the inevitable compaction of the latter

111. *Cliffe Castle, Keighley, the imposing home of Victorian industrialists, was begun c. 1830 and enlarged as a 'castle' in 1875–80. The style is Elizabethan in its general inspiration.*

imposed by the limitations of space in an urban environment. The few remaining examples of eleventh to thirteenth-century houses, all apparently belonging to rich merchants or lords, have, like their rural contemporaries, open halls, service wings and solar ends, though the latter were not always structurally separate. From the fourteenth century onwards more town houses survive and they show a greater variety in the status of the occupants. Those belonging to the wealthiest members of the community still have halls while the lesser ones tend to consist of long ranges which rarely consist of more than two or three rooms and they have chimney stacks and fireplaces built into their side walls. Often, as a result of site restrictions, they are turned at right angles to the street frontage. Such house plans continued little unchanged until the seventeenth or even the eighteenth century. Even the specialized form of urban dwelling—the shop—was adapted from this plan. The front ground-floor room became the shop, with the store room behind, while the owner and his family occupied the upper floors, which owing to a lack of space were sometimes jettied out over the street.

The influence of the double-pile and symmetrical house began to be felt in the early seventeenth century and had spread widely by the end of the century. Most houses of this type, despite their inevitable minor variations still mirrored the rural dwellings with their central doors and entrance hall with rooms arranged symmetrically around. Many older houses, especially those set parallel to the street, which previously had the main door either to the one side of the front elevation or leading off a side passage, were refronted and rearranged internally at this time. A new central doorway and matching windows gave external symmetry while within, an axial passage was flanked by rooms.

Throughout the eighteenth and nineteenth centuries town houses, whether detached or built in rows, all echoed the double-piled plan and symmetrical elevation. Such dwellings were erected in hundreds or thousands in most British towns. From Whitby, where the homes of early eighteenth-century merchants display a severe brickwork, to the villas of south London Victorian businessmen all dwellings conform to this plan. The obvious differences in external decoration and architectural detail tend to be just superficial variations on the theme. Thus, the detached urban or suburban house followed a very similar pattern for almost 200 years.

Yet the seventeenth century also witnessed the development of a new form of urban housing, the terrace. This type of dwelling, which is an essential component of modern town and suburban life, could only be built where relatively large areas of land were available for development or redevelopment by entrepreneurs. Few medieval towns ever had terraces, for the social, economic and physical conditions which allowed their creation generally did not exist. Custom-built rows of terraced almshouses were occasionally provided while in medieval new towns, some terrace-like rows were built piecemeal by the tenants.

The first real terraces tended to provide low-class industrial and semi-industrial housing. There was no overall planning, but merely the construction, in rows, of dwellings which elsewhere would have been built as detached houses. A recent study of the late seventeenth-century development at Frome in Somerset has shown this pattern extremely well. By the end of the seventeenth century the fashion for symmetry had spread to terraces. Because the terraces were developed piecemeal, at first only individual houses had their own symmetry. But later, whole terraces were endowed with symmetry and designed as a piece of architecture. This type of symmetrical terracing culminated at Bath in the eighteenth century, although many other towns, including Edinburgh, Buxton and Cheltenham, contain fine examples. The fashion persisted into the nineteenth century and even beyond, irrespective of the changes in architectural style, but by the end of the nineteenth century, the increasing influence of the speculative developer and builder combined with the increasing demands from owners for houses that were 'different'—if only slightly different—from their neighbours, led to the breakdown of overall symmetry and the appearance of minor irregularities.

The house arrangements behind the terraced façades were, originally, often matters for the owner or speculative builder to decide. But gradually, a standard plan evolved which was, in essence, one half of the typical symmetrical plan and one which also enabled symmetry to be retained externally. It consisted of a front entrance leading into a passage-hall with a staircase which was set on one side of the house, while two rooms were entered from the hall, and with a kitchen wing provided at the rear. The kitchen wing might be merely a lean-to attachment, a single storey block or it could be a rear projection rising to the full height of the house. There was normally also a basement or a cellar.

This basic terraced house pattern became almost ubiquitous but it could be modified to suit all levels of society. The upper-class terraced house was, of course, large, with kitchens and servants' quarters in the basement; a rear staircase to keep the servants' activities apart from the main private circulating area around the hall; large dining-rooms and drawing-rooms on the ground floor; morning-rooms and bedrooms on the upper floors, and servants' quarters in the attics. The middle-class terraced houses were smaller and had far fewer rooms, but the necessity for at least one living-in servant required an attic bedroom. Even the notorious back-to-back industrial buildings which appeared in tens of thousands in the new urban areas of the North and Midlands were really only adaptations of the conventional terraced plan. The side passage was omitted and the front door opened into the living room, while the kitchen was a separate structure at the rear. The staircase usually rose from the living room to the two small bedrooms above.

Thus, in the nineteenth century, terraced housing became the norm for most urban dwellings. Only architectural style and decoration varied. On the more prestigious eighteenth-century terraces there were central pediments, classical half-columns and elaborate doorcases. In the early nineteenth century, windows were typically set in round-headed blind recesses, while doorcases became lighter with decorative fanlights a dire necessity to light the dark halls behind. By the late nineteenth century, bay windows, often crenellated and with much applied mass-produced detailing, became highly fashionable. Only in the mean little industrial terraces was decoration ignored. Each subtle step in the social hierarchy was expressed in the quality of embellishments, the size of rooms and detailed variations to the terrace layout. Thus one's street and even street number address became a reliable guide to social standing.

But by 1900 new changes were afoot. The better-off members of society continued to aspire to detached town houses, set individually in gardens and with at least some external distinction to mark them off from their neighbours. Such houses had long existed on the fringes of towns and during the nineteenth century they became increasingly common. In London, garden suburbs appeared in the early nineteenth century and by the end of the century, every town of substance had its rows of loosely Gothic, Classical, Italianate, or 'vernacular' villas set out along fashionable new streets. The internal plans of the villas were often fairly standardized but the exteriors were as different as resources would allow. Individualism was rampant in this age, and where resources were limited, semi-detached houses as individual as the format would allow were built, each dwelling with its own separate garden space.

Until World War I, individual 'villas', semis and terraced houses continued to be erected. But the 1920s and 1930s produced an explosion of house building based on

112. Industrial terraced housing in Skipton.

completely new demands. The result was the suburban semi which was to become as familiar and as sought after in the 1920s and 1930s as the terraced house had been some fifty years before. Even today, the suburban semi remains as perhaps the most characteristic type of middle-class housing in Britain. How it developed, why it was so popular and how it managed to survive and flourish at all is a fascinating story which has only recently been unravelled. Certainly the semi was a target for continual and often violent criticism. It was denounced on every possible ground: it took valuable land; it was poorly built; badly designed and produced a monotonous and boring environment. Leading architects claimed it failed to take account of good 'modern' design which should have improved its appearance, while those in charge of local authority housing, whether planners, architects or politicians, totally ignored it. Council houses, for example, which were themselves an expression of social change in the twentieth century, were usually designed in a crude, debased, but nevertheless

301

recognizable Neo-Georgian style, even to the extent of being set out in short terraces. Yet such alternative designs were like the critics of the semis, totally ignored.

A middle-class social revolution had taken place. People knew what they wanted and had the power and resources to achieve their aims. They desired a semi-detached house, set in a small garden, with a garage, or space for one, to house their new car. They wanted bay windows at the front, with a little applied 'half-timbering' over it, French windows leading to the back garden and an external symmetry with their near neighbours. Within the general symmetry there should be slight differences, sufficient to distinguish 'home' from the adjacent houses. Inside they demanded a plan modified from that of the old terraced house. A well-lit side hall, a dining-room, a living-room, a small kitchen with labour-saving devices, two or three bedrooms and a bathroom were all required. Basements were unnecessary while servants were no longer needed. A private world geared to the demands of a small family with rarely more than two children was sought and achieved. Middle-class tastes, separate from and almost oblivious to those of the 'establishment', appeared quickly. The middle masses of the British people had become more democratic and individualistic in the 1920s and 1930s and they expressed the changes in their homes.

In the last forty years this trend has accelerated. Even the glory of the inter-war semi has dimmed and the middle-class ideal has gone one stage further in the aspiration for a completely detached house. Even if the home be only nine inches from its neighbour, four freestanding walls is now the aim. Styles too have changed. Neo-Georgian has become popular again. Extra rooms, some for yet more new labour-saving devices, have appeared. Studies, even if they only house a cocktail cabinet, are considered vital. Yet underlying all this there is a strong urge for individual living and an attempt to be in some way different from the neighbours while studiously conforming to their values. These desires and aims have filtered down from the middle to the working classes and in so doing they have refuted almost all the attempts by architects, planners and politicians to pen people in what are considered to be the 'best' dwellings. Economical, space-saving, communal flats and tower blocks have come and gone, collapsing, rotting slowly or being urgently demolished, leaving behind the legacy of social problems and a disfigured environment. More stable are the thousands upon thousands of acres covered by 'little boxes' which have combined as the Harlows, Milton Keyneses and Cumbernaulds of our age. They may offend the architectural purist, be the despair of the environmentalist and drive the planners to distraction. Yet they also reflect the final achievement of a democratic society.

Reflections

The literature and thinking associated with the British home have been rather un-balanced. Since at least the Victorian era, the Fine Art perspective has been paramount, with the more 'important' dwellings being appraised in terms of whether or not they were good and 'significant' or bad and 'debased' exercises in a particular architectural fashion; whether they contained important items of decoration, sculpture or early examples of this or that fitting. Perhaps as a reaction against this preoccupation with arty trappings, recent decades have witnessed the emergence of scholars and groups who have turned the spotlight on vernacular architecture and studied the evolution of humbler dwellings to provide us with important new insights into the detailed development of house-building, the successive use of different techniques in carpentry and the exploitation of different local building materials at different times.

Each of these approaches has much to offer, but when followed too narrowly they are both prone to overlooking the fact that a house is, first and foremost, a home. Here therefore we have attempted to explore the house not so much as a coming together of particular architectural styles and fashions or as a technological complex of materials and craftsmanship in masonry and carpentry, but as a place where a family would perform the plays and pantomimes of domestic life.

We have concentrated on the layout of the house because, whatever fashionable trappings might ice the exterior, the house was for living in. As a result, house designs mirrored the changes in domestic life. They also reflected the links between the principal family, their peers, retainers and servants. Domestic life was not lived in a vacuum and only the poverty-stricken home owner, the eccentric or the recluse could afford to ignore the changes which developments in social norms and behaviour imposed upon the occupiers of great houses. At one time these might require the addition of a long gallery and at another, the conversion of stables into garages. Fortunately, poverty-stricken, eccentric and reclusive owners existed at all periods and so Britain contains many dwellings like Compton Wynyates and Kirby Hall which are particularly expressive of their periods—even though most houses, like most churches, are the accumulations of centuries of fashion following change.

We tend to assume that each turn of the spiral of house design represented an objective improvement upon what had gone before, but this is a misleading view and, for example, a medieval manor house could be much more easily adapted to suit the conditions of twentieth-century living than a nineteenth-century palatial mansion constructed in the era of cheap and abundant servants. A thirteenth-century baron who—in our flight of fancy—might build himself a home according to the layout of a 1930s villa would not have been considered as progressive and visionary by his peers. The absence of a cavernous hall as a venue for feasting, administration, socializing and general living would have been considered anti-social, ungentlemanly and ungracious. The devotion of almost half the accommodation to a number of private bedrooms would have been thought wasteful and prudish, while the bathroom/lavatory would have been considered odd and its fittings weird or, worse, interchangeable. In short, the house would have been totally ill-equipped to meet the social needs of its occupants.

If anything has emerged from our survey it is the dovetailing of social evolution and house planning. And so, more than being a sounding board which echoed to the tune of the architectural fashions or Fine Art fads of each age, the house was above all a vehicle which was adapted and continually readapted to match the changing habits of domestic life. It was essentially a home, even if it was often other things as well.

For all our emphasis on change it is also important to remember the presence of the strong hand of tradition. Conservatism strongly influenced the designs of smaller dwellings, but many traditional features were retained simply because they were useful. Thus, centuries after the abandonment of the long-house in the English mixed farming counties, it was retained in the pastoral uplands because it met the perceived needs of the small livestock farmer who saw good sense in having suckling lambs, a sickly calf or a milk cow close by. The interplay between tradition and progress is nowhere better demonstrated than in the case of the hall and we have shown how it was redefined in the post-medieval period. Conservative values argued for its retention, but it also had continuing uses, even if it eventually degenerated into the entrance hall which is still a component of most modern homes.

We should also be wary of writing off any traditional component of a house. As a multi-purpose, dominating, social, eating and living area, the hall might seem to be as dead as the dodo. But the 1960s and 1970s vogue for open planning which can be custom-built or achieved by disembowelling an older house, reminds us that from Chelsea to converted Pennine barns and the gentrified terraces of Cambridge, the medieval concept of the hall is alive and well.

Although successive changes repeatedly transformed the physical appearance and layout of 'home', the house remained an organic unit which could be remodelled and then changed again to achieve the goal of being what home owners wanted it to be. Only rarely have architects been charged with the brief of designing homes in the image of the priorities of planning and architectural and political lore rather than according to the expressed needs of home dwellers. The ghastly consequences of such policies are evident in most British towns in the form of tower blocks. They are now loudly denounced, not least by the politicians, developers and fad merchants who once proclaimed their virtues and who now find inspiration in the terraces and terraced closes of the first industrial age. As we have seen, the ubiquitous expanses of suburban semis, monotonous in their pursuit of feeble differences but now mellowing in the shade and glow of mature shrubs and gardens, represent a less costly victory of the home desired over the home designed.

Our visions of the past seem to be saying that the home is the product of perceptions and decisions. Some of these derived from architectural visionaries and technological innovators. But much more important were those of the home dweller and owner who took his cues from the practical experiences of domestic life and the expectations and demands of life within the broader society. He sifted through the innovations and fashions and decided which traditional features of the home deserved retention and which new ideas merited inclusion. Each generation makes up its own mind about what home should be. The differences in perception span space as well as time and it is significant that while most continental Europeans seem content in the role of the apartment tenant, private home ownership is a driving ambition of the British. Recent experience suggests that members of the nation will buy anything, at any price, in order to obtain the status and independence which home ownership endows.

PART VII

Landscapes of Recreation

Introduction

The enjoyment of leisure pursuits which have no direct bearing on the physical necessities of life is a characteristic of human history. As a result, vast resources have been devoted to create places of entertainment and recreation, and many of them are preserved in the landscape.

The monuments to enjoyment are very varied, but basically there are two types: those created for the private pleasures of individuals or small groups, and those which society at large—or at least certain classes within society—has chosen to create for mass enjoyment. In the first category are most gardens, be they the grandly formal ones of the seventeenth century or the privet-edged patches of the suburban semis. The second type would include medieval archery butts as well as school playing fields, sports stadia and the venues for village games. Inevitably, the distinction between the two types is often blurred and there are also other factors which should be considered. For example, today recreation is usually clearly defined and separated from other forms of human activity in the way that a typical football ground is used purely for recreational purposes and has no direct practical or ritual significance (although claims for the latter purpose have been made by Desmond Morris).

In earlier times, however, it was more difficult to make a clear distinction between recreation, ritual and practical usages. Archery butts are a good example, for while much fun may have been had, their provision was related to the need for trained archers. In a different field, medieval deer-parks had a recreational function but also had a more important role in providing fresh meat. It was even more difficult to separate ritual functions from recreational ones. In the twentieth century, religion is usually kept quite distinct from most other activities, but in earlier periods and especially in medieval and prehistoric times there was no such division. As a result recreational activities, as well as most other aspects of life, must have been merged with ritual and religion. In this way, the medieval use of churches for social gatherings, like 'church ales', and churchyards for games was not profane but expressed the role of the church as the hub and fount of all ideas and activities. In prehistoric times, the integration of work, belief and play may have been even more complete.

27

Ancient People at Play

We know of no feature in the landscape, nor in the archaeological record, that proves that prehistoric people took part in fun and games. Why should this be so? One might suggest that prehistoric people, living at or near subsistence levels, had no time for such frolics. But this cannot be true. Not only did our distant ancestors sometimes live well above the line of subsistence, but their society was also organized in a way that allowed large numbers of people considerable resources and time to erect massive and complex ritual monuments (see p. 14ff). Perhaps prehistoric people did not organize their recreation, but if so, they were certainly different from any other human societies that we know of, all of which have produced facilities for recreation. The real answer is probably that at certain times of the year, and at certain ceremonies, activities which were basically ritual in meaning became recreational in character. If we wish, therefore, to see the playing fields and fun palaces of prehistoric times we might look at the ancient religious monuments.

Of course, as we know almost nothing of prehistoric religions we can hardly identify their recreational aspects. Nevertheless, it may be worth suggesting possible connections. While the great Neolithic cursuses are now no longer seen as racecourses as the early antiquarians proposed, it may well be that they functioned as processional ways along which people moved to and from certain ceremonies. The slightly later stone rows may also have had similar functions. After all, all religions and sects have, or had, ceremonial occasions which either accidentally or deliberately extended far beyond the central ritual. Even today, in many Latin American countries, the distinction between a religious festival and a fiesta is blurred and it is more than likely that the same overlap occurred in prehistoric times. The great banked and ditched henge monuments were described in Part I and undoubtedly their interiors were used for some form of ritual, while their ditches may well have marked the division between the sacred world within and the profane world outside. The encircling banks may also have provided the seating or viewing areas for the 'laity'. Whether one should see them as the equivalents to the nave of a Christian church, the auditorium of a theatre or both, one cannot tell.

Complex religious rituals and perhaps entertainments too were carried out around burial places. Excavations at the Nympsfield Neolithic chambered tomb in Gloucestershire and beneath Bronze Age barrows have produced evidence of feasting and even of ground stamped down by dancing. What part purer forms of entertainment played in such activities is difficult to know, but as with the traditional Irish funeral wake religious observance and sociable recreation probably merged. Even the entombed

113. *Maumbury Ring, Dorset, a Neolithic henge temple, later developed as a Roman amphitheatre and later still as a gun position.*

beakers which were an essential component of early Bronze Age burial rituals are now thought to have held an alcoholic beverage, so the wake analogy may be particularly apt!

As in so many other areas, the start of the Roman period in Britain marks a complete break with what had gone before; in play, as elsewhere, the ideas of a complex and advanced society were quickly superimposed on the native culture. Roman society had its own specialized forms of recreation and entertainment which were rapidly adopted in Britain. Two forms of recreation left a permanent mark on the landscape. The first type of relics are the remains of public entertainment areas, mainly theatres and amphitheatres which were provided by the Roman authorities as places of public entertainment. But they also had other more important and less obvious functions relating to the society they served. For example, most of the permanent large military bases in Britain had amphitheatres which functioned as 'garrison theatres' to use a somewhat out-dated term. But such amphitheatres had a military function too. They provided a parade ground for drill and weapon training, an assembly place for military display and, no doubt, a venue for morale-boosting addresses; so even here we see the difficulty of attempting to draw clearly defined lines between recreational and other activities. Today our recreational facilities may be used for two hours a week as in the case of a football ground or a few hours every day in the case of our theatres; our Roman predecessors were not so profligate with their resources and probably made much fuller use of their facilities.

The theatres of Roman towns—no town in Britain was fully complete without one—also had a dual function, although here we may see a similarity between our own times and the Roman period. They provided public entertainment for the town dweller and venues for meetings, also, as with our municipal theatres and sports halls, there was a strong element of civic pride and status involved. Like modern sports halls which only cater for a small proportion of the total population, take up huge local resources, and sometimes seem to threaten to bankrupt local authorities, Roman amphitheatres required vast sums of money to build, maintain and run. They were in fact monuments to civic status and pride. Today, when even the best are largely ruinous, they still impress the visitor. The mighty arc of the theatre of St. Albans or the great circular amphitheatre at the legionary fortress at Caerleon stand as major monuments to Roman civic ideals as well as to the ghastly entertainments which debased Roman civilization.

Perhaps the most fascinating of all the Roman amphitheatres is at Dorchester in Dorset. It is much less striking and photogenic than the one at St. Albans, but interesting because it was not built by the Romans. It had been constructed more than three thousand years before the Romans arrived—as a henge monument by Neolithic people. For them it also functioned as a place of ritual entertainment. When the Roman town of Dorchester was founded, the henge had been abandoned for countless centuries. But situated just beyond the walls of the town, it was an ideal and ready-made amphitheatre. With a few minor modifications it took on a new, but oddly related role. Much later, in the seventeenth century, it was again adapted, this time as a gun battery.

114. *The Roman amphitheatre at St. Albans.*

The Romans also introduced into this country the concept of the pleasure garden. This was, for Britain, just as radical an innovation as anything else which arrived at this time. Because gardens are now ubiquitous, it is difficult to imagine their significance in shaping man's attitudes to the environment. A garden is the result of our manipulation of nature to produce contrived patterns of shape and colour to create pleasure. Thus the creator and owner of a garden often expresses his or society's aesthetic aims, values and attitudes in the garden.

Of course, a garden can be much more than simply a source of visual pleasure, but also a place of active recreation, enjoyed in the course of its construction and maintenance. As we shall see, a garden can in addition be an expression of status and power. In the course of two millennia of British horticulture the ideas about the role, proper appearance and function of a garden have changed, and so again we encounter the fickle perceptions of place.

During the Roman period it is likely that all major Roman country houses or 'villas' had gardens, which almost certainly were laid out in the strict Classical traditions of the gardens of the Mediterranean world. Few Roman gardens are known, for they can usually only be discovered by painstaking excavation in the environs of the villas—a task which is not only difficult and time consuming, but also rarely accepted by archaeologists. Nevertheless, at the few villas where this work has been carried out, we are able to see what must have been the standard form of garden in the Roman period. Roman gardens were physically attached to their villas and were generally enclosed, either by walls or by parts of the villa to form courtyards. Within these enclosed courts there were often rectangular arrangements, paths lined with flower beds or low hedges and often with focal statuary or water features at central intersections or along the paths.

The best known of all Roman gardens in Britain was excavated by Professor Barry Cunliffe at the 'villa' of Fishbourne in Sussex. These gardens belonged to a building so far unique in Britain, a palace built around 75 BC for a man of immense wealth and high position who had become familiar with the best of Roman material culture. It has been suggested that the owner was Cogidubnus, a native king, who, as a result of his co-operation with the Roman conquerors, was allowed to retain his throne as a 'client-king'. True or not, both palace and garden were on lavish scales, the palace itself enclosing the garden which was bounded by a verandah or colonnade. Across the centre of the garden ran a wide path, while narrow paths encircled it. The paths were edged by narrow trenches with equally spaced recesses each filled with a rich soil. These were almost certainly bedding trenches for low clipped hedges, probably of box. Other features discovered included the post-holes of timber structures which apparently supported flowering trees or shrubs. Around the outer path, water pipes were found which seem to have supplied fountains or raised basins set in recesses.

Fishbourne is the only Roman pleasure garden known in any detail in Britain. Elsewhere are only tantalizing details, but these support the picture revealed at Fishbourne. At a villa at Frocester, in Gloucestershire, excavations have revealed an approach-drive flanked by grass verges in which were set rectangular flower-beds, while at another villa at Gorhambury, in Hertfordshire, lines of post-holes and trenches on either side of the path seem to be the remains of a contrived walkway with a trellis-work supporting climbing plants.

Other excavations have produced the seeds of box, grapes, plums, apples and sweet cherries, while roses, lillies, poppies and pansies probably grew in the flower beds.

Though gardens and theatrical entertainments were forms of recreation that were to re-emerge and develop at later times in Britain, the Romans introduced another which did not resurface for many centuries: the habit of public or semi-public bathing. The provision of private bath suites in Roman villas or public bath ranges in towns was almost universal. Such baths should not be equated with modern swimming pools, for bathing was a formalized semi-ritual where the opportunity for meeting and talking to people in specialized surroundings was as important, or more important, than the bathing itself. As with theatres and gardens, bath buildings were a vital component of the Romano-British upper class lifestyle. Yet, strangely perhaps, bathing did not again become popular until the eighteenth century, when it re-emerged in a rather different form.

All these forms of recreation were abandoned along with much else when the Roman system declined in the fifth century. As Britain slithered into the Dark Ages there may have been less scope or inclination for play. There is no doubt that the great Saxon halls (see p. 269) had among their important functions that of social entertainment with feasting and story-telling, while the Dark Ages in Saxon and Viking England, Ireland and Wales have left rich legacies of epics, sagas, myths and folk tales which will have had their premières in the dark, alcoholic fug of the feasting halls. However, specific recreational facilities are not recognized until the tenth century when the emergence of a new type of society gave rise to new developments.

28

Medieval Leisure Pursuits

The growth of feudal society, with its well-marked class structure, produced two types of recreational features in the landscape: places of entertainment for the peasant masses, and those created for the pleasure of the élite. On the whole the peasant classes had to invent forms of recreation that were simple, required minimum inputs of resources and did not take up valuable land. As a result, they played crude and boisterous games which required no special buildings, fixtures or land. A few of these have survived in some form as at Ashbourne in Derbyshire, where a violent annual game of 'football' is played through the streets of the town. Frequently paddocks within or adjacent to villages were used periodically for games at times when they were not required for more important agricultural purposes.

These sports fields survive today, but usually only in the form of names. In East Anglia, for example, a very common field name is 'Camping Close' indicating spots where a curious form of football, or 'Camp-ball'—from the word 'Camp' meaning field—was played. Near Cambridge the villages of Girton, Histon, Sawston, Wentworth and Whittlesford all have paddocks with this name. More obvious is the field name 'Football Ground' at North Newington in Oxfordshire or 'Football Garth' at Calverley in Yorkshire. Other less specific names such as 'Playing Close' at Charlbury in Oxfordshire or 'Playsteads' at Westbury-on-Severn in Gloucestershire also indicate areas used for village recreation.

Another significant name is 'Plaistow', 'Plastow' or 'Plaster' as in 'Plastow Green' at Kingsclere in Hampshire and 'The Plasters' at Bromfield in Shropshire. As with all place-names care has to be exercised here, for although *Pleg-stow* means literally 'sport-place' the assemblies which took place at such spots often had more serious functions. Thus, land called 'Plaistow' at Deerhurst in Gloucestershire was also the meeting place of the manor and hundred courts.

Among other names which may also have a deeper original meaning than simple entertainment are 'Dancers' Meadow' and 'Dancing Plain' at Sherbourne and Alresford in Hampshire. However, the name 'Prison Bar Field' at Smethwick, Cheshire, appears to be the land used for the childrens' game of 'prisoners' base' while common names such as Bowling Close and Bowling Leys seems to denote land level enough for and possibly actually used for games of bowls.

As before, the distinction between play, belief and the economics of life was blurred and numerous folk songs and dances endure to remind us of the link between the merry frolics and half-remembered fertility rituals.

On rare occasions, actual monuments survive in the landscape that show a darker side to medieval recreation, far removed from the 'Merry England' of bowls, dancing and football. Just south of the church in the idyllic Dorset village of Stourpaine is a small circular area about 100 feet (thirty metres) across, which is bounded by a low bank and external ditch. This is a 'cock pit' where the medieval and later villagers staged cock fights. Only a few miles away, at Iwerne Courtney, in a remote corner of the parish is a circular pit ninety feet (twenty-seven metres) in diameter, seven feet (two metres) deep and approached by a ramp. This is a bull-baiting pit where this particularly cruel sport was perpetrated.

A nobler sport, and one which in later medieval times was encouraged by the authorities for excellent military reasons, was archery. Able-bodied men were often given special facilities for archery practice which was usually held after church on Sundays. The sport (or training) could take place almost anywhere and needed little more than an open space. Even so, there are few surviving monuments. In the East Yorkshire village of Wold Newton two domed mounds are hidden behind a hedgerow near the pretty green and pond. They were first recorded in 1299, when used as butts for archery practice. However, a word of warning: the extremely common field name 'Butt' or 'Butts' does not usually indicate a place where archery was practised, for the word was normally applied to irregular-shaped pieces of land within the medieval common-fields. Only in a very few instances can the name be surely linked to archery. If butts are rare survivals, yew trees are a common churchyard feature. Yews were certainly planted to produce bow timber but the ubiquitous churchyard yews also owe their presence to tradition, the shelter that they offer and their evergreen symbolism of eternal life.

The pleasures of the medieval upper classes were, as one would expect, rather different; although boisterous or war-like, they still mirrored contemporary society. For these people, recreation was really an extension of the feudal emphasis on war, warriors and 'manly' pursuits. The contrived heroics were blended with lavish entertainments, and tournaments are the best known of such aristocratic sports festivals. The notion of mock battles where the skills and prowess of the warrior knights who formed the backbone of feudal society could be exhibited was apparently introduced from France in the twelfth century and enthusiastically adopted. The early twelfth and thirteenth-century tournaments were serious and often bloody affairs which involved a number of knights fighting as individuals or units over a wide open area of land. Woundings, ransoms and even fatalities were part and parcel of the fun and tournaments of this kind became very popular, posing real threats to law and order. As a result, they were formally legalized and regulated by Richard I in 1194. They could only be licensed by the Crown, the combatants had to pay an entry fee and the events could only be staged at five places in England. Some of these locations are known in general terms: one was between Salisbury and Wilton in Wiltshire; another between Mixbury and Brackley on the Oxfordshire-Northamptonshire border; while a third was somewhere between Stamford and Wansford, now in Cambridgeshire, but the exact locations remain a mystery. Lacking permanent fixtures and being sited on open land, it is not surprising that the tournaments have left no lasting monuments.

Later on in the medieval period, tournaments became more organized and less violent, and this type of formal and regulated jousting, watched by courtiers and fair damsels has secured its niche in the popular imagination. 'Tiltyards' were then specially constructed at certain important castles and manor houses. At Kenilworth Castle in Warwickshire, there is a long narrow causeway, actually a dam, separating two artificial pools and a part of the main approach to the castle. This causeway was used as a 'tiltyard' in the fifteenth and sixteenth centuries. Another one, now much altered by later gardening activities, remains at Dartington Hall in Devon.

The favourite sport of the medieval upper classes was, however, hunting. This had always been the chosen sport of the rich, but under the influence of the early Norman kings it reached new heights of popularity immensely affecting not only the landscape but also the lives of many people. The Norman kings designated large areas of land as 'forests' in which the preservation of the beasts of the chase was the paramount object, and where the hated Forest Laws, quite separate from those which ran in other parts of the King's realm, held sway. Today the word 'forest' implies a large area of woodland. But in legal terms the medieval forest was simply a tract of land which was subject to forest law and which often included not only wooded areas, but also villages, fields and farmsteads. Later medieval kings were less preoccupied with hunting while other lords and magnates also sought rights of hunting. Then, the Treasury's continued shortage of money and the economic value of woodland for other purposes, all led to a gradual

115. *The Rufus Stone (right), erected in 1745 to mark the spot where William II was thought to have been shot while hunting in the New Forest in 1100.*

diminution of the area of the 'forests'. Thus there was the removal of trees for agriculture, the intensive management of surviving woodland for timber, pasture and pannage and a dispersal of rights to hunting and privileges, and Crown lands were sold. Nevertheless, a number of medieval woods still survive, exactly fitting the outline of wood banks which defined their medieval extents and efficient medieval techniques of coppicing, pollarding and felling according to a rota endured into the nineteenth century and in a few woods they are still practised.

The actual creation of 'forests' by the Norman kings had a massive effect on the countryside. The most famous and remarkable of these is the New Forest in Hampshire, an older forest which was greatly extended by William the Conqueror soon after 1066. Here was a huge area of largely open heathland, then as now dotted with small villages and their associated fields. As part of the enlargement of this forest many villages, probably over thirty, were actually cleared away, though many were later to be resettled.

Many surviving woods indicate areas of poor sands or heavy clay, as with the pockets of ancient woodland on the West Cambridgeshire boulder clays. But some woods owe their existence to their establishment as royal playgrounds. Once established such forests had to be administered and managed, initially and primarily to protect game but later for the production of valuable commodities. Former uses may survive as woodland names or physical relics. For example, the large areas of forest demanded administrative sub-divisions for day-to-day management. These were usually called 'walks' or 'bailwicks': forest districts in which a keeper had charge of the game and the woods. The actual woods were often called coppices, for they were managed by 'coppicing' or cutting on a short rotation, and hunting was compatible with most forms of economic management. Between coppices were 'ridings' and 'plains', open and often extensive zones of grass and scattered trees providing herbage for deer. 'Lawns' were enclosed plots of grassland managed to provide hay and pasture for deer and were normally situated close to the keeper's 'lodge'. Such lodges which, by the thirteenth century were often moated for defence against poachers, were scattered in the forest and thus produced a curious dispersed settlement pattern of isolated houses. In Rockingham Forest in Northamptonshire many of the earlier farmsteads, such as Old Sulehay in Nassington parish and Huskisson's Lodge at King's Cliffe, originated not as farming homesteads but as medieval forest keepers' lodges.

There are also many other special areas, all with their own names, which appeared as the complex relationship between recreation and land management evolved during medieval times. 'Purlieus' were areas of land removed from forest law by Edward I, or in

116. *The Barden Tower in Wharfedale. This was one of six lodges provided in the Forest of Barden to accommodate and protect wardens guarding deer. It was rebuilt in the fifteenth century and restored in the seventeenth and eighteenth centuries.*

some cases earlier, but over which royal deer had protection. The owners of purlieu land could themselves hunt royal deer under certain conditions. Thus as Whiteparish in Wiltshire the land still known as 'the Purlieus' was a clearly defined area within the Royal Forest of Melchet over which the adjacent landowner had special hunting rights.

Other important features of the medieval landscape also related to hunting were deer-parks. These were normally much smaller areas of land than forests or chases, though they varied greatly in size. They were privately-owned deer enclosures and were created by the hundred in the twelfth and thirteenth centuries by all nobles who could afford the necessary royal licences. Many of these parks were set in wooded areas, but others were created by the forcible acquisition of existing peasant farmland. The more important the owner the greater the park, for the lavish scale of feasting and visiting demanded ready supplies of venison. One, at Blagdon in Dorset, covered 1300 acres (526 hectares), although the small park at Easton-on-the-Hill in Northampton-shire covered only forty acres (16 hectares). Some had enclosed 'lawns' within them, many had park-keepers' lodges within or attached to them, but all had one common characteristic: they were surrounded by a boundary of such proportions that the agile deer within could not escape. Occasionally, such boundaries were strong stone walls, set on banks, as at the Royal Park at Northampton. More often, the boundaries were massive earthen banks, surmounted by a wooden fence or 'pale' and strengthened by internal ditches, an arrangement which prevented deer from leaping across the boundary. Sometimes sophisticated devices were employed to increase the stock of deer. One was the 'deer leap' which was often an external ramp set against the boundary bank at a point where the 'pale' was absent but the internal ditch dug wider. This enabled deer outside the park to enter but prevented deer from within the park from leaving.

Deer-parks were primarily private game stores. In the very large ones the deer could be hunted within, but in most cases the deer were released on hunting days and chased across the surrounding countryside. Yet, as always, deer-parks had other functions for they provided instantly available prime meat for the traditional and lavish entertainments which were another part of the medieval upper-class life.

Boisterous and violent pursuits were prominent in medieval life but we should not forget that there were other aspects to life in those times which were contemplative and pastoral. One of the physical manifestations of this side to human nature was reflected in the making of gardens which regularly punctuated the medieval landscape.

Only the nobles and leading churchmen could afford the land and labour which gardens demanded, but the peasants' love and understanding of a then unspoilt countryside is reflected in many traditional ballads. The notion that a sensibility to the wonders of nature and landscape was only first discovered by eighteenth-century romantics is quite wrong.

Most medieval gardens had, like most other things, more than one purpose. They produced fruit, vegetables and herbs as well as giving pleasure and thus simple orchards, hardly qualifying as gardens, were very common in grounds of palaces, abbeys and manor houses. Surrounded as they often were by walls, hedges or moats, they were secluded places in which to walk and enjoy fresh air in sunlight or dappled shade, as numerous old documents tell.

More interesting were the more explicit medieval pleasure-gardens which certainly existed in a refined form by the twelfth century at the latest. Henry I, for example, not only had a garden at Windsor but also others at the royal manors at Dunstable in Bedfordshire and Havering in Essex, while at his palace at Woodstock in Oxfordshire he had a small park containing exotic wild animals. From various documentary sources it is clear that throughout the medieval period there were many gardens in Britain, all reflecting a keen delight in the appearance and arrangement of plants and their perfumes as well as the sensuous delights of running water.

What did medieval gardens look like? This is a difficult question to answer for none survives in its original form. At many places we are told that gardens are 'medieval', but this is not true. Gardens, more than any other features of the man-made landscape, need constant attention and are subject to change by alteration or neglect. Thus nowhere in Britain can we see a medieval garden in all its original glory. Even so, from documents it is possible to have some idea of their appearance. Most were very small and usually enclosed by high walls, fences or hedges to provide a setting for private contemplation and pleasure as well as for small social gatherings. Within these

117. *This turret-like building at the palace of the medieval Bishops of Lincoln at Lyddington, Leicestershire, is known as 'the Bishop's Eye' and said locally to have been built so that the Bishop could spy on the affairs of the village. It has now been recognized as the summer house of his walled garden, incorporated into its surrounding wall.*

boundaries, gravel or paved paths divided raised flower-beds and small lawns, while moated islands, small streams, fountains and pools were common features (the pressure for the fountains coming from high-level streams). Terraces, arbours and garden houses also existed. The gardens were often sited immediately beneath the principal private chambers of the adjacent manor house, palace or castle, so that they could also be viewed from window seats. Commonly-planted flowers included roses, lilies, peonies, cowslip, daisy, purple flag iris, hollyhocks and wallflowers. Some like the cowslip and peony were native, others like hollyhocks were introduced from abroad.

Although no medieval gardens remain, in recent years it has been realized that, though now reduced to earthen banks, scarps and ditches, many still exist as field monuments and it is likely that many more still remain to be discovered. One of the best of these abandoned gardens is at Nettleham in Lincolnshire. The site was one of the palaces of the medieval Bishops of Lincoln and was abandoned in the mid sixteenth century. Not only do the grass-covered foundation-walls of the palace itself still exist, so too do the traces of the garden which flanked one side of it. It was very small, only 180 feet across, and its boundary on three sides is marked by a low rubble bank which must be the base of a former high stone wall. The palace ruins form the fourth side. At the upper end of the area above the palace is a slight terrace, and below it is another one. From the centre of the lower terrace a flat-topped rise, just one foot high, extends the length of the rest of the garden. This must have been a raised footpath running between two rectangular flower-beds whose edges are marked by a tiny scarp. Beyond is a similar rectangular area within which was another raised footpath. Though by no means as impressive as many abandoned historical sites, the evidence at Nettleham can give us a vivid impression of what a medieval garden was really like.

29

Recreation in the Sixteenth and Seventeenth Centuries

For the great mass of the population, recreation in these centuries underwent some changes, while at the higher levels of society, although the same basic pleasures remained, new ideas and concepts were introduced which not only changed the settings for recreation but also left a physical heritage of monuments and landscape. Of all the surviving sites gardens are perhaps the most important. As with the medieval gardens, however, few actually survive and most of those ascribed to this period are modern imitations or re-creations. The best reconstructed example is at Hampton Court Palace near London where, on the river side of the palace, a small sunken garden was

118. *The earthworks of the deserted medieval village of Godwick, Norfolk, whose ruined church tower appears lower right, are overlain (upper centre) by the more regular earthworks of an abandoned garden with rectangular divisions. (Cambridge University Collection.)*

laid out between the palace and the elaborate sixteenth-century garden-house cum banqueting-hall.

Though there are numerous contemporary drawings, prints and accounts, to visualize a real garden of this period we have to seek the abandoned remains and attempt to understand them. Hundreds of sixteenth and seventeenth-century abandoned gardens exist and they tell us much about both the visions and desires of the mighty and the efforts of those who sought to imitate them.

Perhaps the best of all abandoned gardens of this period are at Holdenby, Northamptonshire, and were created between 1579 and 1587 by Sir Christopher Hatton. Here, with the help of contemporary plans and descriptions, we can appreciate not only what a great Elizabethan pleasure-garden looked like, but also what was involved in its creation. Hatton, who was Lord High Chancellor of England and holder of many other offices, was one of the most important people in the land; he built a new house at Holdenby, set on a dominating hill-crest. The gardens were intended to be laid out across the slopes of the hill and the flatter ground at the side of the house. However, an obstacle to this plan was the existence then of the village of Holdenby, or rather two villages, one by a hillside parish church and the other near the new house. Hatton swept both away, leaving only the church to be incorporated into the garden. The village near the house was rebuilt according to a new rectangular plan and placed axially to the garden. The views of this new regulated village were obtained by constructing archways in the courtyard wall which fronted the house. In this way Hatton anticipated the Picturesque fashion for remodelled and prettified village 'eye-catchers' by many years.

The construction of the main gardens was carried out at the same time. Below the house, thousands of tons of earth were dumped on the hillside to create a projecting level platform on which elaborate flower-beds were arranged. The edges of some of these flower-beds still survive as scarps in the pasture. On either side of this platform, flights of terraces were dug and planted with roses. At the bottom of one flight was a rectangular pond, while below the other was a long narrow bowling green. Beyond the main courtyard, a large hedged area of lawn, a lake and a two-storey summerhouse and banqueting-hall were built. On the lower slopes of the hillside was a carefully contrived 'wilderness' of trees, with a private hedged flower-garden in one corner, a group of rectangular ponds in the centre and an elaborate arrangement of sloping terraced pathways leading up to a tall circular 'mount' or mound set on one side. All these details still survive as banks, terraces, scarps or ditches and can still be seen to this day.

A garden which is much more easily appreciated is at Kirby Hall, also in Northamptonshire. It dates from the 1680s and was, coincidentally, created by the great grandson of Sir Christopher Hatton. It lies beside the magnificent hall ruins and both hall and gardens are now in the care of the Department of the Environment. Here, the kerbstones edging the elaborate original flower-beds were found, as well as the brick

119. *The restored gardens at Kirby Hall, seen from the top of an original prospect mound.*

and stone revetments of the great terrace which overlooked them. Now restored and planted with roses, these are the best of the seventeenth-century garden remains in Britain.

The relics of a much smaller garden, about which we have scant historical knowledge, lie near the church in the remote village of Hamerton in Cambridgeshire. Here, the hillside is also divided into terraces with a huge central mount on the upper level. The terraces are bounded on three sides by a moat or 'canal' which has a terraced walkway beyond it, while to one side lie the remains of an elaborate moated 'water-garden' consisting of narrow intersecting channels. From these and many other sites we can clearly appreciate the arrangement of the gardens which all the great houses of the sixteenth and seventeenth centuries (see p. 279ff) had. Much bigger than those of medieval times, such gardens still retained many of their medieval characteristics.

They still tended to be enclosed and thus inward looking, and were divided into paths and flower-beds, although the latter were often much more elaborate than before. Water was also important, and was provided in the forms of still water ponds or canals, either arranged in groups or extending along the edges or across the centre of the garden. High level terraces and 'mounts' from which the area could be viewed were also common. A splendid and easily accessible example of such a mount has survived the destruction of the accompanying gardens at New College, Oxford. An even better and more elaborate mount, still surrounded by its original terraces and traces of flower-beds, and dating from 1627–8, is found below Stirling Castle in Scotland. Elaborate detached buildings for banquets, parties and social entertainments were also features of sixteenth and seventeenth-century gardens. The now isolated but quite remarkable Lyveden New Bield (the name means 'new building') and the Triangular Lodge, Rushton, both in Northamptonshire and both built by Sir Thomas Tresham in the late sixteenth century, are fine examples. The former is a veritable country house, with basement, kitchens, dining rooms, drawing rooms and bedrooms, the latter, a small private 'conceit'.

Such buildings reflect the desire for lavish entertainment which was such a feature of high life in the sixteenth and seventeenth centuries. Spectacular and highly symbolic displays to impress guests were constantly organized, despite the sometimes financially crippling costs to those who staged them. Many of these lavish entertainments have left little trace, but David Wilson of the Cambridge University air photography unit has recently discovered the remains of one. They are at Elveham in Hampshire where Edward Seymour, Earl of Hertford, entertained Elizabeth I in 1591. To meet the demands of the occasion the Earl not only rebuilt his house, but created a special garden for a water-pageant. A crescentic lake was constructed in which three islands—one arranged as a ship, another as a fort and the third as a spiral mount—were raised. The whole feature was created for one day of stunning entertainment, and abandoned. Though the land on which the pageant took place is now ploughed, air photography has revealed the outlines of this lake.

Other recreational activities, albeit less elaborate, have also left us their traces in the landscape. As we noted at Holdenby, the gardens included a bowling green. Bowls was an extremely popular game at this period at all levels of society. The story of Sir Francis

120. *Lyveden New Bield, Northamptonshire, a spectacular summer house.*

Drake and his game on Plymouth Hoe is a popular reminder of this and the small bowling greens of this period still survive in many places. In the north-east corner of the town of Wareham in Dorset, tucked neatly into the angle created by the ninth-century defences built by King Alfred (see p. 153), is a small level rectangular area measuring 180 feet (fifty-five metres) by 90 feet (twenty-seven metres) and surrounded by a low bank. It may have been incorporated in a larger garden long since destroyed, but it was, apparently, a bowling green. A rather odd example exists at Great Houghton in Northamptonshire. There, close to the River Nene, is the massive motte of an early Norman castle, known as Clifford's Hill and one of the largest of its kind in Britain. But it was clearly once even taller than now, for in the seventeenth century the summit was cut away to provide a neat sub-rectangular area which was used as a bowling green.

The medieval tradition of hunting, particularly for deer, continued into the post-medieval period, but on a decreasing scale. Most of the old deer-parks had been abandoned, used for cattle grazing, or broken up for arable. The crown also disafforested or abandoned some of the great medieval forested areas, which became more important as economic resources than as recreational areas. Deer-parks, it is true, continued to be created, but with subtle differences. For example, many so-called deer-parks appeared in the mid sixteenth century, but in fact their primary purpose was the breeding of horses at a time when, as Dr Joan Thirsk has shown, there were fears that horses, especially war horses, were going to be in short supply. These 'horse-parks' as they should be called also had deer, while some of them took on a further function, admirably illustrated again at Holdenby. There, as well as building his new house and creating the elaborate gardens already described, Sir Christopher Hatton surrounded both with a huge 'deer-park'. This area had formerly been part of the medieval open fields of the village of Holdenby. Now it was turned over to grass, planted with small groups of trees and copses to become part of the pleasure-grounds of the estate, providing both a pleasing backcloth to the house and garden and an area for riding and walking. In similar ways other landscaped parks began to appear. These modified deer-parks had, of course, well-defined boundaries, but the great banks and wooden pales of the medieval period were superceded by walls and hedges and so the post-medieval parks may be more difficult to recognize today.

The decline in the popularity of hunting was paralleled by a growth in horse racing. From the seventeenth century in particular, partly as a result of Royal patronage, racing became a leading form of recreation and led to major modifications of some landscapes, as we shall describe.

30

Eighteenth and Nineteenth-Century Pleasures

The most important and far-reaching recreational impacts on the landscape in these centuries resulted from the continuing development of gardens and parks. By the late seventeenth century the concept of the garden was changing under the influence of new ideas from abroad, especially from France. Gardens still remained formal in terms of their detailed arrangements of flower-beds, canals or ponds, which tended to become increasingly elaborate. But the garden influence was also expanded into the surrounding parkland, which gradually became more and more a part of the garden

121. *The beautifully landscaped setting of Deene Park, Northamptonshire.*

itself. Avenues of trees or lines of treetopped mounds directed the gaze outwards to the surrounding landscaped setting. These lines of vision often terminated in contrived architectural features or 'eye-catchers'. This tendency towards wider vistas and more extensive backdrops to gardens was aided by the development of the Ha-ha or sunken divide which enabled the garden to be secured from the depredations of parkland deer while offering open views unrestricted by hedges, fences or walls. These 'outer parks' were not, however, the informal landscaped areas of later times. In keeping with the gardens themselves, they were rigidly formal with rectangular copses and intersecting straight lines or avenues of trees reflecting the currents of Classical influence. Few of these parks survive intact, as all were variously modified. Of those fragments that remain the best is that at Blenheim Palace, Oxfordshire, where sections of a great zone of formal avenues still exist. Another less impressive but interesting example is at Eastbury in Dorset. There the formal garden and park were abandoned in the mid eighteenth century before new ideas were exerted. As a result, part of the now grass-grown gardens with their mounts, terraces, and flower-beds survive, as do some of the rectangular copses and a line of mounds which once extended the view from the garden across the park. All these gardens and parks, like those of the sixteenth and seventeenth centuries, were in their various ways expressions of the contemporary vision of nature, society and belief; visions which are also, of course, reflected in the architecture of the period (see p. 279ff).

When in the middle of the eighteenth century these views changed, gardens and parks changed too. The most important of these new ideas was 'Romanticism'. This involved the concept that Nature and flowing natural arrangements were aesthetically more pleasing than a formal ordered world. Eventually great house architecture accepted these ideas, although gardens pointed the way, as the quest for regularity was abandoned. Indeed in the narrow sense, gardens became, to some extent, unfashionable. What was desired was unaltered Nature—or at least what might pass as unaltered Nature—in romantically relaxed vistas sweeping up to and enveloping the great house. So arose the era of 'Capability' Brown and Humphrey Repton, the two most famous and successful members of a numerous fraternity of landscape architects.

Old parks were 'naturalized' and new parks appeared by the score. The landscaped park, so much a feature of England as well as of parts of Wales, Scotland and Ireland, had arrived and in its original form it was a leading product of the Romantic movement.

Nothing that smacked of formalized order was allowed and even the arranged gardens beside the houses were swept away as parks were brought forward to the very walls. Yet, although the goal of landscaping was a 'natural' landscape, the relaxed

122. *An artificial lake and semi-abandoned walled gardens and summer house at Ickworth, Suffolk. Behind stands the isolated church of the emparked village and, to the right, the rotunda of the great house.*

123. *An expanse of relict parkland with various exotic trees surviving at Foelallt near Lampeter long after the accompanying mansion, which appears to have stood on a hillfoot shelf, has disappeared.*

effect was only normally achieved by the most prodigious efforts of engineering and skill: huge dams were constructed to pond back sinuous lakes; mature trees were moved about and planted in 'natural' positions; and, thousands of tons of earth were shifted to achieve smooth contours and contrived views.

Many such parks survive in more or less their original form, while the contrived 'naturalistic' tree patterns betray many former parks, as at Picts Hill in Bedfordshire. One of the most interesting areas of relict parkland lies at the lost mansion site of Foelallt near Llandewi Brefi, where the alien trees endure as outlandish survivors in a lovely Welsh valley.

Some of the most awkward intrusions which faced landscape gardeners in pursuing their aims were the existing living villages. Many of the great houses which were to have landscaped parks stood on the sites of medieval village manor houses. Small medieval and sixteenth and seventeenth-century gardens were often arranged around such houses and their walls kept out the sight and sounds, if not the smells of day-to-day village life. Now such villages were deemed unsightly distractions. No soulfully romantic park could be complete if a normal and truly natural community lived in it to spoil the view and mood. The answer was to remove the village, either entirely, or as much of it as was necessary to achieve the new landscape. As we have already seen at Holdenby, villages were removed for landscaping as early as the late sixteenth century and others were destroyed in the seventeenth century, but the main period of village emparking was after 1750.

In some cases the displaced inhabitants were rehoused in new, planned and model villages; elsewhere they were left to fend for themselves. Hundreds of villages were either destroyed or mutilated between 1750 and 1820 and traces of the former houses and gardens often still remain for the landscape explorer to discover. At one level we may take the example of Milton Abbas where, until 1770, a small market town stood just outside the gates of the great house nearby. Then Joseph Damer MP, later Viscount Milton, rebuilt the house and employed 'Capability' Brown to lay out a new park. The town was entirely destroyed and a new village built some distance away in a small valley, well out of sight of the house. The remains of some of the former streets and even the peasants' gardens still survive within the park.

A less well-known example is that of Moor Crichel in Dorset. At some time in the mid eighteenth century an ornamental lake was built but the village survived and lay beside it. In 1765, Humphrey Sturt, a new owner, enlarged the house and removed the village. The population was resettled in the purpose-built settlement of New Town in the next parish, where three of the cob and thatch cottages still stand. A lower level of destruction can be seen at Madingley Hall in Cambridgeshire, where 'Capability' Brown was also involved. Here the hall stood apart from the village, but the intended view was still spoilt by the peasant dwellings. Brown cut a swathe through the middle of

124. *At Deene, as at many other places, the price of a landscaped park was the removal of a living village. Here we see the old parish church at Deene, its village setting replaced by an ornamental lake and landscaped woodland.*

the village to create two separate settlements and so achieved the unblemished vista.

Even when villages did not intrude, there was often a problem of public roads which passed close to the great house. This difficulty was usually solved by diverting the road in a large loop around the park. Today one will often travel a road that turns sharply opposite the lodge gates of a park and then runs in a broad arc until another sharp bend and set of lodge gates announce that the road has regained its original alignment. Whenever this occurs the traveller can be sure that here there was a road diversion. One of the best examples is Charborough in Dorset where the modern A31 Wimborne–Dorchester Road skirts a huge park which is edged by a continuous brick wall and punctuated by magnificent gateways. On one of the latter, two inscriptions tell the story. One says that 'This road from Wimborne to Dorchester was projected and completed through the instrumentality of J. W. S. Sawbridge Erle Drax MP, in the years 1841 and 1842.' The other: 'This road (through the park) was closed by the orders of the Magistrates, which was appealed against by James John Farquharson Esq. at the Epiphany Quarter Sessions held at Dorchester Jan 4th 1841 and after a trial of three days the order was confirmed by the order of Twelve Honest Jurymen.'

A less obvious example can be seen at West Raynham in Norfolk, where the offending road now forms a deep holloway in the park and where several dwellings were destroyed in the course of landscaping.

Such authoritarian and sometimes brutal actions would not be allowed today, at least if perpetuated by private individuals. Yet the self-indulgence of the mighty has left us a legacy of glorious landscapes which our more egalitarian society has singularly failed to equal when much of what passes for 'art' and 'landscape architecture' merits only a NIB award.

Towards the end of the nineteenth century there was a reaction against the comprehensively landscaped parks. These were often still desired and maintained but the Victorians also loved more intimate, specialized or secluded places, bright colours and often brash and elaborate decorative features. The result was a return to more formalized gardens immediately adjacent to the houses, with terraces, balustrading, ponds, fountains and intricate flower-beds. The gardens seen around most country houses today are of this period despite what the guidebooks may say. Strangely, while Neo-Classical mansions with their surrounding tracts of 'naturistically' landscaped parkland often seem ill at ease in the British countryside, the later Neo-Gothic houses and formal gardens frequently nestle snugly in their settings.

The more violent and extrovert members of the eighteenth and nineteenth-century upper classes also sought pleasure in various sports, some of which affected large areas of the British landscape. One of these was hunting. As we have already seen, hunting has had a long history, but during the eighteenth and nineteenth centuries it was formalized in a way that it had never been before. The familiar and now prudently detested hunting apparel, packs of hounds, and regular 'meets' all evolved as deer, otters, foxes and other helpless creatures were ceremonially chased, tortured and destroyed. The formalization of such a 'sport' required more than just the outward trappings of transparent dignity. It required organization on a large scale. The nineteenth century saw the establishment, on the greater estates, of kennels which not only housed the hounds, but also the necessary horses and the servants. And where, as with fox hunting, the sport took place over land which was cultivated, special measures had to be introduced to produce the supply of victims to hunt. As a result, special copses were planted, often at the corners of fields, to provide cover for foxes. Thus the landscape of, say, rural Leicestershire, with its neat rectangular fields and small copses owes its appearance almost as much to the nineteenth-century hunting fraternity as to the more prosaic Enclosure Commissioners who planned the fields. And the discerning trespasser will often find that deep in some of these woods and copses are large mounds of earth, suitably equipped with drain pipes. These are artificial fox earths carefully constructed to encourage the foxes to live and breed and so provide continuous 'sport'. Though small and prosaic, these little earthworks seem to question our claims to be 'civilized' and undermine the dignity of our species.

Shooting was another recreation which changed the landscape in many ways, sometimes but subtly, but at other times dramatically. In the Midland counties of England, where pheasants were peppered in their hundreds by the guests at huge Victorian house parties, the breeding of these suitably unairworthy birds became an important rural industry, and so it remains in many places. Isolated game keepers' cottages with ranges of necessary outbuildings, specially planted copses with open foraging areas within them are still quite common. Further north, grouse were bred for the guns. These too needed their keepers, but their slaughter also required a curious form of structure which still punctuates the upland moors. The neat lines of stone-walled circular butts which range across the North York moors, Pennines and much of Scotland are essential to the ritual.

In Scotland deer shooting had a greater impact on the landscape. Various grouse moors and deer forests were created in the Highlands, especially in the late nineteenth century, at the expense of many crofting households who were evicted to make way for the gory diversion. Huge baronial mansions appeared in a multitude of architectural styles led by the Neo-Gothic, most of which were only used for the shooting season. Because of its royal connections Balmoral Castle is perhaps the most famous of these, but there are many more.

Racing was another sport, organized by the aristocracy, but in this case enjoyed by all, particularly in the nineteenth century as money, travel and time all became more easily available. The sport was already important in the seventeenth century, while in the eighteenth century racecourses were provided close to scores of towns. One interesting relic of this is at Stamford in Lincolnshire. Just outside the town there is a field whose shape marks it out from its more prosaic neighbours. It is exactly one mile long, but only about fifty yards (forty-six metres) in width and at one end is a now ruinous building of very curious form. The casual visitor might be quite perplexed, but in fact the field is part of the fashionable racecourse of Georgian Stamford which was laid out in 1717. It is the 'mile course' and the building was its grandstand, once an elaborate and distinguished structure with an open loggia on the ground floor, a raked set of seats above and a covered roof-terrace on top.

Again, however, the formalization of racing under the necessary governing body, the requirements for breeding and training, and provision of regulation courses all

125. Deciduous shelter belts lining the approaches to Newmarket shield the racehorses from the noise of passing traffic—an unusual expression of recreation in the landscape.

affected the evolution of landscapes. This is nowhere better seen than at Newmarket in Suffolk, now the headquarters of British flat-racing. On the heath beside the town, are two separate courses whose origins lie back in the seventeenth century. More extensive are the runs or gallops which have preserved large areas of open downland which elsewhere has surrendered to the pressures of modern farming. In addition there are numerous breeding establishments, consisting of extensive stables and other buildings, each set in some of the most remarkable fieldscapes in Britain. The basic regularity of the fields shows that they were laid out in the late eighteenth and early nineteenth centuries as normal Parliamentary Enclosure fields and were intended for agriculture. But here they have been edged by deep shelter-belts of trees, subdivided by further belts and given numerous small protective copses and plantations to protect the delicate animals from the wind. The result is a landscape designed purely for the breeding and training of racehorses. And there is more. The suburbs of Newmarket are full of huge Victorian and Edwardian villas built to house the wealthy visitors who 'came down' for the week's racing, while the main street of the town is dominated by the huge but undistinguished Neo-Georgian structure which houses the Jockey Club itself. Even the railway station at Newmarket is odd. It has numerous platforms and sidings not merely for serving the racing 'specials' but also for assisting the transport of racehorses which, before the arrival of the motorized horsebox, were sent in large numbers by train to race meetings all over Britain. Similar but less extensive landscapes can be seen at Epsom and Ascot.

All these types of recreation take place out of doors. There were other forms of enjoyment which demanded special buildings, notably theatres. Special buildings for theatrical performances existed in the sixteenth century and from then on they became essential in any town with pretentions to civilized life. The earlier theatres had a wide variety of forms, but as always institutionalization and formalization set in, and a fairly standard layout emerged which still endures. Most towns had theatres by the eighteenth century and some of these still survive. Other forms of eighteenth and nineteenth-century upper and middle-class recreation activities have left their mark on towns. Many had assembly rooms and meeting places, erected for the diverse and often lavish entertainments that were so fashionable at that time. At York one can see the Theatre Royal, which, though mainly of late nineteenth-century date, incorporates fragments of eighteenth-century and early nineteenth-century theatres, the first of which was built in 1744. But much more imposing are the Assembly Rooms, built in 1732–5 as a magnificent structure in the Neo-Classical Style, with a great hall ringed by smaller rooms; a mixture based on the prototypes of an Egyptian Hall, Roman Houses and Roman Baths. It encapsulates the recreational lifestyle of a major eighteenth-century provincial town. Also in York is the Festival Concert Hall (now the Museum Chambers) built in 1874 and the de Grey Room, erected in 1841–2 as the annual mess for the officers of the Yorkshire Hussars, but also used for concerts, balls and meetings.

In a much smaller town, Stamford, Lincolnshire, a similar variety of recreational buildings survives. Again there is a theatre of 1768 still intact; Assembly Rooms of 1727; and, most interesting of all, the Stamford Institution. This was built in a 'Greek' style in 1842 and contained a concert and lecture-room with a gallery, a museum, a library and reading-room, newspaper and committee rooms, as well as a laboratory. Later on, an octagonal observatory and *camera obscura* (now demolished) were added. Here we enter the transition from purely recreational functions to the growth of contemporary educational and scientific interest. Even so, much of the spirit of enquiry in both the sciences and humanities on which our own society is based emerged from the recreational pursuits of the eighteenth and nineteenth-century societies—and this is nowhere more evident than in our own fields of archaeology and landscape history.

A very special form of entertainment which had wide-ranging results developed from the fashionable interest in medicinal waters. Places such as Buxton, Tunbridge Wells, Llandrindod Wells, Cheltenham Spa and Harrogate (see p. 223ff) all owe their present importance and position to their development as spas. Irrespective of their debatable medicinal value, the spa waters provided a focus for social gatherings. The baths themselves, the Assembly Rooms, the theatres and town houses all reflected the fashionable pursuit and the social status of the clientele.

The spa towns of the eighteenth century and early nineteenth century were largely developed for the upper classes, while the common folk found their relatively simple pleasures closer to home. But the nineteenth century brought a social revolution in recreation which still has not run its course. There were improvements in standards of living with increased leisure time, and gradually rising wages. In response, some theatres moved down-market and became the grand Victorian playhouses and music halls. At the same time, the development of more benevolent and democratic local and central governments, civic pride and civic authorities produced municipal concert-halls, parks and gardens, which were Victorian in character, usually ostentatious in layout and lavish in decoration. Aristocratic patronage, enlightened social concerns, or both produced other recreational facilities which varied from village halls to the Albert Hall. Sports grounds appeared, whether provided in a village by the lord of the manor in one of the rapidly expanding industrial towns by the new local authority, or by other benefactors. The nineteenth century was also the great age of clubs and societies; a multiplicity of interests were catered for.

The greatest advance, however, resulted from the revolution in transport brought about by the coming of the railways. By the middle of the century it had become possible for all but the poorest of families to travel cheaply to the seaside, and by the 1870s a large proportion of the population could afford at least a week's holiday. The stage was set for the emergence of resort towns for the middle and working classes which extended the spectrum of recreational centres hitherto monopolized by the upper-class spas. Melcombe Regis in Dorset, and Brighton in Sussex had become upper-class resorts in the early nineteenth century when sea-bathing developed as a fashionable diversion. Later, places such as Walton-on-the-Naze, New Brighton, Broadstairs, Weston-super-Mare and Ryde expanded as middle-class resorts. But the arrival of the railway triggered the growth of resorts to the extent that within a few years of a rail link reaching a coastal hamlet, a boom town would appear. Bournemouth, which was merely a few cottages in 1830, grew slowly and with a certain gentility until 1870, when the railways from the Midlands arrived. Then within two decades it had quadrupled in size and Bournemouth had continued to grow to become the largest non-industrial conurbation in Britain. Blackpool and its splendid beaches became accessible by rail in 1846. The town grew slowly at first, but with the passing of the enormously influential Bank Holiday Act of 1871, and the establishment of 'Wakes Weeks' holidays, it rapidly expanded as a resort for the inhabitants of the industrial north west. Most sea-side resorts developed a fairly standard arrangement perhaps best shown at Southsea in Hampshire. The main centre, with the largest and most impressive hotels, lies adjacent to the sea and opposite the very necessary pier with its theatre and other recreational provisions. On either side are carefully ordered municipal gardens, which separate the less grand hotels from the promenade. Behind this imposing façade of a somewhat brash character are neat streets with smaller hotels catering for the lower middle class. Further back again are narrower and meaner streets lined with terraced guest-houses interspersed with shops and other facilities. Further back still lie the even smaller terraces built to house the numerous servants and other workers who were essential to a good resort. Similarly, the railway also enabled racing to develop as a spectator sport for all classes.

The railways helped moreover to produce another feature of the landscape: the major city hotels and restaurants. Although inns and eating places existed long before the railways, the arrival of the latter created a demand for places for overnight stays and so most large railway termini soon developed large and imposing hotels which were soon imitated in other parts of the country.

Until the middle of the nineteenth century, restaurants as we know them today did not exist. For the upper-class males there were clubs, but most people 'ate out' in the dining rooms of inns. The large railway companies had seen the advantages of providing refreshments at large termini or at major junctions, as in the case of the famous Great Western refreshment room at Swindon. Even so, restaurants were slow to arrive. The great innovator was one Frederik Gordon, the son of a decorator, who opened a restaurant in the City of London for businessmen in the 1870s; soon after the Holborn Restaurant for middle-class visitors appeared. The project was a success and soon restaurants mushroomed in every large town and city. By the 1880s and 1890s they were attached to theatres, and had settled down to a standard format which included musical entertainment and special ladies' rooms. Restaurants were soon followed by tea rooms which in turn were adopted by department stores to attract and cater for lady shoppers.

At the start of the twentieth century, the restaurant business broadened its clientele and moved down-market. The trend was marked by the establishment of Lyons Corner Houses, at first in London but then spreading across the provinces as the middle-class fashion for 'eating out' took root. The arrival of the cinema strengthened this trend and in the 1930s and 1940s all good picture-palaces provided a restaurant. Though the more elaborate Victorian restaurants have gone, along with the Corner Houses, the demand for food—preferably fast and fried—has continued. The Wimpey bars and Kentucky Fries are among the latest chapters in the story and they reflect the pace of modern living and the lack of time for leisurely eating.

Today we enthusiastically create visions of a past which never existed. This is expressed in the commuter village with its neatly mown green and twee new village sign and, above all, in the ubiquitous village pub with its exposed timbers and glittering brasses. The timber is often false and there is many a self-proclaimed 'medieval' pub which is a quite recent adaptation of a seventeenth or eighteenth-century dwelling. The real medieval equivalents of the village pub were the squalid cottages where the ale-wives of the village dispensed home brews. The office of village ale-taster was a common feudal appointment, while house inventories of the seventeenth and eighteenth centuries show that home-brewing was universal and most cottages had a 'buttery' chamber which was stocked with the paraphernalia of ale-making. In addition to the ale-parlours in the cottages of the village ale-wives there was a much smaller number of urban or roadside hotels and hostels providing services for a quite different clientele of travellers. A late medieval pilgrims' hotel survives in Glastonbury and some other hotels of the period still exist as private houses—like the fine timber-framed building beside the churchyard in Swaffham Bulbeck in Cambridgeshire. As the coach traffic increased in the later Middle Ages and the centuries which followed, coaching inns became more numerous and many fine old buildings remain as inns or private houses which can often be recognized by their roadside carriage ways which give coach access to enclosed courtyards. 'The Mermaid' in Rye is a vintage example.

Until 1872 the sale of alcohol was largely uncontrolled and many of the larger villages supported a score or more drinking houses, most of them seedy back-parlour establishments or ale-houses advertised only by a post or box bushes. While the clergy

126. Inns have provided the British with agreeable recreation, but few are as old as the Mermaid in Rye, 'rebuilt in 1420' and long associated with smuggling operations. Note the access for carriages, a feature of many genuinely old hostelries.

of the eighteenth or nineteenth centuries probably exaggerated the problem, there is little doubt that drunkenness was rife in Scotland, Wales and Merrie England during and after the Middle Ages. Village life was so arduous and bleak that any dwelling offering a fire, cheap ale and conversation with companions could gather a clientele.

The nineteenth century witnessed an emphasis on spectator sports which was unprecedented since Roman times. This is best illustrated by the case of cricket, the social history of which has been surveyed by John Ford. The sport is rather unusual in that it had parallel origins which lie both in the patronage of aristocrats who employed professional players and were interested in the game as a form of gambling and also in the popularity of the game as a village sport. There was a strong association with inns and as early as 1668 the 'Ram' in Smithfield had its cricket field. The growth of popular spectator sports like cricket, prize fighting and racing was checked by local legislation since the Justices were often fearful that sports gatherings provided the pretext for riotous assemblies and political uprisings. Some 4000 spectators are said to have gathered for a cricket match at Boomb Hole in Kent in 1753, but in 1726 a JP and constable dispersed a crowd of spectators in Essex and in 1764 the magistrates of Westminster considered doing the same.

The increase in attendances at cricket matches in the nineteenth century was remarkable. A crowd of 12,000 gathered to watch England play twenty-two of Sheffield in 1825, while the record attendance for a county game was set in 1892, when 30,760 people watched the first day's play between Surrey and Nottinghamshire at the Oval. The early matches were played in fields where temporary marquees were erected around the boundary to provide food, drink and shelter for the ladies. In the course of the century, the organization of the game, the problem of crowd control and the incursions of dogs and horses resulted in the construction of permanent arenas. The first Lord's cricket ground was on land leased by Thomas Lord in 1787 in an area that is now Dorset Square. A brief occupation of ground now cut by Regent's Canal was followed by a move to the present ground in 1811, where the tavern and pavilion were opened in 1814. Of other major grounds, the Oval dates from 1845, when it was built on a vacant market garden; Old Trafford in Manchester from 1857; Headingley near Leeds from 1892, while Trent Bridge in Nottingham was one of the first permanent cricket grounds to be created outside London and an older cricket field there was enclosed in 1838. Although the eighteenth-century prohibitions on spectator sports had been lifted, the old social class divisions were enshrined in these grounds with their segregated members' enclosures and separate facilities for amateur 'gentlemen' and professional 'players'.

31

Modern Recreation

The economic and social foundations for mass recreation and entertainment were established in the Victorian era, while in the twentieth century new technologies have had profound effects. The early decades of the twentieth century witnessed the ultimate development of the music hall with the appearance of some lavish and flamboyant interiors. However, the halls were fated to be eclipsed by the cinema which brought totally new forms of architecture to the High Streets and suburbs of Britain. During the grim years of the Great Depression, the cinema provided a cheap passport to a dream-world and most families visited the local picture-house at least once or twice a week. By 1934 the British cinema could claim an annual tally of 900 million visits and in 1942 the figure had risen to one and a half billion and was still growing. No form of mass entertainment had ever been so successful.

Cinema architecture reflected the unreal celluloid world, both in the interior decoration and outlandish façades of the ubiquitous Odeons, Regals and Gaumonts which mushroomed on prime urban sites. They were lavishly appointed within, with 'wave' curtains, chrome fittings, stucco or textured paints, fluted light covers and triumphantly ascending theatre organs, while externally any architectural style might be adopted—provided it was imposing and slightly unreal. Neo-Georgian, Neo-Classical, Italianate, Egyptian, and modernistic designs appeared, often in bizarre combinations. These outrageous buildings, now often enduring in reduced circumstances as bingo-halls or supermarkets, strikingly express the attitudes and dreams of the mass of British people in the 1920s to 1940s. They range in size and ostentation from the Granada, Woolwich, with its ultra-modern brick and concrete exterior and exotic interior pastiche of Continental Gothic to the crazy structure at Moordown near Bournemouth, where an outsized Classical pediment sits on a Jacobean façade and is crowned by an oddly Moorish cupola.

Now, of course, the cinema has been replaced by an intimate and domestic form of entertainment: television. Yet even television leaves its mark on the landscape, not only in the forests of aerials, but in the huge transmitting towers that, of necessity, have to be set on lofty hills, often in areas of outstanding natural beauty. It is a reflection of television's dominance of modern life that few people object to the disfiguration of, for example, North Hessary Tor on Dartmoor, by a massive television tower while often justifiable public outcries accompany local quarrying applications.

A new transport revolution has recently transformed the pattern of British recreation and produced unprecedented levels of mass mobility; the consequences for the environment are profound. The availability of cheap motor transport has allowed both the enjoyment and destruction of some areas of outstanding natural beauty, while many outstanding monuments are threatened. Recreational management and crowd control has become a major growth industry with government, in the guise of the Department of the Environment, struggling against the tides to control the flow of visitors to an élite minority of ancient monuments. This is particularly a problem at Stonehenge, where the unique site has been eroded by the feet of throngs of tourists. Local authorities have set up massive country parks, often seeking to cater for every taste. A successful example is the Hampshire County Council's Queen Elizabeth Park near Petersfield where downland has been conserved and there are excellent display areas and reconstructions. The more enterprising members of the landed aristocracy have opened their houses, gardens and parks to visitors, providing them with every conceivable enticement and so producing the Longleats and Woburns of this world. Provincial dynasties, which formerly competed in the pursuit of domestic opulence,

127. *Canal barges in an old industrial setting at Skipton, Yorkshire, are now converted to accommodate holiday-makers.*

now bid in lions or giraffes, and whales or aardvarks may soon be trumps. A more gentlemanly presentation of the heritage is offered by the National Trust. All these individuals and institutions are now engaged in the long and seemingly endless battle between the freedom of the public to see and enjoy what it wants and the potential destruction which results from the extremes of popularity.

And yet the needs of mass outdoor recreation have had a benign influence on the landscape. The very fact that people feel a need to visit historic houses or places of great beauty has fuelled the lobbies that seek to protect such places from the ravages of industry, afforestation and agriculture. Individuals have been drawn together to preserve and protect facets of our threatened landscapes and there have been some valuable successes. The restoration of the Kennett and Avon Canal or the preservation of the Worth Valley railway are good examples, although many more good causes have been lost. Another aspect is the impact of activities like coarse fishing and dinghy sailing. The pursuit of both help to preserve and revitalize canals which would have been abandoned and to achieve the rehabilitation of hundreds of otherwise useless and disfiguring gravelpits. Sadly, as is so often the case with recreation, different pursuits conflict. Thus, while both anglers and boaters seek to preserve the Norfolk Broads from further agricultural destruction, fishing and boating seem to be incompatible pursuits and anglers are tending to desert the Broads.

The twentieth century has also seen the development of the small private garden as an essential adjunct to every suburban house or country cottage. Space is limited and layouts are often unimaginative and stereotyped, partly as a result of the control exercised by commercial nurserymen who offer only limited choices of the most 'commercial' plants, and partly by the influence of the designs of municipal parks and gardens. These latter gardens are also often uninspired in design though stocked with expensive and well-cultivated plants.

Yet even with suburban gardens we see the power of a democratic society to overcome ideas and concepts imposed from above. The early twentieth-century gardens were walled or hedged with privet and, no matter how small, were an extension of the private domain. Later planning and landscape architects have often tried to impose new ideas of space and unity. They demanded open-plan gardens flowing into each other and on to the street, and the abandonment of the territorial hedge. In many cases their attempts at unity have foundered as owners have erected new boundaries to guard their gardens or squabbled with neighbours and the owners of disrespectful dogs.

Hedges and walls have reappeared or, where not allowed, they have been substituted by neat flowerbeds or shrubs which still provide a symbolic partition between the private and public worlds. In their protective shadow, pools, gnomes and concrete rockeries mark every man's idea of a garden for pleasure.

Reflections

Our need for play has recently been explored by psychologists, sociologists and the like. In the animal kingdom, juvenile play is often a preparation for sterner pursuits in adult life—as anyone who has watched the pouncing, kicking and stalking antics of kittens will know. Man is much more sophisticated and complicated, and one of the most attractive and simple explanations of human play holds that its main purpose is to stimulate the emotional backwaters that day-to-day activities do not reach.

In our present political and economic climates, recreation tends to be regarded as a second-rate activity which policy-makers can largely disregard, while focusing on the supposed priorities of work and production. Enjoyment and enlightenment are out of fashion. Periodically, through World Cups, spectacular Test Matches and holiday traffic jams, the public asserts its own priorities. The modern tendency to divorce recreation from the other spheres of life is artificial and in discord with past experience. In the prehistoric and medieval periods, recreation and religion were closely linked, while even the cinemas of the 1920s and 1930s were secular palaces which impacted on the senses of their working-class patrons in almost the way that the medieval parish church stood as a glittering sanctuary amidst the squalor of the surrounding hovels. In some countries football has become a religion as well as an outlet for the aggressive tribal emotions which the ritualized battles with outsiders release.

Recreation and politics also overlap, and from medieval times almost until the modern period, authorities and establishments have sought to encourage those recreations like archery which can be used to buttress the status quo, while discouraging events and contests which generate crowds or unrest. Even today, football suffers grievously because the crowds and contests provide cover for Neo-Fascist hooligan mobs.

Sport has also tended to mirror rather than breach the social barriers of the class system. Aristocratic privileges were used to win and monopolize recreational resources; in the medieval period this involved the establishment of forest laws and deer parks; in the sixteenth to nineteenth centuries, the removal of villages and fields to create landscaped parks and gardens, while today exclusive golf and tennis clubs and fisheries and also the survival of bloodsports in the face of massive popular opposition all testify to the enduring links between sport and class; 'progress' has simply added a racialist dimension.

We have shown how recreation has resulted in the manipulation of the British landscapes. In recent times the emergence of a relatively democratic, affluent and mobile society has produced new problems concerning the organization of the landscape and the conservation of its legacy of monuments, wildlife and scenery. Coherent recreational policies are still sadly lacking. While the urban masses who compose eighty per cent of the British population seek recourse to the countryside and popular interest in landscape history grows at a remarkable rate, the countryside is increasingly festooned with 'No Trespassing' signs, and historic landscapes are dehedged and destroyed at an incredible rate. Meanwhile, a few important and well-publicized monuments are scarcely able to cope with the pressure of visitors and the visitors themselves are jostled, frustrated and denied the tranquility needed to appreciate the wonders displayed. Yet thousands of fascinating sites and monuments are unpublicized and seldom visited. In writing this book we have attempted to introduce some of these places and explain how the remains can be understood and related to the lost generations who created them. We end with an invitation to share, enjoy and improve upon our own visions of the past.

Index